Mastering FreeBSD and OpenBSD Security

Yanek Korff, Paco Hope, and Bruce Potter

Beijing • Cambridge • Farnham • Köln • Paris • Sebastopol • Taipei • Tokyo

Mastering FreeBSD and OpenBSD Security
Yanek Korff, Paco Hope, and Bruce Potter

Published by O'Reilly Media, Inc., 1005 Gravenstein Highway North, Sebastopol, CA 95472.

O'Reilly books may be purchased for educational, business, or sales promotional use. Online editions are also available for most titles (*safari.oreilly.com*). For more information, contact our corporate/institutional sales department: (800) 998-9938 or *corporate@oreilly.com*.

Editors:	Tatiana Apandi Diaz Allison Randal
Production Editor:	Adam Witwer
Cover Designer:	Emma Colby
Interior Designer:	David Futato

Printing History:

March 2005: First Edition.

This book uses RepKover™, a durable and flexible lay-flat binding.

ISBN: 0-596-00626-8
[M]

Table of Contents

Preface

Before I built a wall I'd ask to know
What I was walling in or walling out,
And to whom I was like to give offence.
Something there is that doesn't love a wall,
That wants it down.
—Robert Frost
"Mending Wall"

FreeBSD and OpenBSD are often considered the "other" free operating systems besides Linux. However, in recent Netcraft surveys, the five most reliable web sites on the planet run FreeBSD. OpenBSD, too, is deployed on thousands of security servers around the world. These two BSD-based operating systems are rapidly gaining traction in educational institutions, non-profits, and corporations worldwide.

Plenty of books exist to help you get a FreeBSD or OpenBSD system off the ground. All of them touch on security, but most only dedicate a chapter to it. In sharp contrast, we think it's worth spending an entire book on the subject. FreeBSD and OpenBSD are rife with security "building blocks" that you can use to really take security and "kick it up a notch."

These operating systems have kernel options and filesystem features that go well beyond traditional Unix permissions and controls. This power and flexibility is valuable, but the colossal range of possibilities will leave you dizzy if you don't take things one step at a time. *Mastering FreeBSD and OpenBSD Security* complements existing books on FreeBSD and OpenBSD administration. Where others help you achieve functionality, we help you build security-minded deployments. This book walks you through the installation of a hardened operating system, the installation and configuration of critical services, and ongoing maintenance of your FreeBSD and OpenBSD systems.

Audience

This book is written by system administrators for system administrators. If you're looking for a complete idiot or dummy guide, this book is not for you. We're talking to administrators who have installed a Unix-like operating system before. Almost any will do, but this book is all about what sets FreeBSD and OpenBSD apart from other Unices. You'll get the most out of this book if you're comfortable administering BSD operating systems and want to take your experience one step farther.

Administrators at various skill levels and in organizations of any size can benefit from secure BSD systems. Junior administrators who know how to get a Unix system off the ground can use this book to develop a sound foundation in systems security. Experienced administrators, like experienced cooks, will find new recipes that they can add to their existing repertoire. If you're part of (or all of) a small staff that runs only a handful of servers, you'll see how choosing one of the BSDs can let you spend less time on security concerns and more on your other duties. If you're part of a large staff running many servers, you'll see how BSD servers can be solid pillars in your infrastructure. They're easy to deploy and scale, and maintaining them is a breeze. Securing them is easy enough, too, with the help of this book.

Assumptions This Book Makes

We're really focused on improving the skill set of an established system administrator, so we aren't going to explain a lot of basics. We assume you can find your way to a command line and work your way through the filesystem with speed and grace. We expect that you already have a solid understanding of basic Unix permissions, are comfortable installing and configuring hardware and software, and so on.

If at any time you feel you're in over your head, fear not. Both operating systems have strong followings and easy to find documentation for all the basics. You can look at FAQs, HOWTOs, and handbooks online, or you can buy one of the many good references in print. The "Resources" section at the end of every chapter always lists good resources that provide additional coverage of relevant topics. In many cases, these additional resources provide the foundation in the technology you need to leverage the recommendations in this book.

The Internet is everywhere, and every administrator needs a basic understanding of local- and wide-area networking. We're not going to tell you what TCP/IP is, how DHCP works, or how to cable up your switches and hubs. We'll explain what you need to know when we get into a security topic that is rooted in the deep, dark corners of a protocol specification or some other relatively obscure topic. Network security and configuration are important, but we assume you've already got that under control.

Contents of This Book

We've tried to break the book up into three sections. We begin by establishing a foundation in FreeBSD and OpenBSD, move on to discuss specific deployment scenarios based on this foundation, and we wrap up with a broader look at these operating systems in your existing network.

Part I: Security Foundation

The goal of Part I is to give you the foundation for building and running secure systems with FreeBSD or OpenBSD.

Chapter 1 is an introduction to system security and general security topics that are relevant to the rest of our discussion. It tells you what you're up against and gives you some ideas about how we'll approach securing systems.

Chapter 2 is all about the fundamental building blocks you get for securing systems based on either OpenBSD or FreeBSD. There are some differences, so we highlight those as we go. We cover filesystem features, kernel features, inherent operating system features, and tweaking your kernel to enhance specific security postures.

Chapter 3 augments what you already know about installation. We explore the security-related options, trade-offs, and configurations you must consider when installing. We walk through installing both FreeBSD and OpenBSD, but dwell mainly on areas where choices at installation time can have important security ramifications.

Chapter 4 is a tour de force of administration concerns. You've got it installed, you're running it day-to-day, so now what? We describe controlling access, installing and upgrading software, network security, backups, and system monitoring.

Part II: Deployment Situations

Every server has a specific purpose in life, and FreeBSD and OpenBSD systems are ideal candidates for handling critical infrastructure services like DNS servers, firewalls, mail gateways, and web servers. Part II covers these deployments and how you can leverage specific BSD features to improve the security posture of the services you provide. We don't tell you everything about deploying the specific service, however; just the extra options and special circumstances where you can take advantage of OpenBSD or FreeBSD. The goal of this section is to offer guidelines for securely deploying the software that will run critical services in your network.

With each of these critical network services, we take time to explain the kinds of risks you face, the sorts of attacks you might need to repel, and why you and your organization care about running the service securely. When we talk about installing and configuring software, though, we refer back to the general techniques and building blocks that we laid out in Part I. You'll want to be at least passingly familiar with the techniques, because we combine them in interesting and sometimes subtle ways.

Chapter 5 describes DNS and how to build a secure DNS server. DNS is critical to every Internet service, and getting it right is fundamentally important, so we cover it first. We talk about both BIND and djbdns and how they can be installed, configured, and operated securely.

Chapter 6 covers mail: arguably the most critical electronic communication you support in your organization. We discuss setting up a secure mail architecture as well as filtering and rejecting unwanted mail. We describe both Sendmail and Postfix and how to securely install, configure, and administer them.

Chapter 7 offers a wealth of information on securing Apache-based web servers. We cover risks and threats, configuration and installation, and managing what options your users can set. We also describe `thttpd`, a small, fast, no-frills web server that can perform admirably in certain situations. In the end we talk about some interesting combinations of FreeBSD's jails and web servers to isolate and contain lots of web sites in their own sandboxes.

Chapter 8 is about building firewalls. OpenBSD and FreeBSD make excellent choices as firewall platforms. Getting a firewall operational isn't too hard, but making sure that it's appropriately secured needs to be done carefully. In this chapter, we'll talk about `ipfw` on FreeBSD and `pf` now available on both platforms.

Chapter 9 outlines the topic of intrusion detection system (IDS) on FreeBSD or OpenBSD. We cover the purposes for using IDSes as well as alternative approaches such as log analysis and intrusion prevention. We give you some good guidance on how to build an effective architecture and monitor it for nefarious activity.

Part III: Auditing and Incident Response

Auditing and incident response are topics in system administration theory that are critical but often overlooked. They are not specific services that you run as much as concerns you keep in the back of your mind all the time.

Chapter 10 talks about managing the audit trails. A properly configured system should be warning you about suspicious activity, but how do you manage all the alerts and warnings? We talk about what you want to log, how you can log it securely, and how to manage the logs you generate.

Chapter 11 describes incident response and computer forensics. When the inevitable happens and you have an incident to respond to, how will you do it? We talk about responding to attacks, and tracking down how the attack succeeded, through forensic analysis.

Conventions Used in This Book

We use both typography and common Unix documentation conventions to give you additional information in the text.

Typographic Conventions

Plain text
: Indicates menu titles, menu options, menu buttons, and keyboard accelerators (such as Alt and Ctrl).

Italic
: Indicates new or technical terms, system calls, URLs, hostnames, email addresses, filenames, file extensions, pathnames, and directories.

`Constant width`
: Indicates commands, options, switches, variables, attributes, keys, functions, types, objects, HTML tags, macros, the contents of files, or the output from commands.

`Constant width bold`
: Shows commands or other text that should be typed literally by the user.

`Constant width italic`
: Shows text that should be replaced with user-supplied values.

This icon signifies a tip, suggestion, or general note.

This icon indicates a warning or caution.

There are times when it is very important to pay attention to the typography because it distinguishes between two similarly named, but different concepts. For example, the `host` command and the */etc/hosts* file, or the *jail(2)* system call versus the `jail(8)` command. Sometimes the typeface is an important clue to help you remember which one we're referring to in a given context.

Conventions in Examples

You will see two different prompts in the examples we give for running commands. We follow the time-honored Unix convention of using `%` to represent a non-root shell (e.g., one running as your normal user ID) and `#` to represent a root-equivalent shell. Commands that appear after a `%` prompt can (and probably should) be run by an unprivileged user. Commands that appear after a # prompt must be run with root privileges. Example P-1 shows three different commands that illustrate this point.

Example P-1. Several commands with different prompts

```
% ls -lo /var/log
% sudo ifconfig lo0 127.0.0.2 netmask 255.255.255.255
# shutdown -r now
```

The `ls` command runs as a normal user. The `ifconfig` command runs as root, but only because a normal user uses `sudo` to elevate his privileges momentarily (`sudo` is discussed in detail in Chapter 4). The last command shows the # prompt, assuming that you have already become root somehow before executing the `shutdown` command.

Using Code Examples

This book is here to help you get your job done. In general, you may use the code in this book in your programs and documentation. You do not need to contact us for permission unless you're reproducing a significant portion of the code. For example, writing a program that uses several chunks of code from this book does not require permission. Selling or distributing a CD-ROM of examples from O'Reilly books does require permission. Answering a question by citing this book and quoting example code does not require permission. Incorporating a significant amount of example code from this book into your product's documentation does require permission.

We appreciate, but do not require, attribution. An attribution usually includes the title, author, publisher, and ISBN. For example: *Mastering FreeBSD and OpenBSD Security* by Yanek Korff, Paco Hope, and Bruce Potter. Copyright 2005 O'Reilly Media, Inc., 0-596-00626-8.

If you feel your use of code examples falls outside fair use or the permissions given above, feel free to contact us at *permissions@oreilly.com*.

Comments and Questions

Please address comments and questions concerning this book to the publisher:

O'Reilly Media, Inc.
1005 Gravenstein Highway North
Sebastopol, CA 95472
(800) 998-9938 (in the United States or Canada)
(707) 829-0515 (international or local)
(707) 829-0104 (fax)

We have a web page for this book, where we list errata, examples, and any additional information. You can access this page at:

http://www.oreilly.com/catalog/mfreeopenbsd/

To comment or ask technical questions about this book, send email to:

bookquestions@oreilly.com

For more information about our books, conferences, Resource Centers, and the O'Reilly Network, see our web site at:

http://www.oreilly.com

Safari Enabled

When you see a Safari® Enabled icon on the cover of your favorite technology book, that means the book is available online through the O'Reilly Network Safari Bookshelf.

Safari offers a solution that's better than e-books. It's a virtual library that lets you easily search thousands of top tech books, cut and paste code samples, download chapters, and find quick answers when you need the most accurate, current information. Try it for free at *http://safari.oreilly.com*.

Acknowledgments

Many people helped make this book possible, some of them in big ways and others in critical, yet nearly invisible ways. We'd like to acknowledge them here.

Yanek Korff

First and foremost, I'd like to thank my wife, whose patience continues to surprise me. This book would never have been possible without her help and her support. Also, although she's not old enough to harbor a grudge or appreciate gratefulness, I'd like to thank my one-year-old daughter. She's only ever known a workaholic father and doesn't realize she should be jealous.

An obvious thank you to my parents for putting me on the road to geekdom back in early 90s, and of course putting me through college. May my educators forgive me for everything I've forgotten.

I'd also like to thank Viren Shah who introduced me to FreeBSD. I wouldn't be where I am today without the support and mentoring he's provided me over the years.

Finally, thanks to my good friend Matt Rowley, owner of much computer junk. Some of that junk and the advice that came with it were integral to this book's creation.

Paco Hope

I'd like to thank my wife, Rebecca, who administered everything that doesn't run FreeBSD (like children, houses, and pets) while I was building Frankenstein's BSD lab in our basement. I am grateful for my time in the Department of Computer Science at the University of Virginia, where I cut my teeth as a system administrator. I thank the folks at Cigital, Inc. for introducing me to risk-based approaches to software and system security. Lastly, I thank Adrian Filipi, who gave me my first BSD/386 floppies back in 1993.

Bruce Potter

I would like to thank my wife for being incredibly understanding throughout the writing of this book and the million other things I had going on in the last year. She was amazing, even when I was not. I'd like to thank my kids, Terran and Bobby, and "Uncle Andy" for giving me time to write. Also, I would like to thank all the members of The Shmoo Group for helping me become the geek I am today. Without their friendship and expertise, I don't know where my career would be today (full of moose, no doubt). The same goes to my folks who supported me through my fits and starts in college. And finally, a specific thanks to Joel Sadler, who gave me my first FreeBSD disk in 1995 telling me, "Here, try this. It's better than Linux."

Our Reviewers

We appreciate all the feedback we received from our technical reviewers. They definitely kept us on our toes and made this book better by lending their expert advice and opinions. Thanks to Flávio Marcelo Amaral, Ren Bitonio, Mark Delany, Adrian Filipi, Eric Jackson, Jose Nazario, Neil Neely, Wayne Pascoe, Viren Shah, and Shi-Min Yeh.

O'Reilly

Finally, we thank the staff at O'Reilly, especially Tatiana Diaz, Nathan Torkington, Allison Randal, David Chu, Andrew Savikas, and the innumerable others who have made this book a reality without our knowledge of their existence. An extra thank you goes to Tatiana for helping us reboot this effort after it locked up in the middle of 2004.

PART I
Security Foundation

The goal of Part I is to give you the foundation for building and running secure systems with FreeBSD or OpenBSD.

- Chapter 1, *The Big Picture*
- Chapter 2, *BSD Security Building Blocks*
- Chapter 3, *Secure Installation and Hardening*
- Chapter 4, *Secure Administration Techniques*

CHAPTER 1

The Big Picture

First we crack the shell, then we crack the nuts inside.
—Rumble
The Transformers: The Movie

Security is hard. We have all heard this phrase as a rationale for insecure systems and poor administrative practices. What's worse, administrators seem to have different ideas about what "security" entails. There are two common approaches to securing systems: some view security as a destination while others see it as a journey.

Those who see security as a destination tend to characterize system security in terms of black and white; either a system is secure or it is not. This implies that you can attain security. You can arrive at the end of a journey and you'll somehow be secure; you win. One problem with this viewpoint is determining where "there" is. How do you know when you've arrived? Furthermore, how do you stay there? As your system changes, are you still at your secure goal? Did you move away from it, orwere you not there to begin with? As you can probably tell, this is not our philosophy.

Instead of being a destination, we think security is best described as a journey—a product of ongoing risk management. Rather than trying to make your system impregnable, you continually evaluate your exposure to risks and keep the system as secure as you need it to be. An appropriate level of security is achieved when the risks facing a system balance against the level of effort spent mitigating those risks. No one buys a $5,000 vault to safeguard a pair of fuzzy slippers. You judge the value of what you're protecting against the kinds of threats it faces and the likelihood those threats will succeed, and then you apply appropriate safeguards. This is a much more practical way to view modern day information security.

When following a risk mitigation process, you will periodically pass up the opportunity to enable certain security mechanisms, even though you're capable of doing so. The additional effort may not be warranted given the level of risk your organization faces. You will eventually reach a point of diminishing returns where you simply accept some risks because they are too costly to mitigate relative to the likelihood of the threat or the actual damage that would occur. Sure, it may be fun to use encrypted filesystems, store all OS data on a CD-ROM, and deploy every other countermeasure you can think of, but do you really need to?

We define security in the context of risk. Risk is present as long as the system exists, and risks are constantly changing, so security cannot be a destination; it must be an ongoing process. "Doing security," then, is an iterative process of identifying and responding to risks. This is the philosophy that we encourage you to take in securing your infrastructure.

As you'll see in the rest of this book, FreeBSD and OpenBSD are robust operating systems that offer myriad ways to maintain secure systems. Throughout the book we provide security-minded walkthroughs of software installation, configuration, and maintenance. Along the way you'll notice that we seem to point out more security-related configuration options than you care to implement. Just because we explore options doesn't mean that you should implement them. Come at it from the perspective of managing risk and you'll maximize the cost-benefit of "doing security."

Before we get ahead of ourselves, however, we need to cover a few concepts and principles. In this chapter, we define system security, specifically for OpenBSD and FreeBSD systems, but also more generally. We look at a variety of attacks so that you, as an administrator, will have some perspective on what you're trying to defend against. We'll look at risk response and describe how exactly you can go about securing your FreeBSD and OpenBSD systems.

What Is System Security?

Security professionals break the term security into three parts: confidentiality, integrity, and availability. This "CIA Triad" is a set of security requirements; if you're not taking into account all three of these concerns, you're not working towards providing security. We offer a lot of recommendations in this book that should help you work towards building secure systems, but we don't tell you how these recommendations fit in with the CIA Triad. That's not what this book is about, and it would detract from the real message. Nevertheless, as you're looking at building encrypted tunnels for transferring files, jailing applications, and so on, think about what part of the Triad you're focusing on. Make sure you've addressed all three parts before your project is done.

Whether we're talking about physical security, information security, network security, or system security, the CIA Triad applies. The question is, exactly how does it apply to system security?

Confidentiality

Confidentiality is all about determining the appropriate level of access to information. Confidentiality is often implemented at the most basic level on FreeBSD and

OpenBSD systems by traditional Unix permissions. There are a variety of files scattered across the filesystem that are readable only by the root user. Most notable, perhaps, is */etc/master.passwd*, which contains hashes for users' passwords. The vast majority of files are readable by everyone, however. Even system configuration files like */etc/resolv.conf*, */etc/hosts*, and so on are world readable. Is this wrong? Not necessarily. Again, confidentiality isn't about having to protect data from prying eyes; it's about classifying data and making sure that information deemed sensitive in some way is protected appropriately.

Filesystem level protections are of course only one facet of confidentiality. Data may be exposed through some service designed to serve information like DNS, or a web server. In these cases, the method you employ to protect data won't necessarily be filesystem permissions; perhaps you'll control what systems are allowed to query your DNS server, or which web-authenticated users are permitted to view a certain document tree. When you need to protect data from eavesdropping as it moves across a network, you'll probably use encryption. When implemented appropriately, it helps ensure that only the intended recipient can read the transmitted data.

Integrity

Data integrity relates to trust. If you cannot guarantee the integrity of some information on your system, you can't trust it. Consequently, resources for which integrity is an important issue need to be identified and appropriately protected against modification.

Confidentiality may not have been an issue for your */etc/resolv.conf* file. Allowing users to see what resolvers your system depends on is okay. Allowing users to modify the list of resolvers is not! Your system's resolvers are a data source. When you access a server providing anonymous CVS access to your OpenBSD sources, your system will ask one of the servers listed in */etc/resolv.conf* to find the IP address for the name you provided. If you can't guarantee the integrity of the data in this file, you can't trust the IP address you get from the resolver. As a consequence, you can't trust the sources you download either.

Like confidentiality, the filesystem permissions model helps enforce data integrity. Unfortunately file permissions aren't enough by themselves. If someone has broken through your filesystem protections somehow, you won't know that your data has been tampered with. That is, not without good auditing. Moreover, you won't be able to restore a known good configuration without data backups.

Data integrity is also an issue during network transfers. How can you be sure that the information has not been modified in transit? The BSD operating systems will provide "signatures," which uniquely identify file distributions. When you download a package or source tarball or install a port, you can check your local files against the remote signatures. If it's a match, your file has not been modified while in transit.

Availability

Often overlooked by administrators, availability is the last key component of security. Protecting your systems from information disclosure and tampering is important but not sufficient. If a user on your system "accidentally" copies his 120GB MP3 music collection to your file server and you run out of disk space on /, your system will suddenly cease being useful. If you had separated your home directories into their own partition, and additionally configured filesystem quotas, this would not have been a problem.

Availability does not only pertain to services, it can also apply to data, though most examples you might immediately think of are really data integrity issues. What would happen if a virus infected your workstation and destroyed the only private keys that decrypt vital data? You probably have a backup of that encrypted file and have otherwise taken care of integrity issues, but suddenly that data may as well have been deleted. It's no longer available for use.

System availability can be one of the most difficult areas of providing system security. The number of ways (both physical and electronic) an attacker can make your server unavailable is staggering.

Summary

So, after all this, what is system security? For our purposes, providing "system security" is about responding to risks that threaten the confidentiality or integrity of data that resides on or passes through our systems, and working to guarantee the availability of the services and data. If you made it through this section, congratulations. This is pretty dry stuff, but it's important. We won't explicitly talk about the elements of the CIA Triad in this book, but we encourage you to keep these principles in mind when working on protecting your systems.

Identifying Risks

We are going to consider a variety of risks that we might face and then talk about how we can respond to them. In this chapter, we lay the groundwork for many general risks. In each of the application-specific chapters, we will identify application-specific risks that make concrete examples from the concepts here. We are not going to give you advice on how to identify lightning strikes as a risk and use FreeBSD or OpenBSD features to help protect your data against them. Instead, we think mostly about hackers and other malicious adversaries and how you identify and assess the damage they can wreak on your infrastructure.

Attacks

An attack against a system is an intentional attempt to bypass system security controls or organizational policies to affect the operation of the system (active attack) or gain access to information (passive attack). Attacks can be classified into insider attacks in which someone from within an organization who is authorized to access a system uses it in an unauthorized way, or outsider attacks, which originate outside of the organization's security perimeter, perhaps on the Internet at large.

Attacks motivate system administrators, supervisors, and organizational leaders into caring about security, but where's the damage in an attack? What kind of major assault is required to wreak the kind of havoc required to get all these people worked up? Despite our definition of attack, we still do not have enough information to determine for a given system, where the risks lie.

In order for active and passive attacks to succeed, something must be at fault. Attacks necessarily leverage fundamental behavioral problems in software, improper configuration and use of software, or both. In this chapter, we examine these classes of attacks including the special-case denial of service (DoS) attack.

Remember that while attacks are necessarily intentional, system disruptions due to software failure or misconfiguration probably are not. In either case, the end result is the same: system resources are abused. In the latter case, however, this does not come as a consequence of someone's malevolence. Fortunately, defending against attacks tends to help defend against unintentional disruptions, too.

At a slightly higher level, it is also important to distinguish between attacks that originate locally on the system and those that may be carried out over a network. Keep in mind that, although this distinction is important when thinking about mitigating risk, local attacks can quickly become network-exploitable if the system can be breached over the network in any way.

In order to provide system security for a single DNS server, a firewall, or a farm of web servers, it is important to understand what you are actually defending against. By understanding the classes of attacks you will come under, and the technology behind these attacks, you will be in a better position to maintain a secure configuration.

Problems in Software

Attacks that exploit problems in software are the most common. Security forums such as Bugtraq and Full Disclosure focus on software problems. These are somewhat high volume lists and over the years have recorded thousands of vulnerabilities in software. The kinds of vulnerabilities recorded vary as widely as the associated impact.

In order to be able to understand a security advisory and react accordingly, it is imperative that you understand the common types of software-based vulnerabilities. This knowledge will prove useful when you build and configure your systems, resulting in a more well-thought-out deployment of your infrastructure.

Buffer overflows

Probably the most widely publicized software security flaw is the buffer overflow. Buffer overflows are discussed on highly technical security lists, mass media, and as a result of this press coverage, by company executives. Buffer overflows are the result of (sometimes trivial) tactical coding errors that often could have been prevented. Exploits can be devastating. Buffer overflows are made even more dangerous when the software is reachable over the Internet. For instance, the Morris Worm (1988), used a buffer overflow in the `fingerd` utility as one of its exploit mechanisms. The Code Red worm, which infected hundreds of thousands of computers in 2001, exploited a buffer overflow in Microsoft's IIS web server to do its damage.

So what is a buffer, and how does it overflow? A buffer is a portion of memory set aside by a program to store data. In languages like C, the buffer generally has some predefined size. The C program will allocate the exact amount of memory required to accommodate this buffer. The developer must ensure that the data put into the buffer never exceeds the capacity of the buffer. If, through programming error and some unexpected input, too much data is inserted into the buffer, it will "overflow" overwriting adjacent memory locations that store other information.

The developer may feel that there is no pressing need to ensure the data being placed into a buffer will fit. After all, if it does not fit, the program will probably crash. The user did something stupid, and the user will pay for it. In Example 1-1, if the user inputs more than 20 characters in response to the `gets(3)` function, the buffer will not be able to store all the data.

Example 1-1. A simple buffer that can overflow

```
int main() {
    char buffer[20];
    gets (buffer);
    printf("%s\n", buffer);
}
```

The excess data will be written sequentially in memory past the end of the buffer into other parts of the processes' memory space. There are not necessarily security ramifications in this case—this example is purely academic.

Taken at face value, running past the end of a buffer seems like a pretty innocuous problem. The data ends up in other parts of the processes' memory space thereby corrupting the processes' memory and eventually crashing the program, right? Well, attackers can use specially crafted data to intentionally overflow the buffer with instructions that ultimately will be executed by the operating system.

One popular attack strategy is to overwrite the return location of the function containing the exploitable buffer. Thus at the end of the function, instead of continuing to execute the program right after that function was called, the program's execution continues from some other point in memory. With a little knowledge and effort, an attacker can first inject malicious code (e.g., *shellcode*) which, if executed, would give the attacker access to the system. Then by setting the return location to point to their injected *shellcode*, the operating system will happily read the overwritten memory containing the new return location and execute the *shellcode* at the end of the function. This is only one example of a how a buffer overflow can lead to some additional access on the system.

Fortunately the BSD operating systems have been extensively audited to protect against these, and similar, software flaws. OpenBSD includes built-in protections that prevent programs from writing beyond their allocated memory space thus preventing the execution of arbitrary code. This kind of protection can be very useful since not all of the third-party programs you install on your systems will have undergone the kind of scrutiny the operating system went through.

For non-programmers, this might seem complicated and difficult to digest. Computer science geeks will probably find this very familiar. Application security experts and others well versed in exploiting software vulnerabilities may already be wondering why we are not covering heap-based overflows in addition to the trivial example above. For the curious, additional resources are plentiful online. To succeed as a security-minded system administrator, understanding buffer overflows to this level should be sufficient.

SQL injection

Although buffer overflow attacks get a great deal of attention, there are many other problems in software that give rise to vulnerabilities. With the increasing number of deployed web-based applications, attackers have become quite savvy at attacking web sites. Web-based attacks may target the web server software, a web-based application, or data accessed by the application. Some web-based attacks may even go right to the core operating system and attempt to exploit the host itself. The most common forms of web-based attacks, however, are those that lead to the manipulation of application data or escalation of application privileges.

Complex web applications often work directly with vast quantities of data. This is almost a guarantee when the web application is used by a financial institution or a data warehousing company but also common with smaller e-commerce sites, online forums, and so on. The only reasonable way to manage a large volume of data is by storing it in a database. When the application accesses the database, it must communicate using some defined database query language, most often Structured Query Language (SQL).

SQL is a tremendously easy language to learn, and web developers often feel comfortable working with it after only a few days or weeks of exposure. Hence, there is an abundance of web applications that dynamically construct SQL statements as part of their response to user requests. In general, these statements are constructed based on what a site visitor has selected, checked, and/or typed into form fields on a web page.

Unfortunately, developers are often unaware of how their SQL query can be abused if the input from the user is not properly sanitized. An attacker can often inject her own SQL statements as part of the input to the web application in an effort to completely alter the dynamically generated SQL query sent to the database. These queries may result in data being changed in the database or may give the attacker the ability to view data she is not authorized to view.

There are, of course, ways to defend against SQL injection attacks from within web applications. One common approach is to parse every value provided by the user. Make sure it doesn't contain any undesirable characters like backticks, quotes, semicolons, and so on. Also ensure that the valid characters are appropriate for the value being returned. To get around the problem completely, developers may be able to use stored procedures and avoid dynamically creating SQL.

Other software problems

We have only scratched the surface of application level vulnerabilities. What follows is a brief synopsis of additional software programming errors that have been known to lead to security problems.

Format string error
: Format strings are used by some languages, notably C, to describe how data should be displayed (e.g., by *printf(3)* and derivatives). Unfortunately attackers can sometimes manipulate these format strings to write their own data to memory on the target host. This attack is like a buffer overflow in that it will allow an attacker to run his own code on the victim host. However, it is not actually overflowing a buffer so much as abusing a feature in the programming language.

Race conditions
: Race conditions exist when there is contention for access to a particular resource. Race conditions are common software engineering problems, but they can also have security ramifications. For instance, assume an application wants to write password information to a file it creates. The application first checks to see if a file exists. Then the application creates the file and starts to write to it. An attacker can potentially create a file after the application checks for the file's existence but before the application creates the file. If the attacker does something interesting, like create a symbolic link from this protected file to a world

readable file in another directory, sensitive password information (in this example) would be disclosed. This specific kind of race condition is referred to as a time-of-check-to-time-of-use or *TOCTTOU* vulnerability.

Web-based attacks
: There are a staggering number of web-based attacks available in the hacker's arsenal. SQL injection, and other code injection attacks, comprise one class of web-based attack. Through poor web application design, weak authentication, and sloppy configuration, a variety of other attacks are possible. Cross-site scripting (XSS) attacks attempt to take advantage of dynamic sites by injecting malicious data. These attacks often target site visitors; web developers and site administrators may be left unaware. Handcrafted URLs can sometimes bypass authentication mechanisms. Malicious web spiders can crawl the Web, signing your friends and family up for every online mailing list available. These types of attacks are so common that there are many security companies that focus specifically on web-based security.

Protecting yourself

As a system administrator or security engineer, you generally do not have control over the security within the software installed on your servers.

FreeBSD and OpenBSD are open source operating systems, as is most application software they run. Although you certainly have the option of modifying the source code of applications, you probably do not want to do that. System administrators rarely have time to properly develop and maintain software. As a result, managing custom code will usually lead to software maintenance nightmares.

You may be able to choose one server product over another: while building a mail relay, you might consider Sendmail, Postfix, and qmail. To help guide your decision, you might want to evaluate the particular software's security track record. Be wary, for much like mutual funds, past trends are not a reliable indicator of future performance. With custom, internally developed code you usually have no options at all; your company has developed custom software and your systems must run it.

At this point, you may be wondering if there is any way to mitigate the risks associated with vulnerabilities in software. As it turns out, there is. Being aware of vulnerabilities is a good first step. Subscribe to mailing lists that disclose software vulnerabilities in a timely fashion. Have a response plan in place and stay on top of patching. Watch your systems, especially your audit trails, and be aware when your systems are behaving unnaturally. Finally, be security-minded in your administration of systems. What this entails is described later in this chapter and embodied by the rest of this book.

Denial of Service Attacks

DoS attacks are active—they seek to consume system resources and deny the availability of your systems to legitimate users. The root cause of a system or network being vulnerable to a DoS attack may be based on a software vulnerability, as a result of improper configuration and use, or both. DoS attacks can be devastating, and depending on how they are carried out, it can be very difficult to find the source. DoS attacks have a diverse list of possible targets.

Target: physical

DoS attacks can occur at the physical layer. In an 802.11 wireless network, an attacker can flood the network by transmitting garbage in the same frequency band as the 802.11 radios. A simple 2.4 GHz cordless phone can render an 802.11 network unusable. With physical access to an organization's premises, cutting through an Ethernet cable can be equally devastating on the wired side.

Target: network

At the data link and network layers, traffic saturation can interfere with legitimate communications. Flooding a network with illegitimate and constantly changing arp requests can place an extreme burden on networking devices and confuse hosts. Attempting to push a gigabit of data per second through a 100 Mbps pipe will effectively overrun any legitimate network traffic. Too much traffic is perhaps the quintessential example of a DoS attack.

Network-level DoS attacks can stop nearly all legitimate incoming and/or outgoing traffic thereby shutting down all services offered on that network. If a network-level DoS attack is conducted using spoofed source IP addresses, victims must often work with their ISPs to track down the source of the flood of data. Even still, this process is extremely time consuming and may not even be possible depending on the capabilities of the ISP. Worse yet, distributed denial of service (DDoS) attacks use different attacking hosts on different networks, making it nearly impossible to block all the sites participating in the attacks. DDoS attacks are difficult to defend against, especially at the host level.

Target: application

Even at the application level, a DoS attack can be devastating. These DoS attacks generally use up some finite resource on a host such as CPU, memory, or disk I/O. An attacker may send several application requests to a single host in order to cause the application to consume an excessive amount of system resources. She may simply exploit a bug in code once that causes the application to spiral out of control or simply crash. Some services that fork daemons at every new connection may be subject to a DoS if tens or hundreds of thousands of connections are made within a short period of time.

These DoS situations may not always come as a result of an attack. Sometimes, an unexpected and sudden increase in the number of legitimate requests can render a service unusable.

Protecting yourself

Physical and network-based DoS attacks are difficult to defend against and are out of the scope of host-based security. At the operating system level, you can do little to mitigate the risks associated with these kinds of attacks. Generally, some form of physical access controls help with physical attacks and specialized network devices like load balancers assist with network-based attacks.

IDS hosts may be used to help detect these kinds of attacks and automatically update firewall or router configurations to drop the traffic. Although this may protect one service, if the sheer volume of data is too much, blocking it at your firewall will not be useful. You will need to coordinate with your ISP.

Application-level attacks are something the security-minded system administrator can do something about. If you've been reading about the other forms of attacks, you might already have an idea of the kinds of mitigation techniques you can use against DoS attacks: secure architecture and build, controlled maintenance, and monitoring logs. Any mitigation techniques you have in place to protect from software vulnerabilities and avoid improper configuration and use will help make DoS attacks more difficult. Additional anomaly detection specific to identifying DoS attacks will go even farther.

Improper Configuration and Use

Even if the software you are using is bulletproof, that does not mean that you are home free. Even good software can go bad when configured or used in an insecure fashion. Security options can often be disabled, user roles can be jumbled together allowing excessive access, and passwords can be sent across the network in the clear. High-quality software configured poorly, can be as vulnerable as poor-quality software doing its best.

Sloppy application configuration

One of the most dangerous forms of improper use and configuration comes at the hands of the administrator. The security of a host is directly affected by the security of the applications running on that host. Careless configuration of installed services will almost certainly lead to trouble.

Let's say you need to build a mail server that supports user authentication so that your users can send mail from foreign networks. If you fail to provide an encrypted session over which the authentication information can travel, you will be exposing your organization's usernames and passwords.

You might also need to deploy a set of DNS servers. Without careful configuration restricting who is allowed to query the servers and how, you may be opening yourself up to denial-of-service attacks or worse. Again, careful configuration will help mitigate these risks.

Chapters 5–8 focus on providing common services from FreeBSD and OpenBSD systems. By understanding the application and the risks associated with providing service, you will be able to carefully configure and deploy these services safely.

Protecting yourself

Insecure configuration and use comes in many shapes and sizes. There are nearly an infinite number of ways to misconfigure a host or an application and compromise its security.

Again, as with application security, auditing is vital. But in this case, it is not simply to catch attackers. In order to maintain a controlled configuration on production hosts, you must have a configuration management process. At a technical level this means structured change control, and possibly even revision control procedures. In even more formal environments, a daily meeting where production changes are discussed and approved can go a long way toward keeping configuration changes sane. Auditing hosts that are under configuration management allows you to detect when changes have been made. Any unauthorized changes will be discovered and can be backed out before they cause security problems.

Change control procedures are more extensively discussed in Chapter 4.

Accounts and permissions

At the heart of the Unix security model are users and groups. The concept is pretty straightforward. Files and directories on a Unix filesystem are protected by user, group, and other (often referred to as world) permissions. The user represents the finest resolution of access control. Users can also be members of a group that has specific access rights over filesystem data. To make things more flexible, a user can be a member of multiple groups. Finally, the world permissions apply to all users on the system, regardless of group membership. Permissions are further broken down into access modes specific to the owner, the group, and world. Each class may have read (`r`), write (`w`), and/or execute (`x`) rights to the file. These filesystem permissions are likely familiar to anyone with background in Unix operating systems. However, despite being well understood, it is imperative that filesystem permissions are closely monitored.

One particularly dangerous set of permissions can make user and group ownership sticky. The *set-user-identifier* permission (*setuid* or *suid*) causes a program to assume the user ID of the owner of the file, not the person who executed the file. The *setuid* permission is represented by an `s` in place of the user execute bit. For instance, the `traceroute(8)` program that is included with FreeBSD 5.x is *setuid* by default.

```
-r-sr-xr-x   1 root  wheel     23392 Jun  4 21:57 traceroute
```

When a normal, non-root user runs `traceroute`, the process nevertheless runs as root. This is done because `traceroute` needs access to low level network capability that a normal user does not have. Similarly, the *set-group-identifier* (*setgid* or *sgid*) permission can be set to change the group owner of a file or directory.

While all this can be useful for making programs work in certain ways, it can lead to mistakes. The *setuid* bit should only be applied to programs that absolutely need it. *setuid* root files are often the target of attackers who try to make the program do something it should not. If a *setuid* program can be made to execute arbitrary code, or clobber files, it will do so as root. This could easily lead to escalated privileges on the system. Programs should never have *setuid* bits applied to them after the fact—the fact that they will be running *setuid* should be part of the application design process.

To find *setuid* and *setgid* files on your BSD system, run the following command:

```
% find / -type f \( -perm -2000 -o -perm -4000 \) -print
```

If non-root users on your system don't need to run these *setuid* executables, the *setuid* and/or *setgid* bit can often be safely removed. OpenBSD administrators will be happy to know that the OpenBSD team has spent considerable time reducing the number of *setuid* binaries on the system, and using privilege separation to mitigate the risks of the remaining ones.

The BSD-based operating systems also have a special group: wheel. In order for users to use the `su(1)` command to launch a root shell, they must be in the wheel group. Other than controlling access to the root account, several files and devices on the operating system are group-owned by wheel. Be very careful about who you add to this group.

According to Eric Raymond's jargon file (*http://www.catb.org/~esr/jargon/*), the wheel group was derived from the term "big wheel," which means "a powerful person." When Unix hosts were less common and far more expensive, being in the wheel group was really a position of power. With the advent of free BSD-based operating systems that run on cheap x86-based hardware, being in the wheel group on your home PC does not seem like the honor it once was.

In general, permissions on files and directories should always be carefully controlled and audited. Administrators are often tempted while debugging problems to change the permissions on files or directories to 777 (everyone can read, write, and execute the file or change into the directory) in trying to determine whether the problem is permissions related. In some cases, especially in test environments, this may not be a terrible thing to do—as long as permissions are quickly restored to normal. Unfortunately, in many cases the administrator will have made several changes at once; when the application starts working again he might be tempted to leave everything as it is. This can lead to a very dangerous situation, especially on production systems.

Passwords and other account problems

Beyond permissions, accounts themselves can be the source of security problems. First and foremost, weak passwords are a bane to any security-minded system administrator. Make an effort to enforce strong passwords on your systems and for your applications.

> **Strong Passwords**
>
> Strong passwords are generally at least eight characters in length and should contain a variety of letters (both lowercase and uppercase), numbers, and special characters. Avoid passwords that closely resemble dictionary words, proper nouns, or other words and numbers with any personal significance. Here are a few quick examples.
>
> `Donut` is clearly a lousy password. The introduction of some number substitution in `D0nut1` may make you feel better but will not really improve the strength of the password very much. The password `sremrofsnart` may look good at first glance, but it is merely transformers spelled backward. Likewise, substitution in `sremrofsn@rt` does not significantly improve the password. A mnemonic such as `Tsij6wl!` (This song is just 6 words long!) is a better all-round password than the others. Arbitrary choices of letters, numbers, and special characters that are easy to type are often also good candidates. Finally, passwords should be something easy enough to remember that they do not have to be written down.
>
> Your goal in enforcing strong passwords that satisfy the aforementioned requirements is to prevent passwords from being cracked or guessed. To better understand this concept, explore password crackers and develop an understanding of how they operate. These are the tools that will be used against your password database, given the opportunity.

As time passes, even good passwords can lose strength, in a way. There is a continually increasing chance that a given password has been stolen. This can be accomplished by sniffing traffic on the network, watching users type them in, or compromising a host and running a password-cracking program against */etc/master.passwd*. After some period of time, your password should be changed. For some organizations this period is annual, for others it is monthly.

Improper use of accounts is another common problem on production machines. Administrators will sometimes create a single account for many people to use. This happens often in technical support groups where turnover is high. Rather than finding an easier way to perform account maintenance, an administrator may make a single account for all tech support people and give everyone the password. It is also commonplace to use system accounts with a generic name such as *www* and let several web developers log in under this user ID.

The practice of assigning multiple human beings to one account on the system makes auditing impossible. There is now no way to know what human being performed what actions on a given host because, from the perspective of the operating system, there is only one user involved. Changing passwords on these kinds of accounts is also a hassle as it must be done whenever someone leaves, and everyone must be told the new password immediately.

We continue to discuss managing user permissions in Chapter 4.

Network Versus Local Attacks

We know that attacks can target faults in software, faults in configuration, or both, and this helps us tell how attacks might succeed, but it's also important to consider where attacks come from. A buffer overflow that allows for code execution on a host can lead to a host being compromised. However, if the buffer overflow vulnerability exists in some *setuid* binary that is only accessible to logged-in users, the risk associated with the vulnerability is severely limited. In fact, any vulnerability that requires local access is difficult to exploit, unless would-be attackers can gain access to the host.

On the other hand, if a buffer overflow exists in software that is reachable from the network, `ftpd` for example, then the danger is much greater. Simply being connected to the Internet exposes this vulnerability to everyone on the Internet. The risk associated with remotely exploitable vulnerabilities is often so much greater than with local exploits that administrators tend to respond much more quickly to these kinds of problems.

Just because network-based attacks are more dangerous does not mean you should ignore, or even put off fixing, local vulnerabilities. System administrators, due to lack of time, carelessness or both, sometimes patch the most critical vulnerabilities early and leave the rest "for later." Eventually, a few months or years down the road, this practice is likely to lead to a compromise. It may become possible to combine a vulnerability that had previously only been locally exploitable with another, remotely exploitable, vulnerability to compromise the system. An attacker may be able to break into the system through this service's vulnerability and gain a shell prompt. At this point, just one of those "minor," locally exploitable vulnerabilities is exactly what the attacker needs to gain escalated privileges and compromise the host. From there, other presumed minor vulnerabilities (in services accessible only if you are already behind the firewall, for instance) become prime targets and a means to compromise the rest of your network.

The lesson here is to follow your instincts in patching the most critical vulnerabilities first. However, if you fail to also patch minor software issues in a timely manner, they will be exactly what the attacker needs to own your network.

Physical Security

From boulders to armed guards, physical security can take many different forms. However in most organizations, physical security and information security are controlled by two separate parts of the organization. Firewall administrators usually do not take care of giving out physical keys for the office doors. Sometimes it's tough to remember that physical security is an integral part of computer security.

If physical security breaks down, nearly all computer security constructs are rendered useless. An attacker who has physical access to a host has completely bypassed any network protections in front of the host. No one has invented a firewall (yet) that will detect a physical intruder, remove itself from a rack, and beat the intruder senseless.

Once physical security has been breached, an attacker can remove hard drives, or force a machine to boot to alternate media in order to subvert the core operating system. This will obviously cause a service interruption for the host, but a truly motivated attacker with physical access may not care about completely destroying a host in order to steal data or simply wreak havoc.

While this may seem abundantly obvious, security professionals often lose sight of the importance of physical security. We constantly weigh risks, decide which firewall configuration is best, or determine how best to handle groups on a server. However, decisions like that may be pointless if the data center holding your hosts is in an unlocked or an unattended building. Remember to take physical security into account when weighing risk. It would be a shame to get `ipfw` or `pf` configured on your BSD firewall only to see some guy running down the street with it the next day.

Summary

At this point, you should have a pretty good idea of the attacks your system will face after you attach it to a network. Throughout this book we point out how you can defend against these attacks: where you should go for software updates, how to keep track of and respond to security advisories, and how to be diligent and careful in your system administration practices. In the next chapter, we'll describe in detail some of the building blocks the BSD operating systems provide to further mitigate the risks of system compromise. Before we get there, though, we close the loop on the topic of risk.

Responding to Risk

Risk mitigation starts at the top. If you're working in an environment where you identify systems that need protection, determine how much effort you will put forth to protect systems, and perform the subsequent remediation, then you're doing too much.

In order to be able to respond to risk, the first step is to identify the resources that are important. Your organizational leadership is responsible for providing this high level assessment of information system criticality. Once this is done, senior security professionals get involved so that management can understand the kinds of risks given resources will face and perform a cost/benefit analysis for risk remediation.

The Security Policy

One important artifact that comes from the discussion about risk by management and security professionals is the organization's security policy. This document provides a very high level overview of security requirements for the organization.

If your organization does not yet have a security policy, now is a great time to push for its development. The security policy is a document driven by requirements at the highest level of the organization. With organizational leadership supporting a policy, the administrator has the motivation from management to provide a security infrastructure and the support to do so from management.

There are a variety of resources to assist in the development of a security policy. RFC 2196 provides a guide to setting up security policies. The SANS Security Policy Project at *http://sans.org/resources/policy/* will help you develop a security policy by providing templates and guidance.

So how is this analysis done? If you work for a fairly small organization, you may be very involved in this process. So, let's take a moment to look at how to decide how much security is the "right amount." This is useful both in the context of defining priorities for the organization and at a smaller scale. For instance, your security policy may state that your DMZ systems must be protected by "strong authentication." Security policies in general are not much more explicit than this. It's up to security (and possibly also system) administrators to figure out how to get this done.

How Much Security?

There are two considerations that influence how much time you spend "doing" system security: risk/consequence considerations and usability. The greater the risk or the higher the consequence, the more effort you must spend securing your systems. With respect to usability, if your application of security principles makes administration more difficult—worse yet, if it discourages administrators from maintaining systems because of the hassle—you may have gone too far.

Be careful to differentiate between inappropriate security requirements and lazy administration. Not every administrator who shirks at jumping through a few hoops is pointing out your paranoia.

Risk and consequence

The role of your system combined with its exposure to risk helps you determine to what lengths you should go in locking down your system. If you are building a server that provides DNS functionality to your network, a failure or compromise of this system would easily lead to widespread problems. An incident involving a server that provides only NTP however may merely disrupt clock synchronization until the service can be restored, but may not *immediately* affect the rest of your network.

The location of your system both physically and logically on your network is also an important consideration. Systems located on a perimeter network are exposed to external attacks frequently. A computer providing Internet access at a library may have hundreds of users a day—and not all of them trustworthy. Servers on an office network are only directly exposed to other systems on that network.

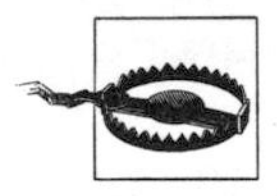

Be careful here! Many administrators blithely assume an internal system is not prone to attack and spend almost *no* time or effort securing the system. This is why the few attacks that originate within the organization so often succeed.

So, what if there were a compromise of a system? What would the impact be to you and your organization? Your organization may suffer from bad press and/or loss of revenue. You may be deemed incompetent and then fired. The effects of a security compromise are not always obvious. The higher the cost of a security breach of the system currently being built, the more time you need to spend securing the system.

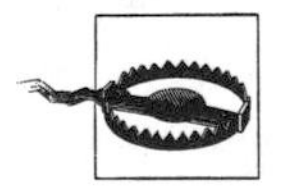

Some argue that, because the system they are building is not that important, the security of that system is not worth any great effort. However, compromised systems often are not an end in themselves; instead they provide attackers with a staging ground from which to initiate further attacks.

From a risk perspective, the amount of effort you must put forth "doing" system security relates directly to the amount of risk involved and the expected consequences of risk realization. Table 1-1 summarizes the effect that probability and impact have on risk.

Table 1-1. Relationship between risk and probability/impact

	Probability		
Impact	**Very probable**	**Possible**	**Very unlikely**
Disasterous	HIGH RISK	HIGH RISK	Medium Risk
Significant	HIGH RISK	Medium Risk	Medium Risk
Moderate	Medium Risk	Medium Risk	Low Risk
Minimal	Medium Risk	Low Risk	Low Risk

This makes sense. Buying a house on an eroding precipice is a high risk proposition. The chances of your house sliding into the abyss are pretty likely. The impact to your house and your belongings certainly qualify as "disasterous." Maybe you'd rather build a house on a mountain. The chances of being buried under a mudslide or avalanche are probably on the low side, depending of course on the mountain's history. The impact would likely be fairly significant though. We're looking at medium risk proposition here. You get the idea. The higher the impact and/or probability, the higher the risk.

Security versus functionality

You might wonder why you don't just use every security tool you have on and around every system. Security costs something. At the very least, the time you spend performing security-related tasks is one kind of cost. The associated loss of functionality or convenience is another form of cost.

Envision building a webmail gateway so that users are able to access internal email even when they are offsite. This has the potential to expose private email to users on the Internet, so you may decide that a few extra notches of security are necessary. So you lock down the webmail system. You remove all webmail plugins except those that are absolutely necessary. You enable HTTP-digest based authentication in your web server. You require that users also come through a proxy server that requires a different layer of authentication. Finally, you mandate that users carry around signed certificates so that their identity can be validated to the server.

This example may be contrived, but security overkill is not always so obvious. In our example, users will become so frustrated with the passwords they must remember, the USB drives they must carry, and the overall hassle that they will eschew webmail altogether. Instead, they may very well start forwarding all their corporate mail to their personal account, which is far more accessible. As a security-minded system administrator, you have just lost: security came at too great a loss of convenience. Similar problems arise if the balance between security and maintainability is lost.

In less structured environments, administrators often have a lot of leeway. If you choose to boot your OpenBSD system from CD-ROM and store all binaries and libraries on this read-only media, you may have gone a long way to keeping your system inviolate. However, what happens when a critical vulnerability is announced and you have to immediately patch vulnerable servers? It will take a great deal of effort to build a new standard configuration onto a CD, test it in your QA environment, and finally deploy it in production. This effort may make you want to wait to perform the upgrades later, delaying your response to a critical event. The maintenance hassle of making your security posture "go to 11" just increased the window of opportunity for attackers.

The danger here is obvious. If you put off patching known vulnerabilities because of the effort required to do so, then you can be worse off than if you had spent a little less effort on your secure configuration. In some very strict environments, you may not have a choice and be required to build, test, and deploy new CD boot images that night.

Choosing the Right Response

After the important resources have been identified and some cost/benefit analysis has been performed to figure out what it's going to take to secure the resource, it's time to decide whether to do it or not. It's pretty obvious what you do when the cost is low and the benefit is high: you act! But what about when the cost is high? If the benefit is high, do you do it anyway? The following outlines what you can typically do with risks after you've identified them.

Mitigate risk

If the fallout from a realized risk is significant and the costs of mitigation can be tolerated, you should take action to mitigate the risk. Some, but perhaps not all, tasks will fall to the system administrator. She is responsible for things like patching vulnerabilities to keep attackers at bay and system backup to prevent accidental or intentional data destruction.

Accept risk

These risks are identified, evaluated, but not mitigated. The realization of these risks fails to significantly affect the organization, the likelihood of risk realization is too low, or no mitigation can be enacted for some reason. For example, a university might categorize the potential for an outside observer using intelligence-grade surveillance equipment to remotely observe the registrar's grade entry as a risk. The likelihood of this occurrence is as low as the cost of mitigation is high. Should the risk be realized, the consequences are probably not dire. Therefore, the risk remains and the university will accept the ramifications if this risk is realized.

Transfer risk

Risk transference is a form of mitigation in which the risk is transferred to another party. This might involve outsourcing a system or process, or keeping it in-house while taking out insurance to cover potential loss. If your system is processing credit card information, there is a risk that the credit card numbers stored on your systems could be stolen by an attacker or insider. Standard mitigation techniques (firewalls, strict access control, and encrypted data) may keep out external eyes, but a rogue employee with access rights may be able to steal and sell this information. The costs associated with the realization of this risk are too immense for the organization to handle, but the likelihood of it happening is low to moderate. A risk like this is a good candidate for being transferred to another entity, like an insurance company.

Security Process and Principles

We now have an idea of the kinds of attacks your host will face. Management has made it clear what resources are important, what must be protected, and what is too expensive to protect. What we're left with is a bunch of risks that need mitigation. We know that to mitigate the risks, we have to balance security needs against required functionality and convenience. We also know that the more critical the resource, the more effort we should go through in securing systems. So let's bring this all into focus in terms of FreeBSD and OpenBSD system administration.

This book is about "doing security" for your BSD systems. This book presents one major framework for building security into your BSD system deployments: security through the system lifecycle. What does this mean? Well, this is a daunting undertaking, to be sure. To make these kinds of tasks easier, we break them into discrete parts; building a secure initial configuration, performing ongoing maintenance, and auditing and incident response.

Initial Configuration

Secure initial configuration is an obvious topic when discussing system-level security. And why not? A host with a secure initial configuration is more likely to stay that way. Careful installation and good decisions early on will leave you with a well-configured, fairly secure system. There is a strong motivation to be diligent in ongoing maintenance because it is easier to maintain a clean slate than it is to solve security issues while not breaking functionality. Furthermore, well-maintained systems who were built from secure initial configurations assist in containment. An attacker that manages to break into a well-maintained box somehow will have a hard time continuing his assault because unneeded services are disabled, file permissions are carefully controlled, and applications are tightly secured.

Properly configuring a host requires a solid understanding of the technology at hand. Unless an administrator knows the ins and outs of the core operating system and the applications running on it, she will not be able to know what actions to take to lock down the host. While there are plenty of host-lockdown templates on the Web for various operating systems, none of them is a one-size-fits-all solution. Administrators often blindly follow security templates only to make their host so secure that it becomes unusable. Or, they follow a template that doesn't apply well to their actual situation. It gives them a feeling of added security because they took proactive security initiatives. But its poor applicability means they have left important weaknesses unaddressed. We urge you to understand the service you are trying to provide and the risks associated with it. From there you can figure out how to appropriately lock-down your system.

Initial configuration is a common area of focus for many books. Configuration is very tangible and the myriad options can be very confusing. Every application has its own unique options and architecture considerations. On any modern OS, there are many applications and aspects to the core system that require specific attention. Authors and readers find it easy to focus on these issues because there is so much ground to cover.

However, securing the initial configuration is not the only aspect of system security. System security is a complicated subject, users rarely see the big picture. Even systems that are thought to have a secure initial configuration can be administered poorly, eventually causing gaps in the security stance of the machine. It is important to look beyond secure configuration options and think about the broader security picture.

Building a secure initial configuration, as far as the operating system is concerned, is the primary focus of Chapter 3. Every application-specific chapter in this book will also focus on the secure initial configuration of the relevant application.

Ongoing Maintenance

Regardless of the role a host plays, once it is deployed, it begins to change. Managing this change is key in maintaining the integrity and security of the host. Assuming you have paid attention to the details of configuring the host, it is in a known good state when it is deployed. Every service request, attempted attack, applied patch, and administrative login has the potential to change the security stance of the machine.

Staying ahead of this change requires a disciplined and coordinated effort. For instance, patch management procedures need to be in place long before you start applying patches. Vendor patches are often released in response to a vulnerability discovered and announced in a public forum. From the point a vulnerability is discovered to the point your systems are patched, the security of your host is a matter of chance. A worm may be written to automatically crawl through the Internet exploiting this vulnerability. An attacker may use the vulnerability to target your organization directly. Thus response to security advisories must be quick and effective.

While this may sound simple as a concept, in practice, patching can be very disruptive. Patches may interrupt service when they are installed. They may even have adverse effects that force you to roll the patch out of your systems until the effects can be mitigated. Successful patch management is not simply composed of technical aspects like how to download and install the patch. Patch management includes regression testing the patch in a lab, getting buy-in from stakeholders and assuring them that the patch will not interfere with organizational operations, and being prepared to roll back when necessary. By understanding the subtleties in patch management, you are helping ensure the security of a host over the long haul.

Other issues, such as using secure transport mechanisms when accessing a host for administrative purposes and proper user management, are also vital for the long-term security of a host. Understanding the ins and outs of secure management is critical on any platform. Implementing these secure management processes can vary dramatically depending on the operating system and applications being used. Luckily, FreeBSD and OpenBSD have a long history of being very maintainable systems. These operating systems are implemented in a manner that makes keeping them secure straightforward and relatively easy to upgrade when security vulnerabilities are discovered.

System maintenance with a goal of maintaining system security is the primary topic of Chapter 4.

Auditing and Incident Response

Sometimes, bad things will happen to good hosts. Even with a secure initial configuration and proper administration techniques, an attacker will periodically successfully bypass the security perimeter of a host. At the very least, auditing will help you determine when you're dealing with an incident. You then need to be prepared to ensure service is restored as rapidly as possible and the damage contained.

Proper incident response relies on both technical and business knowledge. On the technical side, individuals responding to a security incident must have a playbook already created that describes how to get machines redeployed in a secure fashion. Every incident will differ to some extent causing changes in the original plan to restore service. By understanding the core operating system, the applications running, and the manner of attack being executed, an administrator responding to an incident can modify the path to recovery to match the attack that was used.

From a business perspective, the administrator needs to understand the impact the attack has on the business and react accordingly. For instance, if a new product has recently been deployed on the web servers, restoring service immediately may take precedence over preserving the attacker's footprints. Or if an attacker has a history with your organization, you may want to verify that you have a complete audit trail of her actions before restoring servers to known good states. Security is a means to an end. The organization's goals are the ultimate end in most cases, so your actions when responding to an incident should reflect that.

After an incident has been contained through proper response, there may be forensic work required. Some organizations choose to analyze the technical aspect of every incident in an effort to learn what actions the attacker took. This allows them to determine the real loss caused by the attack as well as whether or not civil and criminal chargers should be pursued. Other organizations generally do not do forensic investigation unless the attack is obviously damaging enough to pursue legal action. These types of organizations have determined that the reward for the investigation does not normally warrant the effort required to determine what the attacker has done.

Regardless of your organization's stance on incident response, you may be called upon to perform forensic analysis of a compromised host. The level of diligence required when performing analysis will vary depending on if the investigation is internal or if the data will be used in a court of law. However, from a technical perspective, performing a forensic analysis requires deep technical knowledge of the structure and operation of the operating systems and applications in question. It also requires understanding of the tricks attackers may use to hide or store data and processes.

Forensic analysis is really detective work. It involves looking for clues and understanding the motivation of the attacker. It also involves knowledge of how things work. The lead character in any TV detective show is not just a good interrogator. These fictitious detectives generally have years of broad fictitious experience they can leverage to solve heinous fictitious crimes. Examining a compromised host is very similar; but your experience had better be real and the more you know when you start the analysis, the better analysis you will be able to perform.

Auditing and incident response are the major focuses in the last section of this book.

System Security Principles

Security through the system lifecycle is a useful framework for understanding how security can be woven throughout your administrative duties. This lifecycle is "what you do" for system security. It's time to turn our attention to "how you do it."

We've talked about building a secure system, maintaining it in a clear and controlled way, and responding to threats. Following this system administration lifecycle helps us maintain a secure environment and maintain our organizational operations. However, the details of how to actually conduct these lifecycle activities are not nearly as straightforward.

Understanding how to build, deploy, and maintain a secure system involves technology specific information. In this book, we will give you a great deal of information on

FreeBSD and OpenBSD, arming you with the "domain expertise" required to use these operating systems securely. But beyond that, you must have the right mindset. To be a security-minded system administrator, you need to have the right set of guiding principles. The principles outlined in this chapter should be applied at every stage of a system's lifecycle. Whether you're designing your system or dealing with an ongoing incident, these principles should be valuable in making the right decisions along the way.

As we walk through the system lifecycle in this book, you'll notice that in making decisions or justifying claims, we refer to a variety of security principles along the way. In the book *Building Secure Software* (Addison Wesley) by Gary McGraw and John Viega, the authors present 10 guiding principles for software security. Our focus in this book is not specifically on writing secure code (software security) but in building secure FreeBSD and OpenBSD systems. Nevertheless, many of these principles map directly to secure administration practices and we present them explicitly here.

Apply Security Evenly

The application of security must be consistent across everything you do. The "weakest link" principle means that the strength of your overall security posture will be no stronger than the weakest link. This makes sense. We've already looked an example of this. If your information security stance is strong—your host has been defended against all network-based and local shell-based attacks—you're in good shape. But if your server is located in an unattended or unlocked co-location facility, all someone really has to do is walk up and take your machine away.

Practice Defense in Depth

One of the most important and frequently touted principles is *defense in depth*, also referred to as the "layered approach." Defense in depth suggests that multiple levels of security are better than one single layer of protection. In our example of the physically unprotected server, to apply defense in depth we would move the system to a co-location facility that is locked. Not only should the building be locked, the system should be in a locked cage. Cameras should monitor arrivals and departures. Guards should also be posted to discourage would-be attackers.

Will all of this make our server impenetrable? No, but every additional layer of security makes compromise less likely.

Fail Safe

In case of failure, fail in a safe way. Err on the side of caution. If our server that's now in a guarded vault performs virus checking for your organization's incoming mail, what should happen when the server fails? Should your mail servers simply say "Hmm... my virus-checking host is unreachable. Well, the mail must go through!" Ideally, no. If your organization can tolerate a slight delay in mail delivery, your mail server should probably allow mail to spool until the virus-checking host is available again.

Enforce Least Privilege

Least privilege is the concept that an entity, be it a person, process, or otherwise, is given the bare minimum privilege required to carry out a particular task. The idea is relatively straightforward.

Let's say you send one of your interns to go fix the broken server, but the server is in the same cage as a bunch of your organization's financial systems. The principle of least privilege would indicate that you make sure that the intern you're sending can access the broken server and nothing else. Perhaps you could ask the co-location facility staff to disconnect the host and leave it in a room with a crash cart and a network drop so your intern can work on it without having access to anything else.

One useful way to build least privilege into your infrastructure is to approach deployment and configuration with a default deny mindset. In a firewall context, this means your first rule is to block all traffic. On a system, you only add a user account if and when a specific user needs access. By default, the user is placed into a group that has no access to anything on the system. Should the need arise, the user can be added to additional groups. Even the now well-guarded co-location facility follows this strategy. By default, they will not let anyone access the systems they host for you. You need to specifically authorize users.

Segregate Services

When it comes to system security, don't put all your eggs in one basket. When given the opportunity, separate the services running on systems as much as possible. In some cases, you may want to give one single role to multiple systems so that if one system fails, the service can still be available.

We might have been foolish enough to put our financial data on the same system that performs virus checking. Perhaps, given the volume of mail we receive, virus checking is barely utilizing the resources of the system. Coupling virus checking with data storage at least allows us to use some of that barren 200GB of mirrored disk space that came with the host. It's a good thing we didn't do that. When the system failed, not only would our mail flow have been temporarily interrupted, our financial group would have been unable to issue invoices, reconcile their registers, or (heaven forbid) perform payroll processing!

Simplify

Complexity is a bane when it comes to maintenance. It is easy to maintain a system that is configured in some sane way. When you create too many interdependencies and complex configurations, however, maintenance quickly becomes a nightmare. You're more likely to break something when you touch the machine than fix something.

When your intern finally gets to the system to repair it, he might need to find out what went wrong. If it's a standard FreeBSD install on a pair of hardware-mirrored (RAID 1) drives with packages where one would expect to find them, he stands a good chance of figuring out the problem. What if, on the other hand, you decided that installing using ports or packages wasn't good enough? You compiled your virus scanning software from source and linked all the binaries against custom libraries. If your intern hasn't been fully briefed as to how this works, he'll never discover that the last system upgrade wiped out your custom binaries and that's why the virus scanning software broke.

Keeping things simple ensures that anyone with the right skill set will be able to fix the problem. When complex configurations are unavoidable, they can be simplified through comprehensive documentation.

Use Security Through Obscurity Wisely

People say that security through obscurity is no security at all. Sure enough, if obscurity is your only means of providing security, you are not providing security after all. On the other hand, there are a variety of tactics you can use to be a little more secure in conjunction with other secure configuration and administration techniques. These are generally less effective than "real" security, but a little additional obscurity (defense in depth) doesn't hurt.

Let us suppose that after your intern finishes fixing your virus scanning server, you tell him that he needs to reconfigure the web server on the same system that acts as a frontend management tool for the virus software. Instead of running this server on port 80, he should make it listen for connections on 4000. Like most security-through-obscurity techniques, this alone has limited value. While some vulnerability scanners might just wander across systems finding systems with a listening port 80, most probe thousands of ports per system. Moving your web server is of minimal use because network probes will eventually find it anyway. If he were to also configure the web server so that it doesn't announce what kind of service it is, network scanners will have a little more difficulty telling the person running the scan what kind of service is listening on port 4000.

The key here is that you shouldn't waste time on obscurity when you can spend your time constructively on security. Secure your systems and your services. Document your configuration. If you happen to have a few extra seconds to obscure some information an attacker could otherwise get for free, then by all means do so.

Doubt by Default

If you can help it, don't trust anything. Seems a little paranoid, and taken to the extreme, paranoia will certainly be more of a hindrance than an aid. Still, a little doubt by default will go a long way.

Examples of this are everywhere. If you were to receive a phone call from a director you've never talked to before, and she's asking for the dial-up password—would you tell her? No. At least, not until she's verified that she is who she claims to be. When you visit an SSL-enabled site, does your browser automatically install the certificate and consider it trusted? Of course not. The certificate needs to be signed by a trusted certification authority, it must be valid, and the name on the certificate must correspond to the name of the site you are visiting. Finally, will the co-location staff let your intern in simply because he says he works with Doughnuts, Inc? No way. They'll check his ID and cross-reference his name with their access list.

Every system you build will have services that interact with other systems and users. Think about what you can do to help your running services doubt by default.

Stay Up to Date

Being up to date applies both to your systems and to administrators. Both OpenBSD and FreeBSD are easy to maintain through well-documented upgrade processes. Upgrading application packages can also be a straightforward procedure with tools like *portupgrade* in FreeBSD. Keeping your systems up to date will help ensure vulnerabilities get patched.

The resources available to the system administrator are vast. As it turns out, Google (or your other favorite search engine) is one of the best tools you have at your disposal for information gathering. Keep up to date on what's happening with FreeBSD and OpenBSD. Stay abreast of trends, subscribe to mailing lists, and receive security advisories. Research products thoroughly before you decide to install something. Last, but not least, talk to your peers and share knowledge and ideas. You'll learn something. They will, too.

Wrapping Up

System security is a complex problem. It requires knowledge of the underlying operating systems, the applications running on the host, the network infrastructure, the business goals, and your potential attackers. System security is also divided into phases revolving around the lifecycle of a host. All these aspects must be pulled together in an attempt to keep a host secure and the system usable. As complicated as this may sound, there is hope. Many resources are available to assist in understanding the scope of system security. This book will help you install and configure a secure FreeBSD or OpenBSD system to provide critical services for your organization and hopefully provide insight that will be useful to you as you attempt to tackle the problems that you face.

Resources

The following is a list of resources pertaining to the topics covered in this chapter.

General Security Resources

- *Building Secure Software*, John Viega and Gary McGraw (Addison-Wesley), 2001
- Full Disclosure: *http://lists.netsys.com/mailman/listinfo/full-disclosure/*
- Security Focus (BugTraq et al.): *http://www.securityfocus.com/*
- "Smashing the Stack for Fun and Profit," Elias Levy, Phrack 49: article 14 (*http://www.phrack.org*)

General Security-Related Request for Comments (RFCs)

- RFC 2196: Site Security Handbook
- RFC 2504: Users' Security Handbook
- RFC 2828: Internet Security Glossary
- RFC 3013: Recommended Internet Service Provider Security Services and Procedures
- RFC 3365: Strong Security Requirements for Internet Engineering Task Force Standard Protocols
- RFC 3631: Security Mechanisms for the Internet

CHAPTER 2

BSD Security Building Blocks

Phenomenal, cosmic power! Itty-bitty living space.
—The Genie
Disney's *Aladdin*

FreeBSD and OpenBSD provide unique and powerful features that make excellent building blocks for any secure deployment. This chapter gives you a tour of the most important ones and describes how you can get the most out of them. We will be uncovering functionality that has been in these operating systems for years, yet you may never have known it was there. In the end, you'll have a whole new set of tools you can apply to the different security challenges you face.

The goal of this chapter is to provide you with a set of building blocks that will become rudiments in your security repertoire. In later chapters we discuss how to combine these different rudiments to create more complex security structures that protect individual processes or whole systems. We group our building blocks into five categories.

The filesystem
: If you've worked with any kind of Unix filesystem in the past, this chapter will start in familiar territory. It's only a stepping-off point, however. The BSD systems offer significantly advanced features in their filesystems that are not duplicated on many other Unix-like operating systems. We explore these new features in depth, tell you how to use them, and describe some of the situations where they apply well.

The kernel
: The BSD kernels provide a variety of tunable options, many of which can help us secure our systems. We cover what they do and how to modify the kernel's behavior to use the features you want.

User process controls
: There are a variety of controls that are on the border between the kernel and user applications that help us isolate what our applications can do. We explore

two technologies, namely *chroot(2)* and *jail(2)*, for protecting user-level processes from each other.

Inherent protections
: One of the reasons OpenBSD and FreeBSD make such phenomenal choices for critical infrastructure systems is because of a slew of inherent security-related enhancements. The BSD development teams are working to create systems that are secure by default. We tell you about some of the benefits you "get for free" by running the BSDs, like buffer overflow protections in OpenBSD and hardware cryptography support in both operating systems.

Optimizations
: Related to our discussion of ensuring system availability in Chapter 1, there are ways to make sure your system allocates its resources and attention to the jobs that are most important to you. For example, you can emphasize file I/O or network transactions instead of just running a general-purpose system.

Remember that there is no magic security pill and no single prescription that repels all ills. You will combine these blocks in whatever ways make sense in your situation.

Filesystem Protections

Anyone familiar with Unix operating systems knows about standard Unix file permissions that have been around since the earliest days. They specify what one user, one group, and everybody else may do with a file, directory, or device. They identify only three possible actions: read, write, and execute. It's somewhat sad that after so many years, there are no more sophisticated means of controlling permissions that are standard across all Unices. A variety of proprietary controls have been developed over the years, but each is typically implemented in only one Unix. Most operating systems are still unique in what filesystem permissions they offer, and only the three read-write-execute bits are common to all.

Overview

FreeBSD and OpenBSD (along with NetBSD and Mac OS X) use some derivative of the BSD "Unix filesystem" (UFS). In addition to the standard Unix permissions that are common across all Unices, these BSD systems also implement special filesystem flags that can change the operating system's behavior with respect to certain files. The flags help a system administrator protect key files from misuse and corruption.

In recent years, FreeBSD has evolved UFS to Version 2 (UFS2), incorporating POSIX 1/e access control lists (ACLs) at about the same time. These more advanced discretionary access controls add further, fine-grained control over permissions. Different users can be given different sets of permissions without relying on traditional Unix groups.

The intended use of your system will determine where and when flags or ACLs make the most sense. If you're maintaining a server with many interactive users, ACLs probably make sense because of their flexible permission structure. If your system is more like a dedicated server, the flags will probably be all you need. Flags are one-size-fits-all by nature.

UFS Filesystem Flags

Flags are coarse-grained, but very carefully defined, controls on how a file can be modified, and how it should be handled in backups. Unlike traditional permissions or ACLs, flags enforce the same behavior for all users. If the immutable flag is set on a file, for example, no one can write to it—not even root. The BSD kernel is responsible for enforcing these controls, and your ability to adjust varies, depending on your kernel *securelevel* (see "Kernel Security Level," later in this chapter). In particular, several flags cannot be unset once the kernel *securelevel* is raised above zero. If your system runs at a *securelevel* less than 1, the flags are of only moderate value. An attacker who can compromise the root account can unset these flags at will, but they will certainly impede automated attacks like rootkits. Although you can't turn them off whenever you want, you can set flags on an unflagged file at any time, regardless of the kernel's current *securelevel*.

Manipulating flags

Flags are set with the `chflags(1)` command. Naming a flag will set it, and prepending "no" to the flag's name will unset it. For example, to set the system immutable flag on */kernel*, you run **`chflags schg /kernel`**. To unset it, you run **`chflags noschg /kernel`**. The *nodump* flag is an exception to this convention, since its primary function is to prevent files from being dumped (see "nodump flag," later in this chapter). It is turned on with *nodump* and turned off with *dump*. For example: **`chflags dump /var/db/foo`**.

Specifying **`0`** in place of a flag name will turn off all the flags on a file. It's an inelegant little shortcut, but it works. For example, **`chflags 0 foo`** will turn off all the flags on the file *foo*.

To view the active flags on a file, use the `-o` argument to the `ls(1)` command. Example 2-1 shows a */var/log* directory with a variety of file flags highlighted. Note that this is a contrived example: logfiles with flags set this way could not effectively be rotated, deleted, or otherwise archived.

Example 2-1. Example output of ls -lo in a contrived /var/log

```
-rw-------  1 root  wheel  sappnd  1862 Sep 30 22:39 auth.log
-rw-------  1 root  wheel  sappnd 38374 Sep 30 22:45 cron
-rw-------  1 root  wheel  nodump  3157 Sep 30 03:06 dmesg.today
```

Example 2-1. Example output of ls -lo in a contrived /var/log (continued)

```
-rw-r--r--  1 root  wheel  sappnd 28056 Sep 30 22:39 lastlog
-rw-r--r--  1 root  wheel  -          0 Jun  4 21:57 lpd-errs
-rw-r-----  1 root  wheel  sappnd  2160 Sep 30 03:06 maillog
-rw-r--r--  1 root  wheel  sappnd 15547 Sep 30 22:47 messages
-rw-r-----  1 root  mail   sappnd   628 Sep 30 03:06 sendmail.st
-rw-r-----  1 root  mail   schg    3455 Sep 29 22:00 sendmail.st.0
-rw-r-----  1 root  mail   schg    5543 Jun  4 21:57 sendmail.st.1
```

Table 2-1 lists the flags, who can set them, and a brief description of what they do. They are listed in relative order of usefulness, with the most useful flags first.

Table 2-1. UFS filesystem flags

Flag	Can be set by	Behavior
schg	Root only	System immutable. No part of it can change, not even metadata. Root cannot unset this flag unless the system is in single-user mode or the system is at securelevel 0 or less.
uchg	Owner or root	User immutable. Like the *schg* flag, above, but can be set and unset by root and the file's owner.
nodump	Owner or root	Skip `dump`. Tell the `dump(8)` program not to include a file when it backs up a filesystem.
sappnd	Root only	System append only.No one may truncate the file or write to it at any point other than its end. It can be read at any point, but only written at the end.
uappnd	Owner or root	User append only. Like the *sappnd* flag, above, but can be set and unset freely, both by root and the file's owner.
sunlnk	Root only	System unlink. No one, not even root, can unlink (delete) the file, regardless of the permissions on the parent directory or file.
uunlnk	Owner or root	User unlink. The owner cannot unlink (delete) the file, regardless of the Unix permissions on the parent directory or file.
opaque	Owner or root	Opaque directories. Set only on directories. Makes them opaque when directories are *unionfs* mounted on top of them, i.e., underlying filesystems will not "show through," just like a typical mount-over.
arch	Root only	Archive. The archive flag is not used.

System immutable flag (schg)

This flag is the workhorse of filesystem security. Despite the fact that its abbreviation, *schg*, is derived from "system change," it is universally referred to as the "immutable" flag. When the system immutable flag is set on a file, nothing can modify any part of it. Its metadata (modification times, permissions, owner, group, and so on) cannot be changed, nor can its contents. It cannot be renamed, unlinked (i.e., deleted), or moved, either. Nothing about it can change.

Directories can be made immutable also. They will be just as unalterable as a file, but this will have broader ramifications to the maintenance of the system. If your */usr/local/bin* directory, for example, is immutable, then you won't be able to install any software in that directory while your system runs at a non-zero security level (see

"Kernel Security Level," later in this chapter). The way around this limitation is to reboot into an insecure security level, unset the immutable flags, and then perform the installations. Once the installations are complete, you can run `chflags` to re-enable the immutable flags and then run `sysctl(8)` to increase the kernel security level to its normal level (see "Tweaking a Running Kernel: sysctl," later in this chapter).

User immutable flag (uchg)

The user immutable flag is a kinder, gentler immutable flag that is not affected by the kernel *securelevel*. Users can set and unset this on their own files and directories, just as root can. Unlike the system immutable flag, this one can be unset at any time. In order to be able to set this flag, you must be either the file's owner or root. A user with write access via Unix groups or ACLs, for example, still cannot set this flag.

This flag serves as a useful additional hurdle for an attacker and as a reminder to an administrator. The automatic tools favored by "script kiddies" will probably not account for the possibility that files are set immutable. Failures in their tools, then, give you an opportunity to spot their activities before they completely succeed, and it might even be enough to keep the unsophisticated script kiddies out entirely. When an administrator bumps into this flag, it helps to serve as a reminder that "the file you're changing is important. Be sure that you know what you're doing."

The one place all FreeBSD systems use this flag is on the kernel. It's added mainly as an extra security measure. It helps keep anyone, even root, from accidentally clobbering the */boot/kernel* file. However, rather than inflict a system immutable file on an unsuspecting populace, the FreeBSD maintainers simply made it user immutable. It helps keep the novice administrator from doing something careless, but it doesn't prevent an experienced administrator from getting his job done.

Nodump flag (nodump)

Normally all files in a filesystem are backed up when the `dump(8)` program runs. The *nodump* flag tells the backup system not to include the given file in the dumps. Interestingly, it only affects incremental backups (dump level 1 and above) by default. To tell `dump` to honor the *nodump* flag, specify `-h` on the `dump` command line. If you want files to be omitted from backups entirely (i.e., not even included on full dumps), then you need to specify **`-h 0`** on the command line.

Unfortunately, the *nodump* flag is binary, which makes it hard to have any mixture of behaviors. That is, it's hard to have some files completely omitted from backups while others are omitted only from the incrementals. If you really wanted to, though, you could make this work with some clever automated scripts.

Note that if you use *Amanda* (see *ports/misc/amanda-server*) or a similar software system to automate your backups, it may be a bit tricky to get the `-h` argument onto the command line.

Why would you use such a flag? One set of executives at a major educational institution has their email mailboxes explicitly omitted from the backup schedule. In their case, they are concerned about legal liability. Anything that exists on disk or backup tape can be the subject of a subpoena. These executives want email to be truly deleted if they delete it.

Database files are another example of files that might benefit from the *nodump* flag. They tend to be very large and always changing. They are not very useful to back up with `dump`, however, unless the database server is in a quiescent state while `dump` runs. The files are not usually in a consistent state if the database is actively reading and writing to them. Database files are often among the largest individual files on a system, and they have always been modified recently, so they always get included in incremental backups. This increases the time backups take to run, but they will not actually be very useful for restoration. To back up databases, you have to use a database replication scheme that is aware of the actual needs of backing up databases. Once that is in place, the *nodump* flag can be set on the database files to keep the `dump` program from doing a lot of needless work.

You can also set the *nodump* flag on directories that contain temporary data that is not worth preserving. For example, */tmp* probably has nothing of long-term value in it. You probably don't need to back up */var/run*, either. Then again, depending on your system, you might not save much time or tape space by omitting these directories.

System append-only flag (sappnd)

The append-only flag prevents files from being modified, much like the immutable flag, with one exception: data can be appended at the end of the file. The archetypal use of the append-only flag is for logfiles on secured servers or perhaps for root's *.history* file to help catch unwary hackers (see "Candidates for append-only," later in this chapter).

Note that when a file is marked append-only or immutable, it cannot be removed either. The only difference between immutable and append-only is the ability to append to the file. The flags are the same in all other respects.

User append-only flag (uappnd)

The user append-only flag performs exactly as the system append-only flag described above. The only difference is that this flag can be unset by both the owner and root at any time, regardless of the kernel *securelevel*. The fact that the flag can be unset does not make it useless for security purposes. It helps keep programs from clobbering logfiles or datafiles even when the Unix file permissions would allow it. It also allows non-root users to make use of this kernel feature for their own software. If you do not have non-root interactive users, you may not see a lot of use of this flag on your system.

System no unlink flag (sunlnk)

This flag is a little weaker than the *schg* flag. It simply prevents the deletion of a file. It is arguably most useful in its "user" version, *uunlnk*. It does not prevent truncation of the file or modification of its contents, its permissions, or any other aspect. It merely prevents the file from being removed.

Like other "system" flags, it can only be set by root, and it cannot be unset when the kernel security level is greater than 0. This flag exists only in FreeBSD.

User no unlink flag (uunlnk)

This flag allows a user to indicate that a file may not be deleted, regardless of the actual Unix permissions on its parent directory. Normally, if a user has permissions (through user, group, or ACLs) on the parent directory, she can delete any file in the directory—even files she does not own. That's because, in Unix filesystems such as UFS, the permission for deleting a file is a function of modifying the directory, not the file itself. However, with this flag, the permission to unlink a file can be controlled by the file itself. A user can prevent his file from being deleted, even when the Unix permissions would otherwise permit it.

This flag can be set and unset freely by the file's owner and by root, regardless of the current kernel security level. This flag exists only in FreeBSD.

Opaque flag (opaque)

Opaque flags are used on directories or files that are involved in *unionfs* mounts (see `mount_unionfs(8)` on FreeBSD or `mount_union(8)` on OpenBSD). Union mounts allow one directory or filesystem to be mounted over the top of another directory *while retaining* visibility into the underlying directory. Thus, when you look in the top-level directory, you see the union of the two directories (hence the name). A file that exists in one place but not the other (XOR) will be visible. If there are files or directories of the same name in both places, the "uppermost" one is the one that is accessible.

When a directory is marked opaque with the *opaque* flag, it only shows files that actually exist in its level. That is, it makes the union mount act like a regular mount; files in the corresponding directory of a lower layer will be invisible.

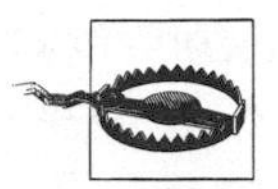

The *unionfs* filesystem is not complete under FreeBSD. It does not fully work and it is dangerous to use. Do not use this feature until you check the documentation and see that it is supported and functional.

Archived flag (arch)

This flag has no official or default function. The `dump` program (you'd think `dump` would care) and all other programs ignore it. The fact that standard programs ignore it doesn't prohibit you from making use of it. It's like another bit that you can set and add your own meaning to.

Common Uses of Flags

It's probably obvious by the preceding discussion and by the functionality implemented in the flags that they were designed with specific tasks in mind. There are a few standard uses of flags that are worth mentioning.

Candidates for system immutable

There are many files that are commonly set system immutable. Your SSH configuration files in */etc/ssh* are good candidates. If your SSH key is ever compromised, all your communications (which might include root passwords or other privileged passwords) can be compromised. Unless you suffer a major compromise or perform a significant upgrade to SSH itself, the SSH keys should remain the same for the life of the system. Likewise, root's *.ssh/authorized_keys* file (if it is used) or administrators' *.ssh/authorized_keys* files could be made immutable. This will stop an attacker from inserting her own authorized key or removing your access to the system by removing your key.

A workstation will probably have fewer files immutable than a core infrastructure server. The exception to this is if you establish a network filesystem infrastructure where software installations are all on a networked disk. In that case, the workstations can be locked down more tightly because the changes that users request probably take place on that networked fileserver, rather than at their desktops. Depending on how tightly you lock down the workstations, you may or may not choose to apply some of the following suggestions, which are more appropriate for core servers.

Lock down and make immutable all the directories that contain software binaries and libraries. These include:

/bin	*/sbin*	*/usr/bin*
/usr/sbin	*/usr/lib*	*/usr/libexec*
/usr/libdata	*/usr/X11R6/bin*	*/usr/X11R6/lib*
/usr/local/bin	*/usr/local/sbin*	*/usr/local/lib*
/usr/local/libexec	*/usr/local/libdata*	

You probably will not have all of those directories, unless you are working on a user-oriented workstation. A system whose sole purpose is a VPN concentrator, for example, would probably not have the X11R6 directories.

There's an important difference between `chflags -R schg /bin/*` and `chflags -R schg /bin`. The former does not set the immutable flag on the directory itself. This allows an attacker to insert files in the directories. A malicious program named `mroe` in */bin* is a devious, subtle attack if the administrator is prone to misspelling.

It's sometimes also useful to create "blocker" files that are immutable to prevent file-creation exploits from creating holes. Imagine a file-creation exploit that creates a *~root/.rhosts* file containing +. Your `rsh`/`rlogin` daemons (that for some crazy reason you didn't disable yet) will now permit root logins from any system with no password (see *rhosts(5)* for more information). If you create the file, make it empty, and then make it immutable, you protect yourself from an attack like this. There is an equivalent *~root/.shosts* file that is used by `ssh`; it could also be blocked this way.

Sidestepping Immutability

An aggressive administrator might mark all of the files in */etc* immutable, make the */etc* directory itself immutable, and enforce the flags by running in securelevel 2 (see "Kernel Security Level," later in this chapter). It turns out that, without rebooting, an attacker who achieves root access can still slip past these protections with a little bit of diligence. The following attack will allow you to take over an OpenBSD system that has been locked down this way. FreeBSD 4.x is similarly vulnerable, but FreeBSD 5.x is not.

1. Make a copy of */etc* (or whatever important directory you want to own). Be sure to use a tool or options that do not duplicate flag settings. Something straightforward like `cp -pr` is bad, but `tar` should work.
2. Modify the files in your */etc* copy to suit your needs.
3. Mount an MFS filesystem over the existing */etc*. For example:

```
sudo mount_mfs -s 8192 /dev/wd0a /etc
```

4. Copy your modified files into your clean-slate MFS */etc*.
5. Send HUP signals to any daemons whose configurations you replaced.

The daemons will reread their configuration files from your new version of the */etc* directory, and they will follow your new configuration. This just goes to show that even options that seem pretty rigid, like filesystem flags, can sometimes be circumvented.

FreeBSD 5.x is not vulnerable because `mount` fails in any securelevel greater than 1.

Candidates for append-only

Remember that append-only is the same as immutable, except that the file can be appended. Your immediate intuition would be to set this flag on logfiles. If you did that, though, the files could not be rotated on an automated schedule. Append-only logfiles cannot be renamed, deleted, or moved—just like immutable files. Being able to rename, move, or delete a logfile is tantamount to editing it. So, in general, you probably will not be setting your basic logfiles, like */var/log/maillog*, to be append-only.

There are a few places where append-only files make sense. If you have specially designed your logging infrastructure so that you have a very large logging disk, and you want to be sure that your log is safe, the append-only flag can help. You could only rotate the logs at boot time, so that might motivate you to reboot on a somewhat regular schedule.

Finding files with flags

The `find(1)` command understands flags if you give it the `-flags` argument. For instance, this command finds all files that have the *uunlnk* flag set in user paco's home directory: **`find /home/paco -flags +uunlnk -print`**. Here's how you might do something interesting with find's flag awareness.

Remember how we said you could use clever scripting with the *nodump* flag to get some files included only in full backups, while others excluded entirely? You could use the *arch* flag (which has no defined purpose right now) to indicate the files that should be included in the full backups. Set the *nodump* flag on files that should never be dumped at all, and set both the *nodump* and the *arch* flag on files that should be included only in full backups. Always run `dump` with the `-h 0` argument so all files with the *nodump* flag set will be excluded. On nights that you run full backups, run a find command like this before you run `dump`: **`find / -flags +arch -exec chflags dump '{}' \;`**. That finds all files that have the *arch* flag set, and turns off their *nodump* flag. After `dump` does its work, you can run a similar command to reverse these effects: **`find / -flags +arch -exec chflags nodump '{}' \;`**. Whenever you want to remove a file from your incrementals, you merely set the *arch* flag on it, and this scheme handles the rest.

POSIX Access Control Lists (FreeBSD Only)

Access control lists (ACLs) extend the well-known Unix file permissions to control, at a fine-grained level, the kind of access individual users or groups can have on particular files. They are new extensions to the Unix filesystem (UFS) and UFS Version 2 (UFS2). Both ACLs and UFS2 are only available under FreeBSD. The permissions governed by ACLs are still the traditional read, write, and execute permissions of Unix filesystems, but they can now be specified for arbitrary lists of users and groups. You're no longer constrained to set permissions for three populations: the owner, one group, and everybody else.

ACLs can be a boon for administrators who manage multiuser systems because users can manage the ACLs on their own files just like the administrator can. With ACLs, a system administrator doesn't have to know what federations of users are forming from week to week and then create Unix groups for them. Individual users can give and revoke access to whomever they choose, whenever they choose.

Enabling ACLs

Before anyone can use ACLs on any filesystem, you must make sure your kernel has the `UFS_ACL` option enabled. The generic FreeBSD kernel does, so unless you took it out when you built a custom kernel, you don't need to do anything special. This one option is sufficient whether you are using ACLs under UFS or UFS2 filesystems. The only time you have to worry about UFS filesystems, though, is if you are using an older FreeBSD system. UFS2 has been the standard filesystem since FreeBSD 5.1.

Once you have the kernel support built in, there are two ways to enable ACLs: using the */etc/fstab* file or tagging the superblock directly.

ACLs in /etc/fstab. There is an *acls* option to mount that can be specified in */etc/fstab* as shown in Example 2-2.

Example 2-2. Example /etc/fstab file with ACLs for /home

```
# Device     Mount   FStype  Options                             Dump Pass#
/dev/da0s1b none     swap    sw                                  0    0
/dev/da0s1a /        ufs     rw,userquota,groupquota             1    1
/dev/da0s1f /usr     ufs     rw,userquota,groupquota             2    2
/dev/da0s1e /home    ufs     rw,userquota,groupquota,acls        3    3
/dev/da1s1e /var     ufs     rw,userquota,groupquota             2    2
/dev/acd0c  /cdrom   cd9660  ro,noauto                           0    0
```

As you can see, the */home* partition in this case has ACLs enabled.

ACLs in the superblock. Tagging the superblock is actually the preferred way to enable ACLs on the filesystem. It can only be done, however, using the `tunefs(8)` command; and `tunefs` can only do its job on an unmounted filesystem. If you want to do this, you will have to take your system down to single-user mode, or umount the idle filesystem, in order to run it. For example, to enable ACLs on the */home* filesystem, you would umount it, and run **`tunefs -a /home`**. The superblock tag is the best way to enable ACLs because it cannot easily be removed from the filesystem. A typo in */etc/fstab* or filesystem changes could inadvertently cause the `acls` flag to be omitted at mount time. However, the ACL flag in the superblock will never be overlooked by `mount`.

Managing ACLs

The setfacl(1) and getfacl(1) commands allow you to manipulate the ACLs on files. Entries in the ACL can either be replaced wholesale or can accumulate. Each time setfacl is run, it can append a new access specifier to the access control list, replace an existing entry on the list, or replace the entire list with a new list specified on the command line.

As an example, let's assume we have a file *book.pdf*, and we want three users (paco, yanek, and bruce) to have read and write access to it. Let us also suppose that the Unix group editors should have read access to this file, and no one else should have any access. In traditional Unix, we could not actually enforce such permissions—there is no way to give three users write permission while giving a Unix group read-only permission. With ACLs enabled, Example 2-3 shows the series of commands that will establish exactly that permissions structure on *book.pdf*.

Example 2-3. Setting ACLs with setfacl(1)

```
% setfacl -b book.pdf              # Erase any existing ACLs
% setfacl -m u:paco:rw book.pdf    # Add Paco's access
%  # Now do Bruce and Yanek in one (contrived) command
% setfacl -m u:bruce:rw -m u:yanek:rw book.pdf
% setfacl -m g:editors:r book.pdf # Give the Unix group editors read access
% setfacl -m o:: book.pdf          # Nobody else gets any permission at all
```

The specifier for the ACL entry is three elements delimited by colons: a letter, a user or group, and then the access to grant that user or group. The letters u, g, and o are very similar to chmod(1) and indicate what you'd expect: user, group, and other, respectively. Naturally there is only one "other" entry. There can be an arbitrary number of user or group permission entries. The specifier in between the colons is either the name of a user, the name of a group, or nothing. In the case of a user or group entry, omitting the user or group name implies that the ACL entry applies to the file's current owner or group. For symmetry, the "other" ACL entry has two colons, but nothing can go between them. After the second colon come the permissions—specified with r, w, and x, again just like with chmod.

To see the ACL for a file, use the getfacl command as shown in Example 2-4. It shows the access control list for the *book.pdf* file we established in Example 2-3.

Example 2-4. Viewing the ACL of book.pdf using getfacl

```
% ls -l book.pdf
-rw-rw-r--+ 1 www  www  0 Nov 23 04:12 book.pdf

% getfacl book.pdf
#file:book.pdf
#owner:1001
#group:100
user::rw-
user:paco:rw-
```

Example 2-4. Viewing the ACL of book.pdf using getfacl (continued)

```
user:yanek:rw-
user:bruce:rw-
group::r--
mask::rw-
other::---
```

ACLs are subtle in a few ways. The only hint you have that a file has an associated ACL is a + after its Unix permissions in the output of `ls -l` as shown in Example 2-4. They also invisibly supercede the standard Unix file permissions. The output of `ls -l` might show a file readable by the `editors` group, and user `gnat` might be a member of `editors`, but if there is a specific ACL entry that denies user `gnat` read privileges on the file, he will be denied. Only the output of the `getfacl` command will explain why.

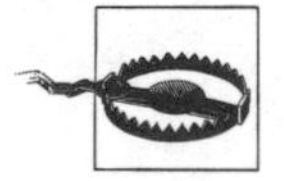

Both ACLs and flags can be confusing if they are used on an NFS file server. The NFS protocol has no means of transmitting ACL information from the server to the client. So the client will be denied permission because the ACL or the flags deny the action, but the client will have an incomplete picture of why it happened. Commands like `getfacl` and `ls -lo` will appear to work, but they will not actually show the true ACLs or flags. Commands like `setfacl` and `chflags` will fail on NFS mounted filesystems.

Tweaking a Running Kernel: sysctl

As the BSD kernels have evolved, many of their internal data structures have become more exposed to the administrator. Modern BSD kernels can now be tuned while they run, using a program called `sysctl(8)` that displays and sometimes alters the value of a variable in the running kernel. Most `sysctl` variables control highly specialized and localized functionality in the kernel. Your server's role, and the environment in which it deployed, largely determine which of these variables—if any—you need to set. A very active database server might need more open files per process than usual. A very active web server will often need various TCP/IP variables tuned. An Internet server that is in a hostile network will need options set that are unnecessary for an intranet server on a friendly network.

These variables might indicate the default settings in a kernel module or device driver (e.g., `net.inet.ip.ttl=64`). Sometimes they offer low-level tuning on things like buffer sizes (e.g., `kern.ipc.maxsockbuf=262144`). Some of them are read-only and dynamic to provide a snapshot in time of some kernel state that is constantly in flux (e.g., `vm.loadavg=0.04 0.08 0.08`). Others merely offer a convenient way to get information out of the kernel. Changing these values is a fundamental skill that will be required as part of most significant tasks discussed in this book.

> **sysctls Change**
>
> The names and behaviors of sysctl variables change from time to time. New versions of the operating system introduce new variables and retire old ones. In this chapter we discuss FreeBSD 5.3-RELEASE and OpenBSD 3.6. There have been significant changes in FreeBSD, for example, from the 4.x versions to the 5.x versions.
>
> There are several places to find all the names and values for variables. The definitive source, of course, is to run **sysctl -a**. That will list all of the sysctl variables known to the current kernel, and it will show their current values. It does not, however, indicate which values can be changed, nor what would happen if they were changed. The *sysctl(3)* and sysctl(8) manpages indicate whether particular values are changeable. Some values are not changeable at runtime, but can be altered from their defaults at boot time by entries in */etc/sysctl.conf(5)*.

Setting sysctl Values

Reading sysctl values is easy: just run **sysctl variablename**. Any user can read all kernel values. Setting variables is equally easy. Just add an equals (=) sign and the new value: **sysctl kern.securelevel=2**. Only root can set values. Once you have a set of sysctl values that you like and want to make default, you can add them to *sysctl.conf(5)* in a simple variable=value format. The only values that can go in */etc/sysctl.conf*, however, are those that can be set once the system is up and running multiuser. FreeBSD allows some values to be set at boot time, but not later. Those go in */boot/loader.conf*. The *loader(8)* manpage lists which variables can only be tuned at boot time in this file.

> sysctl is a very powerful tool and it has no error checking. Tweaking the wrong variable the wrong way can send your system spiraling downward quickly. Fortunately, sysctl values are not permanent, so a simple reboot will fix a badly set sysctl value. Be sure to test them before codifying them in a file like */etc/sysctl.conf*.

Kernel Security Level

There are several sysctl variables that are important to overall system security. Probably the single most important sysctl variable in the entire system is the variable kern.securelevel, simply referred to as its *securelevel*. Its value has diverse effects across a wide variety of functions and features.

Table 2-2 summarizes the various ways in which the kernel *securelevel* affects system operations. They are explained in detail in the following sections.

Table 2-2. Kernel security levels

System property	Securelevel -1	0	1	2	3†
System immutable and append-only flags can be changed	✓	✓	–	–	–
Raw disk devices for mounted file systems can be written*	✓	✓	–	–	–
/dev/mem and */dev/kmem* can be written	✓	✓	–	–	–
Kernel modules can be loaded and unloaded	✓	✓	–	–	–
Non-mounted raw disk devices can be written*	✓	✓	✓	–	–
Filesystems can be mounted	✓	✓	✓	–‡	–
Time can be adjusted more than one second forward or back	✓	✓	✓	–	–
IP filtering and firewall rules can be changed	✓	✓	✓	✓	–

* Raw disk devices only exist in OpenBSD.
† Securelevel 2 in OpenBSD is equivalent to 3 in FreeBSD.
‡ Filesystems can be mounted under OpenBSD, FreeBSD 4.x , but not under FreeBSD 5.x.

Root can raise the *securelevel* at any time, but it can never be lowered. You must change your configuration file and reboot to run at a lower level.

Level -1: "permanently insecure"

If the system finds itself in *securelevel* -1 at the end of the boot process, it will not raise the *securelevel*. Thus, setting your default level to -1 is how you get the system to stay insecure at boot time. At various times in later chapters we will recommend that you "reboot to a lower *securelevel*" in order to accomplish something that can only be done that way. Setting your default *securelevel* to -1 is how you'd do that.

In FreeBSD, you may also specify **`kern_securelevel_enable="NO"`** in */etc/rc.conf* to boot into securelevel -1.

At kernel *securelevels* 0 and -1 the operating system behaves as like any traditional Unix: root is supreme and can do all things. All filesystem flags are enforced but can be both set and unset. All devices can be read and written to as their permissions indicate. Firewall rules can be set and unset at will, and the system clock can be set arbitrarily.

Production systems that have any sort of security requirement should normally run with a *securelevel* higher than 0. It's worth noting that even if you immediately promote your system to *securelevel* 1, you'll still be able to configure everything without difficulty. It's only after flags have been set on something you want to change that the *securelevel* may interfere. You can install new packages and set flags on the newly installed files without worrying about the *securelevel*.

Level 0: transitional security level

There is no operational difference between secure level 0 and *securelevel* -1. The system only runs in level 0 briefly during boot time and when it is in single-user mode. Generally systems boot at level 0 and then switch to a higher level after booting, or they boot at -1 and stay there.

Securelevel 0 is unusual in that you can lower the *securelevel* back to -1 if you want to. If your OpenBSD system normally runs at *securelevel* 1 or 2 and you want to boot to a lower level just once, you can do so without modifying your configuration file. Boot to single-user mode and you will find your system in *securelevel* 0. Set the *securelevel* to -1 by running **`sysctl kern.securelevel=-1`**. When the system boots, it will not increase the *securelevel* to its default.

Level 1: improved operational security

At level 1, the kernel imposes stricter security constraints than a traditional Unix system. Write access to raw disk devices (which exist on OpenBSD and FreeBSD 4.x) is denied, even to root-equivalent processes, if the raw device corresponds to a currently mounted filesystem. On FreeBSD, though raw devices don't exist, similar constraints apply. You cannot write to the disk device of the mounted filesystem.

In traditional Unices there are two styles of devices: "raw" and "cooked." The raw devices do not use buffering in the kernel, but instead perform their I/O directly to the device. The kernel mediates access to cooked devices. It might prefetch more data than a program asks for and store the extra in a buffer, or it might buffer data that a program writes until it has enough to make a call to the real device. Raw devices are used by programs like `fsck(8)`, `dump(8)`, `mount(8)`, and `newfs(8)` to read and write data directly off of disks.

The kernel also enforces the system append-only and system immutable flags (see "Filesystem Protections," earlier in the chapter). The */dev/mem* and */dev/kmem* devices cannot be opened for writing, which helps protect against rogue processes writing into other processes' memory.

Kernel modules cannot be loaded or unloaded in any level greater than zero, and this might occasionally interfere with your maintenance. The BSD kernels have become increasingly modular in recent years, which helps reduce the amount of RAM the kernel uses. They don't load device drivers for devices you don't have. For example, most dedicated servers rarely mount CD-ROMs. The ISO-9660 filesystem driver, therefore, is not built into the kernel. It is available instead as a kernel module. The first time you try to use a CD-ROM on a system running at *securelevel* 1 on higher, the `mount(8)` command will automatically try to load the kernel module and fail. If the ISO-9660 driver is something you need often, you will have to either add a command to the boot process to load the driver at boot time, or compile the driver into the kernel. For dedicated servers, this is rarely an issue after the server is configured the first time.

Just be aware that you cannot add certain module-based functionality to a server with a non-zero *securelevel*. You have to reconfigure the system so it will boot into a lower *securelevel*, reboot, and then do the work that requires the kernel module.

Level 2: high security

Each level of security includes all the protections of all the lower levels. At level 2, all of the level 1 protections remain, but several are expanded. For OpenBSD and FreeBSD 4.x, no raw disk device can be opened for writing at all once you're in level 2. This means, among other things, that the `newfs(8)` command cannot be used to create filesystems. Additionally the `growfs(8)` command will not run at this level. Even though FreeBSD does not use raw devices anymore, these same restrictions are implemented in FreeBSD on the so-called "cooked" devices.

It's interesting to note that mounting an MFS filesystem will fail in securelevel 2 in FreeBSD 4x and in FreeBSD 5.x, but for different reasons. In the first case, it will fail because `newfs` cannot run. In the latter case, you just can't mount filesystems in securelevel 2.

This protection is selective, so devices such as tapes and network devices are still accessible to processes with root privileges. Additionally, the protections are only for writing to raw disk devices, not reading. If reading from raw devices were restricted, then `dump(8)` and `fsck(8)` would not be able to run. Programs like FreeBSD's `camcontrol(8)` and anything else that tries to directly manipulate the SCSI bus would fail, though. Interestingly `mtx(1)`, a tape library control program available in *ports/misc/mtx*, will not work at this *securelevel*, but the built-in `chio(1)` library control program will. The reason is that `mtx` tries to use */dev/pass0*, a device that directly reads and writes on the SCSI bus, whereas `chio` uses API calls in the operating system. If direct reads and writes to the SCSI bus were allowed, then disks could be written and manipulated—bypassing the *securelevel*.

Time is also carefully controlled at level 2 and higher. It cannot be adjusted forward or backward by more than 1 second at a time. This restriction on time has two beneficial effects. It makes log entries more trustworthy because the time cannot be modified to make events look like they happened in the future or in the past. Accurate time also affects digital signatures. If any processes on the system use asymmetric cryptography to apply digital signatures (e.g., PGP or S/MIME email), the accuracy of the clock is critical to the validity of the signature.

Restricting time adjustments is not normally a problem when you keep your time synchronized using `ntpd(8)`. At boot time, before the *securelevel* is set, the system calls `ntpdate(8)` (or `ntpd -q`) to adjust the clock however much it needs to be adjusted. Then the system starts the ntpd daemon, to continuously synchronize the local clock with the public time servers. Although your typical Intel-based PC system clocks tend to drift significantly, even the worst can be kept in check by ntpd.

Level 3: network security

This level only exists in FreeBSD. The protections it offers in FreeBSD are duplicated in OpenBSD at *securelevel* 2. At kernel *securelevel* 3, two network features—the firewall rules ipfw(8) and *ipfirewall(4)* as well as the *dummynet(4)* traffic shaping parameters—become immutable. This is most beneficial when the system is acting as router, performing network address translation, or is some other core network device. It helps prevent an attacker from opening holes in your firewall to allow malicious network traffic through. These are the only differences between level 3 and level 2. If you do not have concerns about firewall rules (for instance, if you do not use the firewalling features), there is no particular value in running in *securelevel* 3.

Setting the securelevel for FreeBSD

The FreeBSD *securelevel* is controlled by two variables in */etc/rc.conf(5)*. A typical configuration looks like:

```
kern_securelevel_enable="YES"
kern_securelevel="2"
```

By default, kern_securelevel_enable is set to NO in */etc/defaults/rc.conf*, which causes the system default of 0 to be demoted to -1 at boot. You may find additional details about securelevels in the manpage for init(8).

Setting the securelevel for OpenBSD

The OpenBSD *securelevel* is configured to be 1 by default. To change your default *securelevel*, edit */etc/rc.securelevel(8)* and change the line securelevel=1 to a new value. OpenBSD documents its behavior in the *securelevel(7)* manpage.

Thoughts on using securelevel

Making *rc.conf* or *rc.conf.local* immutable in a *securelevel* greater than 1 is the only way to prevent an attacker who gains control of your system from lowering its security level. The only way to reduce the security level of your system in such a configuration is to interrupt the boot process at the console and enter single-user mode.

Before trying to "make your system go to eleven" on the kernel *securelevel*, however, think about whether the hassle in maintenance is worth the additional security. We would argue that the additional security is mostly illusory, but the maintenance hassle is absolutely real. The additional security is minimal because your attacker's goal is probably not to reboot the system to a lower *securelevel*. Instead, she really wants to modify database records, set up back doors into the system, and so forth. If she gets into the system at all, you will need more than directory permissions and *securelevel* to protect your assets. Don't look at *securelevel* as a silver bullet that cures all security problems. Security levels can make administration more complicated and time-consuming in addition to making systems safer. Sometimes all the work of raising the *securelevel* can be bypassed somewhat, too. See the sidebar "Sidestepping Immutability," for an example of bypassing *securelevel* in FreeBSD 4.x or OpenBSD.

The more volatile your filesystem, the harder it is to run at a high security level all the time. Each time you install software, you will be installing files in potentially sensitive areas. For instance, if you use something like Osiris (*http://osiris.shmoo.com/*) to capture all the attributes of files on the filesystem, that database will need to be updated after a software install. If that database is stored on the system itself, it will probably be immutable, and the *securelevel* settings will make it impossible to update it without rebooting into a lower *securelevel*. Clearly software installation in such an environment requires a deeper depth of planning and staging than a non-*securelevel* installation. The more sensitive your users are to system reboots, the more planning and staging you'll need.

The above considerations notwithstanding, no server that needs to be secured should omit the kernel *securelevel* setting. It is one of the distinguishing features that sets FreeBSD and OpenBSD apart from similar free Unix-like operating systems.

Other Security-Related Kernel Variables

Several additional variables are available that each add some small value to securing a server. Not all of them are appropriate to all environments.

Random PIDs

A number of exploits, such as race conditions, make use of the fact that process IDs (PIDs) have historically issued sequentially by the operating system. Process ID 1 is assigned to `init`, and then all the others are issued incrementally. If the server launches the BIND nameserver at boot time, for example, the `named(8)` process probably gets the same PID (plus or minus a few) every time. Unless something unusual happens and the nameserver is killed, an attacker can count on `named` having that PID on his target. Of course, every server will be slightly different, but once you learn PIDs for a particular system, they will only change a little each time the server boots. Other processes, such as *sendmail(8)*, fork often. If a process runs with root privileges and it forks, there is a second copy of it (the child process) running with root privileges for some small instant of time. Typically the child sheds its root privileges as quickly as it can, but sometimes the child process is vulnerable to some outside influence like creating a temporary file named the same as one it plans to open. By knowing the PID of the child process and how to influence it, attackers can try to exploit these kinds of race conditions.

FreeBSD allows you to choose to assign PIDs to processes randomly by setting the kern.randompid variable to 1. PID 1 still goes to init, but everything else is random. OpenBSD does not offer a choice for this behavior. It always assigns random PIDs, except to init.

Controlling core dumps

When a process crashes, or when it is sent certain unhandled signals, it might "dump core" in an attempt to aid in debugging what went wrong. More often than not, this core file is large and useless for the system administrator. It is a snapshot of the memory the program was using at the time the program crashed, along with various register values like the stack pointer. If you are the program's developer and you have the source code and motivation, you can use the core file to help track down just what was happening when the program crashed.

Most of the time, system administrators and system users have no use for core files. More importantly, such files can inadvertently leak important information to a malicious user. Imagine, for instance, a situation where an attacker can cause the web server process to dump core. Perhaps there is a buffer overflow that causes a segmentation fault, or some kind of unhandled exception. If the web server dumps core while it has, for example, the server's SSL private key unencrypted in memory, that key will be in the core file. While the core file probably will not be dumped somewhere visible in the web hierarchy, the attacker may have some other means of getting the *httpd.core* file from the web server (e.g., perhaps the attacker has a login account). If he does get the core file, he can rummage through the core file to extract the SSL private key, and now he can decrypt all that server's traffic! A lot of things have to go wrong for such an attack to actually succeed, but you can see the potential.

Table 2-3 describes some sysctl variables that control core dump behavior. In general, core dumps should be turned off unless you have a very specific need for them. Note that two of these are FreeBSD specific, and the last one performs the same role, but is named differently in FreeBSD and OpenBSD.

Table 2-3. Core dump controlling sysctl variables

Variable name	Default	Usage
kern.coredump (FreeBSD only)	1	Enables core dumps by programs. If they are enabled, the core file will be named according to the kern.corefile template below. This can virtually always be disabled safely.
kern.corefile (FreeBSD only)	%N.core	Template for core filenames. %N is the name of the program that crashed.

Table 2-3. Core dump controlling sysctl variables (continued)

Variable name	Default	Usage
`kern.sugid_coredump` (FreeBSD)	0	*Setuid* and *setgid* programs are especially likely to have sensitive information in memory, so they do not dump core by default. You would only enable this if you were actually trying to get a core file from such a program for debugging or forensic purposes.
`kern.nosuidcoredump` (OpenBSD)	1	

Reducing visibility in the network

Two related variables tweak behaviors in the TCP/IP stack to make a system less visible to probes. This helps you keep a low profile in the presence of automated scanners, and it helps reduce the amount of resources the kernel spends responding to such probes. The variables are `net.inet.tcp.blackhole` and `net.inet.udp.blackhole`. To use them, put the following lines in */etc/sysctl.conf*:

```
net.inet.tcp.blackhole=2
net.inet.udp.blackhole=1
```

Network Scans: What Are They?

When your system is available on the Internet, it will definitely be the subject of one or more probes. If the system is behind a firewall, the firewall can block the majority of the probes. Otherwise, your system will receive a lot of weird traffic that malicious people send. They are trying to figure out what operating system and software you are running and whether there are any known exploits for it. They do this in a variety of ways.

Someone who is scanning usually just picks IP address ranges and starts sending packets to ports on those IP addresses. There are a number of tools such as `nmap` (*http://www.insecure.org/nmap/*) that automate this process. Once he knows what ports your server listens to, he will probe those ports more specifically. For instance, he will connect to port 22 to determine if the version of OpenSSH you run is vulnerable to any number of vulnerabilities OpenSSH has had over the years. He may also send packets with the *SYN* and *FIN* bits set. Such packets are not used in normal TCP/IP connections, but malicious scanners use them regularly. It turns out that most operating systems are idiosyncratic in how they process such packets, so the system's response can often identify what operating system is running.

You will never completely defeat such scans, since you have to have some connectivity. Giving away as little information as possible, though, is a good practice.

These variables cause the kernel to drop packets when another system attempts to connect to a TCP or UDP port where no process is listening. The normal kernel behavior would be to compose a TCP reset packet, or an ICMP port unreachable message, and send it as a response. When the two "blackhole" sysctl variables are set, the kernel does nothing when it receives connection attempts on non-listening ports. The probing system gains no information about your system. It cannot distinguish a non-listening port from a timeout in the network. This will slow an attacker down some because he will wait some amount of time after each probe packet is sent. His scan will take a lot longer. Turning on these variables also reduces the amount of resources consumed by the kernel's responding to such probes. Any system that is subject to a lot of random port scans or probes should have these variables on. Any system that is connected to the Internet is subject to just such scans and so should have these variables enabled.

Dropping "synfins"

A similar variable `net.inet.tcp.drop_synfin` will cause the kernel to drop all TCP packets that have the SYN and FIN bits set.

See the sidebar "Network Scans: What are They?" for more information on *synfin* packets and how they are used.

These so-called "synfin packets" are often used by programs like `queso` and `nmap` to "fingerprint" an operating system. Some believe that dropping such packets (i.e., not responding to them) violates the TCP specification, but there are vigorous compelling arguments on both sides. Some system and network administrators are not comfortable with dropping them. It is unlikely, however, that failing to respond will have any adverse effect on the operation of your server.

Dropping SYN+FIN packets requires that you change your FreeBSD kernel configuration. Unless you add the `option TCP_DROP_SYNFIN` statement to your configuration and recompile your kernel, the `net.inet.tcp.drop_synfin` variable will not be honored. Consult Chapter 9 of the *FreeBSD Handbook* (O'Reilly) for a thorough walkthrough of kernel configuration and compilation.

The Basic Sandbox: chroot

As Unix systems evolved over time, more and more defects were found in critical system software. When software ran with elevated privileges, those defects could often be parlayed into security compromises. Sometimes a program might divulge the contents of a protected file, and sometimes it would execute a system call with unauthorized parameters. The change root (*chroot(2)*) system call was invented as a defense against this sort of attack. If the privileged software goes awry, this secondary defense tries to limit the damage that might result.

Be aware that both *chroot* and *jail* have two different sets of manpages. There are *chroot(2)* and *jail(2)* system calls as well as `chroot(8)` and `jail(8)` commands.

The principles behind chroot are simple. A process running in a chrooted environment sees a normal filesystem, but it in fact has a virtual root directory. The goal is to prevent the process from accessing files outside its sandbox. So, if `ntpd` runs in a chrooted environment, for example, and an exploit is discovered that causes it to overwrite a file, files in the real filesystem should be protected. The daemon perceives a / directory and will write relative to that directory, but on the real filesystem, the directory is something like */var/ntpd*, and the daemon cannot actually reach the real / directory.

The archetypal use of chroot is for the FTP daemon, `ftpd(8)`. It allows anonymous users to traverse part of the filesystem and download files. For obvious reasons, it should not allow them to traverse the entire real filesystem anonymously. To run correctly, however, the daemon needs more than just the files it is supposed to serve. It needs files like */etc/passwd* and */etc/group* to map numeric UIDs and GIDs to user login names and groups, */etc/localtime* to display times in the correct time zone, and */etc/motd* to define a "message of the day" to users who connect. In order to get the FTP daemon to run correctly in a chroot environment, then, it takes some configuration and planning.

Creating a chroot Environment

It takes a bit of work, and sometimes some in-depth knowledge of the software you're installing to properly build a chroot environment for it. Figure 2-1 shows an example of a real filesystem, with a chroot virtual filesystem beginning at a */jail* directory on a real filesystem. Most software that is amenable to chroot will tell you, in their manpages or other documentation, what they require in order to run correctly. If they don't give you explicit instructions, expect to spend some time in trial-and-error attempts. We discuss some techniques for determining software needs in the section "Managing jails."

First, you must create a directory hierarchy with all the subdirectories that need to exist. In this case, */jail* with subdirectories *bin*, *etc*, *lib*, *usr*, and *web*. We're chrooting a web server, so we're going to put all the web server's binaries, configuration, and data in the *web* directory.

Then copy the software and all its data into the chroot area. Depending on how the software will execute, this usually requires copying shared libraries (e.g., the C runtime library */usr/lib/libc.so.4*), configuration files, and datafiles. If the software normally expects its configuration files to be in */etc/software.conf*, then install the file in */jail/etc/software.conf*.

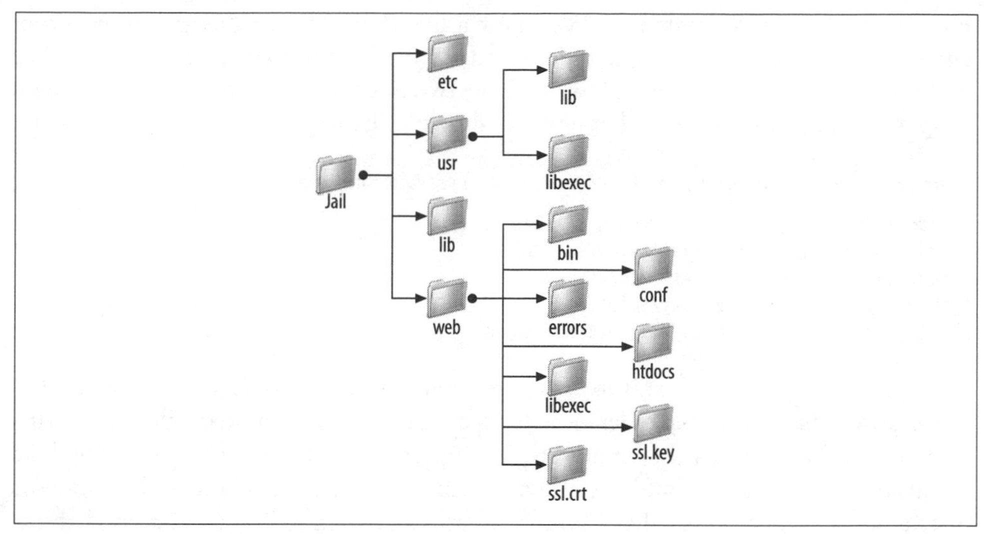

Figure 2-1. A chroot filesystem

Most software capable of taking advantage of chroot will save you some of this effort. Either by statically linking at compile time, or by dynamically loading all its shared libraries before calling *chroot*, it reduces the number of files that have to be stored in special chroot filesystems. BIND 9, for example, does exactly this, alleviating the need to copy a bunch of dependent libraries into a virtual filesystem.

An Example: chrooting ntpd

When a program does not have native support for *chroot(2)*, the way BIND and `ftpd` do, you can use the `chroot(8)` command to impose the restrictions on it. To show how this is done, we will take a program in FreeBSD, `ntpd`, that does not support chroot and launch it chrooted. There have been historically very few bugs with `ntpd` relative to its ubiquity, and OpenBSD has already imposed privilege separation on its `ntpd`, so this is a somewhat contrived example. We start out by creating a */jail/ntpd* virtual filesystem. Normally we would create a separate user associated with `ntpd` and make all the files in the jail owned by that user (OpenBSD has an `_ntpd` user for this purpose). In this case, we can't do that because only root can change the clock. The `ntpd` process needs to run as root.

If the process must run as root to set the clock, what is the `_ntpd` user for? The OpenBSD team wrote their own NTP daemon that prominently features privilege separation. It drops its privileges for most mundane operations (like DNS lookup and parsing network messages). This is an excellent example of how a simple design and the application of a security principle can obviate the need for complex, error-prone configurations.

First, let's just take a crack at it. We know a few things have to exist in our chroot environment: the */usr/sbin/ntpd* binary and its configuration file */etc/ntp.conf*. We make our virtual root directory with these two files and run the command with proper syntax just to see what happens, as shown in Example 2-5.

Example 2-5. Make an ntpd chroot environment and see what happens

```
% sudo mkdir -p /jail/ntpd/usr/sbin /jail/ntpd/etc
% sudo cp /usr/sbin/ntpd /jail/ntpd/usr/sbin
% sudo cp /etc/ntp.conf /jail/etc/ntp.conf
% sudo chroot /jail/ntpd /usr/sbin/ntpd
ELF interpreter /libexec/ld-elf.so.1 not found
```

This tells us two things: first, the program is dynamically linked; second, we have to track down its library dependencies. If `ntpd` were statically linked, all the instructions would be stored in the binary file. The operating system would essentially load the `ntpd` file into memory and execute it. Because it is dynamically linked, it borrows instructions from various other libraries. Normally dynamic linking is a good thing. It makes the programs smaller on disk and in RAM. This lets your system benefit more from its caches because the same RAM pages and disk blocks are being used by multiple programs. When dealing with a chroot (or, as we will see, with a jail), dynamic linking makes it a little harder to isolate the program. We have to identify every library that `ntpd` loads, and we have to put a copy of the library in the virtual filesystem.

Rather than find all the libraries by trial and error, use `ldd(1)` to interrogate the binary as shown in Example 2-6.

Example 2-6. Using ldd to determine library dependencies

```
% ldd /usr/sbin/ntpd
/usr/sbin/ntpd:
        libm.so.3 => /lib/libm.so.3 (0x280ae000)
        libmd.so.2 => /lib/libmd.so.2 (0x280c8000)
        libcrypto.so.3 => /lib/libcrypto.so.3 (0x280d2000)
        libc.so.5 => /lib/libc.so.5 (0x281c7000)
```

Copy */libexec/ld-elf.so.1* and these other library files into */jail/ntpd* and try again. You'll see that it works! Now, `ntpd` is a pretty straightforward program, so chrooting it was equally straightforward. For other programs, you often need more files than just the shared libraries. If `ntpd` had complained about other missing files, we would have used some of the techniques described in the next section, "Finding Other Dependencies."

You might wonder if you gained anything by chrooting `ntpd`. While chroot is potentially escapable, especially if the process runs as root, you did create an additional hurdle for an attacker who would exploit your `ntpd`. He must not only create a successful exploit for the daemon, but he also has to customize his attack to escape your chroot environment. This is just another layer of defense, in line with our defense-in-depth principle.

A dedicated hacker who is specifically targeting your system for some reason might spend the extra time and effort to break out of a chroot. The so-called "script kiddies," on the other hand, who run automated discovery and exploit tools will probably pass over your system since they'd rather spend their time on low hanging fruit. Ultimately, you have to consider the level of hostility you face and decide whether the increase in security was worth the effort of chrooting.

Finding Other Dependencies

If you try to run programs in a chrooted environment and they fail mysteriously, the `ktrace(1)` and `kdump(1)` commands come in handy.

To use `ktrace`, simply put it on the command line first, like you would for `sudo(8)`. A file named *ktrace.out* will be produced in the directory in which you run `ktrace`. You can then use the `kdump` command to parse that file. The first things to look for are files that the program you're trying to chroot is attempting to open. Look for the name-to-inode (*NAMI*) translation (e.g., **`run kdump | less`** and then search interactively for "NAMI"). This makes a good starting point because you often see files that you know don't exist and you can work on installing those files into your virtual filesystem.

See Table 2-4 for some red herrings that you don't need to track down.

If the *NAMI* translations don't give you enough of a clue to figure out what files you need in the virtual filesystem, look more interactively at the `kdump` output for more information. Example 2-7 shows some of the output from trying to open a file named *foo* that is not readable by the current user:

Example 2-7. kdump output

```
52240 cat      CALL  open(0xbfbffc8c,0,0)
52240 cat      NAMI  "foo"
52240 cat      RET   open -1 errno 13 Permission denied
```

Often the kinds of problems you run into when trying to install software into chroot are configuration files or shared libraries that do not exist in the right path. By running `kdump` and `ktrace` multiple times, you can zero in on the files you need and where they need to be. If you're working with a daemon process like Sendmail or Apache that forks child processes, you can run **`ktrace -di`** to follow its descendents. Also check for application-specific options that may prevent the program from running in daemon mode. Many daemons have options to stay in the foreground and log extra information.

Sorting through kdump's output

You don't have to track down each and every file that the program tries to open. Sometimes, for example with *libcrypto.so*, you'll see the program try opening it in a variety of different directories until it finally finds it. The library is ultimately found, so it really doesn't matter where it's found. Other files, like */etc/malloc.conf*, don't actually matter most of the time. They should only exist if you really are trying to modify *malloc(2)*'s behavior in your chroot or jail environment. Table 2-4 lists files that you'll frequently need in either a jail or chroot environment. It also lists some files that you might see in the output of `kdump` that aren't usually important. If your program dies because it can't open a file, look at the last error in the `kdump` output and work backward from there. Don't start with files that aren't found if the program keeps running after failing to find the file.

Table 2-4. Files related to chroot and jail

Filename	Description
/lib/ld-elf.so.1 (FreeBSD) */usr/libexec/ld.so* (OpenBSD)	The runtime loader for the operating system. If you intend to run any dynamically linked programs, you will have to provide this file in this location inside the virtual environment. You will also need one or more dynamic libraries.
/lib/libc.so.5 */usr/lib/libc_r.so.5* */usr/lib/libstdc++.so.4* */lib/libm.so.3* */lib/libcrypto.so.3* */lib/libcrypt.so.2* */usr/lib/libpthread.so.1*	Dynamic libraries that you frequently need on FreeBSD, including the C and C++ runtime libraries, the standard math library, the cryptography library, and pthread library. The *libc_r.so.5* library is a reentrant version of the standard C runtime environment that is used by programs that use FreeBSD's native threads instead of pthreads.
/usr/lib/libc.so.34.1 */usr/lib/libstdc++.so.33.0* */usr/lib/libm.so.2.0* */usr/lib/libcrypto.so.11.0* */usr/lib/libpthread.so.6.0*	Dynamic libraries that you frequently need on OpenBSD, including the C and C++ runtime libraries, the standard math library, the cryptography library, and pthread library.
/etc/pwd.db	A hashed version of the traditional */etc/passwd* file. Used frequently to map numeric UIDs to names. Does not actually contain encrypted versions of passwords.
/etc/spwd.db	A hashed version of the */etc/master.passwd* file, just like *pwd.db*, but has encrypted versions of passwords. Might be needed if software in your *chroot* environment needs to authenticate users (e.g., an IMAP daemon).
/etc/localtime	Specifies the local time zone. Allows log entries to carry a properly localized timestamp.
/var/run/ld-elf.so.hints	A hints file used by the runtime loader (`ld.so`). It speeds up the loading of programs slightly, if it exists, but you don't have to have it.

Table 2-4. Files related to chroot and jail (continued)

Filename	Description
/etc/libmap.conf (FreeBSD only)	An optional file that changes how *ld.so* loads dynamic libraries. Again, you might use it in unusual circumstances, but most normal installations won't use it and it will show up as a file not found in the `ktrace` output.
/etc/resolv.conf	Sometimes you might want DNS resolution to act differently inside your chroot or jail than for the rest of the operating system, or you might have software (e.g., Postfix) that requires this file.
/etc/malloc.conf	This file controls options for the *malloc(2)* system call. See the *malloc.conf(5)* manpage for more information.
/dev/null */dev/random* */dev/urandom* */dev/srandom* */dev/zero* */dev/mem* */dev/kmem*	These are device files that you commonly need in a chroot environment. Don't create them all just in case. Create just the ones you need.

Making device nodes

If you run **`ls -l`** on the device you're interested in, you'll see everything you need to know to make a copy of it. For example, if your software needs */dev/random* in */jail/dev*, Example 2-8 shows how you look up the major and minor modes and then run the `mknod(8)` command with the right parameters.

Example 2-8. Making devices in chroot environments

```
FreeBSD% ls -l /dev/random
crw-rw-rw-  1 root  wheel  249,   0 Nov 25 14:04 /dev/random
FreeBSD% sudo mknod /jail/dev/random c 249 0

OpenBSD% ls -l /dev/random
crw-r--r--  1 root  wheel   45,   0 Nov  3 17:15 /dev/random
OpenBSD% sudo mknod /jail/dev/random c 45 0
```

Limitations of chroot

For almost as long as it has been around, chroot has been the focal point of an arms race between hackers and programmers in the Unix world. The programmers try to make chroot inescapable (hence their frequent use of the term "jail" to refer to it), and hackers invent increasingly complex ways of escaping.

For instance, directory and file handling in chrooted processes has traditionally been a source of chroot escape tricks. Directories and files that were open prior to calling *chroot(2)* remain open and available to software after calling *chroot*. If the software is not fastidious about closing them all before calling *chroot*, it may be possible later to use open directories to break out. Another technique for reading files outside the chroot environment involves calling `mknod(8)` to create a disk device file (e.g., an `rwd0a` or `da0s1a` node) and then opening it and finding the superblock for the filesystem. The primary superblock is always at a well-known offset (sector 32) from the start of the disk partition. The process can traverse the full filesystem of that device by manually decoding inodes and seeking to the right blocks on the disk. The inode number for the root directory is also always 2. This means that processes can always tell, simply by looking at the inode number of the root directory, whether or not they are seeing a virtualized filesystem.

Even though a chrooted process sees a virtualized filesystem, it is otherwise unrestricted. This means that, if it runs as root, it can do almost anything it wants. For instance, a chrooted process can still send signals to other processes using *kill(2)*, or create device nodes using *mknod(2)*. Under FreeBSD, you can set the `sysctl` variables `security.bsd.see_other_uids=0` and `security.bsd.see_other_gids=0` to hide processes that do not have the same UID or GID as the chroot'ed process. But this only helps a little. If the chroot'ed process knows the PID of another process it wants to signal, it can still use `kill()` to send the signal. These `sysctl` variables make it harder to find processes, but they don't limit the interprocess interactions. By default, FreeBSD allows all chrooted processes to see all other processes on the system. On OpenBSD this level of control is not supported.

As a rule, chroot is most effective when the chrooted process closes all its open files and directories and drops all its privileges as soon as possible after calling *chroot(2)*. It is worth mentioning that shells are notoriously hard to chroot, even shells that innately try to be restrictive, like `rsh`, `rbash`, and `rksh`. With their willingness to manipulate files and filehandles, plus their rich built-in commands and scripting capabilities, shells are hard to limit.

Jail: Beyond chroot

The well-known defects and deficiencies in *chroot(2)* motivated FreeBSD developers to develop a more thorough sandbox, which they call *jail(2)*. Whereas *chroot* works the same on both OpenBSD and FreeBSD, *jail* exists only on FreeBSD.

New Limitations

Poul-Henning Kamp and Robert Watson created a whole new system of sandboxing processes. They actually modified the FreeBSD kernel in a variety of places to specifically close loopholes that had been historically used to escape chroot environments. The intent of a jail is to create a different environment, and one that cannot be so easily escaped. While the kernel is minimally aware of chrooted programs, it has dozens of checks in all sorts of subsystems that are related to keeping programs in a jail.

Jail Versus chroot

For many years, the only technology available for putting processes in sandboxes was the chroot mechanism. Since "chroot" is a somewhat hard to pronounce, the term "jail" is often used. The terms *chroot* and *jail* are interchangeable to most people. You will frequently see documentation and literature talk about "putting a process in a chroot jail" or "jailing a process with chroot." It's somewhat unfortunate, then, that the authors of the *jail(2)* system call in FreeBSD chose the term they did. In FreeBSD, *jail* and *chroot* are totally different implementations that achieve similar goals. Because this text deals significantly with both technologies, we are very careful with our usage. When we text say *chroot*, we refer to the *chroot* system call and when we say *jail*, we mean the *jail* system call.

Limited process interaction

One of the most significant and interesting ways that jail is different is that it creates a whole new identifier associated with a process and its permissions: the *jail ID*. All processes have always had an effective user ID (UID) and group ID (GID). With the advent of jails, all processes now have a jail ID (JID) as well. Traditionally one process could affect another process if the UIDs of the two processes matched. This is true even in chroot environments. In a system using jails, however, the JID must also match. Even though a process with JID 2 has UID 0 (i.e., a root-equivalent process in jail 2), it cannot send signals to, read information from, or even detect the existence of a process that has a different JID. As you might expect, JID 0 corresponds to the main operating system. A process with UID 0 and JID 0 can kill any process whether the victim process is jailed or not.

Limited access to network resources

Jail addresses network issues that are completely unaddressed by chroot. Although a privileged chrooted process sees a virtual filesystem, its access to the network is unmediated. It can send and receive arbitrary data, *listen(2)* on a *socket(2)*, create raw sockets, spoof packets, and perform similar nefarious activity. Every jail, on the other hand, has a single IP address and hostname associated with it. Processes in that jail will only be able to send packets with the IP address assigned to the jail. Ethernet MAC address spoofing is not possible within a jail, either. Jailed processes cannot access promiscuous mode on Ethernet drivers (or the *bpf* packet filtering device in general). The kernel explicitly checks the process's jail ID before allowing such things. Raw sockets, MAC spoofing, and such activities are only permitted to non-jailed processes. These restrictions on networking set jail apart from chroot already, but the improvements do not stop there.

Devices and mknod

Jail and chroot both create a virtual filesystem, but with jail, the process's ability to perform disk-related activities is severely restricted. A jailed process cannot call *mknod(2)* (meaning `mknod(8)` also fails) to make device nodes. Because of this restriction on making devices, all the devices must be made in the jail's */dev* directory before launching the jail. Although processes cannot create new device nodes, they can read any devices that already exist in the jail. Thus, it's very important to create only the device nodes that the processes will need. Chances are good that no process that needs a jail will also need access to raw SCSI devices (such as `pass(4)`), for instance. You might be surprised to find that */dev/mem* and */dev/kmem* are needed, since they appear to create a quick path to information disclosure. As it turns out, the kernel device drivers related to those pseudodevices don't allow jailed processes to read or write the memory areas associated with processes having a different JID.

In FreeBSD 5.x, the old *MAKEDEV* way of handling devices is gone in favor of *devfs*. */etc/devfs.conf* controls the permissions for each device in the */dev* directory and can hide device nodes that are undesirable for one reason or another. When you make your jail, you can create an */etc/devfs.conf* file in it that will create just the right devices that your processes need. You can also expect the normal devices to appear, and simply hide the ones that you don't want visible in your jail. If you're thinking about making this filesystem immutable, *good for you*.

Creating Jail Environments

There are two different styles of jails: "thin" and "fat." Thin jails are just like chroot, but better. You set them up the same way you set up a chroot environment, but you get all the additional protections from jail. Fat jails, on the other hand, are almost like virtual systems. You install a subset of the operating system in them and then you can use and manage them like a separate host. We talk about both, but it's safe to say that thin jails and chroot really differ mainly in the syntax of the command you use to launch them. Everything we described in "Creating a chroot Environment" applies to creating a thin jail. The rest of this section explores creating fat jails and the motivations for doing so.

The manpage for `jail(8)` covers creating jails very well. In particular they offer the following sage advice:

> It is a lot easier to start with a "fat" jail and remove things until it stops working than it is to start with a "thin" jail and add things until it works.

Given that as a starting point, there are a couple of realistic ways to create reasonable fat jails: We can build the whole OS from scratch or we can use the binaries on a distribution CD.

Building jails from source

The manpage for jail(8) recommends the procedure shown in Example 2-9 for building a jail from source. We build it in */jail/master* because, as we discuss in "Make a builder jail," it's often useful to have a fat jail where you build all the software that will run in your other jails.

Example 2-9. Building a jail from source

```
% D=/jail/master
% cd /usr/src
% sudo mkdir -p $D
% sudo make world DESTDIR=$D
% cd etc
% sudo make distribution DESTDIR=$D
% sudo mount_devfs devfs $D/dev
% cd $D
% sudo ln -sf dev/null kernel
```

If you take this approach, make sure you use your */etc/make.conf* file (see Chapter 4 for more about */etc/make.conf*) to exclude a lot of the optional modules (e.g., *sendmail*, *BIND*, *ISDN4BSD*, etc.) that you don't need in your jails. This may lead you to create a couple of *make.conf* files, one for building your system in general and one for building jails.

Installing from a distribution CD

If you have your distribution CD mounted at */cdrom*, you'll find the base OS distribution at */cdrom/base*. There is an *install.sh* shell script that obeys the DESTDIR environment variable. Example 2-10 shows how to install the base OS into a jail from the CD.

Example 2-10. Creating a jail from a distribution CD

```
% cd /cdrom/base
% sudo sh install.sh DESTDIR=/jail/master
```

You can add other distributions located in */cdrom/distribution_name* in the same way.

Launching Jails

Launching jail requires a few more command-line arguments than chroot because the *jail* system call requires more arguments than does *chroot*. In addition to the virtual root of the filesystem, you must also supply the one IP address and hostname that the jail will use. Ideally, this hostname appears in DNS matched to the IP address in use for the jail; but, if you use an */etc/hosts* entry, it will work fine. Lastly, you must provide a command to run in the jail.

Fat jails as virtual machines

You may get to the point where you have an */etc* directory, `sshd`, and a variety of other binaries installed in your jail. In this case, you can run */etc/rc* to start up something that looks and feels like another instance of FreeBSD but isn't really. In this case, after the jail is up and running, you can actually use `ssh` to log into it and manage it. Since processes you launch will be children of `sshd`, which is a child of the jailed */bin/sh*, they all have the same JID. This means they all see the same virtual filesystem, use the same IP address, and can interact with each other.

Of course, if there are processes in your jail that listen on the network, attackers can attack the jail in much the same ways as they can any other host. Still, even if they actually succeed in logging in, the amount of damage they can do is significantly limited. They probably can't see any part of the filesystem other than what is in the virtual filesystem, and they can't interact with any processes running outside the jail. Of course, they might be able to use the jail environment to participate in distributed denial-of-service (DDoS) attacks, but the complex network address spoofing that some DDoS attacks use won't work.

Jail security options

There are special `sysctl` variables that control certain behaviors of jails. They control whether jailed process can affect the jail's hostname, use certain network protocols, and whether or not System V interprocess communication (IPC) is allowed. These options have security ramifications that might need to be relaxed in order for certain software to work as expected.

Normally, jails only have permissions to work with local sockets, routing sockets, and IPv4 sockets. Only these sections of the networking part of the kernel are fully jail aware. Thus, it's possible that a jailed program with access to a different protocol family (e.g., IPX or ATM) could do malicious things with those protocols. The `security.jail.socket_unixiproute_only` variable controls whether jails can access all protocols, or just the jail-safe protocol families. Change the default value to 0 to enable the non-jail-safe protocols.

System V IPC allows processes to communicate through several mechanisms and to use a variety of synchronization primitives like semaphores. Unfortunately, this is another section of the kernel that is not jail aware in a sophisticated way. System V IPC is not permitted from within a jail by default, but you can enable this functionality by setting `security.jail.sysvipc_allowed` to 1. Unfortunately, it's an all or nothing proposition. If enabled, a jailed process can see all semaphores, shared memory segments, queues, and other System V IPC data structures. This means that root-equivalent processes will have access to all System V IPC data structures, jailed or not. Such broad access allows a jailed process to have effects outside its own jail, which obviously has security implications and weakens one of the goals of the jail in the first place. In general this option should retain its default disabled status unless you have a specific reason to enable it.

Managing jails

A variety of commands make working with jails easier. For instance, the output of `ps(1)` does not indicate which jail a particular process is in, but the `jls(1)` command does. After you know a JID, you can use `jexec(1)` to add a new process to an already running jail. If you need to `kill` a process, you can do so from outside the jail (if your shell has JID 0, of course). If you want to `kill` an entire jail, you can combine the `kill(1)` command (assuming */bin/kill* or */bin/sh* exists in the jail) with `jexec`. For example, you can `kill` every process in jail 3 by running **`sudo jexec 3 kill -1`**.

Installing Software in Jail

This section of the text discusses the FreeBSD packages and ports system extensively. If you are unfamiliar with them, see Chapter 4 of the *FreeBSD Handbook*. We also talk a lot about them in Chapter 4 of this book.

When you try to put a program in a jail, especially if you are trying to install only the minimal subset of files it needs, you may have difficulties getting the right files in the right places, as we described previously. Instead of hunting down dependencies, consider using the ports system to create packages that can be installed in the jail. For custom software, you have a couple of options: you can just wing it, or you can leverage the ports system to make a new port of your custom software, and then all the packaging and tracking comes along for free.

Make a builder jail

If you make your software from source, using the ports tree, you can still install the software into the jails using packages. The best option is to create a fat jail that looks just like the jail where you will be installing the new software, except that it has a compiler and the ports system installed in it. Build software inside that jail and then run **`make package`**. The FreeBSD ports system cannot make a package from your newly built binaries unless they are first installed in the main operating system, so you definitely want to do this in your builder jail to avoid interfering with your base OS.

For this example, we assume that the target jail is rooted at */jail/web* and there is a special building jail named "master" already configured at */jail/master*. The whole session would look something like Example 2-11.

Example 2-11. Using a jail to build software for other jails

```
main-system% sudo ifconfig lo0 alias 127.0.0.2
main-system% sudo jail 127.0.0.2 master /bin/sh
builder% cd /usr/ports/www/apache2
builder% make
[... make messages omitted ...]
builder% sudo make install
builder% sudo make package
builder% sudo kill -1
main-system% sudo pkg_add -R /jail/web \
    /jail/master/usr/ports/www/apache2/apache-2.55.tgz
```

Note that we have to create an IP address and associate it with some network interface (the loopback, in this example) even though we won't be doing any networking.

Install from binary package

Copy the package file you've just made (and the pkg_add executable and associated dependencies, if they're not already in the jail) into the jail's filesystem. If the jail is not currently running, you can install the software by using the jail command to run pkg_add, as shown in Example 2-12. Notice that the first thing to do is to copy the package file into some location that will be visible inside the jail.

Example 2-12. Installing into a jail from a package file

```
% sudo cp ports/packages/All/apache-2.55.tgz /jail/web/tmp
% sudo jail 10.1.0.2 www.example.com /jail/web pkg_add /tmp/apache-2.55.tgz
```

Getting custom software installed in a jail

If you download some source code that is not supported by the ports and packages infrastructure, you have a few options for getting it in jail. One option is to make a port out of it. It takes a little effort to start with, but it's effort well spent. Once your software is correctly installed through a port, it is very little work to keep it up to date. You can use the portupgrade program to maintain it, and you can run **make package** to make a binary installable package out if it. All this functionality is free after you create the port infrastructure.

The other option is to figure out its dependencies through trial and error. The section "Finding Other Dependencies" discusses a lot of good techniques you can use to find and satisfy dependencies. Remember that you can also RTFM and look at the source code. If you're trying to jail some interesting software, you're probably not the only person to try it. Check the mailing lists both for your operating system and for the application itself and see if anyone has had luck or can at least warn you about the problems you'll face. You'll probably find it most helpful to do this trial-and-error work inside your builder jail, because it presumably looks the most like the jail in which your software will ultimately run.

NFS-Based Jails

Jails offer the possibility of creating lots of virtual environments for specialized jobs and segregating them into separate independent sandboxes. However, in order to run correctly, a lot of the operating system might need to be installed in the jail. This creates a scalability problem for large numbers of jails. Not only do they require copies of the operating system files, but those copies must all be kept synchronized and updated. Updating a large number of jails is difficult, as is detecting changes in them. You can use read-only NFS to solve several of these issues, making dozens or hundreds of jails scalable.

Creating a single NFS master jail

Create a master jail filesystem that contains the right set of files for your applications. If you plan to use just one master for dozens or hundreds of jails, then this may end up including a superset of files that are not needed in all jails. Share this filesystem as read-only to localhost (127.0.0.1) only. Likewise, make a temporary area that every jail can write to for its */tmp* and */var* partitions. Share these as read/write to *localhost* also. Have each jail mount the single read-only master jail root filesystem, and writable */var* and */tmp* filesystems from *localhost*.

If you use this approach, you probably want to create a "package master" jail of some kind into which you can freely install software and create packages. The master jail in this example is too important to screw up.

There are many advantages to the read-only NFS master jail. All the upgrades can be done in just one place and take effect immediately. The filesystem is read-only from the point of view of the jail. Even if the jail is compromised, a rogue process cannot overwrite the NFS-mounted files. Lastly, disk caching in the operating system can still help with performance. If you make 10 copies of all your binaries and data, then you will get lower disk cache performance than if you have 10 jails all requesting the same binary off the disk.

Inherent Protections

FreeBSD and OpenBSD provide excellent foundations for secure servers. They have security underpinnings that other operating systems don't. Just by choosing FreeBSD or OpenBSD, you automatically benefit from built-in protections. OpenBSD distinguishes itself especially along these lines. Its "secure by default" mantra means you frequently don't get choices about security options: you're given the most secure option by default and you'd have to go out of your way to be less secure. FreeBSD tends to be a little more flexible about security. It doesn't force your configuration one way or another, but gives you some of the same options and lets you choose. It also doesn't always activate the most secure settings by default. It's up to you, with either operating system, to figure out what works best for your environment and set the options appropriately.

This section discusses several inherent security-related technologies, some are available in both operating systems and some are available only in one. Some of them are optional, and others are mandatory.

Fighting Buffer Overflows

OpenBSD incorporates two technologies into its kernel that fight the dreaded buffer overflow. They are utterly transparent to programs running on OpenBSD because they are integrated into the operating system and the compiler. They significantly limit the damage that's possible from the classic buffer overflow problems. The first is W^X memory protection and the second is ProPolice stack protection.

W^X memory protection

One of the fundamental principles exploited by a buffer overflow attack is the fact that data (on an Intel i386-based system, anyways) can be executed. That is, an attacker can change the value in the instruction pointer to the address of any location in memory and the CPU will execute the bytes it finds there as instructions. Some non-Intel CPU architectures prevent executing code on memory pages that are not marked executable, but Intel hardware does not support that behavior. Since the hardware can't help us, OpenBSD incorporated a software technique into its kernel.

The W^X (pronounced "write XOR execute") technique tries to make memory pages either writable or executable, but never both. That is, if you can write to the memory page (i.e., it contains some data for the program like its heap or stack), then the page can't be executable. If you can execute the page (that is, if it contains instructions), then it will not be writable. This functionality is implemented by extensions to the compiler that work in concert with specific features in the runtime loader (*ld.so*) and the kernel itself. The kernel itself keeps track of this quality for each memory page.

The goal of W^X is to make a program crash if it attempts to write to an execute-only page or execute code on a write-only page. The kernel and the loader try to make sure that a program's instructions are always allocated on pages marked executable, and data (e.g., the program's stack and heap) is always allocated to pages that are writable but not executable. It's not flawless, but it sets up a significant barrier to misusing buffer overflows. W^X frequently turns a high-impact problem, like privilege escalation through stack smashing, into a low-impact problem: badly written programs crash. While you'd rather not have an important program crashing a lot, it's a lot better than it being exploited.

ProPolice stack protection

The W^X technique is a good one, but keeping "defense in depth" in mind, the OpenBSD team didn't stop with just that one protection. They also incorporated stack protection called "ProPolice" by Hiroaki Etoh at IBM. As an extension to the GCC C/C++ compiler, ProPolice rearranges buffers and variables on the stack in a variety of ways to thwart would-be hackers.

Another principal that hackers use when crafting exploits is the fact that programs are loaded into memory in exactly the same way every time. Creating an exploit that loads just the right machine instructions into the right memory location is a time-consuming process and it always involves a little trial and error. Once he has figured out what inputs to send, though, the hacker knows that, given the same inputs, the program will perform the same way each time. ProPolice breaks this fundamental assumption. It inserts a random "canary" value into every function frame. When a program returns, code that has been added by the compiler checks to make sure the canary value has not changed. If it has, the program will log an error and crash.

It's almost impossible to defeat this system unless the hacker can guess the canary value and insert it into his attack input. However, there are essentially 2^{32} (about 4 billion) possible canary values, and a *different one* is chosen for each and every function call. You might think he can just keep trying his exploit over and over with the same value in the canary position, and eventually—through luck—his canary value and the random one used by the program will match. That's true. Mathematically speaking he will have to attempt it billions of times before he succeeds. In this case we are counting on detecting his attempts through some means (perhaps the logs) before he makes billions of attempts. Don't forget—there's still W^X to get around.

Cryptography

Cryptography is a critical component in most security architectures. Performing cryptographic operations quickly, safely, and correctly is vital to the entire security infrastructure that is built on top of cryptography. SSL web connections, SSH, IPv6, VPN connections, and many other security tools need cryptography to work correctly. OpenBSD and FreeBSD excel at supporting not just software cryptography, but hardware-based cryptography. Rather than having hacked up drivers for a random assortment of cards, they have a cryptographic framework, allowing them to integrate cards from different vendors and provide a uniform application programming interface (API) to software.

OpenBSD and FreeBSD support essentially the same list of hardware cryptographic coprocessors, which basically consists of boards using several HiFn chipsets as well as the Broadcom Ubsec chipset. You can find HiFn cards under the "PowerCrypt" and "XL-Crypt" names from a company called GTGI. The Broadcom chipset appears in cards that bear the NetCryptX name. Information on how to purchase the cards and how much they cost is scarce.

Both OpenBSD and FreeBSD integrate these cards directly into the *crypto* framework (see *crypto(4)* on OpenBSD and *crypto(9)* on FreeBSD), which is a uniform set of kernel APIs for performing cryptographic operations. Once the card is installed, OpenSSL and the *ipsec(4)* infrastructure will all use the hardware-provided algorithms. If the card provides a random number generator (not all do), the kernel will use it as its source of randomness. Some newer versions of the cards support cryptographic algorithms like AES that are not yet exported through the *crypto* API. Taking advantage of a hardware cryptographic accelerator, however, is about as painless as it possibly could be.

Code Review

Both BSDs have excellent security track records, though it is arguable that OpenBSD has a few more bragging rights. Both FreeBSD and OpenBSD review code before it is committed to the operating system. The OpenBSD team, however, takes it a step further. They audit software before it is added to the ports system, too. You will notice in later chapters that we sometimes have to recommend that you install software from source on OpenBSD because no port exists. With so much software and only a limited number of people who volunteer time to review software for security issues, the OpenBSD team cannot review everything that everyone would like to run. It's actually quite remarkable how much software they *have* reviewed.

The OpenBSD team, during its audits, routinely discovers buffer overflows, format string problems, and a host of other common programming errors. They share their findings with the software developers and sometimes create a solution or workaround so that the code can safely be integrated in OpenBSD. Very often the version of software that you run in OpenBSD is not exactly what the software's original author distributes. Patches are applied to impose privilege separation, make the software run under a specific user by default, or to correct unsafe behavior.

As a general principle, you want to run as much software out of the base operating system as you can to take advantage of the efforts of the teams that audit the software. Although there are plenty of places where we recommend considering software that is not installed by default, you must be conscious of what you might be giving up and what you are gaining.

OS Tuning

Both FreeBSD and OpenBSD have a variety of options to help you tune the operating system to support the specific needs of your application. As with most BSD configurations, a great deal of the pertinent options are set with *sysctl* options in */etc/sysctl.conf*. Some FreeBSD options available at boot time are set through */boot/*

defaults/loader.conf. OpenBSD is less flexible than FreeBSD in this regard. Some options can only be set or modified by adjusting your kernel configuration and recompiling your kernel from source.

> **To Tweak or Not to Tweak**
>
> There may come a time, whether you are using FreeBSD or OpenBSD, that your current server and its configuration just do not give you enough performance to meet your needs. You may want faster response time, higher overall throughput, or a higher maximum concurrent connection count. There are definitely options that you can tweak to get more performance from a server. However, they are likely to gain only incremental improvements. Will you double your throughput or triple your concurrent connections? Possibly, but not very likely unless your starting configuration is abysmal.
>
> If you're looking for small increments of improvement, consider the tuning options presented in this section. Some specialized servers (e.g., a busy VPN concentrator) may need some simple tweaking to increase kernel resources dedicated to networking. However, if you are looking for substantial leaps in capacity, consider whether your budget for equipment and staff time can support adding one or more redundant servers. You can spend a lot of time fine-tuning a server, only to eke out a small incremental gain in the end.

It is worth mentioning, especially in the case of FreeBSD, that most of these options automatically tune themselves at boot time. The kernel is aware of your RAM, CPU speed, and total virtual memory. It scales many values based on predefined, carefully worked formulas. All the FreeBSD kernel developers recommend that you avoid tuning these variables unless you really understand the interdependencies and implications. The OpenBSD developers even discourage rebuilding your kernel, because you can create configurations that they have not tested and find yourself using an unstable kernel. If you still really want to get under the hood and tune, read on.

maxusers: Basic Influence

In the very old days, the kernel's `maxusers` variable was one of the only readily accessible variables. By tuning it, you would set maximum values for a wide variety of filesystem resources, network resources, and other in-kernel data structures. It was statically compiled in and required rebuilding the kernel to change. In OpenBSD, it is still done this way.

FreeBSD recently moved to a dynamically set `maxusers` variable by default. When it is left unchanged (set to zero), a variety of formulas are used at boot time, based on physical RAM, to determine how large most data structures should be. Generally speaking these calculations are probably right for you. But you can explicitly define `maxusers` to be something nonzero in your kernel configuration if you are not happy with the automatic calculations.

Increasing Maximum Values

If your server is very busy, you may find that it cannot open enough files to serve all the requests being made. This is an easy issue to diagnose because the error messages are logged to the kernel facility via syslog and are quite clear. Set the variable `kern.maxfiles` to a number that is large enough, but be careful. Tune it gradually, and only to a value high enough to stay above your high-water mark.

You may also want to tune the maximum number of inbound TCP connections you can handle. In FreeBSD, the variable that controls this threshold is `kern.ipc.somaxconn`, whereas in OpenBSD it is `kern.somaxconn`. Tuning this value high will increase the memory used by the kernel data structures associated with network connections. Tuning it too high can reduce performance. Consider carefully before tuning it. If possible, evaluate your changes in your test environment before putting them into production.

Network Buffering

You can also tune the amount of memory available to buffer data going in and out of the network subsystem in the kernel with `net.inet.tcp.sendspace`. This controls the buffer size available to outbound network flows; increasing it allows more data to be queued up, decreasing context switches to fetch more data from disk, allowing more efficient sending of data. If you predominantly send data in small chunks (e.g., a dedicated DNS server), increasing the size of this buffer will have no beneficial effect. On the other hand, if you are running a popular FTP mirror and routinely provide very large downloads to users, you may find this worthwhile.

If your server receives many large inbound requests, it might make sense to tune `net.inet.tcp.recvspace`. Candidates for large inbound network data might be mail servers that handle a lot of mail and deal with a lot of unusually large messages or web servers that deal mostly with very large file uploads. Again, this variable is only valuable if your traffic patterns are substantially dominated by specific kinds of well-characterized traffic. If you see a general mix of big and small, inbound and outbound traffic, then tuning these variables will have limited effect.

Novices often ask about tuning the number of *mbufs* available in the kernel because they see messages in their logfiles about running out of *mbufs*. In the modern network infrastructure of the kernel, no variable can be tuned in isolation; each affects another. However, FreeBSD does allow some influence over the *mbufs* by tuning the `kern.ipc.nmbclusters` variable. Before deciding that you need to tune this variable, though, you should run **`netstat -m`** to see if you are anywhere near your limits. Even on busy servers, the kernel generally picks good values for this variable.

In OpenBSD, the number of *mbufs* allocated is a function of the `maxusers` variable. This is a more coarse method of tuning than you might desire. If you are willing to reconfigure and recompile your kernel, you can set the `NMBCLUSTERS` variable in the kernel configuration file directly.

Wrapping Up

We've covered a number of security-oriented features that make FreeBSD and OpenBSD unique among Unices, as well as among operating systems in general. These features give you an edge in securing your system. By adding a few `sysctl` variables to your standard configuration, you can tune the behavior to fit the security posture that you need. You can reduce your visibility in the network, help thwart scans and denial-of-service attacks, and reduce the amount of resources malicious folks can consume on your network. By combining the kernel *securelevel* and UFS filesystem flags you can more strongly protect many critical pieces of the operating system. If your users need the flexibility of ACLs, you can give them ACLs as well to specify filesystem permissions with finer granularity.

Your options are not quite as diverse on OpenBSD systems. Still, it's clear that the effort the development team has gone through to follow the defense in depth, least-privilege, fail-safe, and other principles yield great rewards. Careful code audits, privilege separation whenever possible, service-based users, W^X, and ProPolice—it's all good stuff.

As you read through the chapters in this book, look for places where the building blocks in this chapter can be put to good use. Feel free to play around with them and find a solution that works for you.

Resources

TrustedBSD (http://www.trustedbsd.org/)
: The TrustedBSD project is an effort to add options to FreeBSD that make it compliant with the Common Criteria for Information Technology Security Evaluation. ACLs were implemented as part of this effort.

ProPolice Stack Protection (http://www.trl.ibm.com/projects/security/ssp/)
: "GCC extension for protecting applications from stack-smashing attacks."

Posix.1e (http://wt.xpilot.org/publications/posix.1e/)
: The IEEE 1003.1e standard that was used as a reference when designing FreeBSD's ACLs. The standard itself has been abandoned by IEEE, but some vendors continue to use it as a reference.

CHAPTER 3
Secure Installation and Hardening

So the combination is one, two, three, four, five.
That's the stupidest combination
I've ever heard in my life. That's the kinda
thing an idiot would have on his luggage.

—Dark Helmet
Spaceballs

Securing a system doesn't necessarily begin with a running system. Given the option, it's a good idea to start thinking about system security early on: before and during installation. In this chapter, we step through the installation process for both OpenBSD and FreeBSD and address some of the security implications of your early decisions.

If you are not comfortable with the install process for either operating system, now is the perfect time to read the relevant documentation. For FreeBSD, read Chapter 2 of the *Handbook*. For OpenBSD, see section 4 of the FAQ. If you have not signed up for the FreeBSD and OpenBSD security lists, do so immediately. Links to these lists are available in the "Resources" section at the end of this chapter.

Throughout this chapter we will be following the fundamental security principles laid out in Chapter 1 of this book. Keep in mind that in the context of system security it's not always true that "more is better." The consequences of increased security often include greater administrative overhead in maintenance and installation, more complicated configuration, and a general decrease in flexibility and convenience. Balance the trade-offs appropriately for your environment to arrive at a solution that meets both your usability and security requirements.

This chapter is divided into three sections. The first section, "General Concerns," covers some of the decisions you should make and security issues of which you should be aware before beginning the install. As the name implies, this section is applicable to both FreeBSD and OpenBSD administrators. The second section provides a security-minded installation walkthrough: first for FreeBSD and subsequently for OpenBSD. Feel free to skip the part that doesn't apply to your system and proceed to the last section of the chapter: platform-independent security concerns in "Post-Upgrade Hardening."

General Concerns

Before grabbing a floppy or your BSD distribution on CD, there are a few decisions to be made that apply to both FreeBSD and OpenBSD installations.

What Are You Building?

The first and most important question you have to ask yourself before starting to build a system is, "What am I building?" A clear idea of the role this system will play in your environment is vital. The following system classes help define the role of your system.

Workstation

The BSD workstation is a daily use system usually with a list of installed packages at least two or three pages long. These systems almost always have the X Window System installed. They might not be upgraded or maintained other than by the end user and at her whim. At businesses, these systems are almost always found behind a firewall. These systems are generally out of your control after (or even before) system build, so user education is your best bet to keeping them secure. You may also want to consider an organization-wide "image" of FreeBSD or OpenBSD that has been preconfigured (locked down) and tested by security-minded system administrators.

Workgroup server

By definition, a server provides some kind of service to users. Servers can be shared development machines, exporters of filesystems, intranet development systems, etc. Workgroup servers generally interact with a variety of users and are not treated as carefully as infrastructure servers, though they do tend to be administered and upgraded by a system administrator. These are the familiar multiuser Unix systems. Rolling these systems into your patching and upgrade process for infrastructure servers is usually a good idea. These systems could exist on the same protected network as workstations, or better yet, on a separate network accessible to internal users.

Infrastructure server

As the title implies, these systems provide some kind of critical infrastructure service: name service (DNS), network time (NTP), dynamic address assignment (DHCP), email, external web presence, and so on. Infrastructure servers are often protected from both users on a local area network and users on the Internet by one or more firewalls. They are critical to the proper functioning of the network and have the bare minimum software installed. System administrators who are responsible for the *specific services* provided by a given server are often the only users granted access, and they perform patching, upgrades, and software installs.

In some cases, service operators may request access to the system for publishing content (i.e., in the case of an external web presence), or administering the particular service for which they're responsible. If possible, provide restricted access via one of the following means:

Automated synchronization
: It may be possible to set up an internal repository for content or configuration and periodically synchronize this data with the external server. This may be achieved using tools like `rsync`/`rdist`, or by building an internal CVS repository and performing regular checkouts from the infrastructure server. For more information about secure file distribution techniques, see Chapter 4.

FTP
: Running a chrooted FTP daemon on an interface only accessible from the internal network will provide an acceptable means for file transfer. Of course, FTP is a clear-text protocol and other options should be pursued first.

SCP only (SSH denied)
: The `scponly` product is available from *http://www.sublimation.org/scponly/* and will restrict access so that operators are only able to transfer files and not gain a shell.

Service-specific remote maintenance
: Some services offer innate remote maintenance capabilities. BIND, a popular DNS server, may provide the requisite remote administration capability via the `rndc` utility. You could also create a stealth master nameserver to which configuration changes are made but that is not directly queried for data.

System jails
: Ensure operators log into a jailed environment on the system that provides access to the files and directories.

Bear in mind that one of the main reasons service operators desire access to production infrastructure systems is to ensure that their changes do not produce any undesirable results. This end may also be achieved by providing service operators systems on the internal network or on a test network that mimic the behavior and support the identical configuration as a production counterpart.

Multipurpose system

When you must get the job done, but do not have the money to build 20 specialized servers, you need to combine functionality. Behold the multipurpose machine! An unfortunate product of budgetary constraints, this class of system can incorporate any combination of the aforementioned classes of systems. When a multipurpose machine fails, is subjected to an attack, or merely needs to be rebooted, you lose several services all at the same time. These machines can be made more secure with careful use of chrooting, jails, good monitoring, constant auditing, and patching. However the effort and painstaking care involved in maintaining a multipurpose machine is immense. These days, reasonable workstations capable of providing key services can be purchased for very little. Plan a migration process away from multipurpose systems by removing services one by one until the original system can be decommissioned or reassigned to a single task.

Be aware, however, that there are dangers in segregating all services onto separate machines. There are several criticisms you may face when presenting this option to your supervisors or peers, and we will address the most common concerns here.

More systems require more administration
: Unless you can develop a standard system configuration and upgrade process, you may experience an unnecessarily high total cost of ownership (TCO) as a result of maintaining many specialized servers. Standardizing and automating will go a long way to making system maintenance easy and reducing TCO. Combining services onto one system can make sense as long as you retain the system class concept. Finally, remember to take into account the cost of failure of several critical services at once. As always, there is a tradeoff between security and convenience. Pick a solution that meets your security and usability requirements.

Cheap or used systems tend to have faulty hardware
: Although it may sound trite, avoid buying cheap or used systems, or using them over the long term. The migration away from a multipurpose server may be a time-consuming process for budgetary reasons. If you feel you can find cheap or used hardware now that will last at least a year (presumably you will have additional funds at that time), it may be worth the risk. If desirable, build two machines to serve the same purpose instead of one either as a hot-failover system or a cold spare. The services you plan on deploying on the server and the state of your current multipurpose machine will help you decide when to take the plunge.

Names will have to change everywhere
: It can be quite problematic to place a particular service (such as email, internal web, DNS, etc.) on a server with a new name. This is a valid complaint, but is also a problem that needs resolution anyway. Prepare for migrating services by creating alternate and more general namespaces for your services. Use canonical names (CNAME records) in DNS instead of hostnames in client and server configuration files. After the system configurations have been updated across the organization, service migration may begin.

This is by no means a comprehensive list of attacks against the multi-server model, but hopefully should provide you enough ammunition to convince management and your peers that the pain is worth the effort.

Media and Network

Once you have a good idea of the kind of system you are building, it is time to look at your media options for installation. Both operating systems offer a variety of media options, the most common being bootable floppy or CD and network installs. With all installs, there are two major security concerns: data integrity and host vulnerability.

In order to ensure the highest integrity of data, a CD install is safest. If the CD has been acquired from a reliable source (authorized vendor) you can be reasonably confident that the contents do not pose a security risk. In most cases you will want to use the latest release of the operating system available. When working with critical pieces of infrastructure, you would not be overly cautious to fall back a few releases.

With FreeBSD, significant changes occur at the turn of the major version number of the operating system (i.e., between 4.x and 5.x). In this case you might want to stick with the latest 4.x release until the new version has sufficiently matured. The tradeoff here is that you will need to plan a major release upgrade sooner, rather than later.

OpenBSD, on the other hand, releases on a strict calendar schedule that is somewhat independent of feature changes and technology. Thus, version numbers do not tell you what major changes you face when upgrading. For example, OpenBSD's i386 architecture switched its binary format from *a.out* to *elf* when it released Version 3.4. Upgrading by building from source was not possible from Version 3.3 to Version 3.4. Peruse the "What's New" section of the release announcement to see if there have been major introductions that you would rather avoid on vital systems.

To be networked or not to be networked

If you choose to have your network interface up during the install process, whether for the purposes of installing the operating system or merely because the interface happens to be plugged in, you may be exposing yourself to needless risk. If your system uses its network interface during the install process, you're placing implicit trust in the network to which your system is attached.

When your system needs to contact another on your network, it issues an `arp(8)` (address resolution protocol) request. A response is received with the hardware address of the target system. But what if a malicious system were to answer instead and provide you the *wrong* hardware address? Your system may then send subsequent requests to the malicious system instead. This kind attack is known as *arp poisoning* and facilitates a *man-in-the-middle attack* (MITM).

This may sound implausible, but a careless roaming user who brought in his wireless access point and attached it to the network may have unwittingly created a back door and facilitated this attack.

A MITM attack may also be possible if someone has compromised a DNS server for an organization you wish to contact, or your local DNS server. Looking up the IP address of *ftpx.freebsd.org* may return the wrong IP and you may start downloading binaries that seem legitimate but are actually riddled with Trojans.

Admittedly, there may be perfectly legitimate cases where a network install is both appropriate and desirable. If you have the infrastructure in place that provides a reasonably secure copy of the operating system distribution, you may want to use this local repository as your FTP source. If your network is isolated or you are well protected behind a firewall, the risks of remote host compromise are minimal. After all, as soon as your system is built, you're likely to perform an upgrade—you'll need to place trust in your network at that point anyway.

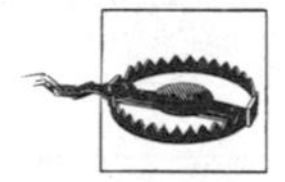

Having a firewall does not mean you are safe. A firewall controls what traffic is allowed into and out of your organization. Firewalls can be poorly configured, or may allow legitimate traffic to a service that can be compromised with specially crafted (but valid) input. Other means of entry and exit are possible and a source of great concern to security administrators. Blindly trusting the security of your network is never sound planning.

One final thought: if the system you're building will eventually live outside of your innermost firewall, perhaps on your DMZ, or completely beyond your security perimeter, consider performing the installation and hardening on a more protected network. When the system has been locked down to your satisfaction, move it out to the perimeter network. A few tweaks to */etc/resolv.conf*, */etc/hosts*, and the *rc.conf* or *rc.conf.local* startup configuration file should be all you need to configure the system on the new network.

Media verification

Ensure your media was acquired from a reliable source. Retail, shrink-wrapped software is *generally* safest, and moderately stale local copies of FTP repositories are the next best bet. It is not often you hear about an FTP distribution server being compromised, but it is not unheard of. Consider using tools like `md5(1)` against your downloaded CD images to verify that the hashes match those provided as reference on trusted FTP distribution servers, as shown in Example 3-1.

The Dangers of DHCP

If you do choose to build a server on a local network, you are given the option to automatically configure your network interface using DHCP. Although this may be convenient, it poses certain security risks and may interfere with subsequent configuration.

DHCP is without authentication or a sanity check. A network may contain any number of DHCP servers, and nothing says they have to be working in tandem. Even in a trusted networking environment, a user could bring in a wireless device with DHCP enabled providing a means for intruders to enter your protected network and for your system to be inadvertently placed on this insecure network during system build!

If you use DHCP during the install process and you are 100% confident that you have acquired your network configuration from the correct server, you may still run into problems later when you rebuild your kernel. We go into more detail when we cover kernel reconfiguration for FreeBSD later in this chapter.

For these reasons, we recommend you choose a static address when building servers. Workstations generally remain configured with DHCP and on the network on which they were built.

Example 3-1. Verifying the md5 checksum of a FreeBSD .iso

```
% fetch http://ftp2.freebsd.org/pub/FreeBSD/ISO-IMAGES-i386/5.3/CHECKSUM.MD5
CHECKSUM.MD5                                    100% of  278  B  366 kBps
% fetch http://ftp2.freebsd.org/pub/FreeBSD/ISO-IMAGES-i386/5.3/5.3-RELEASE-i386-disc1.iso
5.3-RELEASE-i386-disc1.iso                      100% of  644 MB  315 kBps
% cat CHECKSUM.MD5
MD5 (5.3-RELEASE-i386-bootonly.iso) = e370ae39bb34f0789c638b6ad50038a2
MD5 (5.3-RELEASE-i386-disc1.iso) = fbcbfdff31f27de396f257e0a37a78b8
MD5 (5.3-RELEASE-i386-disc2.iso) = 21874a5663022768336e4cc73d1dd30d
MD5 (5.3-RELEASE-i386-miniinst.iso) = 96124b2608ba481693e04d364d485e3c
% md5 5.3-RELEASE-i386-disc1.iso
MD5 (5.3-RELEASE-i386-disc1.iso) = fbcbfdff31f27de396f257e0a37a78b8
```

Preexisting Vulnerabilities

Choosing your installation media is a decision that should never be taken lightly. Even before installing FreeBSD or OpenBSD on a system, you should check out the appropriate web page to determine whether you're about to install software with known vulnerabilities. FreeBSD lists security advisories chronologically on their security page at *http://www.freebsd.org/security/*, and you'll find analogous information for OpenBSD on the Errata page at *http://www.openbsd.org/errata.html*.

FreeBSD and OpenBSD release versions of the operating system on a semiregular basis. Just because you received a CD of OpenBSD or FreeBSD in the mail a week ago does not mean that you are about to install the "latest version" of the operating system. Any bugs or security issues discovered shortly after release have likely been announced on OpenBSD security-announce or FreeBSD security-notifications *and* been addressed in the source tree.

If you are installing an even older distribution, you can almost guarantee that upon installation there will be vulnerabilities (possibly remotely exploitable) in the system. Avoid installing particularly old software if you can. Be very conscious of your network connectivity and potential exposure if you must install a dated distribution.

Knowing about the existence (or absence) of security issues will help you decide whether you should bring your network interface up during the install process. You may discover that you need to wait until after the install and after you have turned off some or all of your listening services before connecting the system to your network.

Performing a CVS update procedure may open the door to MITM attacks and Trojaned code. While software systems have been built to automatically download file signatures or hashes with files with the intention of guaranteeing data integrity, a good cracker will replace both these server-provided hashes and corresponding files making these automatic solutions ineffective. The only means to realistically increase confidence that the file you download is legitimate is to perform out-of-band tests. These might include:

- Visiting the vendor's primary web site and comparing the hash there to the hashes on all the mirror sites, especially the site from which you obtained the file. They should all be the same.
- Confirming with other administrators or software providers on mailing lists that the hash is a valid one.
- Downloading a file to a local repository once and waiting a month or so to see if anyone has identified rogue data within that timeframe before performing an upgrade.

Of course, few administrators have the time necessary to follow any of these steps. In this case, functionality requirements may outweigh security concerns. Be cautious.

Slicing Up Your Filesystem

It may seem out of place to be reading about filesystem slicing in a chapter about a secure installation and hardening. However, availability is inexorably tied to security, and proper filesystem portioning can affect data and service availability, so we must address this issue.

Your first step will be determining whether your system will contain anything besides BSD during the `fdisk(8)` table setup. Servers from vendors such as Dell and Compaq ship with maintenance or utility partitions that provide disk management tools and hardware test suites. You will probably want to keep these handy in the event of a system malfunction. For an infrastructure server, dual-booting with another operating system should be avoided.

The Whats and Whys of CVSup

CVS (Concurrent Versions System), is a software source code version control system. Developers use CVS and other version control systems to track changes as they work with source code. The entire FreeBSD and OpenBSD source trees are housed in CVS repositories so that when developers check out a file, modify it, and check it back in, changes to the file are recorded. This later facilitates looking at change history or performing rollbacks to previous versions of a given file.

Getting the latest sources for your FreeBSD operating system is most often achieved by using CVSup. This is a highly optimized network distribution package for CVS repositories. If you already have an "old checkout" of a CVS repository, running `cvsup(1)` only transfers data if a file has changed, and then only the changes to the file, not the entire file.

`cvs(1)` is used by OpenBSD to check out sources just as a developer would need to in order to modify code. Direct access to this facility allows changes made locally to be merged in with changes made to the code base by the OpenBSD development team. Likewise, the command **`cvs update -dPA`** performs a file update similar to `cvsup`.

After installing a FreeBSD or OpenBSD system, you will need to update it. Both installation procedures below describe the steps involved in performing a system upgrade. Bear in mind that the steps involved (`cvsup`, `make`, installation) are all fairly time consuming.

The `cvsup` or `cvs update` procedure will download all the source code for your operating system. If you installed from CD, it's beneficial to install the CD's copy of the sources so that you only have to download updates. Either way, the sources should end up in */usr/src*.

After you have the source, you will need to run some form of `make`, which prepares new binaries for your system based on the updated code base. When this is done, you may begin the install step, which does exactly what you think it does. If you have not been through a system upgrade before, set aside plenty of time. On a fast (1+ Ghz) system, you may need an hour or more. On a slower system (300Mhz), the `make` step can easily consume 6 hours.

For more information about `cvsup(1)` and `cvs(1)`, read the manpages for each.

One of the first steps you must take after successfully installing your system is to retrieve/update your operating system's source tree (usually using `cvsup(1)` or `cvs(1)`) and upgrade or patch the operating system until all known issues have been addressed. Immediately following the installation, you won't know if the running services have ***known security issues***, unless you've consulted the appropriate resources.

If you are not already familiar with what kinds of data are stored in which directories, spend a moment reading the *hier(7)* manpage. You will find a complete description of the filesystem hierarchy and the kind of files you are liable to find in any given directory.

After `fdisk`, define your partitions. Laying out your filesystems properly from the start will save you grief down the road. It's almost always a good idea to have separate filesystems for */*, */tmp*, */var*, */usr*, and perhaps */home*, as shown in Figure 3-1. You may also want others specific to your situation.

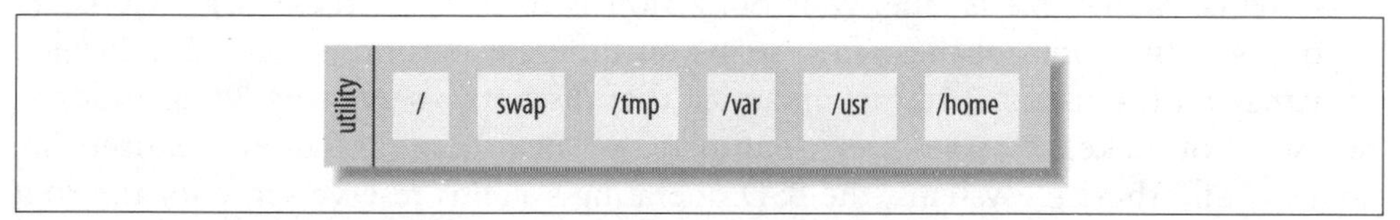

Figure 3-1. A possible disk layout of distinct filesystems

There are four major motivations for not simply creating a large root volume.

Integrity
: A system that experiences a power loss runs the risk of losing or corrupting data. This may limit itself to a few files, a directory, or the entire filesystem. The branches of the file hierarchy store different kinds of data as described in the manpage for *hier(7)*. The */home*, */usr*, */tmp*, and */var* filesystems, for instance, are fairly dynamic to varying degrees and experience many frequent changes. The root filesystem (excluding the others) tends to be fairly static. The chance of corruption in the event of a power or system failure will relate directly to the filesystem's volatility.

Availability
: You can't divorce availability from security. Running out of space in the root filesystem will interrupt service. When done maliciously, it is a form of denial of service attack. The likelihood of overextending available space on the root filesystem is significantly reduced when frequently written-to filesystems (such as */tmp* and */var*) are separated from the root. A rogue application or user will only be able to fill filesystems on which write access is granted.

Security
: Mount options such as disabling the interpretation of character or block special devices, disabling *set-user-identifier* (a.k.a. *set-user-id* and *setuid*) or *set-group-identifier* (a.k.a. *set-group-id* and *setgid*) bits, disallowing execution of any binaries altogether, and setting a filesystem as read-only are all possible when separate filesystems are defined. With a monolithic filesystem, none of these options could be applied. On the other hand, slicing out a partition such as */var/log* on a centralized logging host would enable you to apply all these options to the filesystem.

Performance

On a system with a great deal of disk activity, it can be useful to isolate frequently written-to filesystems near the perimeter of the drive platters to isolate them from more frequently read filesystems. Incorporating these directories as part of a larger filesystem places no constraints on the physical location of data stored within—in this case, fragmentation may cause a marked decrease in performance.

Arguments against filesystem slicing assert that a system will not behave as expected when */tmp* and */var* are filled and therefore there is little value in slicing out those filesystems. While this is true, your obligation is to mitigate these risks. Consider putting subdirectories of these filesystems on different partitions (such as */var/mail* or */var/spool* for instance) so that an attack that disrupts a service by filling a filesystem will not make the server itself nonfunctional. Bear in mind that even if users are able to "fill" these filesystems, the BSD operating systems reserve space for the root user, thus it is not uncommon to see "full" filesystems over 100% capacity. To configure how much space is reserved, look at the `-m` command-line argument to `tunefs(8)`. Avoid changing this value unless you really know what you are doing.

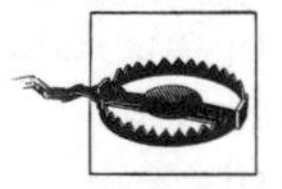

Take special care with the */tmp* and */var* filesystems. These are frequently written to by non-root processes and are more liable to fill. The multipurpose */var* directory is especially important as it not only stores critical system logs, name server configuration, and system database files, but also your print spool and mail queue. These data may constantly vie for space.

FreeBSD 4.4 and OpenBSD 3.4 introduced `growfs(8)`. With this utility and the availability of cheap hard drives, running out of space on a filesystem is not an issue. It is now common for system administrators to leave the majority of a disk unallocated so that space is available when a filesystem needs to be grown.

In the event that you have multiple disks at your disposal and wish to use them in a non-RAID configuration, the install processes of both operating systems allow you to mount your partitions from both drives. In this case, you may also want to create swap partitions on both drives. The following excerpt from the *FreeBSD Handbook* provides the rationale.

> On larger systems with multiple SCSI disks (or multiple IDE disks operating on different controllers), it is recommend that a swap is configured on each drive (up to four drives). The swap partitions should be approximately the same size. The kernel can handle arbitrary sizes but internal data structures scale to 4 times the largest swap partition. Keeping the swap partitions near the same size will allow the kernel to optimally stripe swap space across disks. Large swap sizes are fine, even if swap is not used much. It might be easier to recover from a runaway program before being forced to reboot.

When you have finished deciding how to slice up your disk, you may end up with a layout similar to the one in Figure 3-1. In this case, a utility system existed on the first slice of the disk, which was maintained. The rest of the disk was devoted to the operating system. Within this second slice separate partitions were made for each of the filesystems mentioned previously.

XFree86

The X Window System is rarely found installed on servers that house critical services. X is an extremely large and complex collection of binaries and libraries that introduces a huge code base from which vulnerabilities emerge from time to time. XFree86 is an open source implementation of the X Window System that is distributed with a variety of contemporary open source operating systems including Linux and the BSDs.

The X Window System is based upon the X protocol that takes the client-server model up to the application level. The goal of this protocol is to provide a graphical user interface within and between systems transparently. While this design improves look and feel, portability, and performance, all the security issues of the client-server model add to the already long list of application vulnerabilities.

That said, the XFree86 development team has done a phenomenal job over the years improving the security architecture of their implementation of the X Window System and it is today far safer to run X on servers than it ever was before. However, the goal of X is and always has been to provide a convenient graphical user interface.

Infrastructure servers are typically remotely accessed machines and provide only very specific services over clearly defined protocols. The only "use" of the server is by the administrator, and administration is usually console based.

You might think of workgroup servers as systems that need X. Sure enough, they may need to support the execution of X applications. What is referred to as the "X Server," however, allows locally executed applications to appear on the server's display. This means local memory allocated to the video card adapter and the PCI bus needs to be accessed. When direct memory access is being provided to an application, a vector for attack is introduced. The bottom line: the X Server rarely needs to be installed on workgroup servers.

Given the security ramifications of installing the entire X distribution, we recommend against doing so for workgroup and infrastructure servers. As needs arise for users to run X applications, these applications may be installed as packages or through ports. In the latter case, dependant packages will be automatically retrieved and installed. This assures you that only the software *required* to make a given application function is installed, but no more.

Users and Passwords

At the end of the installation, you're prompted for a password for the root user. In the case of FreeBSD, you are also prompted to create an additional user. Do it. This will be *your* user account, and could be added to the "wheel" group if you will need to su(1) to root. For OpenBSD, create an additional user account after installing the OS.

It's very important that you create an account for yourself instead of running around the system as the root user. Operating as a nonprivileged user protects you from you. Poorly thought out commands or even typographical errors as root can send you scrambling for backup tapes. Even seasoned administrators can get a little spacebar happy and turn the command **rm -rf** ***/my/dir/prefix**** to **rm -rf** ***/my/dir/prefix ****. If your current directory happens to be */usr*, by the time you press Ctrl-C, all manner of vital system files may be gone.

The two typical ways to gain super-user privileges are su and sudo(8). The former is available in the base installation of both operating systems, and the latter is included in the base install of OpenBSD and as a port/package in FreeBSD. When a user is a member of the wheel group, that user can use su to become root. However, doing so introduces an enticement: now that the user is root, why spend extra keystrokes to drop privileges again? The sudo command solves this problem by running only a single command at a time as root and logging the command as it runs it. You are immediately returned to your nonprivileged shell after the command has executed.

For more information about the differences between su and sudo, and some of the motivations for and pitfalls of each, see Chapter 4.

When creating a user account, take the time to develop a *strong* password both for root and any users you create as described in Chapter 1.

Summary

At this point you should know what you are building and where it is going in your network. You are armed with the installation media (and method) you have chosen and have thought about the risks associated with those decisions. Without further ado, let's dig into the not-so-glorious installation processes for FreeBSD and OpenBSD.

If you will be installing FreeBSD, keep reading. If you want to follow the weapon laden puffer fish, skip ahead to the section entitled "Installing OpenBSD" just ahead!

Installing FreeBSD

The FreeBSD install process brings you to the `sysinstall(8)` main screen (see Figure 3-2). If necessary, change your *keymap* or adjust install options. If you are booting from an older FreeBSD CD yet performing an FTP install, you may need to point the install elsewhere by changing Release Name under Options. That done, choosing the standard install is probably your best bet.

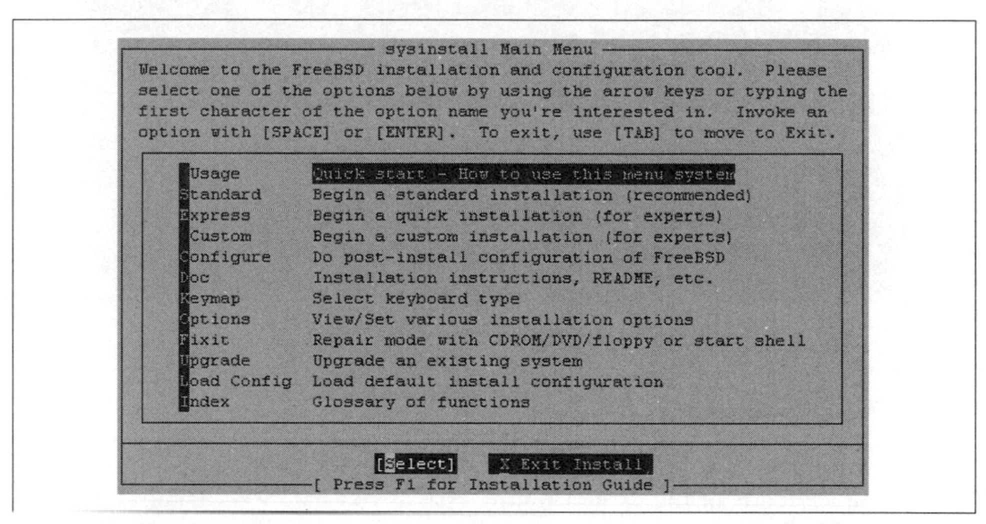

Figure 3-2. The sysinstall main screen

Preparing the Disk

Your first step will be to put into effect decisions you have already made regarding filesystem slicing. Having these written down in advance helps ensure you haven't made any mistakes.

Select your drive, decide whether or not to dedicate the entire disk or to leave aside some space for a maintenance partition, and move on. If you are not dual-booting, a standard boot loader is all you need. Finally, choose a filesystem layout that is appropriate for your system's task, as shown in Figure 3-3.

FreeBSD 5.0 added support for UFS2 filesystems and, in fact, this is the default. These filesystems provide improved performance during `fsck(8)`, support for larger filesystems, and extended attributes for native discretionary (ACLs) and mandatory access control (TrustedBSD MAC Framework). There are no particularly compelling reasons to fall back to the UFS1 filesystem.

```
                              FreeBSD Disklabel Editor

Disk: ad0          Partition name: ad0s1     Free: 0 blocks (0MB)

Part        Mount            Size Newfs   Part        Mount           Size Newfs
----        -----            ---- -----   ----        -----           ---- -----
ad0s1a      /               128MB UFS1    N
ad0s1b      swap            128MB SWAP
ad0s1d      /tmp            128MB UFS1+S  N
ad0s1e      /var            256MB UFS1+S  N
ad0s1f      /home          1024MB UFS2+S  N
ad0s1g      /usr           4485MB UFS1+S  N



The following commands are valid here (upper or lower case):
C = Create          D = Delete      M = Mount pt.                W = Write
N = Newfs Opts      Q = Finish      S = Toggle SoftUpdates       Z = Custom Newfs
T = Toggle Newfs    U = Undo        A = Auto Defaults            R = Delete+Merge

Use F1 or ? to get more help, arrow keys to select.
```

Figure 3-3. The disklabel(8) editor

Choosing Distribution Sets

This is the meat of the FreeBSD install process. It is here that you get to pick and choose the key parts of the base operating system you will need. Figure 3-4 shows the "canned" distribution sets that FreeBSD provides. While the Minimal option seems like a good bet, it is possible to install more without sacrificing security.

Keep your finger away from the Enter key! If you're familiar with `sysinstall`, you know that hitting the Enter key at the wrong time is usually shortly followed by hitting the reset button in frustration. Keep your fingers on the arrow keys (for navigation) and spacebar (for selection).

The Minimal distribution set includes both the base FreeBSD operating system and basic encryption services (`ssh` and SSL-related binaries and libraries, `pam`, `kerberos`, etc.). If you select Minimal, you can further customize which distributions are installed by subsequently selecting the Custom option.

Making a system more secure will likely simultaneously make it less convenient to manage, but the converse is not true: making system administration an arduous task does not imply that your system is more secure. Install the *man*, *catman*, and *info* distributions. If your environment requires *kerberos*, then by all means install the [eBones] *krb4* or [Heimdal] *krb5* distributions. Alternately, the MIT version may be installed from ports (*ports/security/krb5*) after the install.

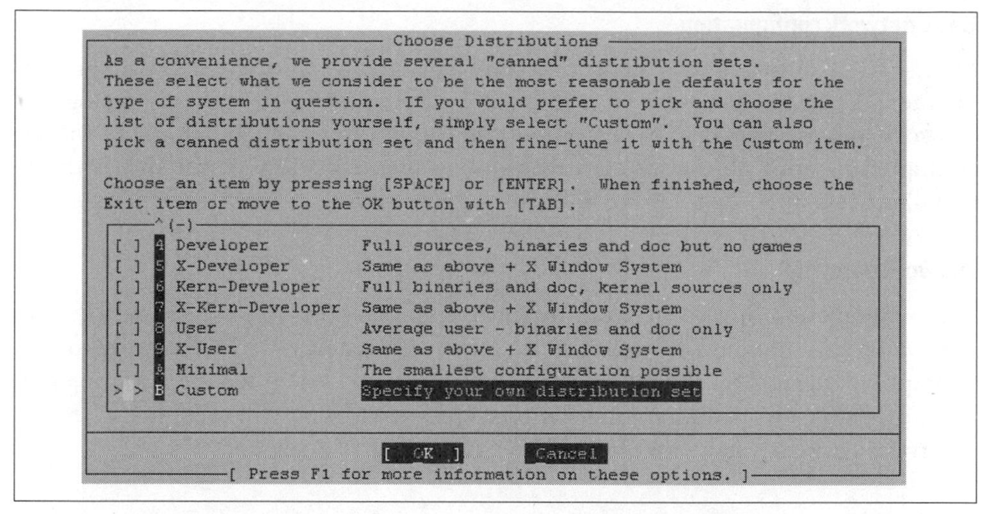

Figure 3-4. Choosing a distribution set

If you plan to rebuild your kernel or perform a local upgrade (as opposed to over NFS), install the *src* distribution. Installing *ports(7)* is a matter of preference. Some prefer to install binary packages instead of compiling ports locally. Others write scripts to pull down only the ports in which they are interested. It is your call. In either case, if you plan to cvsup to the latest versions of either the entire *src* or *ports* distributions, it makes sense to install them now and pull down only differences. The examples we provide in this book will always favor *ports* over packages.

Take note that in FreeBSD 5.x *perl* is a separate distribution. If you'll have need of a Perl interpreter (and you probably will, especially if you're going to be installing software from *ports*), install the *perl* distribution.

As was mentioned previously, you will rarely find X installed on servers. For an infrastructure server, command-line tools are usually adequate for administration. If you are building a multiuser development system or workstation, pieces of the X distribution may be required and may be installed later.

Choose your desired distributions, click OK, and FreeBSD will begin installing.

Post-Installation Configuration

The following section describes the various choices during the FreeBSD install process. Any prompt that may affect the security of your system is described below. The post-installation configuration begins by prompting you to enable your network interface.

Basic network configuration

Using DHCP during the install process can be dangerous, as discussed earlier in this chapter. When building servers, it is often easier to start with statically configured network information than worry about the implications of DHCP. You will be prompted to bring up the interface you just configured before continuing with the install process. It is safe to do so, if you trust your network or are not connected.

Network gateway

Upon completion of your network interface configuration, you are prompted: "Do you want this machine to function as a network gateway?" The answer to this prompt will depend on the role of your system. If your system will be a routing firewall, provide network address translation (NAT) services, or will for some other reason route packets, you will want to answer yes. Otherwise, say no.

inetd

If you are not providing one of the services `inetd` spawns, skip configuration of this super server during the install process. Even if you will be providing a service that runs from `inetd` (e.g., `ftpd(8)`), it's easy enough to configure it later, after you have hardened your system. Say `No` here for now.

sshd

It is very convenient to enable `sshd` at this stage. It means you will not need to sit with a console attached to the system while you configure it. If you have been paying attention to the security mailing lists and are confident that `sshd` listening on your newly installed server is safe (it has no known vulnerabilities), leave it on.

Security profile (FreeBSD 4.x only)

FreeBSD 4.x installs provide a set of prepackaged security profiles available only during installation. These profiles consist of a variety of changes to system defaults (specifically, in */etc/rc.conf*) that are outlined in Table 3-1. These profiles are termed Moderate and Extreme, though the term Medium is used interchangeably with Moderate.

Table 3-1. FreeBSD security profiles available during sysinstall

	Moderate	Extreme
sendmail	Enabled	localhost:25 only
sshd	Enabled	Disabled
portmap	Enabled if NFS client is enabled	Disabled
NFS server	Enabled if selected earlier	Disabled
securelevel	-1	2

Following the defense in depth principle, a security-minded system administrator would opt for the most secure configuration, enabling only services that are required instead of disabling services that are not: she would choose the Extreme security profile.

If you choose a Moderate security profile, you will gain the ability to upgrade your system after the install while still in multiuser mode. If you choose the Extreme security profile, you will have to drop to single user mode to perform the upgrade; this is the recommended approach anyway.

> There may be files on your newly installed filesystem with the system immutable (*schg*) flag set. Files with this flag will not be overwritten and in securelevel 1 or higher, not even the root user will be able to unset these flags. Therefore you will need to reduce your security level either by going into single user mode or by choosing the Moderate profile.

When your system has been installed, you can switch to the holographic shell provided for you on vty4 (press Alt-F4), and disable all unnecessary services by modifying your startup configuration file, */etc/rc.conf*.

After the installation is complete and your system is up and running, you can turn any necessary services back on after you are sure there are no known vulnerabilities in these services.

Anonymous FTP

The same rules apply to Anonymous FTP as to `inetd`. Even if you plan to be providing unauthenticated FTP access, deployment of this service should be performed carefully and after the system has been prepared. Before configuring this service, you should set up a `jail(8)` as described in Chapter 2.

NFS

NFS is a primitive protocol that provides file-sharing capability. Unfortunately it also provides little in the way of authentication and no encryption by itself. Deployment of NFS in a perimeter network or beyond the firewall should be avoided. Deployment anywhere else should probably also be avoided. See Chapter 4 for a more extensive discussion of the pitfalls of NFS and some possible alternative approaches.

Time zone

Consistent time is vital in a networked environment. For piecing together an audit trail, debugging mail or web application logs, or authenticating using Kerberos tickets, you should care about the system time. Resist the temptation to put your system's clock in Africa (unless, of course, your server *resides* in Africa).

System time is very important for troubleshooting and forensics. To ensure that the time across all your systems is consistent, develop a sound Network Time Protocol (NTP) architecture as described in Chapter 4.

Linux compatibility

You may need Linux compatibility for building workstations and servers that must run proprietary commercial binaries available only for Linux (such as for audio and video streaming) and other non-BSD operating systems. If you do not foresee the need, follow a minimalist approach and skip Linux compatibility for now—you can always add it later.

XFree86

A graphical user interface is appropriate on workstations and development servers. Workstations will require a full complement of X-related binaries, libraries, and user interface applications; development servers often only need enough libraries to be able to run self-built GUI programs and compiling tools. Infrastructure servers do not generally run X but sometimes have X libraries installed. For example, an installation of Apache for a production web server at an ISP may also require a variety of graphics suites that rely on the existence of X libraries. In this case, the X libraries in question may be installed through dependencies in the *ports* installation process.

Packages

The packages available during the install process are generally of similar age as the release. If you're installing an older version of FreeBSD (knowing full well that you will be upgrading in a moment), the packages you install in this step will be equally antiquated.

However there is one package you should install now: `sudo`. We mentioned `sudo` briefly earlier in this chapter and will cover the tool in far greater detail in Chapter 4. For now, either bear with us here as we ask you to blindly install this package or become familiar with `sudo` by reading the relevant sections in Chapter 4 and return here. Either way, scroll down to the security category, find `sudo`, select it, and install it.

Finishing up the install

Finally you're given the option to create a user account and set a root password. As discussed previously, it's important to create a user account instead of running around as root, and the passwords you set both for yourself and the root user should be strong. Many administrators like to add themselves to the wheel group at this point. However, you don't need to do this to gain root level access since you're using sudo. After these two steps, you find yourself at the end of the sysinstall process. Congratulations!

FreeBSD Hardening: Your First Steps

As you know by now, you can't just "turn on" security. System security is like a collection of switches and knobs that you must constantly adjust. Many of these controls were introduced in Chapter 2. Deciding which switches to flip and which knobs to turn will depend a great deal on your environment: security policies and procedures imposed upon you, your own security requirements, the nature of the data on the system, and the administrative overhead you are willing or required to tolerate. This section provides numerous suggestions to improve the security of your freshly installed FreeBSD system. Some steps are more important than others, and in a lot of cases, this too varies between environments.

Step 1: Configure sudo

We'll make this step brief since we cover sudo extensively in the next chapter. For now, all you need to do is ensure that the user account you created has fairly liberal rights when it comes to running privileged commands through sudo. In order to configure sudo to allow your account to execute any command as root, edit the *sudoers(5)* file by running visudo(8) without arguments while logged in as root. Append the following line to the file:

```
username ALL = ALL
```

Where of course *username* is the account you created for yourself during the install process. That's it! Save the file, log out, and log back in under your regular account. In order to run privileged commands from here on out, just prepend sudo to the command you'd ordinarily run as root. The first time you use sudo, it will tell you about the power you hold and ask for your (not root's!) password. Thereafter, it will periodically prompt for your password to make sure *you* are *you*.

Step 2: Turn Off Unnecessary Services

Your server is likely to provide one or two critical services to a local network or to visitors from the Internet. Other supporting services may also be running like sshd(8) for remote administration. All other services that listen on a network interface can be disabled. There is where knowing about preexisting vulnerabilities come in handy. With this in mind, it is a reasonable precautionary step to disable these services also.

If you've just installed FreeBSD 5.x, opted to not configure inetd during the install, and chose to enable sshd, you're in great shape. The only services you'll have listening on a newly installed 5.x system are sendmail accessible only on the loopback interface, and sshd. If you did enable inetd, make sure you edit */etc/inetd.conf* and comment out all unneeded components.

If you've just installed FreeBSD 4.x, the state of your system will vary depending on the security profile you chose. If you selected the extreme security profile, you will not have any remotely accessible services enabled and your first step is complete.

A FreeBSD 4.x system configured with a medium security profile will have a variety of running processes listening on several externally accessible ports. If your network card is not plugged in, that's not much of a problem—but you are going to be online sooner or later. Sooner, really, because your second step in this process is updating your system to the latest security branch (for more information about tracking branches, see Chapter 4). So turn off those services by adjusting *rc.conf(5)* as appropriate, and plug in. If you didn't configure your network at all during the install, do so after these services are disabled.

FreeBSD has a handy utility called sockstat to assist you in determining what services are listening on what port. Use the command **sockstat -l** to list all listening services. If you want to limit the results to only IPv4 interfaces, run **sockstat -4l**. For more information, see the sockstat(1) manpage.

Step 3: Update Your System

A freshly installed system is rarely up to date. Chances are good that development has continued since you acquired your software, and numerous bugs (both security and otherwise) have been found and fixed. As we've mentioned before, make sure you're subscribed to the security notifications list, and have checked the security page on the FreeBSD web site for known vulnerabilities. In any case, it's time for your first system update.

Getting the latest sources

Once you have connectivity and are reasonably assured that your system cannot be compromised by a remote attacker, it is time to cvsup your system sources, and rebuild. But wait, in a fit of paranoia you did not install the cvsup package as part of the FreeBSD install! Why did you fail to install something of immediate use? Well, if you have no plans to install XFree86 on this machine, you need the cvsup-without-gui port, which is not available during the install. The cvsup that is available depends on X libraries that you would like to avoid installing if possible. Fortunately the acquisition of cvsup-without-gui is as simple as:

```
% sudo pkg_add -r cvsup-without-gui
```

Typically when impatient administrators use cvsup to update the source tree, they do so as root. Downloading source code shouldn't require root-level privilege. Really, the only reason this level of access is needed is because of default filesystem permissions. The cvsup program will need to store information in */var/db/sup*, and will write into */usr/src*. When you upgrade your system, you'll also need to write into */usr/obj*. The solution here is to adjust the default permissions of these three directories (you may need to create */var/db/sup* first) so that you can write to them without elevated privileges.

How you accomplish this is up to you. If you're the sole administrator in charge of performing system upgrades, you might just want to make yourself the owner of these directories as shown in Example 3-2. Otherwise, you may want to use a special administrators-only group and grant group-write access to these directories.

Example 3-2. Changing ownership of key directories for cvsup

```
% sudo mkdir /var/db/sup
% sudo chown -R username /var/db/sup /usr/src /usr/obj
```

Now that you've got permissions straight, it's time to configure cvsup. First, you will need to create an appropriate *supfile*. This file sets a variety of defaults and will be read in by the cvsup program when you update your sources. Begin with one of the example files in */usr/share/examples/cvsup*, perhaps *standard-supfile*. Look for a line that specifies the release and tag, for example:

```
*default release=cvs tag=RELENG_5_3
```

The tag specifies the branch of FreeBSD you want to track. In general, most carefully administered FreeBSD servers track the security branch which includes only critical bug and security fixes. Thus if you install FreeBSD 5.3, you will always be running FreeBSD 5.3 with patches, and the appropriate tag for this is in fact RELENG_5_3.

If the *supfile* you're working with indicates something other than a security branch, for example RELENG_5 (that indicates -STABLE) or just . (a period, that indicates -CURRENT), adjust the tag as appropriate. After you adjust the *supfile*, save your working file elsewhere, perhaps */usr/local/etc/security-supfile*. Finally, update your FreeBSD sources by running:

```
% /usr/local/bin/cvsup -L 1 -h cvsupx.freebsd.org \
  /path/to/your/chosen/supfile
```

Be sure to replace the ***x*** in **cvsupx.freebsd.org** above with a number corresponding to a cvsup mirror close to you.

Do not directly modify any of the example *supfiles*. If another example cvsup configuration file better suits your needs, use it instead. If you need to make drastic changes to any of these files, save a modified copy of the file elsewhere. You do not want to accidentally lose your changes during a system upgrade.

While it is possible to track the -STABLE branch, be aware that system upgrades may include more changes than you bargained for. Some administrators have had success carefully tracking the -STABLE branch by performing upgrades to noncritical servers and subsequently upgrading other servers (using source from the exact same time) after a great deal of testing. Other administrators have been badly burned by tracking this branch. Unless vital features or fixes exist in the -STABLE branch, stick with the security branch. Finally, forget about tracking -CURRENT on production infrastructure. It is too volatile and unreliable and is better suited to systems with which you tinker but not on which you rely.

After you have successfully performed an update, you have the opportunity to save your update preferences for later use. To do this, add a block similar to the following to */etc/make.conf(5)*:

```
SUP_UPDATE= yes
SUP=        /usr/local/bin/cvsup
SUPFLAGS=   -L 1
SUPHOST=    cvsupx.freebsd.org
SUPFILE=    /path/to/your/chosen/supfile
```

After doing this, you may update your sources by running **make update** from */usr/src*.

For more information about cvsup including (and especially) using *refuse* files to tune which files or directories you retrieve, see the FreeBSD manpage for cvsup(1) and Appendix A.5 of the *FreeBSD Handbook*. To learn more about tracking branches of FreeBSD, see the relevant discussion in Chapter 4.

Kernel configuration

Before upgrading your system, you will probably want to fine-tune your kernel, both for security and performance reasons. Customizing your kernel configuration is typically recommended for FreeBSD systems, and only needs to be done immediately after the system is built and when you introduce new hardware. Given an environment where there are few hardware changes and consistent hardware across an infrastructure, the one time cost of fine-tuning yields rewards over the long term.

Creating a custom kernel configuration is almost never done from scratch. Typically you start from a *copy* of the */sys/conf/GENERIC* kernel and remove options as necessary. In some cases it may be necessary to add hardware support from */sys/arch/conf/NOTES* (In FreeBSD 4.x this file was *LINT*). As with installing distributions and packages, the following adage holds true: if you do not need it, do not install it. In a kernel context, this means if you do not need the kernel option, delete the configuration line and it will not be compiled in. The fewer drivers and options compiled into the kernel, the less always-running code there is to exploit.

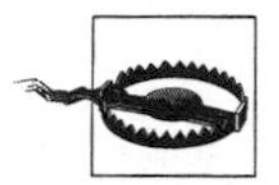

Be careful with what you remove. It may not be obvious that some options are mandatory. For many releases, the `COMPAT_43` option had the somewhat vague comment "Compatible with BSD 4.3" in the *GENERIC* file. Few administrators understood why they would want to be compatible with BSD 4.3 and removed this option. Then they discovered that their systems would no longer boot, and the comment now includes "[KEEP THIS!]."

The process of configuring a custom kernel is exceedingly well documented in Chapter 9 of the *FreeBSD Handbook*. While you need not actually compile or install your kernel in this step (we will do that in a moment as part of the system upgrade), now is a good time to create a configuration file for your custom kernel. The following list of options includes some of the changes you may want to make to the generic kernel for security reasons.

`BPF`
: The Berkeley Packet Filter option in the kernel allows packet sniffers such as `tcpdump(1)` to function. On many servers, the *bpf* pseudodevice is probably not necessary. Some key exceptions are DHCP servers/clients and IDS hosts. Access to information provided by this pseudodevice relies on the user being able to read from */dev/bpf**. If you want to restrict snooping on network interfaces, remove the *bpf* device from your kernel configuration.

`CD9660`
: Removing this option from the kernel will relegate the ISO9660 filesystem drivers to a kernel module. In a securelevel of 1 or greater, this module will not load, and access to a CD will require that you bring the system to single user mode or reboot. In a hostile physical environment, this may be desirable. In other cases, the administrative hassle will probably outweigh any security benefit.

`DEBUG`
: This option is disabled by default and should remain that way on production servers. Turning this option on would cause symbols to *not* be stripped after linking yielding a larger kernel, larger core dumps (unless you have disabled core dumps using `sysctl` as described in Chapter 2), and more information in those core dumps.

`IPv6, gif, faith`
: Falling under the category of "if you don't need it, don't install it," if IPv6 is not being used in your environment, there is no need to compile it into your kernel. Removing this option will shrink your kernel and allow for the removal of *gif* and *faith* devices that provide tunneling and relaying support for IPv6. Compiling without this option will also ensure that ports you build on your system after installing your new kernel do not have IPv6 support compiled in by default.

`KTRACE`
: The `KTRACE` option in the kernel will provide for kernel tracing using `ktrace(1)` and `kdump(1)` as described in Chapter 2. This option is enabled by default. `ktrace` assists with debugging and providing empirical data regarding the types of I/O operations a program is requesting and arguments to these operations. As a result, `ktrace` can assist in leaking sensitive information to the individual running `ktrace`. Unless you plan on using `ktrace` for one of the purposes discussed in Chapter 2, it is probably best to leave this option out of the kernel.

`MSDOSFS`
: The MS-DOS filesystem drivers will, like the ISO 9660 filesystem drivers, be compiled into a kernel module if this option is disabled. As with `CD9660`, the kernel module will not load at securelevel 1 or higher. In addition, even without this kernel option, `mtools` (in the FreeBSD ports collection) provides a means to access MS-DOS media without the support of this filesystem.

`NFS`
: NFS between systems is rarely used on production systems with direct exposure to the Internet. Support for NFS and `NFS_ROOT` can be safely removed from your kernel configuration unless you plan to provide a locally accessible and read only master `jail` as described in Chapter 2, or your system is on a LAN and the situation calls for it.

`UCONSOLE`
: This option allows non-root users to own the system console device (*/dev/console*). On an infrastructure system, there should be no need for users whatsoever. On a workstation or other server running X however, it is likely users will want to grab the console using programs like `xconsole`. Your situation will determine whether you want to leave this in.

`USB`
: USB devices are invaluable on workstations. Some servers these days ship without integrated removable media bays at all and rely on the availability of USB floppies and CD-ROM drives. Your hardware will in large part determine whether USB devices should be supported by your kernel. In an untrusted environment, automatic support of USB media may not be desirable.

Remember that just because the functionality is not compiled into your kernel, you may still have access to it. Much of the kernel is modular, so even if you do not compile it in, you can load the appropriate module later, provided your system is running in a securelevel below 1.

Once you have decided how to build your custom kernel, save the configuration file with the other files in */sys/arch/conf*. Be sure not to replace the original `GENERIC` configuration file, but instead, save your changes into another file, e.g., `MYKERNEL`.

Your first upgrade

With the latest sources sitting in */usr/src* and a custom kernel configuration file ready, you're prepared to upgrade the system. This entire process has been comprehensively covered in Chapter 21 of the *FreeBSD Handbook*, so we will not waste time with the entire process here. Instead, a few do's and don'ts of upgrading your FreeBSD system.

- Do read */usr/src/UPDATING*. Failure to do so could cause you to miss a step, rendering your system in a less-than-ideal state.
- Do create *make.conf(5)* for your system. If you plan to run a mail transport agent or nameserver installed from ports or ask a package, you would be well advised to configure *make.conf* so these binaries are not replaced during a system upgrade (this is less important during your first upgrade). Example 3-3 shows values in */etc/make.conf* that might be appropriate for an i386 AMD based server with DNS software installed through ports instead of in the base system.

Example 3-3. Example /etc/make.conf for FreeBSD

```
CPUTYPE=    k6-2
CFLAGS=     -O -pipe
COPTFLAGS= -O -pipe
NO_BIND=    true     # no BIND
NOGAMES=    true     # no games (games/ subdir)
NOPROFILE= true     # no profiled libraries
KERNCONF=   MYCONFIG
BOOTWAIT=   3000
```

- In addition, your *make.conf* can assist with updating your source tree via **make** update by pointing it to your *supfile* and `cvsup` binary as described previously. For a full description of the options available in *make.conf*, see the *make.conf(5)* manpage.
- At this stage, don't worry about `mergemaster(8)` clobbering your configuration files. You haven't made any configuration changes yet. If you've never run `mergemaster` before, read the manpage. Table 3-2 describes options that may be useful to you in running `mergemaster`.

Table 3-2. Important mergemaster options

Option	Description
`-i`	If a file does not exist in */etc* (it is being introduced as part of this upgrade), automatically install it.
`-p`	Pre-*buildworld* mode. Compare files essential to the success of the *buildworld*/*installworld* process. Run this before *buildworld*.
`-v`	Increase verbosity, useful the first time you run `mergemaster`.
`-t [arg]`	Specify an alternate temporary root from which to make comparisons.

Step 4: Wrapping Up

With your FreeBSD system upgraded, it's time to turn your attention to some final system lockdown activities. Because this process is so similar for both FreeBSD and OpenBSD, it has been placed at the end of this chapter under "Post-Upgrade Hardening." If you decide to complete some of these steps before running `mergemaster`, you will have to be careful when selecting to install, delete, or merge configuration files you may have changed. Best of luck!

Installing OpenBSD

One of the hallmarks of OpenBSD is the incredibly low number of remotely exploitable vulnerabilities in the *default* install. As a method to this madness, the OpenBSD team has built the install process to achieve this goal: the options provided during the install are few, and security options are enabled where possible by default. What this all means is that the OpenBSD install is simple, swift, and painless. Following the prompts will get you from zero to fully functional in very little time. That said, let's move quickly through the steps.

Preparing the Disk

The first step in an OpenBSD installation is to indicate that you are, in fact, installing and not upgrading or in need of a shell for maintenance or recovery. Enter **`I`** for install, pick your terminal and keyboard emulation, confirm, and it's time to pick a disk and slice it up.

If you have no maintenance partition and do not plan to dual boot, you can use your entire disk for OpenBSD. Create your partitions according to the decisions you made before starting the install process, quit, and write the new disk label.

Remember, if at any time you feel lost, provide the installer **`?`** as input. You will be provided help. You may also get the entire manpage for `fdisk(8)` and `disklabel(8)` by typing in **`manual`** or **`M`** for each application respectively.

If you have chosen to separate the most common filesystems, the installer will automatically flag your filesystems as shown in Table 3-3. This saves you a little bit of work later.

Table 3-3. Default flags for mount(8) set by the OpenBSD install

	nodev (no devices)	*nosuid* (no set-uid/gid)
/usr	✓	
/tmp	✓	✓
/home	✓	✓
/		
/var	✓	✓

The nodev option may cause you a little grief later on if you are running a chrooted process within */var*. A DNS server like named(8) for instance, chrooted in */var/named*, will want to use devices like */var/named/dev/null* and */var/named/dev/log*. If you plan to chroot daemons in */var*, you may want to remove this flag.

Configuring Your Network

Network connectivity during the install process is really your call, as described previously in this chapter. If you are building a server, you are unlikely to be using DHCP to configure your network interface. Provide values at the prompts and proceed.

During network setup, you will be prompted for a nameserver and whether that nameserver should be used immediately. Be sure this is a trusted resolver. The last thing you need is to be a victim of a MITM attack and directed to a malicious site when you try to download patches via FTP or cvs!

After network configuration, you are prompted to enter a root password. Make it a *strong* password. OpenBSD does not prompt for the creation of a new user; we'll do that soon.

Choosing Your Distribution Sets

Here we are at the meat of the OpenBSD install process. At this point, you choose which file sets to install. Each set is a portion of the OpenBSD distribution and it is named according to its contents and version. Figure 3-5 shows file sets of the OpenBSD 3.5 distribution. The only required sets are the kernel (*bsd*), the base OpenBSD system (*base35.tgz*), and the files from the */etc* filesystem (*etc35.tgz*). You may also want to install the compilers (*comp35.tgz*) and the manpages (*man35.tgz*).

If you are building an infrastructure server, you will probably want to avoid installing any X file sets. In the case of a development server, the base install for XFree86 (*xbase35.tgz*) may be appropriate.

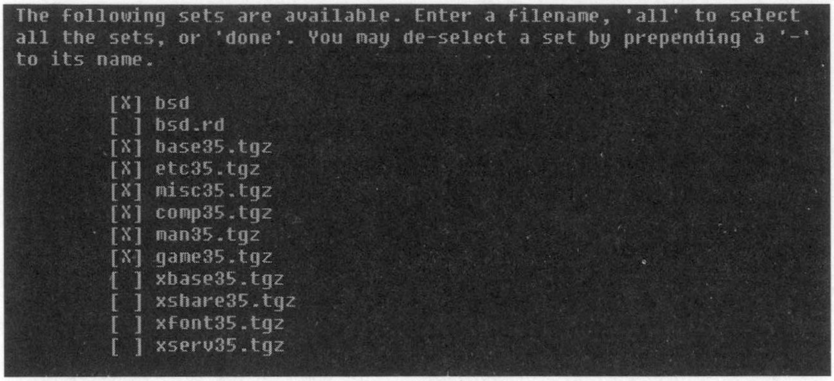

```
The following sets are available. Enter a filename, 'all' to select
all the sets, or 'done'. You may de-select a set by prepending a '-'
to its name.

        [X] bsd
        [ ] bsd.rd
        [X] base35.tgz
        [X] etc35.tgz
        [X] misc35.tgz
        [X] comp35.tgz
        [X] man35.tgz
        [X] game35.tgz
        [ ] xbase35.tgz
        [ ] xshare35.tgz
        [ ] xfont35.tgz
        [ ] xserv35.tgz
```

Figure 3-5. Choosing OpenBSD 3.5 file sets

Activating sshd

After installing file sets, you are asked if you want to enable `sshd(8)`. The convenience of enabling `sshd` at this stage is high. It means you will not need to sit with a console attached to the system while you configure it. If you have been paying attention to the security mailing lists and checked the OpenBSD Errata page to ensure that `sshd` listening on your newly installed server is safe, leave it on.

An Innocuous Question About X

You are subsequently asked if you plan to run X on the system. If you're building a workstation or, heaven forbid, a multipurpose machine that might serve as someone's desktop, the answer to this may be yes. If you're building a development server so that users can launch X programs from the server but have them displayed on their system, you do not need to enable this.

Answering this question in the affirmative will modify */etc/sysctl.conf* such that `mdachdep.allowaperture` is set to either 1 or 2 (depending on your platform). When your OpenBSD system boots after the install, the system's *securelevel(7)* is incremented to 1. This restricts, among other things, applications from being able write to the physical address space and I/O ports corresponding to your VGA adapter and some general PCI configuration registers. The aperture driver (see the *xf86(4)* manpage) */dev/xf86* was introduced to OpenBSD so that the X server can have the access it needs to this address space and these registers even when the system is running in a securelevel higher than 0.

From a security standpoint, it's important to know that the aperture driver will allow any one process to bypass the restrictions imposed by the system's security level. Usually this process is the X server, but before the X server is able to load, a malicious user or application *could* use this driver to do some damage. Granted, this is a not very easily exploitable window, but if you want to get rid of it altogether, answer no to this question, and do not run X.

Finishing Up

Finally, it is time to set your time zone and prepare to reboot your system. Before you do so however, do you know what services will be running at the end of the reboot? To find out, there are two files you will need to look at: your startup configuration file, *rc.conf*, currently in */mnt/etc* and your system startup script */mnt/etc/rc*. If you run:

```
# cat /mnt/etc/rc.conf | egrep "(_flags|=YES)" | grep -v =NO
```

You will get a list of directives that may spawn services. Results from the command above, however, do not necessarily mean a service will start. A given service may be disabled in the same configuration file by a later directive set to NO, or the service's start is dependent upon some other factor, such as the existence of a configuration file or directory in the filesystem. To determine if this is the case, look through */mnt/etc/rc* for the flags directive in question and determine under which conditions the service will start.

Don't bother trying to disable `syslogd(8)`. By default, the system logger will not accept incoming UDP datagrams unless running with the –u (insecure) flag.

If you decide to disable services, place overrides to the startup configuration file in *rc.conf.local*. This file is sourced right after the *rc.conf* file in the system startup script.

If the procedure above seems too cumbersome to follow (and it should), you have two options for mitigating the risks of having listening services when you reboot:

- Disconnect your network interface. This is by far the easiest and most reliable choice.
- Disable services you know (through some other means) will be running on your OpenBSD system.

If you are comfortable with the set of services running post-install and know they have no known vulnerabilities, go ahead and reboot your system. Your OpenBSD install is complete!

OpenBSD Hardening: Your First Steps

OpenBSD's proactive "secure by default" approach to security results in a very secure system immediately after install. The goal here is to ensure system administrators start from a system that is not open to remote compromise. Therefore few services will be running after a fresh install, and these services will have undergone rigorous review. If you have followed the recommendations in this chapter, you will have taken things one step further. You have ensured that there are no listening services or have verified that any listening services are not vulnerable to remote exploit.

Nevertheless, system security is an ongoing process, and there is more work to be done. The following two steps are essential to bringing your system into a more secure state, and continued diligence will keep it there.

If you are not familiar with the administration of OpenBSD, please spend a little time immediately after the install reading the *afterboot(8)* manpage.

Step 1: Create a User

When you first log into an OpenBSD system you are admonished for logging in as root. The default *.login* file from which commands are executed under the default c-shell (`csh`) includes this warning. It's a bad idea to run around your system as root; a stray typo could send the system into an unrecoverable state. Instead, create a local user account for yourself and use `sudo(8)` to execute privileged commands. This will accomplish three things:

- It will keep your system safe from you.
- It will ensure that you think about the privileged command you are about to execute before blindly typing it in and hitting enter.
- It will provide a valuable audit trail of privileged commands executed.

Both `adduser(8)` and `vipw(8)` will allow you to create a user, though the former command is a little more helpful and will allow you to set a user password. Many administrators like to add themselves to the wheel group at this point. However, you don't need to do this to gain root level access since you're using `sudo`.

Step 2: Configure sudo

We'll make this step brief because we cover `sudo` extensively in the next chapter. For now, all you need to do is ensure that the user account you created has fairly liberal rights when it comes to running privileged commands through `sudo`. In order to configure `sudo` to allow your account to execute any command as root, edit the *sudoers(5)* file by running `visudo(8)` without arguments while logged in as root. Append the following line to the file:

```
username ALL = ALL
```

Where of course *`username`* is the account you created for yourself in the previous step. That's it! Save the file, log out, and log back in under your regular account. In order to run privileged commands from here on out, just prepend `sudo` to the command you'd ordinarily run as root. The first time you use sudo, it will tell you about the power you hold and ask for your (not root's!) password. Thereafter, it will periodically prompt for your password to make sure *you* are *you*.

Step 3: Turn Off Unnecessary Services

Looking at the process list after login (by running **ps ax**) will show you what's running on your system. Checking the output of **netstat -a** on a freshly installed OpenBSD 3.5 system will show that sshd, and a few basic services provided by inetd (identd(8), daytime, time), are remotely accessible. In addition, sendmail and comsat(8) are listening on the loopback interface. Depending on the kind of system you are building, some of these services may not be necessary. Let's go through each of them and discuss whether you need to adjust or disable these running services.

sshd

The secure shell daemon is of fundamental importance. It serves as your primary means of remote shell access to your system and it is rare you would ever want to disable this service. However, by default, the sshd daemon will allow logins as root. You have already created a user that has sudo rights, so there's no reason to continue allowing logins as root. This can be disabled by setting PermitRootLogin in */etc/ssh/sshd_config* to **No**. For more information about tightening security around sshd, see the "Post-Upgrade Hardening" section, later in this chapter.

inetd

There are several programs running "out of" inetd by default. For the most part these services are trivial and not prone to attack. However, they are also not particularly necessary and can probably be disabled on most systems. If you are building a workstation, services running out of inetd such as identd and comsat may be useful. inetd with a default configuration, however, is best disabled on infrastructure servers by placing **inetd=NO** in your */etc/rc.conf.local*. You may revisit this decision later.

Sendmail

There is little harm in keeping sendmail running in its default configuration on OpenBSD. It listens only on the loopback interface and as such, is only vulnerable to attack from the local host. If your system provides many user accounts, however, you need to ensure that your locally listening services are patched. Alternately you could replace sendmail with another MTA—See Chapter 6 for more information on building a secure mail server.

Step 4: Update Your System

It's time for another look at the Errata page on the OpenBSD web site. Here you will find a list of security and reliability issues that have been identified since the latest release and ways to resolve them. The role of your system will determine how you want to approach the topic of system updates now and in the future. OpenBSD has three options available for system update: patch manually, track the patch branch (otherwise known as stable), or track the current source.

Any of these options are viable for OpenBSD workstations, but servers (especially infrastructure servers) must be treated with more care. It's a good idea to limit your updates of servers to the patch branch. For more information about OpenBSD's branches of development, see the relevant discussion in Chapter 4.

So, let's begin by getting a cvs checkout of the appropriate patch branch. First ensure that */usr/src* is owned by you or writable by a group to which you belong. Then retrieve OpenBSD sources as follows:

```
% setenv CVSROOT anoncvs@some.server.somewhere.tld:/cvs
% cd /usr; cvs checkout -P -rOPENBSD_X_Y src
```

Where X_Y (e.g., 3_5 for OpenBSD 3.5) is the patch branch you wish to track. For a list of anonymous CVS servers, see *http://www.openbsd.org/anoncvs.html*. Once the source has been downloaded, rebuild your kernel and **make world**. For a walk-through of an OpenBSD upgrade procedure, see the OpenBSD patch branch documentation at *http://www.openbsd.org/stable.html*. OpenBSD does not encourage that you develop a custom kernel configuration unless you have specific hardware requirements. The following is an excerpt from the OpenBSD FAQ:

> Under most circumstances you will NOT need to compile your own kernel. The GENERIC kernel will usually be all that you need. In fact, there are several reasons why you do not want to create your own kernel. The main reason is that it is very easy to make changes to the kernel configuration which look logical, but do not work. This is your danger sign. If something does not appear to work properly, please try the GENERIC kernel before sending in a bug report. Developers will usually ignore bug reports dealing with custom kernels, unless the problem can be reproduced in a GENERIC kernel as well. You have been warned.

As a result we do not cover the process of building a custom kernel configuration. Should the need arise, there's plenty of information for you in the FAQ.

Step 5: Wrapping Up

Once your system has been updated and is running only those services that you require, you can turn your attention to some of the more fine-grained security controls. These steps are fairly similar for both OpenBSD and FreeBSD, so the following section, "Post-Upgrade Hardening," covers both operating systems.

Post-Upgrade Hardening

At this point, you are ready to start locking down your system configuration. As we repeat throughout this book, disabling features and creating limits does not always increase the security of the system. It generally makes sense to take a "bang for the buck" approach to hardening. Deal with the most critical yet easily handled issues first before moving on to more complicated security with diminishing returns. The following steps provide one approach to system lockdown, but it is not the only way.

Configure Users and Groups

If your system will be serving multiple users, allowing logins, providing FTP accounts, and so on, spend some time thinking about how to structure your users and groups. For workstations with many users, configuration of different sets of users and groups on each machine may be impractical. However, through the use of a centrally managed authentication and authorization mechanism, users and groups can be administered in a scalable fashion.

The most important group on a BSD system is, of course, wheel. Members of the wheel group have a variety of read rights in */dev* that normal users do not and are the only users allowed to `su(1)` to root (with knowledge of the root password, of course). You may choose to make yourself and other administrators members of the wheel group, but if you're using `sudo`, there's little motivation for doing so.

With FreeBSD 5.x and the introduction of ACLs, the reliance on Unix groups has diminished. In some cases (such as a file server) ACLs may be a more appropriate access control than groups. See Chapter 4 for additional information about user/group administration and access control for users and administrators. See Chapter 2 for more information about how ACLs work and how to use them.

Toor (FreeBSD only)

FreeBSD includes a toor (root spelled backward) account, which has been historically used to gain root access with an alternate root shell. The rationale being, should the system need to boot in single user mode, root (with statically compiled */bin/csh*) would still be able to log in.

This user has since been made somewhat moot given two changes. First, when FreeBSD boots into single user mode, the administrator is prompted for a shell—even if the default root shell is `/usr/local/bin/bash`, for instance, the administrator could enter `/bin/sh` and log in. Second, FreeBSD has introduced a fully dynamic system (binaries in */bin* and */sbin* are not statically linked, but rely on libraries elsewhere on the filesystem). A collection of static binaries for recovery have been placed into */rescue*.

In any case, you shouldn't be logging in as root unless you're performing system recovery, thus the toor account may be safely deleted.

Adjust Mount Options

The following mount options can affect the security of the system. Turning on all options for every filesystem will render your system unusable, so do not do that. Look closely at what the options do, and consult the manpage for `mount(8)` for more information.

As mentioned previously, OpenBSD administrators may have some of these options already set depending on the filesystems that were sliced out during the install process.

`noauto`
: This option, when specified for a filesystem in */etc/fstab*, will ensure that the filesystem is skipped for **`mount -a`** (run during system startup). This can be useful for filesystems you want handy, but not mounted all the time such as CD-ROMs.

`nodev`
: As the name implies, this option prevents character or block special devices from being interpreted as such when found on the filesystem. While all but the root filesystem are good candidates for this option, remember that chrooted or jailed services often require */dev* inside their pseudo root filesystem.

`noexec`
: Binary executables will not be loaded and executed from the filesystem if this option is set. All but the root and */usr* filesystems are candidates for this option. Remember, however, shell scripts will continue to work just fine. On a system with developers, setting `noexec` for */home* will ensure you get beat up in the parking lot on your way home.

`nosuid`
: This option prevents the `setuid` or `setgid` bits from taking effect. Programs will run as the executing user. As the manpage for `mount` mentions, this option has little use if a `setuid` or `setgid` wrapper is installed and publicly executable on the filesystem.

`rdonly`
: Nobody can write to a filesystem mounted read-only. It may be tempting to consider this option instead of using immutability flags, but root can easily get around the read-only option by running **`mount -uo rw`** ***`filesystem`***. The system must be rebooted into a securelevel of less than 1 if the immutable flag is to be circumvented.

`suiddir` *(FreeBSD only)*
: `suiddir` allows files in a directory with a `setuid` bit set to inherit ownership from the directory. Thus if the directory has the `setuid` bit set and is owned by root, other files created in that directory will also be owned by root. The manpage for

mount provides good additional information about this option. Be wary whenever you enable suiddir.

There are a variety of other options available for mount, and you should seek them out. It's fairly obvious, though, that while these options are useful, they are by themselves not as strong as some of the other security features of FreeBSD. For a system built according to a defense-in-depth strategy, however, they're well worth using where appropriate.

Lock Down sshd

Authentication is the way systems are convinced you are who you say you are. By default, the secure shell daemon (sshd(8)) accepts a variety of authentication mechanisms including via password, public key, and through some alternate challenge-response mechanism. This may not be ideal.

Password authentication

Users are very familiar with password authentication: you provide your username and your password. If the password on file for the username you provide matches the one you provide, you have successfully authenticated. All you need is a valid username and password to get into a system configured to allow password authentication through SSH.

Public key authentication

To configure public key authentication for ssh between two systems, you must first generate a pair of keys for yourself: a public and private key. This is accomplished using the ssh-keygen(1) utility and will, by default, create a *~/.ssh/id_dsa* private key and a *~/.ssh/id_dsa.pub* public key. When your public key is placed on a target host in the *.ssh/authorized_keys* (or *.ssh/authorized_keys2*) file in your home directory, and you have in your possession (on the source host) the private key, you may successfully authenticate after typing in a *passphrase*. Note not only do you need something in your possession (the private key), you also need to know a *passphrase*. This is known as two-factor authentication and is a significant improvement over password authentication.

We strongly recommend reading the sshd(8) manpage to better understand how this form of authentication works. Suffice it to say that it is stronger than mere password authentication and should be required of users and administrators alike.

Challenge response authentication

By itself, this is not a single form of authentication. FreeBSD and OpenBSD treat challenge response authentication support in different ways as described below. This allows sshd to point to an alternate authentication framework. In the case of

FreeBSD, this framework is Pluggable Authentication Modules (PAM). In OpenBSD, login classes determine possible authentication information. For more information about PAM and login classes.

Workstations on a protected LAN usually benefit from having a variety of authentication options available. Servers, on the other hand, should have a more restricted set of possible authentication mechanisms, we recommend limiting authentication to public key only. Below are configuration changes in */etc/ssh/sshd_config* you may want to consider. See the *sshd_config(5)* manpage for more information.

Allow/deny groups and users
: Specifying `AllowUsers` tells `sshd` to only allow logins by the listed users. Likewise, specifying groups after `AllowGroups` limits logins to users who are in the listed groups. The inverse options, `DenyGroups` and `DenyUsers`, do what you would expect.

`ChallengeResponseAuthentication`
: This option specifies whether or not PAM should be used for authentication in FreeBSD and whether to allow the authentication styles described in */etc/login.conf* to succeed in OpenBSD. It is enabled by default, and can be disabled if you are not using any of the authentication mechanisms specified in FreeBSD's */etc/pam.d/sshd* or S/Key on OpenBSD. Setting this to **`NO`** alone does not disable password authentication on FreeBSD.

`PasswordAuthentication`
: Password authentication for `sshd` is weaker than the other options and should be disabled on production servers where possible. At the very least, on infrastructure servers, enforce public key authentication by setting `PasswordAuthentication` to **`NO`**.

FreeBSD only: setting this to **`NO`** will still allow authentication through PAM, including password authentication. You will want to remove *pam_unix(8)* from */etc/pam.d/sshd* or set `ChallengeResponseAuthentication` to **`NO`**.

`PermitRootLogin`
: While this option accepts the arguments **`YES`**, **`NO`**, **`WITHOUT-PASSWORD`**, and **`FORCED-COMMANDS-ONLY`**, allowing users to log in as root makes accountability impossible. It becomes very difficult to tie people to logins, which is vital to successful auditing. Set this option to **`NO`**.

`Protocol`
: If possible, restrict SSH connections to protocol 2 only. The SSHv1 protocol is vulnerable to a MITM attack for which many easy-to-use kits exist. In an environment where the SSHv1 protocol is still prevalent, develop a migration strategy to move users over to SSHv2 and change this option to read **`Protocol 2`**.

`StrictModes`
: This is enabled by default, but it is important to know what it does. `StrictModes` checks file permissions before accepting login. Not doing this can introduce security problems should users leave their private keys unprotected.

`UsePrivilegeSeparation`
: This tells `sshd` to *fork(2)* an unprivileged child process to handle the session. This child process runs as the user making the connection mitigating the risks of privilege escalation. It is enabled by default and is a good thing.

`VerifyReverseMapping`
: This enforces RFC931 compliance. That is, the IP address making the connection to the server reverse resolves into a hostname, which in turn resolves to the IP address making the connection to the server. Turning this option on (it is disabled by default) will make people unhappy if they need to connect from environments where they have no control over DNS mappings. Use with care.

`X11Forwarding` *and* `X11UseLocalhost`
: When both `X11Forwarding` and `X11UseLocalhost` are enabled, the server on which `sshd` is running provides a proxy display on the wildcard address instead of the loopback address. This exposes the proxy display to requests originating from outside the `ssh` tunnel. `X11UseLocalhost` is set to **`YES`** by default. Allowing X11 forwarding at all may expose the client system's X server to attack.

If you do not already have an SSHv2 key, generate one now. Resist the temptation to keep using your old key or password because of the hassle. With widespread support of the SSHv2 protocol in both open source and commercial software for most platforms, there's little reason to support either the older protocol or passwords.

Configure Basic Logging

Logs form the basis of your audit trail. Without them, there is little hope you will be able to track down what happened on a system after a security breach or malfunction. An incomplete set of logs will yield an incomplete picture when you are trying to recreate the series of events leading up to a security incident. Having logs by themselves may not even be enough. You need to be sure that your logs have not been tampered with and contain all the information you are interested in tracking.

First, decide what you are interested in tracking on the system. On a single-purpose machine such as a mail server, this is fairly easy: you want to know about important system events and have detailed mail logs. Next, make the appropriate configuration changes to */etc/syslog.conf* (read the manpage for *syslog.conf(5)* for more information) as shown in Example 3-4 and HUP `syslogd`. If you have a `syslog` *loghost* server, do not forget to send your logs to it.

Example 3-4. Sample syslog.conf for a mail server

```
# Facility/Level specification                Log Destination
*.err;kern.debug;auth.notice;mail.crit        /dev/console
*.notice;kern.debug;mail.crit;news.err        /var/log/messages
security.info                                 /var/log/security
mail.info                                     /var/log/maillog
cron.info                                     /var/log/cron
auth.info                                     /var/log/ssh
*.emerg                                       *
*.info                                        @loghost
```

Bear in mind, you may have to revisit this step after installing ports or packages should you decide to track logs from that application in a different file or by using one of the reserved local facilities. You also want to configure log rotation via *newsyslog.conf* to ensure that your logs do not fill up your filesystem. `newsyslog(8)` can be configured to zip up old logs at a certain time or size and reset permissions on new logs it creates. It will even maintain a certain number of logs so you do not have to spend time cleaning up after old logfiles.

Once you have your key logs identified, you may be tempted to use the append-only file flag (*sappnd*) so that your logs cannot be truncated. If you end up using this flag and you are running in a securelevel greater than 1, however, `newsyslog` will fail when it tries to delete the old log and create a new one.

For a more comprehensive treatment of logging and building audit trails, see Chapter 10.

Create Login Banners

In U.S. courts, the waters of computer crime and trespassing have only barely been tested. Advising users of your systems that their activities may be monitored and that only authorized users should log into the system only strengthens your position if you wish to use your audit trail in a U.S. court of law. Login banners are fairly easy to create and put into place, so there's no good reason to omit this step from your security checklist. Login banners should, at the very least, warn all users who attempt to access your system that they have no expectation of privacy, and that they implicitly consent to monitoring by using the system, and so on. Consult with a lawyer regarding words that are appropriate for your organization.

The message of the day file, *motd(5)* is an ideal place to enter a login banner. Various services print *motd* at login. If login banners are required before authentication (this is a good idea), the problem must be solved on a case-by-case basis. For services that are connection oriented (TCP) and are compiled with *libwrap*, (e.g., `inetd`) *tcpwrappers* can be used for login banners. There are three requirements for this:

- In the case of `inetd`, you'll need the **`-w`** option.
- */etc/hosts.allow* must contain the `banners` directive (see the *hosts_options(5)* manpage).

- A file must exist in the directory specified as an argument to the `banners` directive above of the same name as the service for which the banner should be displayed.

A sample *hosts.allow* configuration may look like this:

```
ALL: PARANOID : RFC931 20 : deny
ALL: ALL: banners /etc/banners
```

Files containing login banners would then need to be named *in.telnetd*, *ftpd*, and so on, and placed in the directory */etc/banners*.

`sshd` may be configured directly by using the `Banner` configuration option. If you choose this option and provide your *motd* as an argument, you should also turn off `PrintMotd`, or users may start complaining of banner overload.

Configure NTP

Keeping your system's time accurate is vital. This is why changes in the system clock are limited to ±1s per second at securelevel 2. Without a reliable timestamp, analyzing logs moves from the realm of "art" or even "science" to sheer futility. There are two parts to configuring `ntpd(8)`: initially (and roughly) setting the system clock and keeping it accurate. On FreeBSD systems `ntpdate(8)` is used to initially change the system clock to the correct time, often at boot. OpenBSD administrators may be more used to `rdate(8)`. In order to keep the clock accurate, `ntpd` periodically polls time servers and nudges the system clock back toward the right time, should it fall out of sync.

`ntpdate` on FreeBSD systems may be configured either through `sysinstall` after installation is complete or manually. `rdate` on OpenBSD systems may be configured after the install by setting `rdate_flags` appropriately in */etc/rc.conf.local*. You may need to look up NTP servers in your geographic vicinity. A list of public NTP servers is available at *http://www.eecis.udel.edu/~mills/ntp/servers.html*.

Remember that `ntpdate` and `rdate` do not take into account network latency, will only query one server, and drastically adjust the system clock. This is useful to eliminate any large discrepancies that would preclude `ntpd` from running, but will not provide accuracy beyond a tenth of a second. `ntpd` uses sophisticated algorithms and multiple servers to keep sub-millisecond accuracy.

It's vital that you set the system clock before the system's securelevel is promoted during boot. This is easily accomplished on FreeBSD by adding the following to your */etc/rc.conf*:

```
ntpdate_enable="YES"  # FreeBSD Only
ntpdate_flags="-b public-ntp-server.domain.tld"
```

OpenBSD administrators would similarly add the following to */etc/rc.conf.local*:

```
rdate_flags="-n public-ntp-server.domain.tld"
```

The ntpdate utility is approaching deprecation, which means it will eventually be removed from the operating system. To prepare for its impending doom, set ntpdate_program to **/usr/sbin/ntpd** and ntpdate_flags to **-q**. This will have the same effect as running ntpdate but will use ntpd instead.

ntpd is configured to run by specifying **ntpd_enable="YES"** in FreeBSD's */etc/rc.conf*, or **ntpd=YES** in OpenBSD's */etc/rc.conf.local*. Do not forget to create a configuration file according to the manpage for *ntp.conf(5)*. At a minimum, you must specify one or more servers you wish to contact for time. For more information about configuring and securing ntpd, see the section entitled "The Importance of Time (NTP)" in Chapter 4.

Tune Your Kernel

A variety of kernel variables can be adjusted on the fly using sysctl as described in Chapter 2. Now's a good time to refer to that list of variables and choose a subset that is appropriate for the system you are building. If you are uncertain about how your change may affect the system or applications you install down the road, skip this step for now and come back to it after your applications are installed. You may then adjust one parameter at a time and ensure that things are working as you would expect.

Set File Flags

Beyond the append-only flags available for system logs, there are a variety of file flags that can be set using the chflags utility. Again, these flags were discussed in depth in Chapter 2. While you might be able to set many of these flags now, it is probably safest to wait until you have installed additional packages. When the time comes, write a script to set and unset the flags—this will help you make widespread changes without trying to remember later what files need to have which flags applied or removed. The mtree(8) tool may help you take such snapshots of your filesystem permissions for use later.

Local Security

Local security is often overlooked by system administrators. Systems are not always located in airtight vaults, guarded by trained personnel, and behind other whiz-bang authentication devices. Even in supposedly secure co-location facilities, other organizations may send their administrators into your "cage." Even if you can afford your own cage, there may be other personnel whom you cannot completely trust with the keys to your system. And servers aren't the only systems vulnerable to local attack—providing for local security in a computer lab at an educational institution protects both your campus network and the previous user of the system.

The bottom line is that, when a system is placed in an untrusted environment, additional steps need to be taken to prevent snooping. Mind you, you will be able to do little against someone armed with a bucket of water and some lithium, but you can at least protect your data to some extent. Consider the following steps to help protect your system from local abuse.

On the screen

When you walk away from a system, you leave behind some information about what you were doing. If you happened to be running privileged commands, there is a risk of information disclosure. There are a number of ways around this including:

Disabling scrollback buffers

In FreeBSD, the following options can be set to adjust the behavior of your default console driver *syscons(4)*.

```
SC_NO_HISTORY          #disables back-scrolling in VTYs
SC_DISABLE_DDBKEY      #disables the debug key.
SC_DISABLE_REBOOT      #disables the ctrl-alt-del key.
```

Disabling the scrollback buffer cannot be done in OpenBSD, though Ctrl-Alt-Del is disabled by default.

Screen blanking

It can be useful to ensure that your screen is blank when you walk away and the system is idle. In FreeBSD, the *splash(4)* manpage describes the changes required to */boot/loader.conf* and */etc/rc.conf*, provided there is support in the kernel. OpenBSD provides *wsconsctl(8)* that allows you to adjust key *wscons(4)* variables. It is also possible to blank the screen at logout by adjusting */etc/gettytab* from:

```
P|Pc|Pc console:\
        :ht:np:sp#115200:
```

to:

```
P|Pc|Pc console:\
        :ht:np:sp#115200:\
        :cl=\E[H\E[2J:
```

Auto-logout

Automatic logout may be achieved system-wide in various ways depending on your shell. Adjusting */etc/profile* and adding **`export TMOUT=`*`seconds`*** will affect `bash` users, and placing the command **`set autologout=`*`minues`*** into */etc/csh.login* will affect `csh` (and `csh`-derivative shell) users. You may also enforce that `tcsh` users authenticate after spending several minutes idle and be subsequently logged out if they fail to do so by specifying **`set autologout=`*`(x y)`*** where ***`y`*** is the number of minutes to wait before prompting for authentication, and **x** is the number of total minutes to wait before logging the user out. FreeBSD's csh shell is actually tcsh, and this configuration would apply to root in this case.

Adjust /etc/ttys

Find the line specifying the console. This should be easy, it's near the top. Change the word **secure** to **insecure**. This will require that users enter the root password even when booting into single-user mode. In the same vein, you may want to consider assigning a BIOS password so the OS cannot be circumvented by removable media—just don't require a password for internal hard drive boot.

Wrapping Up

At this point you are probably gnawing at the bit, ready to dive into software installation. Fair enough. With a careful installation and subsequent hardening of the system, you are well on your way as a security-minded system administrator to building an OpenBSD or FreeBSD server that's very resistant to attack. Keep in mind that security consciousness is not something you can forego after your system has been "locked down." Staying abreast of vulnerabilities and patching are invaluable.

Resources

The following is a list of resources pertaining to the topics covered in this chapter.

FreeBSD

- FreeBSD mailing lists: *http://www.freebsd.org/doc/handbook/eresources.html#ERESOURCES-MAIL*
- The FreeBSD Handbook: *http://www.freebsd.org/handbook/*
- FreeBSD web site: *http://www.freebsd.org/*
- *The Complete FreeBSD*, Fourth Edition, Greg Lehey (O'Reilly), 2003

OpenBSD

- OpenBSD mailing lists: *http://www.openbsd.org/mail.html*
- OpenBSD web site: *http://www.openbsd.org/*

CHAPTER 4

Secure Administration Techniques

When we slip by their early warning systems in their own shuttle and destroy Autobot City, the Autobots will be vanquished forever!
—Megatron
The Transformers: The Movie

Whether the obligation for maintaining a system has just fallen into your lap, or you've recently completed building a system, your job as a security-minded system administrator has only just begun. A system built, configured, and hardened today cannot be called "secure" forever. At best, you can claim it is fully patched and hardened such that it has no known exploitable vulnerabilities. A few months from now, without your intervention, that statement will probably no longer hold true. System modifications may result in an even more vulnerable system given too much administration coupled with too little care. Even if nobody has logged into the system since deployment, recently discovered programming errors or new tools and techniques will have given rise to exploitable vulnerabilities.

Given that a server you build is liable to be used for at least a few years, careful and well thought out system administration will save you and your organization headaches. To some people, maintenance is an ugly word. Who wants to spend time maintaining a system when building new systems is more fun? This attitude often leads to lazy or sloppy administration, which will eventually lead to a compromised system. Dealing with cleaning up a compromised system or network usually involves careful analysis, lots of overtime, and being at the wrong end of the accusatory finger. This is a lot less fun than regular and careful maintenance.

In this chapter, we look at security administration practices and decisions over the long term. We begin by looking at access control. Carefully controlling who can do what to your systems helps you maintain a known, secure, configuration. We then turn our attention to handling maintenance necessities in a secure fashion: performing software installations, upgrading the system, and mitigating vulnerabilities through patching. Because FreeBSD and OpenBSD systems are often used as some kind of service provider to the rest of the network, we examine the associated risks of some common services and, of course, how we can mitigate those risks. Finally we turn our attention to system health as a means of establishing known behavior and observing deviations.

Throughout this chapter, we approach standard system administration tasks with a security focus. Doing so allows us to evaluate our actions from a security standpoint and ensure that our actions will not reduce the overall security of the system.

Access Control

Granting users and administrators rights on the system is a deceptively easy task, and one of the most basic facing the system administrator. Controlling system access, begins with basic Unix accounts, group membership, and file permissions. Recent additions such as ACLs and mandatory access controls in FreeBSD can make managing access quite complicated. Take a little time to think about the design of your access control systems to ensure you have granted the access needed, without sacrificing security.

Controlling User Access

Users fall into several categories, depending on the system involved. Generally, only administrators have accounts on infrastructure systems—and in higher security environments, only administrators responsible for the service that system provides. Add developers to the list of allowed users and you have a workgroup system.

Traditionally, local user accounts represent two classes of users: those who have shell accounts on the system, and service users. Service users don't usually need a valid shell (they do not log in) but do have an associated group. The user and group named on an OpenBSD system (BIND in FreeBSD), for example, allows the DNS server to run as someone other than root. In this case there is no human being associated with the user and it should stay this way. Do not set a password and shell for system users or use the account as an administrative one. It is permissible, however, to add DNS administrators to the named group for the purposes of administering nameserver configuration files without needing privileged access.

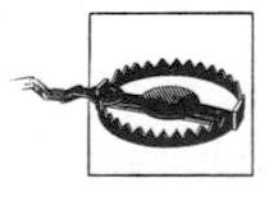

Be careful in OpenBSD that you do not add ordinary users to the staff group. This is an administrative group and has fewer restrictions based on the predefined login classes on OpenBSD systems. See *login.conf(5)* for more information.

Infrastructure systems should provide shell access only to administrators; therefore these systems require few user accounts and groups beyond the system defaults.

Workgroup systems, however, benefit from careful user and group planning before the creation of the first user account.

Most Unix users are familiar with the user/group/other permissions model found in most Unix operating systems. OpenBSD and FreeBSD continue to provide this basic access control functionality by user and group membership. Granting access by group is fairly flexible in that you are able to control access by moving users into and out of groups instead of changing the permissions of files and directories. Thus group permissions are often used more than user permissions for controlling access to data. As such, how you allocate users to primary groups is a very important decision. There are three typical approaches: using a catch-all primary group, using project-based primary groups, and using per-user groups. We favor the last approach, as you'll see.

Using a catchall primary group

One way to organize users into groups involves creating one group for all users (e.g. *users*) and placing all users into this group. Create additional groups on a per-project or role basis and assign users to these secondary groups for finer grain access control. This paradigm suffers one conceptual drawback: the users group is almost equivalent to world permissions because this group contains all users. In addition, files created by users will be group-owned by the users group and, depending on the user's umask, may be group readable by default.

The key difference between world permissions and a catchall users group is that system users like nobody, sshd, and so on will not be in the users group you create. This is a good thing. User accounts used by system daemons should be granted minimal access to files and directories on the system.

Project-based or role-based primary groups

Project-based or role-based groups as primary groups also allow for effective access control. This method, like the method described above, fails to cover one scenario. There is no way to add users without automatically giving them access to some subset of data already present on the system. In environments where contractors or guest users are periodically given user accounts, this can pose a problem.

Per-user groups

Per-user groups are one way around this drawback, and this solution fits in well with the least-privilege paradigm. In this scenario, you create a new group every time you create a new user; thus there is a one-to-one mapping of users to groups. Following this strategy, users do not automatically have access to any data when they first log in. Only if they are subsequently added to another group will they have any group-based access. This effectively nullifies group permissions by default for all users, allows for more granular access control, and may therefore be your ideal choice for managing users and groups. The only drawback to this approach is the small administrative inconvenience of creating new groups when you create new users.

Login classes

With a system to manage users and groups in place, you can turn your attention to putting in place resource limits, environment variables, and session accounting on a per-user or per-group basis. Login classes provide an effective means of doing this. As you create groups for the users of your systems, reevaluate the preexisting limits imposed in */etc/login.conf* and see if additional restrictions may be appropriate for the group you are creating.

umasks

The user file-creation mask (`umask`) is of fundamental importance in any discussion about access control. Setting a `umask` affects the default permissions on all newly created files. Most administrators and users expect files they create to be readable for everyone (user, group, and other) but only writable for themselves. Likewise when directories are created, they expect that anyone should be able to change into the directory and list contents (user, group, and other read/execute), but only the creator should be able to write files.

FreeBSD and OpenBSD set a default `umask` of `022` for users. It is this setting that creates the behavior described above. For users, this may be acceptable. For the root user, a more restrictive `umask` is preferable. A more appropriate `umask` would enforce full user rights but no group or world permission upon file, a `umask` of `077`. You may adjust the default `umask` on your system by modifying */etc/login.conf* appropriately. Be advised that users can freely overwrite the default `umask` by using the *shell-builtin* command `umask` either on the command line or in their shell startup configuration file (*.[t]cshrc* for `[t]csh`, *.profile* for `[ba]sh`, etc.).

The danger of ACLs (FreeBSD only)

User and group permissions used to be all there was to worry about on BSD systems. Now, however, FreeBSD 5.x offers support for filesystem access control lists (ACLs). With these discretionary access controls, it is now possible to grant much more fine-grained permissions based on arbitrary collections of users instead of granting permission by preexisting groups. With this increased flexibility comes the need for more careful administration. Arbitrary and haphazard assignment of permissions can make it extremely difficult to determine who has access to what and manage permissions in general. In some cases, it may be preferable to administer your system using standard Unix permissions.

On the other hand, it can be frustrating to see carefully crafted group-based permissions changed by users to a world-readable or, heaven forbid, a world-writable state. In many cases, users see this as a convenience and prefer it over tracking down the administrator with a change request. Whichever paradigm you choose, understand the risks involved in either approach and make a conscious decision instead of "going with the flow."

If you decide discretionary access controls are not appropriate in your environment, perhaps mandatory access controls are for you. The mandatory access control (MAC) framework was introduced with FreeBSD 5.x and allows the administrator to assign security-relevant labels to data. This type of access control imposes limits based on data classification and user rights, both of which are controlled by the administrator.

Bear in mind that the MAC framework is considered experimental and careful consideration must be given to the use of this feature on production systems. It is also only available on UFS2 filesystems.

Neither ACLs nor MAC is supported in OpenBSD.

Controlling Administrator Access

Perhaps even more important than controlling the access users have on your systems is limiting and auditing administrator access. On systems with multiple administrators or service operators who need certain administrative rights, don't provide access by passing around the root password during lunch. Infrastructure systems generally provide one or two major services and you may be able to grant rights by making key files group-writable. On some systems, the only privilege certain administrative users may need is the ability to restart key service. Allowing some non-root users to do this is easy using `sudo`. Even on systems where multiple administrators operate at the same system-wide level, it is important to carefully audit what administrators do to enforce accountability. The rest of this section outlines some of the approaches you should take to grant administrator access while limiting and auditing the use of escalated privileges.

Disable and avoid clear-text access

The first place to look for ways to mitigate the risks administrators pose is in their access method. `telnet(1)`, `rsh(1)`, `rlogin(1)`, etc. are clear-text protocols. Your username, password, and every bit of data displayed or typed into a session is easily readable by anyone else on the local network. Administrators should never use clear-text protocols. This should be a done deal, as the default on both FreeBSD and OpenBSD systems is to have these clear-text protocols disabled.

Connect using SSH

Both OpenBSD and FreeBSD provide secure shell (`ssh(1)`) services as part of the base installation. Leave `telnet` disabled and use `ssh`. Configure `sshd(8)` to accept remote connections based on public/private key cryptography instead of the weaker password-based authentication. Ensure all administrators accessing your servers are generating `ssh` keys using the `ssh-keygen(1)` utility. The public half of their keys may then be placed in their *~/.ssh/authorized_keys* file on every system to which they require access. See the "Post-Upgrade Hardening" section of Chapter 3 or the *sshd_config(5)* manpage to learn how to disable password authentication altogether.

> Password authentication is a form of single-factor authentication. This means the user merely needs to know something to gain access. Public key authentication requires that you not only know a passphrase, but also that you have the private key. This is known as two-factor authentication and is stronger than single-factor authentication.

When the number of systems involved reaches hundreds, thousands, or tens of thousands, managing `ssh` keys scattered across machines can become a nightmare: both for distribution and removal. In this case, `ssh` using public key authentication might not be an option, so consider deploying a Kerberos infrastructure which provides for secure, centralized authentication and kerberized `ssh`. Kerberos eliminates the need for distributing `ssh` keys while still providing encrypted access. Without additional software, however, Kerberos reduces the authentication from two-factor back to one.

Privileged access using ssh

Administrators gain root-level access to a system in one of three ways:

- They place their public keys in *~root/.ssh/authorized_keys* (or list their Kerberos principals in *~root/.k5login*) and `ssh` directly into the root account from remote systems.
- They use a nonprivileged account to `ssh` into the system and then `su` to gain a root shell.
- They use a nonprivileged account to `ssh` into the system and then use `sudo(8)` to execute privileged commands.

The first option requires that you allow root logins via `ssh` and no human being can be directly tied to login events. This is far from ideal. The second option allows you to disable root logins, but after the administrator gains a root shell, she is unlikely to relinquish it and subsequent commands are not audited. The third option provides accountability, enables auditing for every action, and is generally considered the most secure way to gain privileged access.

General sudo Configuration

Once administrators are using an encrypted means of access to the system, and not logging in as root, you may turn your attention to the execution of privileged commands. This is, after all, what sets the administrator apart from the user.

sudo is available with the base operating system in OpenBSD and may be installed out of FreeBSD's ports from *ports/security/sudo* or during the install process. It allows the users of the system (or other administrators) to execute commands as other, often more privileged, users. It also allows for the dissemination of granular administrative rights with comprehensive auditing (by logging every command run through sudo) instead of "keys to the kingdom" without any accountability. In a nutshell, sudo operates by accepting entire commands as arguments to itself, consulting the *sudoers(5)* configuration file to authorize the user attempting to run the command, and then executing the command in an alternate user context.

Creating a customized *sudoers* file is one of the first steps the security-minded system administrator takes on a newly installed system. Like it's counterpart `vipw(8)` for the *passwd* files, `visudo` locks the *sudoers* file and provides some syntax checking after editing. Since the *sudoers* file defines how users can execute privileged commands, errors in the file can be very dangerous. Always use `visudo`.

sudo configuration is fairly straightforward. You define aliases for commands, hosts (useful if you distribute a single *sudoers* file to multiple hosts), users who should be allowed to run privileged commands, and user accounts under whose context certain commands should be executed (sudo can run commands as non-root users with `-u`). Aliases, found at the bottom of the *sudoers* file, specify *which* users are allowed to execute *what* commands, *where* (which host), and potentially, as *whom*. We do not go into any more detail about general sudo configuration, as configuration is extremely well documented in the *sudoers(5)* manpage. Instead we turn our attention to secure configuration guidelines and pitfalls.

Avoid dangerous commands

Be extraordinarily careful about the binaries to which you grant access. Be aware that many binaries (like `vi(1)`) let you spawn a shell. When `vi` is executed with superuser privileges, any commands it runs (such as a shell, or `grep`, or `awk`) will be too! Likewise, `less(1)` (which is the opposite of `more(1)`) on FreeBSD and OpenBSD can invoke the editor defined by the `VISUAL` or `EDITOR` environment variable when you press **v** while paging through a file—if this variable is set to `vi`, a root shell is just a few keystrokes away. To allow users to view certain sensitive files, allow privileged execution of the `cat(1)` binary; `more` can run in the user's context. In Example 4-1, the first command runs `more` as root, the second runs `more` in the user context and `cat` as root.

Example 4-1. Viewing files with sudo

```
% sudo more /root/private_file
% sudo cat /root/private_file | more
```

There are innumerable commands that can gain unrestricted elevated privileges when provided certain keyboard input, file input, or environment variables. Some examples include find(1), chown(8), chgrp(1), chmod(1), rm(1), mv(1), cp(1), crontab(1), tar(1), gzip(1), and gunzip(1). As it turns out, configuring sudo without "giving away the barn" is no easy task!

Remember that liberal sudo rights should only be assigned to administrators who would otherwise have root. Otherwise, allow only very specific privileged commands by following the guidelines in the rest of this section.

Use explicit paths

Explicitly providing a path ensures that identically named binaries elsewhere in the path are never executed with elevated privileges. While there are ways to control how the PATH is used in sudo, including the ignore_dot and env_reset flags, the safest and most foolproof way is to always use explicit paths to binaries.

The env_reset flag resets the PATH environment variable among others. Read the *sudoers(5)* manpage to determine whether this flag would work well in your environment.

Be very specific

As mentioned previously, several system commands can be used to gain elevated privileges when combined with sudo. To combat this, be very specific about not only allowed commands but also the allowed arguments, as shown in Example 4-2.

Example 4-2. Commands with arguments

```
Cmnd_Alias WEB = /usr/local/sbin/apachectl, \
                 /usr/bin/chgrp [-R] www-devel /web/*
```

In this case, the alias WEB is created as a set of commands for the administrators of the web server. They have unrestricted use to the Apache control script apachectl(1), and may change group ownership of any files in */web/* to *www-devel*, while optionally providing the recursive argument to chgrp.

Use NOPASSWD sparingly

A useful feature of sudo is the ability to allow certain users to run commands without having to provide a password. If users ask for this functionality, you should feel comfortably within your rights as an administrator to deny their request. Forcing a password prompt sends a message (both literally and figuratively) to users that they are about to run a command in root's context and they should be careful and responsible.

In some cases, service accounts need to run privileged commands, and there may not be a human being around to enter a password at the time. In these cases, it becomes acceptable to use the NOPASSWD option as shown in Example 4-3.

Example 4-3. Service account using NOPASSWD

```
nagios    localhost = NOPASSWD : /usr/local/etc/rc.d/nagios.sh restart
```

In this case, the nagios service account under which some daemon or script runs is able to run the `nagios.sh` startup script with the restart argument. Since this daemon is running without user intervention, should the need arise to restart `nagios`, it will be able to do so without needing to provide a password.

Be realistic

Finally, avoid being too draconian. Service operators are likely to get angry and spend time trying to find ways to gain unrestricted escalated privileges if you provide too few means for them to do their jobs. This wastes time and, if they succeed, will defeat your auditing strategy.

Comparing sudo and su

The BSD operating systems favor `sudo` over `su`. We take a moment here to outline some of the advantages and disadvantages of both approaches. We have tried to capture the salient differences in Table 4-1.

Table 4-1. Security related characteristics of sudo and su

Characteristics	sudo	su
Advantages		
Single password required for root access		●
Logging of executed privileged commands	●	
Fine-grained administrator privileges	●	
Simple revocation of privileges	●	
Distributable configuration of access rights	●	○
Disadvantages		
Can accidentally grant root access	●	
Elevates importance of administrator's password	●	●
Encourages laziness	●	●

Bear in mind that the satisfaction of the named characteristics may be affected by the number of administrators on the system in question.

Single password required for root access

One major advantage the default configuration for `su` has over `sudo` is that only one authentication token (root's password) can grant a user root access. On a system with multiple administrators and `sudo` configured to grant `ALL` rights to users in some administrative group, several username/password combinations can lead to root access.

On a system with only one administrator, root's account may be locked and the administrator's password may be the only root-capable password. Bear in mind this relies on the fact that sudo prompts for a password, which may be overridden in *sudoers*. In the event of a system crash, all filesystems will need to be checked before sudo may be used. If your system has been configured to prompt for root's password in single user mode, a BSD bootable CD will be necessary to gain root access.

This must be mitigated on systems with sudo by a password policy that documents guidelines for exceptionally strong passwords for all administrators.

Logging of executed privileged commands

All commands passed as arguments to sudo are logged by default to syslog's local2 facility. Successful authentication and subsequent execution of a privileged command are logged at priority notice, and authentication failures result in a log entry of priority alert. In addition to what one might expect in the log for sudo, you will find the full path of the command executed, which can alert you to potentially unsafe or malicious executables. Once su is run, however, no subsequent commands are reliably auditable.

For more information about configuring logging, see Chapter 10.

Accountability is one of the most vital parts of system security. Having a history of all privileged commands executed on a system is invaluable. This is one of the greatest benefits of sudo.

Many administrators choose to group administrators who should have full root access into the wheel or other administrative group. They may subsequently configure sudo so that these administrators have full root access by using a configuration line similar to the following:

```
%groupname ALL=(ALL) ALL
```

Remember that this grants administrators the right to run shells as an argument to sudo or through sudo -s, which invokes the command specified in the SHELL environment variable. In both of these cases, auditing will cease.

Fine-grained administrator privileges

Unlike su, sudo enables the administrator to allow only very specific commands. This may be ideal in environments where users should have administrative rights over key applications under their respective jurisdictions.

Simple revocation of privileges

Removing a user's ability to execute privileged commands is trivial with sudo: simply remove the user from the *sudoers* file. If su is your only means of administrator access control, the departure of an administrator will require changing the root passwords on all systems for which that administrator knew the root password.

Distributable configuration of access rights
: The only access right "distributable" with `su` is full-fledged root access. To grant users the ability to `su`, you would need to add them to the wheel group. To centrally control access, you would need to either have consistent group files everywhere, build a system to push files, or use YP/NIS. The fine-grain control possible with `sudo` may, however, be distributed to systems using a variety of automated mechanisms for simple centralized administration like `rsync(1)` and `rdist(1)`.

Can accidentally grant root access
: It is difficult to accidentally tell someone a complex root password. Simple mistakes in the *sudoers* file, however, can lead to less-than-desirable effects. Take extreme care when working within the *sudoers* file to ensure you are not granting users the ability to gain escalated privileges.

Elevates importance of administrator's password
: Administrators treat root passwords with great sensitivity. Unfortunately, they are not always as careful with their own. Novice administrators sometimes utilize the same password in administering systems as they do for local intranet sites. In the former case, the password is being transmitted over an encrypted tunnel. In the latter case, it may not be.

When restricted to using `su`, knowing an administrator's password will allow you to log into an account in the wheel group. This may result in privilege escalation through abuse of group-level permissions or by cracking the root password by brute force. When using `sudo`, knowing an administrator's password is equivalent to knowing the root password, if the administrator has the ability to invoke a root shell in some way.

Encourages laziness
: Certain activities become a little cumbersome with `sudo`:

- Redirection of command output into a directory or file not writable by the caller
- Chained commands (e.g., **`sudo`** ***`timeconsuming_command`*** **`&& sudo`** ***`quick_command`***) may only partially execute due to password timeouts
- Repeatedly having to type in `sudo`
- Working with directory hierarchies not executable by you

In these cases and with `su` in general, the temptation exists to stay in a root shell once you're there, for the sake of convenience. An errant space-asterisk-space in a quickly typed `rm` command may suddenly lead to hours of recovery time. This can be avoided. Stay in a root shell for as short a period of time as possible.

Even when you have configured `sudo` to grant fine-grained permissions, the root account, of course, still exists. This account represents "keys to the kingdom" and is a goal of many attackers. This account must have a strong password that is known by few, and protected well, or it should be locked.

When administrators are supposed to have full-fledged root access but choose, or are required by policy, to use `sudo`, the root account may be safely locked. In this case, administrators invoke a shell through `sudo` to gain root-level access. Remember, however, that whenever shell access is provided, every administrator's password is as important as the root password would be since it effectively grants the same privileges.

Safeguard the Root Password

Root passwords should be stored in a secure location available to a non-administrator in the event of an emergency. This is most often accomplished in at least two ways for redundancy.

The most common and straightforward way to be able to securely recover root passwords is very nontechnical. Write the passwords down on paper and store the sheet offsite with other system configuration documentation. Be sure to clearly define who has access to these documents.

m of n Cryptography

Decryption that requires a subset of a known group of people is known as *m of n* cryptography. As long as any *m* people out of a pool of *n* can get together, they can decrypt the file. You want to pick the right *n* people to prevent collusion (e.g., vice presidents, corporate officers, managers, etc.) and a large enough *n*, relative to your turnover rate, that *m* of them will always be around.

Picking *m* (i.e., how many people need to be present, since any group of *m* people will be sufficient) also requires good planning. You probably do not want *m* to be 1, since that is the same as giving the root password out to all *n* people. Values of 2 or 3 are good for *m*. Unfortunately, *m of n* cryptography is only available in commercial products, such as PGP, RSA's Keon server, and Sun's iPlanet.

One bank requires any three (*m*) out of its eight (*n*) vice presidents to type passphrases to decrypt the keys that are used by the SSL-enabled web servers. When the servers crash and have to be restarted at 02:00, the vice presidents actually drive to the operations center to restart them. This serves as a significant incentive for both business owners and administrators to run a reliable system.

The root password may also be encrypted by a combined key such that multiple people are required for decryption. For instance, if none of the administrators to whom the file has been encrypted are able to perform root functions (e.g., due to vacation, illness, or death), passwords should be recoverable only by the combined efforts of some collection of relevant supervisors, IT managers, and/or executives.

Protecting the root password in these ways is more important when no other individuals are able to gain physical access to the system. Where physical access exists, someone should be able to boot the system from removable media and change root's password from the console. Nevertheless, an alternate means of root password access should be possible to save time in the event of an emergency.

The root password, however, is not sufficient for a non-administrator to do something useful in an emergency. Remember to include some disaster-reaction documentation (such as how to shut down the key servers before the UPS runs out of power) where non-administrators can refer to it.

Security in Everyday Tasks

Even with the careful assignment of rights to administrators, system security needs to be in the forefront of every administrator's mind as the system ages. A carefully built system can start off pretty secure—and then you put it online and start installing software. After that, you might add accounts or configure the system so that it can be accessed anonymously. The following section in the chapter focuses on software installations and updates that may have an impact on the security of your system.

Installing Software

Installing software on your OpenBSD or FreeBSD system is accomplished using packages or the ports system. Individuals who have taken on the responsibility of being a port or package maintainer try to ensure that the latest or best version of the software will build correctly on the operating system and will install according to the operating system's scheme. They don't necessarily audit the software for software vulnerabilities.

Installing a port is often as simple as typing in **make** with a few command-line arguments based on your functionality requirements. Package installs are even easier. Dependencies can be automatically installed. Downloading source tarballs and configuring them yourself is certainly also possible but more cumbersome. You run the risk of not having applied the latest patches and you will have to install dependencies first, manually.

Ports and packages

The ports system is one of the most obvious differentiators between the BSD systems and other free and commercial Unix platforms. All platforms offer "binary packages," but only the BSDs offer the flexibility of ports. From a security perspective, there are few strong reasons for choosing one paradigm over the other. Some argue that it is easier to verify file signatures for one precompiled package than for several *.tgz* files used by a port.

For more information about file signatures, see "Preexisting Vulnerabilities" in Chapter 3.

Most administrators who are aware and diligent about verifying file integrity will go no father than checking to see that the signature matches the one provided by the same site from which they obtained the package. As it turns out, this trivial check is conducted by the ports system every time a file is downloaded. Few administrators take the time to check the signature of a package at all, much less cross-reference it with the site that originally provided the package. In an ideal world, administrators would cross-reference signatures with several mirror sites and the main distribution site to verify file integrity. Few administrators have the inclination or the time.

The greatest advantage of a port is that it offers complete flexibility in configuring your ported applications. Packages can be compiled to support no related software, some related software, or *all* related software, and you may not always find the exact combination that you seek. Ports, on the other hand, offer options for linking with specific pieces of software to provide additional functionality. In FreeBSD, this is often accomplished with a small menu during the configuration of a port or the definition of some environment variables. OpenBSD allows administrators to set a `FLAVOR` for a port before installation. You will see examples of both throughout this book.

If the goal is to have compiled binaries, why not just install precompiled software and be done with it? This is, in fact, the main argument against using the ports system. Ports require more system resources than packages. Not only must source code be downloaded and extracted, it must also be compiled and linked to produce binaries, which are finally installed. In many cases, this proves to be a compelling argument, but when flexibility is needed, ports are often the answer.

The OpenBSD ports system actually compiles a port and installs it into a *fake root* form, which it builds a package using the `-B` option of `pkg_create(1)`. This has certain advantages for the administrator including not having to install dependent ports that are only required during build time.

Most of the examples in this book will describe the ports style of installation, as the package may be either not available or trivial to install. Nevertheless, there are two things to watch out for when working with the ports system.

Ports ownership

The ports hierarchy usually lives in */usr/ports*. Because only root can write to */usr*, administrators often install the ports hierarchy from CD or via cvs as root. Unfortunately, this means that whenever the administrator needs to build a package, she must do so as root (via sudo, for instance). This is not a safe practice. Small errors in *Makefiles* can result in very interesting behavior during a make. Malicious *Makefiles* have also been known to exist.

This presents a valuable opportunity for the separation of responsibilities. Before updating your ports tree, ensure */usr/ports* is writable by someone other than root. Make this directory group-writable if a group of people install software, or change the ownership to the user responsible for installing software.

FreeBSD administrators who use cvsup to update their ports tree will also need to create a */var/db/sup* directory that has similar permissions.

You may now update your ports tree and build software as an ordinary user. When your **make** or **make install** needs to do something as root, you will be prompted for the root password. To adjust this behavior somewhat, set SU_CMD=sudo in the file */etc/make.conf*. Now while installing ports, sudo will be used instead of su.

This mostly works. There are some cases in which the authors have observed problems using this non-root-owned methodology in building ports. We hope these problems are ironed out of the ports system soon.

FreeBSD administrators who use the portupgrade utility to manage ports will want to provide the -s or flag. This makes portupgrade use sudo when it needs to perform actions as root.

OpenBSD administrators should set SUDO=sudo in */etc/mk.conf*. *Makefiles* know when certain commands need to be run by root and will automatically run these commands as arguments to the program specified by $SUDO.

Ports and base conflicts

In FreeBSD, some software in the ports system has already been installed with the base system. Prime examples are BIND, ssh, and various shells. The version in ports is often more recent than the version in the base distribution, and you may decide that you want to overwrite the base version. Newer is not always better, however. The version included as part of the base distribution is likely older, but will have all relevant security patches applied to it and will have undergone more widespread scrutiny longer. The version in ports will include functionality that has probably not yet been extensively tested. Use the version from ports when you need additional functionality, but stick with the base for reliability and security.

Ensure that if you install the version from ports, it either completely overwrites the base installation or you manually eradicate all traces of the base version to avoid confusion. The method to do this will vary based on the package. The *Makefile* for BIND9 on FreeBSD systems understands a `PORT_REPLACES_BASE_BIND9` flag, which will overwrite the base install for you (this is described in detail in Chapter 5). The *Makefile* for the FreeBSD *openssh-portable* port looks for an `OPENSSH_OVERWRITE_BASE` flag, which does about the same thing. Other ports may require that you manually search for installed binaries, libraries, and documents and remove them.

OpenBSD includes applications such as Apache, BIND, OpenSSH, and sudo in the base distribution and does not provide a means to track this software through ports. After all, the installed applications have gone through rigorous security review. If you want, for instance, to use Apache Version 2 or a different version of BIND, you must fetch, compile, and install the package manually. Otherwise, updates to software within the OpenBSD base distribution may be installed by tracking the stable branch as described later in this chapter.

Multiple versions installed (FreeBSD only)

If you do choose to manage your installed software using ports instead of with your base, you may run into version problems. Let's say you installed Version 1.0 of port *foo*. After installation, you modified some of the files that were installed with the port in */usr/local/etc* and used *foo* for several months. When you learn of a security vulnerability in *foo*, you decide to upgrade to Version 1.1, but instead of uninstalling the old version first, you install v1.1 on top of the old version. The package database now lists two versions of *foo* installed, but that is not really the case.

The installation of v1.1 does not clobber your configuration files in */usr/local/etc* because they were modified since the install of v1.0, but it *does* replace binaries, libraries, shared/default configuration files, and so on, provided they were not modified since the installation of v1.0. So far, so good. The new version of the port is in fact properly installed and may be used, though you might have had to update the configuration files.

You may choose at some point to uninstall *foo* v1.0. All installed files that match the MD5 checksums of the files distributed with v1.0 will be removed. Any shared/default configuration files that were identical in Version 1.1 will also be removed, resulting in a broken *foo* v1.1. You will need to reinstall v1.1 to replace these files.

The same kind of situation may arise if *foo* v1.0 depended on *libbar* v2.0 but v1.1 of *foo* depended on *libbar* v2.1. While uninstalling *foo* v1.0 before installing the new version would avoid problems down the road for that port, *libbar* may be in trouble. As you can see, the ports system's tracking of dependencies is handy, but it only goes so far.

You can find the recursive list of dependencies of a port by running **`make pretty-print-build-depends-list`** and **`make pretty-print-run-depends-list`** from the port's directory. For more information about working with the ports tree in general, see the manpage for ports(7).

To avoid these situations, ensure you uninstall installed ports before installing new ones, or, better yet, use the *portupgrade* port to manage upgrades of software installed from the ports tree. This handy utility will make these dependency problems moot and save you time and headache upgrading ports. `portupgrade` is well documented in its manpage and should be considered mandatory for any system with more than a few ports installed.

Packages on OpenBSD will refuse to install, by default, if a previous version is already installed. This means that ports, which are compiled into packages before installation, will also fail to install. This is good.

Change Control

Software gets installed. Software gets upgraded. All this administration is important but must be audited in some way so that other administrators and managers can answer questions like:

- What recent change caused this new (or broken) behavior?
- Was the system or application patched, or was a workaround put in place to protect against a given vulnerability?

Detailed change control procedures are generally designed around organizational priorities and therefore are beyond the scope of this book. Nevertheless, change control is an important aspect of system administration. As you build your FreeBSD or OpenBSD systems, ensure you have a written list of requirements (both security-related and functional) to which your system must conform. As you build your system, document the steps you've taken to achieve these requirements. These documents will form the basis of your configuration management doctrine and will help you rebuild the system in the event of a system failure and transfer ownership of the system to another administrator should the need arise.

As time goes on, you will find a need to change your system configuration or upgrade installed software. If you have a test environment in which you can put these changes into effect, so much the better. Carefully document the steps you take to accomplish these upgrades and configuration changes. When you're done, you will be able to test your system to ensure it continues to meet the requirements you already have documented. Should problems arise, you will likely be able to quickly isolate the change that gave rise to these problems.

Although describing complete change control procedures is out of scope, FreeBSD and OpenBSD do provide tools to help administrators carry out change control policies on system configuration files.

Tracking Changes

FreeBSD and OpenBSD are large software projects with developers scattered around the world. Building an operating system without keeping a close eye on changes is impossible. From a user perspective, we see software version numbers that continually increase, but in the background, developers are regularly "checking out" files from some development repository, modifying them, and checking them back in. All of these files also have version numbers, which continually increment as they are modified. For example, examine the following snippet from */etc/rc.conf* on an OpenBSD system:

```
# $OpenBSD: rc.conf,v 1.95 2004/03/05 23:54:47 henning Exp $
```

This string indicates that this file's version number is 1.95. It was last modified at late on the fifth of March by user henning.

Both FreeBSD and OpenBSD development teams have chosen to use the Concurrent Versions System (CVS) to manage file versions and ensure changes are closely tracked. CVS uses the basic functionality of the Revision Control System (RCS) to track changes to individual files and adds functionality to manage collections of files locally or over a network. This may seem a little far afield for system administration, but tracking changes is as important to developers as it is to system administrators.

Imagine if every configuration file you touched were managed in this same way—you could know what changes were made to any given file, by whom, and when. You would also be able to get a log of comments of all changes as entered by those who made modifications. Best of all, you could trivially roll back to a previous configuration file without having to pull data off of a tape. In cases where multiple modifications are made in a day, that kind of information will likely not be found on a tape.

As it turns out, setting up a CVS repository is fairly straightforward.

If you do not already have a firm grasp of the version control concept, consult the manpages for `cvs(1)` and `rcsintro(1)`.

Before creating your repository, you should create a CVS administrative user and corresponding primary group, which will own the files in the repository on some tightly secured central administration host that has very limited shell access. We'll call both the user and group *admincvs*. Ensure this account is locked. The home directory can be set to */nonexistent* (this is a service account, not meant for users), and shell can be `/sbin/nologin`. Once this is done, initialize the repository as shown in Example 4-4. This example assumes the user under which you are operating can run the commands listed via `sudo`.

You will note that this user can run `mkdir`, `chmod`, and `chown`. Being able to run these commands can result easily in privilege escalation, so the only users allowed to run these commands should be those who have full root access anyway.

Example 4-4. Initializing a CVS repository

```
% sudo mkdir /path/to/repository
% sudo chmod g+w /path/to/repository
% sudo chown admincvs:admincvs /path/to/repository
% sudo -u admincvs /usr/bin/cvs -d /path/to/repository init
% sudo chmod -R o-wrx /path/to/repository
```

At this point, you must configure your `CVSROOT`. This environment variable lets the CVS program know where the repository is. If you will be working with a CVS repository on the local system, you may set the `CVSROOT` to be the full path to that directory. Otherwise set your `CVSROOT` to ***`username@hostname:/path/to/repository`*.**

If you choose to access the repository from a remote FreeBSD or OpenBSD system, your cvs client will attempt to contact the server using `ssh`. Thus, CVS may cause `ssh` to ask for your password, passphrase, or just use your Kerberos ticket, depending on how you have `ssh` configured.

Whether the repository is local or remote, your access will map to some account on the target system. In order to be able to check items in and out of CVS, you (and everyone else who needs to use this CVS repository) must be a member of the admincvs group. If you have not already done so, add yourself to this group. You are then ready to perform your first checkout of the repository, as shown in Example 4-5.

Example 4-5. First checkout of a CVS repository

```
% mkdir local_repos_copy && cd local_repos_copy
% cvs checkout .
cvs server: Updating .
cvs server: Updating CVSROOT
U CVSROOT/checkoutlist
U CVSROOT/commitinfo
U CVSROOT/config
U CVSROOT/cvswrappers
U CVSROOT/editinfo
```

Example 4-5. First checkout of a CVS repository (continued)

```
U CVSROOT/loginfo
U CVSROOT/modules
U CVSROOT/notify
U CVSROOT/rcsinfo
U CVSROOT/taginfo
U CVSROOT/verifymsg
```

Finally, you're ready to add projects into the repository. Simply make any directories you would like under your local copy of the repository (*local_repos_copy* in our example) and add them using **`cvs add`** ***`directory_name`***. Files may be created within these directories as needed and added to the repository via the same **`cvs add`** mechanism. In order for files to actually be copied into the repository, and subsequently whenever you make modifications to the file, you will need to issue a **`cvs commit`** ***`filename`***. If you have made widespread modifications, you may simply run **`cvs commit`** from a higher level directory, and all modified files under that directory will be found and committed en masse.

Once your CVS repository is created, you are left with two problems.

- How do you organize the contents of your CVS hierarchy?
- How do you take configuration files from within CVS and put them on target hosts?

Unfortunately, both of these topics are beyond the scope of this book. We can provide a few tips, however.

- The more sensitive the files in your repository, the more careful you must be in providing remote access and configuring local filesystem permission.
- Everyone who has access to this repository is in the admincvs group, so you shouldn't put any non-administrator content in this repository.
- `ssh` can be used to copy files to target hosts. If you have disabled `PermitRootLogin` in the CVS server's `sshd` configuration, you will need to copy files as another user into a remote staging area and have another root-owned process periodically check this location for new files to install.

We go into more detail about the general problem of secure file distribution in the "Network Service Security" section later in this chapter.

- Every file you copy to a target system should include a header describing where the master file is in CVS, when it was last modified, who copied the file to the system, and when. This will help prevent other administrators (or you, if you forget) from making modifications to configuration files directly on target systems. You could automatically prepend such a header instead of storing the headers within the files themselves.

If security requirements in your organization prevent you from using CVS in this way to track changes to documents or copy them to target systems, you may also opt to track changes directly on the system. You could create CVS repositories on every system, perhaps in some consistent location, precluding the need for configuration file transfer. You may also use RCS—a far less fully featured revision control system, which merely tracks changes to a given file in *./RCS* (RCS creates subdirectories in every directory that contain RCS-controlled files). If you choose this route, you may want to evaluate tools like `rcsedit` and `rcs.mgr`, which turn up quickly in a web search.

After you have solved these problems, you will be in a much better position to handle changes to system configuration than you were before. You will then be better prepared to turn your attention to more significant system changes like patching and upgrading.

Data Recovery

Data backup and recovery typically serves several purposes:

Disaster recovery
: When a system is completely ruined, perhaps due to a hard drive crash or similar event, it needs to be restored to service.

Data recovery
: Sometimes a user or an administrator makes a mistake and needs to restore an old version of important files or directories. This might include restoring a few user data files, the firewall configuration, or an older version of a program.

Forensics
: If you are pursuing an intruder who has been on your system for more than a day or two, you may find evidence of his activities in your backups. Incriminating files that he eventually deleted may have been backed up before he deleted them.

Legal compliance
: If your organization is involved in a legal matter, your boss (or law enforcement personnel) may come to you with a subpoena requiring the organization to turn over a lot of data. Common examples include email, memoranda, or perhaps internal documents related to the subject of the case. Very often you will have to resort to your backups in order to fulfill the demands of the subpoena.

FreeBSD and OpenBSD administrators typically turn to one of two pieces of open source software for performing data backups: `dump(8)` or the Advanced Maryland Network Disk Archiver (Amanda). For the most basic jobs, `dump` is probably adequate. It gives you the ability to record a complete snapshot of a filesystem at a given point in time. Amanda is largely an automation suite built on top of tools like `dump` and `tar(1)`. If you need a complex tape rotation or want to automate the use of a multi-tape library, Amanda can save you a lot of work.

When it comes time to read data off your backup tapes, however, the tools of the trade are `restore(8)` and `tar`. Of course `tar` is `tar`'s own complement as it supports both creation of tape archives with `-c` and extraction with `-x`. The `restore` program is the complement to `dump`, and it reads the data format that `dump` writes. Amanda uses `dump`, so `restore` will be the tool you use to retrieve data from tapes whether you use `dump` directly or use Amanda.

Data completeness

If you want to be able to restore your complete system from a hard drive crash, it is critical that you use `dump` to make your backup. Other techniques like `tar(1)` and `cpio(1)` will fail to capture critical filesystem information that you will want when you restore. Although they both capture symbolic links and can work with device files, their support is problematic in some corner cases.

For example, for compatibility across platforms, `tar`'s datafile format uses some fixed-sized fields. FreeBSD uses device numbers that cannot be accommodated in `tar`'s format. Thus, if you use `tar` to backup your root partition, the devices in */dev* will not be stored correctly. Although it is easy to fix them during a restoration, it is a detail worth considering. You might think that FreeBSD's use of *devfs* (a filesystem that automatically creates devices in */dev* based on your system's hardware) means that you have few, if any, device files to back up. However, if you have followed the guidelines in this book, you have probably created jails and/or chroot environments for various mission-critical services. You will have created device files in those environments that are not automatically created by `devfs` and are not correctly backed up using `tar`. Similarly, "hard linked" files, which share a common *inode* (as opposed to "symbolically linked" files), are stored twice in a `tar` or `cpio` backup, instead of once in a `dump` backup.

If you have a dedicated server that only runs one critical service, such as DNS, you may find complete system dumps more work than they are worth. If you have all your service-specific data backed up (e.g., the whole */var/named* directory and configuration files from */etc*), you might be able to recover from a disaster simply by installing fresh from the CD. You reinstall the service, `restore` your service-specific data, and reboot. If you plan to perform restorations this way, you will have to write much of the backup and restoration procedures yourself, although they may not be very elaborate.

Data confidentiality

Your backup data is a snapshot of all the data that is in your filesystem. It probably contains a variety of critical files that should not be disclosed to anyone. Most backup files, however, can be read by anyone who has access to the media. Unless you go out of your way to add encryption to your backup scheme (neither `dump` nor `tar` have innate support for this), your data is easily readable from a medium that has no concept of permissions or privileges. Thus, if you store your backup tapes somewhere without strict physical access control, unauthorized people may be able to walk off with all of your data.

Barring physical theft of data, however, there are still confidentiality concerns related to how you manage your backups. If you use Amanda to back up over the network, it will spool the data up on a local hard drive as part of the process. Although this improves your tape drive's performance by allowing it to stream at its maximum data rate, it means all your confidential data will temporarily exist on the tape server, until it gets written to tape. If the tape should jam or fail to write, this file will remain on the hard disk until it is successfully flushed to tape by an administrator. If you assign backups to a junior administrator because they are tedious (what senior administrator does not do this?), remember that the junior administrator may effectively gain read access to all the data that the backup server sees. This may not be what you want.

Data retention

If your organization does not have a data retention policy that governs the storage of backup tapes, you might want to consider establishing one before an external event forces the issue. If your organization is not involved in any sensitive activities, perhaps you do not need to worry as much. Most organizations, however, are surprised to realize how much they care about old data. If the CEO, chairman, or other leader of the organization deletes a sensitive file, she probably thinks it is gone for good. However, you know that it lives on your backups for some amount of time, and you can retrieve it if you are compelled to.

Filesystem access

On a typical server (either OpenBSD or FreeBSD), the raw disk devices are owned by root, but the group operator has access to read them. This allows the operator group to bypass the filesystem and its permissions and read raw data blocks from the disk. This is how `dump` is able to take a near image of a disk device. If you rebuild a filesystem with `newfs(8)` and then `restore` your files, the files will be restored almost exactly, down the *inode* numbers in many cases. The operator group is especially designed for backups this way. If you look in */dev*, you will find that operator has read access to almost all significant raw data devices: floppy disks, hard drives, CD drives, RAID controller devices, backup tape drive devices, etc. Furthermore, the operator user's account is locked down in a way that the user cannot log in. If you run backups, either by custom scripts or by Amanda, you should use the operator user and/or group. The default Amanda configuration will do just that.

Note that operator's home directory is not created by default. You will have to create it and set its ownership to the operator user and group. For both dump and Amanda, you will need operator's home directory.

Network access

Generally we assume that you will have a small number of servers that have tape drives installed (possibly just one) and data will traverse the network from clients to these servers. This transfer happens via either a push or a pull paradigm. Since the tape host knows how many tape drives it has and whether or not they are busy, most systems favor having the tape host pull data from data hosts.

Amanda and other methods of remotely collecting data will send the contents of your filesystems in the clear over the network. Regardless of where your backup server is in relation to the backup clients, your data may be observable while in transit. This is clearly a problem, and you should establish some means of protecting the data in transit, either through a VPN, SSH tunnel, or some other form of encryption.

One of the most powerful ways of restricting (and encrypting) backup connections is by using `ssh`. It is possible to use `ssh` keys that have been configured on the client side to only allow connections from the backup server, not provide a *pty*, and run only one command (e.g., some form of `dump`). This is accomplished by creating a specially crafted *authorized_keys* file as shown in Example 4-6.

Example 4-6. The operator's ssh key in ~operator/.ssh/authorized_keys

```
from="backupserver.mexicanfood.net",no-pty,command="/sbin/dump -0uan -f - /" ssh-dss
base64-ssh-key OPERATOR
```

If a backup client is configured in this way, the backup server needs only to `ssh` to the client and pipe output from the `ssh` command as follows:

```
% ssh operator@backupclient | dd of=/dev/nrst0
```

Of course, the target command could be a script, which, based on the day, would perform a different level `dump`.

It is also possible to perform secure backups initiated by the backup client by setting the RSH variable to `/usr/bin/ssh` and subsequently running `dump` as follows:

```
% /sbin/dump -0uan -f operator@backupserver.mexicanfood.net:/dev/nrst0
```

If you choose to use the operator account for `ssh`-enabled backups, not only will you need to create a home directory for this user, you will also need to change the login shell from `nologin` to `/usr/bin/false`.

Of course, other levels of protection are available to protect access including creating a specific interface used for backup traffic, configuring a local firewall, or using intervening firewalls.

Some organizations use an administrative secondary network interface exclusively for backups. If you're in this boat, be very aware of exactly what other devices could be listening on this interface. Push for encryption regardless.

It is also possible to use the primitive `rdump` command to backup data across a network. Unfortunately this tool relies on the use of *~/.rhosts* files and programs like `rcmd` and `ruserok`. There are severe security implications to using these tools and providing reasonable security is more trouble than it is worth. Given the ease with which Amanda and `dump` can be used securely, there is little need to use `rdump`.

Upgrading

At some point, you will likely want to upgrade your OpenBSD or FreeBSD server. If you followed the guidelines set forth in Chapter 3 for your operating system installation, you have already performed a trivial upgrade. As you allow your system to remain in operation from a few months to a year or more, upgrades become more challenging. Consider putting in place regular upgrade procedures that ensure you are capturing all security and reliability related updates. In some cases, your regular upgrade schedule may be accelerated by a released security advisory. This section of the chapter covers the steps you take to keep your system secure by patching and upgrading.

Patching Only

One school of thought for upgrading systems can be summarized by "if it ain't broke, don't fix it." Many system administrators adhere to this paradigm and upgrade or configure workarounds only when they run into a problem. Strictly adhering to this approach may have a variety of negative consequences:

- Systems are often in an unknown state, especially if you have been intermittently patching individual binaries as security advisories have been released without documenting all changes.
- It can be tempting to put off the installation of less-critical locally exploitable vulnerabilities when the affected host only provides shell accounts to administrators. These omissions may linger longer than desired.
- Increased care is required in performing an upgrade on an older system—the more workarounds that have been configured, the more painstaking it will be to account for them all during a full system upgrade.

The OpenBSD and FreeBSD security teams release security advisories with source code patches to address issues on a regular basis. As discussed previously, installing patches to mitigate the risks presented by security vulnerabilities is a key component to secure systems administration. However, following a patch-only philosophy, a few months or years down the road you or another administrator may find it difficult to conclusively determine if your system is free of all known vulnerabilities. While patching is vital for rapid response and risk mitigation, regular upgrades are necessary, too.

Tracking Branches

Both operating systems provide a patch branch, which includes only security and critical reliability fixes to a given release of the operating system. This branch offers the highest level of stability by introducing only the most critical security and reliability fixes. The administrator can expect that while tracking this branch, the fewest number of changes have been introduced into her system and only the most significant issues have been addressed.

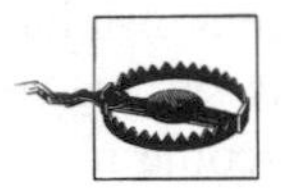

Despite how few changes are made to these production-quality branches, always perform system upgrades in a test environment before upgrading production systems.

Tracking this branch accommodates the "if it ain't broke, don't fix it" philosophy, while at the same time updating the system's configuration to reflect a certain patched state. This allows other administrators to determine whether the system is up to date in an instant.

Determining when to upgrade your BSD system can be tricky. Several factors will play into your chosen paradigm for longer term system maintenance. In more structured environments, your organization's security policy should describe the exact schedule for system patching and upgrades based on your security and availability requirements. The considerations for upgrading your system will depend on the operating system, so we must consider each in turn.

Tracking OpenBSD branches

OpenBSD calls their production-quality branch the stable branch or the patch branch. This is the appropriate choice for most, if not all, of your systems infrastructure. These stable branches are created at every OpenBSD release and are maintained for two releases. Because new versions of OpenBSD are released approximately every six months, you can avoid upgrading for about a year—but you had better not wait any longer than that. Note also that the official upgrade path with OpenBSD does not allow skipping versions. Do not attempt to install 3.6 over 3.4. Upgrade to 3.5 first. Upgrades are most safely accomplished through the construction of a parallel system and subsequent data and configuration migration.

If you do not have the resources and time to dedicate to this process, a binary upgrade is your best bet. That is, you are less likely to run into problems while per-

Release Engineering

There is one important difference when comparing the way OpenBSD and FreeBSD count releases and manage branches. OpenBSD releases are denoted `x.y` where both x and y are equally significant. This means upgrading from 3.3 release to 3.4 release should (in general) be considered as significant a step as upgrading from 3.9 to 4.0. OpenBSD systems maintain a stable branch at every release. These branches are usually maintained for two releases.

FreeBSD releases also have `x.y` notations, but in this case x is the traditional "major" version number, and y is the traditional "minor" version number. A change in the major version number indicates significant and substantial changes are being introduced to the system. Upgrading from 4.4 to 4.5, 4.8, or even 4.9 is not a major undertaking (though certainly the more increments are skipped the more careful you must be). An upgrade from 4.9 to 5.0, even though the two versions appear close, includes extensive changes in the code base.

Be sure to read the mailing lists and learn about what is happening on the major release before you blithely upgrade. Ideally, you should set up a test system where you can install the new version and become familiar with it before upgrading critical servers. Note also that some major versions are more significant than others. The switch from FreeBSD 2 to FreeBSD 3 was a rocky one, and there were some significant bugs in 3.0. As an exception to the rule, the transition from 3.0 to 3.1 included a switch from *a.out* to *elf* binaries—another troublesome change. The transition from 3.0 to 4.0 was much smoother. FreeBSD 5.0 was released with an explicit warning that there were still some instabilities. By Version 5.3, however, the 5.x branch had reached production quality stability for most purposes.

For more information about OpenBSD releases, see Chapter 5 of the FAQ. For details about FreeBSD's release engineering, see *http://www.freebsd.org/releng/*.

forming a binary upgrade than while performing a source upgrade. This was especially true between Versions 3.3 and 3.4, which included a change in the format of system binaries from *a.out* to *elf*. Bear in mind you may need to rebuild applications installed from ports (after updating your ports tree) when you perform a binary upgrade of your system.

On infrastructure systems with very specific purposes like firewalls, nameservers, mail relays, etc., you may find there are few security advisories that expose exploitable conditions for your system. In these cases, frequent operating system upgrades may be overkill. In all other cases, updating your system to the latest stable on a monthly or bi-monthly basis is recommended.

Tracking FreeBSD branches

FreeBSD calls their production-quality branch the security or release branch. This is an ideal choice for most, if not all of your critical production systems. This branch is typically officially maintained for a little over a year.

New minor releases of FreeBSD are shipped every four months or so. The `-STABLE` branch will track through various changes in the source tree, eventually culminating in a code freeze. During this period of time, release candidates are tested and the only changes made to the `-STABLE` branch are critical fixes—much like in the security branch. At the end of the code freeze is the next FreeBSD release. Directly tracking `-STABLE` is only recommended for less important systems, and ideally in a test environment first.

To keep up to date, FreeBSD administrators will generally want to track the security branch for one or two releases. Once a later release has reached maturity (after the release candidates, and perhaps even a month or two after that), it is appropriate to upgrade to this later release and track this new release's security branch. This is a fairly straightforward process described as a post-installation hardening task in Chapter 3.

Finally, new major revisions of FreeBSD come around every few years. Migration to these platforms should never be done for critical systems until the `x.2` or `x.3` release and the introduction of a `-STABLE` branch for that version. If possible, building parallel systems and performing a data and configuration migration is the way to go.

You need not go through an entire `make world` process on all of your FreeBSD systems. Pick an internal host and build binaries there. You may then burn the contents of */usr/obj* to a CD and subsequently mount this CD on */usr/obj* on other systems and perform the install.

Although you may be thinking that the `-STABLE` branch is production-quality, FreeBSD includes performance enhancements, noncritical bug fixes, and sometimes even small features into this branch of code. This is generally more change than you look for on critical systems infrastructure. While these have been carefully tested and should work in most environments, traffic on the *freebsd-stable* mailing lists provides evidence that users do experience problems tracking this branch from time to time. Nevertheless, if you are able to test upgrades to the latest `-STABLE` system to ensure compatibility with your hardware and software, this may be a viable option for all but the most vital of your infrastructure servers.

Security Vulnerability Response

System maintenance periods are typically thought of by users as "the time when IT is working on the system." What are the administrators working on, exactly? Maintenance may involve the introduction of new functionality, attempted resolution of a problem, or hardware replacements and additions. Most users tend not to guess that the administrator is working on patching the system to mitigate the risks of a recently announced security issue, yet it is with this important aspect of system maintenance that we are concerned in this section of the chapter.

Although we focus on the mitigation of risks described in security advisories, remember that the addition of functionality or even hardware can affect the overall security of your system. The security-minded system administrator would do well to always ask himself, "How does what I am doing right now affect the security of my system?"

Keeping Abreast

Without a list of software you care about, how can you possibly know what to patch and when to patch it? Take inventory and document the systems under your jurisdiction. Note the operating systems and applications installed across your organization. With this information you're well equipped to start subscribing to the relevant mailing lists.

FreeBSD lists
: FreeBSD offers a variety of lists that are a great asset to system administrators. Of utmost importance is *freebsd-security-notifications* to which all security advisories are posted. Typically these advisories are also cross-posted to the *freebsd-announce* list, which broadcasts other important FreeBSD related events. Both of these lists are low volume, and subscription should be considered mandatory for any FreeBSD administrator. For a description of all the FreeBSD lists available, see Appendix C of the *FreeBSD Handbook*.

OpenBSD lists
: As with the FreeBSD lists, the OpenBSD team offers a *security-announce* list that should be considered of paramount importance to all OpenBSD administrators. The OpenBSD announce list should also be considered for news about the OpenBSD project (items are not necessarily cross-posted from *security-announce*). Both of these lists are low volume, and subscription should be considered mandatory for any OpenBSD administrator. For more information about the available OpenBSD lists, see the Mailing Lists section of the OpenBSD.org web site at *http://www.openbsd.org/mail.html*.

SecurityFocus lists
: SecurityFocus offers a variety of security-related mailing lists that are operating system specific (Linux, BSD, Solaris, etc.), topical (IDS, Firewall, Secure Shell, etc.), and more general in nature (Security Basics, Bugtraq). In years past, Bugtraq was seen as the authoritative source for security advisories. In recent times, however, the signal-to-noise ratio has increased, rendering this list more

difficult to use effectively. It may be worthwhile to subscribe to the *vuln-dev* (Vulnerability Development) list to get a heads up to potential problems before formal advisories can be released. New security administrators should strongly consider the security basics list.

Application Specific lists
: Most application vendors provide separate mailing lists for users, developers, and those interested in security advisories. Consult your application vendor's web site for more information about the lists provided. There should, at the very least, be a low-volume *announce-only* list, which should be considered mandatory reading if the application is present in your organization. Throughout this book you will be pointed to mailing lists for the applications we cover.

FreshPorts (FreeBSD only)
: FreshPorts (*http://www.freshports.org*) is an excellent resource for administrators to find out when port maintainers have updated the ports tree. Create a FreshPorts account, select the ports you wish to monitor (or upload the output of **pkg_info -qoa**), and specify how often you'd like announcements. FreshPorts will notify you whenever the ports on your "watch list" are updated and will include the port maintainer's comments.

After subscribing to the necessary mailing lists, you should have a flow of information into your mailbox. The next challenge is in knowing how to react to advisories you receive.

Security Advisory Response

After you determine that a security advisory actually pertains to software installed on your systems, you must take action. Your response to a security advisory can be broken down into four distinct tasks: categorization, severity assessment, response planning, and execution.

Categorization

Terms like buffer overflow, race condition, and format string vulnerability should quickly become familiar as you start reading advisories. Understanding what these issues are, how they can be exploited, and what attacks become possible as a result of the exploit will require a little bit of work on your part. Read the advisory carefully and consult Google if you don't understand any of the terminology. After you've developed at least a basic understanding of the vulnerability, you should be able to informally categorize it according to the kind of security breach it represents and the connectivity required for the exploit.

There are several kinds of security breaches for which advisories are issued: arbitrary code execution, privilege escalation, denial of service, information disclosure, and so on. Some require local access for a successful exploit, whereas others may be exploited remotely. The severity of each of these kinds of breaches will vary according to your environment and the system in question, thus categorizing the advisory will help in assessing the potential impact.

Severity assessment

The most important factor in determining the severity of an advisory is understanding how the security breach described by the exploit will affect your organization. Not only does this vary by organization, but also by the type of breach.

Higher visibility companies, financial institutions, and security firms suffer immensely when security breaches that involve information disclosure occur. Organizations that rely on income from transactions or provide critical services to other organizations can lose money when faced with a denial of service (DOS) attack. Smaller organizations often feel that security is less important because they are neither highly visible nor do they provide critical services. These companies do not suffer immediately when their systems are compromised, instead they discover later that their systems were used to attack other more highly visible companies (or a government) and must deal with that situation instead.

Nevertheless, there are cases where immediate service-interrupting response is overkill. If the potential exploit is only able to provide an alternate means of access to data that is already public, the vulnerability may be considered less severe. If a denial of service attack becomes possible against your web server, but your web site availability is not of importance to your organization, patching can wait. Still, do not succumb to neverending procrastination. The vulnerability may have more far-reaching consequences than either you or the writers of the advisory have determined.

Finally, once the exploit has been evaluated to determine its potential effect on the organization, you must determine the likelihood that the breach will occur. If the exploit requires local access on a system to which only you have an account—the risk is minimal. If the attack requires local access on a system that provides anonymous FTP services, there is a greater cause for concern. While you may be tempted to disregard a remotely exploitable vulnerability because you feel there is little value in attacking the organization, bear in mind that exploit toolkits do not differentiate between companies, they merely scan IP ranges for vulnerable systems.

Response planning and execution

When it comes time for mitigation, your job as the system administrator is to solve the problem with a minimum of disruption. How you go about this will vary greatly based on the severity of the vulnerability and the availability of a fix. In general there are six ways to respond to an advisory:

Do nothing
: If the output of your severity assessment is that the vulnerability cannot be exploited in your organization, lack of response may be appropriate.

Upgrade at next maintenance

Organizations often have structured maintenance windows during which systems personnel may perform maintenance. Some organizations lack the structure but nevertheless can schedule a maintenance window for some time in the not-too-distant future so as to minimally impact the business of the organization.

Upgrade tonight

More potentially damaging exploits may need quicker response. In these cases, waiting for a maintenance window poses too much risk and a more rapid response is warranted.

Upgrade now

In rare cases, an advisory is released that describes a vulnerability that is potentially catastrophic if exploited and trivial to exploit. In these cases, immediate response may be necessary.

Mitigate and upgrade later

In some cases, an upgrade is warranted, but a mitigation exists that can yield an immediate, albeit temporary, solution. Mitigation is useful to allow for more time in planning an upgrade, in order to postpone the upgrade until a scheduled maintenance window, or in the event that an upgrade path has not yet been laid down.

Turn it off

In the event that an advisory is released that has no upgrade path and no mitigation strategy, your only option might be to disable the affected service.

The most potentially devastating exploits should certainly evoke rapid response. Be careful not to overreact, however, and cause more damage than the attackers. Plan and test your response before executing. Less critical services and advisories may evoke a more lazy response. While this response may not be inappropriate in all cases, be careful to follow through with your plan at your earliest opportunity. Vulnerabilities left unchecked are quickly forgotten.

Most advisories released by the FreeBSD and OpenBSD security teams are accompanied by instructions for various mitigation strategies. These often include updating to the latest revision of the software, applying a patch to the source code and reinstalling, or even changing a configuration option to disable a vulnerable component. In severe cases where the vulnerability, if exploited, would cripple your organization, reaction to the advisory must be immediate. This does not necessarily mean you unplug the system from the network. It may be possible to mitigate the issue by adjusting your firewall rules, rate limiting connections, or adjusting the configuration of the application. In the worst cases, you will need to disable the service until the problem can be resolved. This should provide you with enough breathing room to carefully plan and test a response that eliminates the vulnerability.

Remember that security advisories are often released for third-party software several days before the ports tree has been updated to reflect the availability of the patched version of that piece of software. It is also not uncommon for source code patches to become available before the new versions of the files have been checked in to the CVS repositories. In these cases, you may need to take immediate action by patching the source code and reinstalling. When the ports tree is updated, you may overwrite your patched binaries by installing the new version of the software.

In rare cases, such as the potentially exploitable buffer management issues with OpenSSH in September of 2003, you will hear rumors of exploit code already in existence long before patches (or even an advisory!) become available. In these cases, you may need to disable the service until the situation becomes clear. If this isn't possible, consider restricting the service in some way to mitigate the risk..

Network Service Security

FreeBSD and OpenBSD systems can provide an extensive list of services. While Chapters 5 through 9 of this book provide detailed information about some of the most common and complex network services, you may find a wealth of more basic services are also useful on your network. The second half of this chapter discusses some of these services, what they provide, how to provide them securely, and in some cases, why you should do so.

inetd and tcpwrappers

The Internet daemon (`inetd(8)`) is a network service super-server. It comes with a bit of a stigma—and this is no surprise since most texts on securing hosts contain a step where you disable `inetd`, yet few describe enabling or even securing it. `inetd` is not evil, and it can be used safely. The services `inetd` is often configured to provide, however, should sound like a list of security nightmares: `telnetd`, `ftpd`, `rlogind`, `fingerd`, etc. All of these services pose unnecessary risk to infrastructure systems, especially when much of the functionality can be provided by `ssh`.

Again, `inetd` is not to blame. As most administrators know, the `inetd` process reads configuration information from */etc/inetd.conf* and listens on the appropriate TCP and UDP ports for incoming connections. As connections are made, `inetd` spawns the appropriate daemon. Unfortunately, there are not a great many daemons traditionally run through `inetd` that are safe to use in today's unsafe network environments. Nevertheless, should you find yourself in a position to provide services through `inetd`, you should know three things.

First, on FreeBSD and OpenBSD systems, `inetd` will limit the number of incoming connections to no more than 256 per second. Unless you legitimately receive this many requests, you may want to lower this threshold by using the `-R` *`rate`* command-line argument.

Second, use tcpwrappers. The manpage for *hosts_access(5)* describes how tcpwrappers may be configured using */etc/hosts.allow* and */etc/hosts.deny* to restrict connections based on originating hostname and/or address specification. We briefly examine a *hosts.allow* file in Example 4-7.

Example 4-7. Sample hosts.allow file

```
ALL : 1.2.3.4 : allow

# SHORT CIRCUIT RFC931 ABOVE THIS LINE
ALL : PARANOID : RFC931 20 : deny
ALL : localhost 127.0.0.1 : allow

sshd : mexicanfood.net peruvianfood.net: allow

proftpd : dip.t-dialin.net : deny
proftpd : localhost .com .net .org .edu .us : allow
ALL : ALL \
        : severity auth.info \
        : twist /bin/echo "You are not welcome to use %d from %h."
```

In this example, all connections are allowed from 1.2.3.4. The `PARANOID` directive in the next line performs some basic hostname and address checking to ensure the hostnames and IP addresses match up. The second part of that stanza utilizes the `IDENT` protocol to verify that the source host did in fact send the request, provided the source host is running `identd`.

The latter lines are fairly straightforward. All connections are allowed from *localhost*. Connections via `sshd` are permitted from both *mexicanfood.net* and *peruvianfood.net*. FTP access from *dip.t-dailin.net* is explicitly denied access (presumably the administrator noticed a lot of attacks from this network and has no users there) while access from *.com*, *.net*, *.org*, *.edu*, and *.us* networks are allowed.

Finally, if the connection was not explicitly permitted or denied before the last line, the user is informed that she is not allowed to use a given service from the source host, and the rejection is logged via syslog to the *auth.info* facility and level.

FreeBSD systems support tcpwrappers compiled into the `inetd` binary. This means that by using the `-W` and `-w` flags to `inetd` (these flags are on by default—see */etc/defaults/rc.conf*), your `inetd`-based services will automatically be wrapped.

To use tcpwrappers on OpenBSD systems, use `tcpd(8)`. Example 4-8 lists two lines in */etc/inetd.conf* that demonstrate the difference between using tcpwrappers for `eklogin` and not using it for `kshell`.

Example 4-8. Using tcpwrappers in OpenBSD

```
eklogin stream tcp nowait root /usr/libexec/tcpd rlogind -k -x
kshell stream tcp nowait root  /usr/libexec/rshd rshd -k
```

Enabling tcpwrappers for `eklogin` but not `kshell` is done here for demonstrative purposes only. If possible, use tcpwrappers for all services run through `inetd`.

The server program field changes to */usr/libexec/tcpd* (the *tcpwrappers* access control facility daemon), which takes the actual service and its arguments as arguments to itself.

Finally, `inetd` spawns other programs using a *fork(2) exec(3)* paradigm. Programmers are very familiar with this, as it is the way a process spawns a child process. There is nothing particularly wrong with this approach, but you must be aware that loading a program in this way is not a lightweight operation. For instance, `sshd` could run out of `inetd` easily enough, but since `sshd` generates a server key on startup (which takes some time), the latency would be intolerable for users. Therefore, when supporting a high rate of connections is a requirement, `inetd` might not be the best solution.

Remember that a variety of daemons utilize tcpwrappers even when they do not run out of `inetd`. To determine if this is the case, read the manpage for the service. You may also be able to tell by running `ldd(1)` against the binary. If you see something called *libwrap*, then tcpwrapper support is available. If the binary is statically linked, of course, your test will be inconclusive.

Network File System

Centralized storage through the use of shared filesystems is a common goal of many administrators. OpenBSD and FreeBSD systems natively support the Network File System (NFS) Version 3. While this service is often used and considered vital in many networks, there are inherent security risks in sharing a filesystem across a network of potentially untrusted systems.

NFS should be avoided if at all possible. We present this section not to describe how you might secure NFS, but instead to illustrate why a secure installation is not possible. If you must have a shared network filesystem, consider more secure NFS alternatives such as the Andrew File System (AFS), Matt Blaze's Cryptographic File System (CFS), or the Self-Certifying File System (SFS).

Implicit UID and GID trust

The greatest security concern in deploying NFS is the minimal amount of "authentication" required to access files on a shared filesystem. By default, when exporting an NFS filesystem, user IDs on the server (except root) map to user IDs on the client. For example, a process on the client running with UID 1000 will be able to read and write to all files and directories on the server that are owned by UID 1000. Yet UID

1000 on the client may not be the same user as UID 1000 on the server. The administrator of the client system could trivially su to any user on that system and be able to access all user-readable files on the shared filesystem. This danger extends to the root user if the -maproot option is specified for the shared filesystem in */etc/exports*.

This danger may be mitigated by forcibly mapping all remote users to a single effective UID for the client. This essentially provides only guest access to the filesystem. If writing to the filesystem is permitted in this case, it will become impossible to enforce user-based permissions as all users essentially become the same user.

Some administrators have made it possible to tunnel NFS over SSH. This ensures all NFS traffic is encrypted. However, this has limited value as it does not eliminate the implicit UID and GID trust issue described here.

NFS export control

NFS is configured by *exports(5)*. That is, what filesystem is exported under what conditions to which systems? This allows for fairly fine-grained control of exports. With the application of the principle of least privilege, you would export filesystems with as many security options enabled as possible. Consider the following examples.

```
/home/users          devbox, buildbox, sharedbox
```

This configuration will export home directories to the three systems specified, all of which are under the control of an administrator that ensures users are not able to access other users' home directories.

```
/scratch             -mapall=neato:    userbox1, userbox2, userbox3
```

This scratch area for project *neato* is shared to all systems, but users from all clients are mapped to user neato. This allows only the specified NFS clients to work with this temporary storage area.

```
/archives            -ro
```

These archives are shared for all users to read, but no users may write to the filesystem. For more information about restricting exports, see the manual page for *exports(5)*. You should now begin to realize that deploying NFS in anything resembling a secure manner will require that you remove much of the functionality that you would have liked to retain.

NFS network restrictions

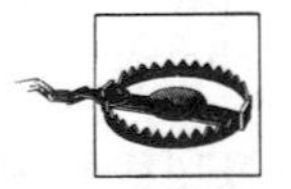

If you find yourself reading this section, you may be suffering from a mandate to run NFS. We again urge you to consider some of the shared filesystem alternatives mentioned previously.

On the network level, there is an additional set of restrictions about which the administrator should be aware. By default, mountd(8), which services mount requests for NFS, accepts connections only on reserved ports. This ensures that only the root user on remote systems may mount shared filesystems. If the -n argument is specified to mountd, requests from all ports will be honored. This allows any user of any system to mount network drives. Do not enable this option unless you have a specific need to do so—the manual page for mountd mentions that servicing Legacy Windows clients may be a motivation.

The ports that NFS needs are managed by the *portmapper*, now called rpcbind(8) (Sun remote procedure call [RPC] implementation) in FreeBSD 5.X and portmap(8) in OpenBSD. In OpenBSD, portmap will by default run as the _portmap user and given the -s flag in FreeBSD, rpcbind will run as the daemon user. In both cases, these services may be reinforced with the use of tcpwrappers so that only given systems or networks can communicate with these applications and hence, use NFS. Since RPC negotiates ports dynamically, NFS is a very difficult service to firewall.

With or without a firewall, it should be clear that NFS, while it may be useful, lacks any real security. Avoid using it if at all possible.

Network Information Services

What was originally Yellow Pages (*yp*) was renamed to Network Information Services (NIS) as a result of trademark issues. Thus, many of the programs related to NIS begin with the letters "yp." NIS, like NFS, is RPC-based but provides centrally managed configuration files for all systems in a NIS domain. Although the configuration details of NIS are beyond the scope of this book, there are significant security implications in running NIS on your network, the least of which is the unencrypted dissemination of NIS maps, such as your password file.

NIS should be avoided if at all possible. We present this section not to describe how you might secure NIS, but instead why you cannot. If centralized authentication and authorization is your goal, consider authenticating using Kerberos and providing authorization via LDAP. Unfortunately this is an extensive topic and would require a book dedicated to it. A more straightforward approach may be to safely distribute password files from a trusted administration host. We describe this latter procedure in the next section.

Password format compatibility

If you have NIS clients that only understand weaker DES passwords (pre-Solaris 9, update 2 for example), your NIS maps will have to contain only DES encrypted passwords. This may be accomplished by ensuring that users make password changes on systems that understand only DES passwords, or by reconfiguring your system to generate DES encrypted passwords by default. Neither of these are good solutions.

Encrypted password exposure

The *master.passwd* file, which contains encrypted passwords for all your users, is easily readable by others on your network when you use NIS. Although the requests clients make for the *master.passwd.byname* and *master.passwd.byuid* maps must come from a privileged port, this is not a significant increase in security. If any users on your network have a root account on any Unix system on your network (or can quickly build a system and plug it in), this restriction becomes irrelevant.

It gets worse. NIS is frequently used in heterogeneous environments and, as described above, passwords may need to be stored using the much weaker DES encryption rather than the default *md5* or *blowfish* encryption of FreeBSD and OpenBSD respectively. As if this weren't bad enough, some older operating systems will not support the concept of shadow passwords. In this case, NIS must be run in `UNSECURE` mode (specified in the appropriate *Makefile* in */var/yp*). With this configuration, encrypted passwords are exposed in the *passwd.byname* and *passwd.byuid* maps. Perhaps not so terrible because the security involved in the "low-port-only" concept was weak to begin with.

Limiting access to NIS maps

At the heart of NIS is the `ypserv(8)`, the NIS database server. It is this daemon that accepts RPC and dutifully provides database contents upon request. Host and network specification in */var/yp/securenets* can be used to limit the exposure of your password maps through RPC. The `ypserv` daemon will read the contents of this file and provide maps only to the listed hosts and networks. Given a network of any meaningful size, you may configure an entire network range in this file for which RPC should be answered. With *securenets* configured in this way it is trivial to bypass by merely connecting to the network in question. Specifying only a handful of hosts in this file, however, could effectively provide NIS maps to a group of servers while limiting "public" access.

On the client side

If you have chosen to lock NIS down to a handful of servers, `ypbind(8)` can use some attention. This daemon searches for a NIS server to which it should bind and facilitates subsequent NIS information requests. All systems running NIS should have statically configured NIS domain names and servers, so that instead of attempting to find a server by broadcast, `ypbind` immediately binds to a known NIS server. This prevents malicious users from setting up alternate NIS servers and perhaps providing password-free *passwd* maps.

When is NIS right for you?

If all systems involved in the NIS domain support shadow passwords and can understand `md5`/`blowfish` encrypted passwords, some of the risk associated with NIS is mitigated. If NIS is being provided only to a handful of closely administered servers via `securenets`, the risk is further mitigated.

However, NIS still relies on the difficult-to-protect RPC and operates without encryption. Avoid NIS altogether if you are working with heterogeneous or not completely trusted networks. Instead, develop another, more secure, way to distribute user, group, or configuration files.

For basic configuration information about YP/NIS see the *yp(8)* manpage and Chapter 19.9 of the *FreeBSD Handbook*.

Secure File Distribution Using scp

One alternative to NIS is file distribution over `ssh`. In fact, this paradigm will work not only for password and group files but also for other arbitrary configuration files. The secure copy (`scp(1)`) program is included as part of the `ssh` program suite and is included in the base distributions of both OpenBSD and FreeBSD. Secure copy, as the name implies, copies files between networked systems and guarantees data integrity and confidentiality during the transfer. Authentication for `scp` is the same as for `ssh`.

In order to put in place secure file distribution, you will need a management station to house all files that are distributed to other hosts as shown in Figure 4-1. This host should be exceptionally well protected and access should be restricted to only the administrators responsible for managing file distribution, in line with our principle of least privilege. Transferring configuration files to remote systems is a three-stage process:

1. Put the files in staging area on the management station.
2. Distribute the files to systems.
3. Move the files from the staging area on target systems into production.

Initial setup

Initial setup will vary depending on the environment. The following steps provide one example of preparing for secure file distribution. Your requirements may dictate changes to the approach presented below.

1. Create `ssh` keys for authentication.

   First, create a pair of `ssh` keys for copying files over the network on the management station. For the purposes of this discussion, we will name these keys *autobackup* and *autobackup.pub* and place them in */root/.ssh*. These keys should be generated using `ssh-keygen(1)` and may be with or without a *passphrase*. For pros and cons of these two approaches, keep reading.

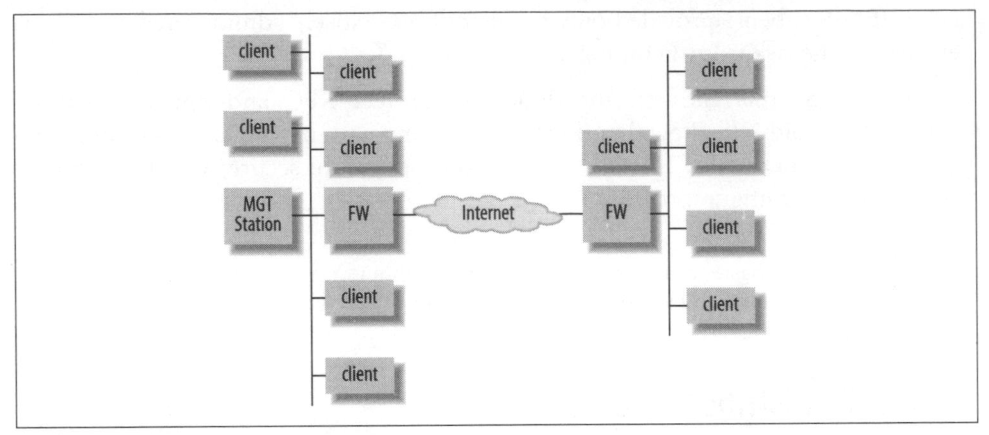

Figure 4-1. Secure file distribution architecture

2. Create a staging area from which files will be copied.

   Next, if servers to which files are being transferred have differing configuration requirements, it becomes necessary to gather files into a staging area before the transfer. In most cases, workgroup servers and infrastructure servers to which you are copying files will permit login from different sets of users. You may need to write simple scripts to extract a subset of accounts from your *master.passwd* and *group* file instead of copying the entire contents.

   If you are copying a *master.passwd* file from the management station to remote systems, bear in mind the root password on the remote systems will become the same as that of the management station. In most cases, this is not desirable, and the root account should be stripped from *master.passwd* using a program like sed or grep before transmission.

   Also note that the *master.passwd* and *group* files may not be */etc/master.passwd* and */etc/group*. You may keep syntactically correct organization-wide master files anywhere on your system. In fact, this is preferable since you do not want to grant everyone in the organization access to your management station.

   This staging area may be anywhere on the management station. Simply declare a directory as a staging area, and begin writing scripts to collect configuration files.

3. Write scripts to gather files.

   Once the staging area has been assigned, you must write the necessary scripts to gather configuration files from the system. In the case of *master.passwd*, you may need to customize the contents by extracting only a subset of users. A script to create the necessary files might look something like Example 4-9.

Example 4-9. Script to gather configuration files into a staging area

```
#!/bin/sh

# This ensures the nested for loop iterates through
# lines, not whitespace
OIFS="$IFS"
IFS="
"

# This is where we keep the maps, our "staging area"
# This variable is just a template for various "level" dirs
level_dir=/home/users/netcopy/level

# Make sure our 3 level directories exist and clear them out
# before continuing with the script.
for level in 1 2 3; do
  mkdir -p ${level_dir}{$level}
  rm -rf ${level_dir}${level}/*
done

# Let's make sure /etc and /usr/local/etc exist
# within the staging area
for level in 1 2 3; do
  for dir in /etc /usr/local/etc; do
    mkdir -p ${level_dir}${level}/${dir}
  done
done

# We're going to be writing the contents of master.passwd
# Let's make sure the file's got the right permissions first
for level in 1 2 3; do
  touch ${level_dir}${level}/etc/master.passwd
  chown root:wheel ${level_dir}${level}/etc/master.passwd
  chmod 600 ${level_dir}${level}/etc/master.passwd
done

# Here we grab users from the master.passwd and group
for line in `grep -v '^#' /some/master.passwd | sort -t : -k3n`; do
  IFS=$OLDIFS
  set -- $line
  uid=$2
  gid=$3
  # If the uid is betweeen 1000 and 4999, it's a level 1 user
  if ([ $uid -ge 1000 ] && [ $uid -lt 5000 ]); then
    echo $line >> ${level_dir}1/etc/master.passwd
  fi
  # If the uid is betweeen 5000 and 9999, it's a level 2 user
  if ([ $uid -ge 5000 ] && [ $uid -lt 10000 ]); then
    echo $line >> ${level_dir}2/etc/master.passwd
  fi
  # If the group is 101 (dev), it's a level 3 user
  if ([ $gid -eq 101 ]); then
    echo $line >> ${level_dir}3/etc/master.passwd
```

Example 4-9. Script to gather configuration files into a staging area (continued)

```
  fi
  IFS="
"
done

# Copy additional configuration files
for level in 1 2 3; do
  tar -cf - \
   /etc/group \
   /etc/resolv.conf \
   /etc/hosts \
   /etc/aliases \
   /usr/local/etc/myprogram.conf \
   | tar -xf - -C ${level_dir}${level}
   # Additional files may be listed above the previous line
  cd ${level_dir}${level} && tar -czpf config.tgz etc usr/local/etc
  rm -rf etc usr
done
```

Note that this script copies users based on user ID and group ID. In most cases, a subset of accounts is more easily garnered when distinguishable by group as opposed to user ID range. For ease of administration, pick whichever approach works best in your environment and stick with it. Finally, bear in mind that this script must execute as root and will be working with sensitive files. Be very sure the staging directories and files are well protected.

4. Prepare remote systems.

   After scripts have been written to gather the necessary files for transmission, prepare the remote systems to receive files. Create a designated account to receive the transferred files. In this example, we will call this account *netcopy*. Create a *~netcopy/.ssh/authorized_keys* with the contents of *autobackup.pub* from the management station.

You might be thinking that this is a lot of trouble and it would be easier to merely copy files over as the root user. However, we advise that you disable root logins via ssh in */etc/ssh/sshd_config* and log in under your user account. Permitting remote root logins makes accountability much more difficult.

The remote systems will also need scripts to move files from the staging area into the appropriate place on the system. Given the gathering script in Example 4-9, a trivial tar extraction from the root of the filesystem on the remote system will place all configuration files in the correct places with the correct permissions. This script must also execute as root and should be placed in root's *crontab*.

Pushing files with passphrase authentication

As discussed previously, for increased security, the ssh daemon should be configured to accept only key-based authentication, as opposed to password authentication. Because scp uses the same authentication as ssh, however, requiring keys and *passphrases* can be difficult to automate. However, automation is not always necessary. Even when using NIS, you must issue a make(1) in the */var/yp* directory to push the maps to remote systems. To provide the same functionality, you can (this should sound familiar) write a script to accomplish the push while requiring password entry only one time with the help of ssh-agent(1). Example 4-10 shows how this might be accomplished.

Example 4-10. Script to copy files using an ssh key

```
#!/bin/sh

level1_dir=/home/users/netcopy/level1
level2_dir=/home/users/netcopy/level2

level1_sys=alpha beta gamma delta
level2_sys=mercury venus earth mars

# This runs the ssh-agent which keeps track of ssh keys
# added using ssh-add.  Using eval facilitates placing
# values for SSH_AUTH_SOCK and SSH_AGENT_PID in the
# environment so that ssh-add can communicate with the agent.
eval `ssh-agent`
# This will prompt for a passphrase.  Once entered, you
# are not prompted again.
ssh-add /root/.ssh/autobackup

# Securely transfer the compressed tarballs
foreach system in $level1_sys; do
 scp ${level1_dir}/config.tgz ${system}:
done

foreach system in $level2_sys; do
 scp ${level2_dir}/config.tgz ${system}:
done

# Kill the agent we spawned
kill $SSH_AGENT_PID
```

This script requires a *passphrase* every time it is executed, so a person must initiate the transfer. Admittedly this script could be replaced by one that acts like a daemon, prompting for authentication once and then copying repeatedly at specified intervals. In this scenario, a *passphrase* would still be required every time the script is started—but this would occur perhaps only at boot time.

Pushing files without passphrase authentication

It is possible to generate ssh keys without an associated *passphrase*. These are logically similar to the key to your house door: if you have it, you can open the door. There is an inherent danger in creating keys that provide a means to log into a system without any additional checks. It is vital that the private key in this case is very well protected (readable only by the *netcopy* user).

This risk can be mitigated somewhat with a few options in the netcopy user's *~/.ssh/authorized_keys* file. For example, we could configure remote systems to restrict access not only by key, but also by host, as shown in Example 4-11.

Example 4-11. Restricting access by key and host, disabling pty(4)

```
from="mgmthost.example.com",no-pty,no-port-forwarding ssh-dss base64_key NETCOPY
```

Before our base-64 encoded ssh key, we provide three options and the ssh-dss key type. The first option specifies that not only does the source host have to provide the private key to match this public key, but it must also come from a host named mgmthost.example.com. Moreover, when connections are made, no *pty* will be allocated and port forwarding will be disabled.

Despite the security concerns with using *passphrase*-less keys, it becomes possible to automate file distribution. In this way, modifications can be made to files on the master system with the understanding that, given enough time, changes will propagate to all systems to which files are regularly copied. The script required to perform a secure copy is almost identical to that in Example 4-10, but the ssh-agent and ssh-add commands can be removed.

An scp alternative

We discussed earlier in this chapter a way to track changes to configuration files using CVS. If you have a CVS repository that contains all configuration files for your systems, you already have a staging area from which you can copy files to target systems. You need only decide which system will push the files, and perform a **cvs checkout** of your configuration data onto that system. The rest of the procedure will be very similar.

Alternately, you may prefer a pull method instead of a push. With little effort, you could write a script to check the status of configuration files installed on the system via **cvs status *filename***, and check out-of-date files out of the repository as necessary. Since cvs will use ssh for authentication, you are again in a position to automate this procedure by placing the script in cron and using an ssh key that does not require a *passphrase*. Similarly, organizations with a Kerberos infrastructure might choose to place a service-only *keytab* on systems used for checking configuration files out of your repository.

Wrapping up

The script to gather files and copy files to the remote system may easily be combined into one script. The file copy will occur based on the successful authentication of the netcopy user. A regular `cron(8)` job should check for the existence of the file on all remote systems, and if it exists, extract the contents into the appropriate folders.

Also, be aware we have glossed over an important mutual exclusion problem in the sample scripts here. If, for some reason, either our scripts that collect configuration files or our scripts that un-`tar` configuration file blobs run slowly, the next iteration of the script may interfere with this iteration by clobbering or deleting files. Before building a system like this, make sure to include some kind of lockfile (this can be as simple as touching a specially named file in */tmp*) to ensure that one iteration does not interfere with another.

Although this approach requires a great deal more initial configuration than NIS (because `ypinit` performs the setup for you), the vulnerabilities inherent in NIS are mitigated. This paradigm works well for copying user account information and system configuration and may be easily adapted to copy configuration files for other software like djbdns and Postfix.

The Importance of Time (NTP)

The naïve administrator will assume that once he sets the system clock, he need not concern himself with system time. After all, computers are good with numbers, right? Not so. As any experienced administrator knows system clocks drift. When systems in your network start drifting away from each other, you can run into a variety of problems including, but not limited to:

- Being unable to build a reliable audit trail because it is impossible to reliably determine the ordering of events on different systems
- Checking things into and out of version control repositories
- Authenticating Kerberos tickets
- Working with shared filesystems
- Operating clustered or high availability configurations
- Properly servicing DHCP and DDNS requests
- Creating correct timestamps on emails within and leaving your organization

Fortunately, NTP on FreeBSD and OpenBSD systems is trivial to set up. The `ntp(8)` package is included with the base of both operating systems (as of OpenBSD 3.6), so there is nothing to install. All that remains are security and architecture considerations.

Security

Trivial NTP security can be achieved through the use of restrict directives in the NTP configuration file: */etc/ntp.conf* on FreeBSD systems and */etc/ntpd.conf* on OpenBSD systems. These directives determine how your NTP server will handle incoming requests and are expressed as address, mask, and flag tuples. From a least privilege perspective, you would configure NTP much as you would a firewall: initially restrict all traffic and subsequently describe which hosts should have what kind of access. A base configuration ought to look something Example 4-12.

Example 4-12. Default NTP restrictions

```
restrict default ignore
driftfile /etc/ntp.drift
```

From this point, additional servers may be listed. Example 4-13 is a contrived example that permits unrestricted access from *localhost*, while hosts on 192.168.0.0/24 may query the nameserver, and the final two NTP servers may be used as time sources.

Example 4-13. Specific ntp restrictions

```
restrict 127.0.0.1
restrict 192.168.0.0 mask 255.255.255.0 notrust nomodify nopeer
restrict 10.1.30.14 notrust nomodify noserve
restrict 10.1.30.15 notrust nomodify noserve
```

If you are unfamiliar with the `restrict` directive, these configuration lines might look a little odd. Flags to the `restrict` directive limit access, thus the lack of flags for the *localhost* entry specifies no restrictions rather than being fully restrictive.

This is an adequate solution when providing NTP services to known clients. There are situations where IP restrictions are not enough. In these cases, you may want to consider NTP authentication. Authentication provides a more flexible way of controlling access when:

- You need to provide time service to a limited number of systems across untrusted networks.
- You wish to grant certain entities the ability to query or modify your time server, but cannot rely on a static remote IP address.
- You feel mere IP restrictions that permit runtime configuration are inadequate.

NTP authentication is supported using both public and private key cryptography (via the Autokey protocol). After keys have been generated using the `ntp-genkeys(8)` utility, the server may be configured to use specific keys with specific hosts, be they symmetric or asymmetric. Bear in mind, sensitive symmetric keys will have to be exchanged securely through some out-of-band mechanism. Asymmetric keys contain a public portion that may be exchanged in the clear. Additional details about the configuration of authentication for ntp are beyond the scope of this book but are addressed in the documentation available through *http://www.ntp.org*.

Architecture

As with any other network service, providing time to your organization requires a little planning. NTP is typically woven into a network in tiers. The first (highest level) tier is authoritative time source for your organization. All NTP servers in this tier are configured as peers and use publicly accessible time servers as authoritative time source, or if your requirements dictate, acquire time from local time-keeping devices. The second tier of NTP servers for your organization will derive time from the first tier and provide time services for clients or subsequent tiers.

Unique security considerations exist for every tier. Top level organizational tiers that communicate with external servers are vulnerable to attack. One of the most effective ways to mitigate the risks associated with this exposure is to limit the external NTP servers that can communicate with your systems through firewall rules. This places implicit trust in your external time sources, which in most cases is acceptable. More stringent security requirements will necessitate local time-keeping devices.

Middle-tier systems that communicate with both upper- and lower-tier systems, but no clients should be configured such that only upper-tier systems may be used as time sources, and lower-tier systems may query time. All other requests should be denied. More stringent security requirements may dictate that upper-tier and lower-tier encryption keys must exist to authenticate communications. Smaller environments generally do not have a need for systems in this tier.

Finally, the lowest tier NTP servers provide time to internal clients. These systems should be configured so that only the immediate upper tier systems may be used as time sources, but anyone on the local network should be able to query time on the system.

As with the other tiers, high security requirements may require authentication to guarantee time sources are in fact the systems they claim to be.

Monitoring System Health

Performance monitoring concerns might seem out of place in a book about system security, but system availability is a vital part of system security. After all, denial of service attacks are considered security concerns even though they merely make systems unavailable. Keeping a keen eye on things like disk usage, load averages, or the existence or absence of specific daemons will ensure that you are immediately aware of your systems behaving unusually.

Network monitoring can be a bit of a double-edged sword. Keeping track of what your systems are doing will definitely help you know when they misbehave. Yet to do this, you must invariably allow connections to your system from your management station; and most monitoring suites offer little in the way of authentication. Moreover, these suites often have a long history of vulnerabilities. Ironically you could increase your exposure to risks by installing software that helps monitor for risks. As with any other software you install, you should remain vigilant.

Moreover, a carefully deployed and administered monitoring suite will be a 24/7 guardian over your network. It will have a comprehensive view of every server, service, and vital application. It is imperative that any monitoring solution you deploy is very well protected against prying eyes. Employ the principal of least privilege here and allow very few shell accounts to the monitoring station. Access to any web interface should be tightly restricted and require authentication over an encrypted channel from known hosts. There are few better reconnaissance tools than a monitoring suite carefully configured by a conscientious system administrator.

There are several open source monitoring tools that can be deployed on FreeBSD and OpenBSD systems like Big Brother, which is free under certain conditions, Big Sister, and OpenNMS. There are also a variety of tools to monitor both hosts and network devices using SNMP. All of these are contenders in the network monitoring space, but we will be looking closely at one of the most flexible and widely deployed network monitoring packages, Nagios (formerly NetSaint).

Nagios

Nagios is available in FreeBSD's ports tree or from the Nagios web site, available at: *http://www.nagios.org/*. Nagios implements host and service monitoring for systems across a network. The `nagios` daemon runs on a single server and uses various plugins to perform periodic checks.

The plug-ins distributed with Nagios (in the *nagios-plugins* package) are capable of performing local checks, which monitor load average, disk space usage, memory and swap utilization, number of logged in users, and so on. Of course there is more to system monitoring than only examining the monitoring host. Therefore, plug-ins are also included to monitor the availability of network services on remote systems, as long as a TCP or UDP port is open for probing. When problems are noticed, Nagios can be figured to send out notifications in a variety of ways, commonly via email.

Plug-ins for Nagios are constantly updated, and new plug-ins appear on a regular basis, as needed. Given a particular need in your environment, writing your own plug-in is very simple using just about any programming or scripting language you choose. In addition to plug-ins are add-ons. Add-ons extend Nagios' functionality by providing a breadth of functionality too extensive to mention. One of these add-ons is the Nagios Remote Plugin Executor (NRPE). This daemon is configured on client systems with a variety of local checks allowing the monitoring host to check local statistics on remote systems.

Installation

Installation on FreeBSD starts and ends with a **`make install`** from the *net-mgmt/nagios* subdirectory of the ports hierarchy. This installs both Nagios and the *nagios-plugins* collection automatically. It will also create a Nagios user and group for the execution of the daemon. OpenBSD administrators will need to fetch the compressed tarball and install the software in the traditional way per the documentation on the Nagios web site. The rest of this overview will assume that you have either installed Nagios from ports or have installed it manually in compliance with *hier(7)*.

Configuration

Default configuration files for Nagios are installed to */usr/local/etc/nagios*. Many of these configuration files can be left as they are, after the `sample` suffix has been removed. There are three main configuration files to look at when first configuring Nagios. These are the main Nagios configuration file, the CGI configuration file, and the object configuration files.

nagios.cfg

The main Nagios configuration file, *nagios.cfg* by default, controls the way Nagios finds its configuration and subsequently operates. The sample file is well documented, but you should also consult the documentation on the nagios.org web site as you work through this file. There are sets of options in this file worth discussing.

The first is the `check_external_commands` option, which enables the submission of commands through the web interface. If you feel your Nagios web interface is sufficiently protected (for instance, by using digest, Kerberos, or certificate-based authentication over SSL), you may wish to change this value to 1 to enable external commands. This will allow you to schedule service/host downtime, enable and disable various checks and notifications, delay checks, force checks, and issue other commands through the web interface. These web-submitted commands go into the file specified by `command_file`. Only the web server, users should have access to the directory in which this file is stored.

The second set of options are those that point to the object configuration files `cfg_file` and `cfg_dir`. Each can be specified multiple times and may point to specific files or specific directories. When directories are specified, all files ending in *.cfg* within the directory will be processed. Directory specification allows for a little more flexibility and easier delegation of responsibility.

You will want to peruse the rest of the settings in this file, but most will have reasonable defaults.

cgi.cfg

The CGI configuration file, *cgi.cfg* by default, controls the behavior of the Nagios web interface. This includes how Nagios should build URLs within the interface, and which users have access to various aspects of the Nagios system. These users must be authenticated by the web server and gain access by username.

It is possible to both disable authentication and allow commands to be submitted through the web interface by specifying a `default_user_name`. If you do this, make sure your Nagios web interface is protected in some other way so that only trusted administrators can access it.

Object configuration files

The object configuration files are the heart of Nagios's configuration. These files describe the hosts Nagios will monitor, the services to monitor on these hosts, who will be contacted when problems are detected, when checks are performed, and so on. In order to get Nagios operational, your best bet is to look over all the sample configuration files and move them into a configuration subdirectory after you have modified them to suit your environment. Start with the most basic configuration files like *hosts.cfg-sample*, *services.cfg-sample*, *timeperiods.cfg-sample*, and *contacts.cfg-sample*. You will probably be able to simply rename the *checkcommands.cfg-sample* and *miscocmmands.cfg-sample* configuration files until you have a better idea of additional commands you need to run. Start by configuring Nagios to monitor local statistics. When you feel comfortable with the way that works, start monitoring remotely accessible services on other systems. Once this is done, you will be ready to tackle NRPE.

The information here is a cursory overview of Nagios configuration. For detailed explanations of all the available options, make sure to read the sample configuration files thoroughly and peruse the documentation available at *http://www.nagios.org/*.

Installing NRPE

The Nagios Remote Plugin Executor makes local checks on remote systems possible. NRPE is available in the FreeBSD ports tree in *ports/net-mgmt/nrpe2*. OpenBSD administrators must fetch the port from the addons page at nagios.org. Once retrieved make sure you include support for OpenSSL. This may be done on FreeBSD systems by running **`make WITH_SSL=yes`** from the port directory. OpenBSD administrators will need to pass the `--enable-ssl` argument to the configure script.

Ensuring that NRPE is built with OpenSSL support means that all communications between the `check_nrpe` program on the monitoring host and `nrpe` daemon on client systems will be encrypted. Remember that this is just encryption, not authentication.

Beware of enabling command-line arguments for nrpe. Traditionally, nrpe is configured on client systems with a known set of named commands. The paths to these commands and associated arguments are hard coded on the client systems. Enabling command-line arguments allows the check_nrpe plug-in to not only tell client systems to run a particular check, but also provides the specific command-line arguments. While this allows you to manage your configuration of client checks from the Nagios monitoring host, it has a variety of unpleasant security ramifications. If you have developed a means to securely distribute configuration files as described earlier in this chapter, managing nrpe configuration centrally should be trivial.

On the Nagios monitoring host, once the NRPE package has been compiled, the check_nrpe binary must be copied into */usr/local/libexec/nagios* with the rest of the Nagios plug-ins. On all client systems, copy the nrpe binary to */usr/local/sbin* instead.

Configuring Nagios with NRPE

On the monitoring host, you will need to tell Nagios to use NRPE to run local checks on remote systems. To do this, add the following check_nrpe command to your *checkcommands.cfg* file as follows.

```
define command {
  command_name    check_nrpe
  command_line    /usr/local/libexec/nagios/check_nrpe -H $HOSTADDRESS$ -c $ARG1$
}
```

You will then need to add commands to one of your configuration files or create a new configuration file on the monitoring host that specifies which NRPE checks should be run on which remote systems. This procedure is fully documented in the *README* distributed with NRPE. No other configuration is required on the monitoring host.

NRPE on client systems may then be configured to run out of inetd(8) (or xinetd) to make use of tcpwrappers support and rate limiting. Alternately it may be run directly as a service using the startup script provided in the port. nrpe can be configured with a list of IP addresses from which to accept commands directly.

On all client systems, you will need to install the *nagios-plugins* port and configure NRPE by creating an *nrpe.cfg* configuration file usually located in */usr/local/etc*. This file should contain a list of local commands whose output the nrpe daemon will send back to the Nagios process on the monitoring host.

Fine-tuning

A complete description of configuring Nagios for the variety of environments out there would consume far more pages than we are able to spare, but rest assured, documentation exists. As a newcomer to Nagios, do not expect to get the system operational in a day, or even a few days. With the extensive documentation on the Nagios web site, the FAQ, the forums, and the mailing lists, however, you will not be short on help.

Wrapping up

With Nagios and `nrpe` operational, you have a 24/7 observer of all the systems under your jurisdiction. Configure your thresholds appropriately and you will become immediately aware when unusual activity is detected. For instance, on an `ftp` download-only server, it may be especially important to detect even a small increase in disk usage. This might indicate that the system is misconfigured and allowing people to add content. Watching the number of `smtpd` processes on a mail relay may provide an early warning allowing you to investigate before the system goes down.

What to watch, and what thresholds to set, are questions you will have to answer for yourself. After you have Nagios set up, configure it to warn you earlier rather than later when it detects a problem. If you find that your thresholds are set too low, you can always raise them. Your goal is to know as soon as something unusual is happening on your system, but you don't want to be badgered by useless alerts.

Wrapping Up

Building and maintaining a secure server is a nontrivial and never-ending task for the system administrator. Starting with a carefully built system, it is important to control who has access and what users and administrators can do. Keeping up to date with security and reliability fixes to the operating system and installed software requires that you stay informed and prepared. Finally, keeping tabs on how your systems are running will give you insight into whether any of them might be misbehaving. Following the guidelines set forth in this chapter will help you build a more easily maintained and secure systems infrastructure.

Resources

A list of resources follows.

Operating System

- *BSD Hacks*, Dru Lavigne (O'Reilly), 2004
- FreeBSD release engineering: *http://www.freebsd.org/releng/*
- FreeBSD mailing lists: *http://www.freebsd.org/support.html#mailing-list*
- OpenBSD flavors: *http://www.openbsd.org/faq/faq5.html#Flavors*
- OpenBSD mailing lists: *http://www.openbsd.org/mail.html*
- *Unix Backup and Recovery*, W. Curtis Preston (O'Reilly), 1999

System Monitoring

- Big Brother: *http://www.bb4.com/*
- Big Sister: *http://bigsister.graeff.com/*
- Nagios: *http://www.nagios.org/*
- OpenNMS: *http://www.opennms.com/*

General Security

- *Incident Response*, Richard Forno and Kenneth R. van Wyk (O'Reilly), 2001
- SecurityFocus: *http://www.securityfocus.com/*
- *SSH, The Secure Shell: The Definitive Guide*, Daniel J. Barrett and Richard Silverman (O'Reilly), 2001
- Topics in Cryptography: *http://www.wikipedia.org/wiki/Topics_in_cryptography*

PART II

Deployment Situations

Every server has a specific purpose in life, and FreeBSD and OpenBSD systems are ideal candidates for handling critical infrastructure services like DNS servers, firewalls, mail gateways, and web servers. Part II covers these deployments and how you can leverage specific BSD features to improve the security posture of the services you provide. We don't tell you everything about deploying the specific service, however; just the extra options and special circumstances where you can take advantage of OpenBSD or FreeBSD. The goal of this section is to offer guidelines for securely deploying the software that will run critical services in your network.

With each of these critical network services, we take time to explain the kinds of risks you face, the sorts of attacks you might need to repel, and why you and your organization care about running the service securely. When we talk about installing and configuring software, though, we refer back to the general techniques and building blocks that we laid out in Part I. You'll want to be at least passingly familiar with the techniques, because we combine them in interesting and sometimes subtle ways.

- Chapter 5, *Creating a Secure DNS Server*
- Chapter 6, *Building Secure Mail Servers*
- Chapter 7, *Building a Secure Web Server*
- Chapter 8, *Firewalls*
- Chapter 9, *Intrusion Detection*

CHAPTER 5

Creating a Secure DNS Server

A good name is better than fine perfume.
—Ecclesiastes 7:1, Holy Bible,
New International Version

The Domain Name Service (DNS) is a critical service underpinning the entire Internet. Every nontrivial network has at least one DNS server. In the simplest case, a small organization may simply have a caching server that helps aggregate queries to the outside and answer queries about internal-only systems. Larger organizations operate many servers to handle higher demand for name resolution. DNS is at the heart of email communications, web communications, and SSL/TLS trust. We can't overstate its importance.

Yet, despite its central role in all Internet communications, DNS is surprisingly insecure. As a protocol, it was designed in the good old days of the Internet when servers trusted each other and malicious packets were few and far between. There are significant weaknesses in the protocol, and there have been significant problems with the programs that use the protocol.

In this chapter, we describe the security implications related to operating DNS servers. We outline some of the risks your organization faces related to DNS, and some of the ways to mitigate those risks. We focus on the two most common DNS servers for FreeBSD and OpenBSD: the Berkeley Internet Name Daemon (BIND) and Daniel J. Bernstein's DNS server (djbdns). We will compare and contrast the security postures of the two servers and how they approach the various risks related to DNS.

Having discussed the risks and mitigations, we will describe specific installation scenarios. We will describe how to get it isolated in a sandbox and how to lock down the machine tightly to avoid compromise of the DNS service. Lastly, we will cover routine maintenance procedures and how they can be accomplished securely.

We will also discuss a few of the pros and cons about choosing which server software to run, but ultimately, the decision is yours. Our goal is to help you get it installed and running securely.

The Criticality of DNS

The correct operation of DNS is vital to any Internet network. We rely on it to translate human-readable names into IP addresses both to organize our computers and to make them easier to work with. Of course, DNS is involved in the reverse process, too: mapping IP addresses to names. DNS plays a vital role in a variety of other Internet services. DNS records enable or help prevent several kinds of man-in-the-middle attacks. DNS records are often used to help distribute Internet traffic between different geographical sites. With the increasing use of IPv6, DNS can be invoked to help distribute public keys in an asymmetric cryptography system.

Your organization probably relies on DNS in a variety of ways. If you have any online presence, then DNS enables your visitors to resolve DNS names to your servers' IP addresses. More importantly, the mapping of names and IP addresses in DNS is critical to your customers' trust of the SSL certificate and connection that you offer them. Your company's email is routed via DNS records. Most modern companies rely heavily on email, and their successful use of email depends absolutely on the correct functioning of DNS. Thus, reliable and accurate DNS records are vital for keeping Internet communications open between your organization and others.

Technical Risks Related to DNS

There are a few ways in which DNS can be attacked that relate directly to the software you run or the data in your DNS zones. Sometimes the absence of data, or the presence of a typo, can create a significant opportunity for mischief.

Vulnerabilities in DNS software

Of the two software packages discussed in this chapter, BIND has had the worse track record; numerous and significant vulnerabilities have been found in it over the years. Some have granted root access to remote attackers. With certain versions and certain configurations, the `named(8)` process could inadvertently execute rogue code on the DNS server. Once any kind of rogue code can be executed, it is often possible to invoke a shell on the system. Once a shell can be executed, an attacker can usually escape a chroot environment with only a little more time and effort.

Zone misconfigurations

Zone misconfiguration problems are possible with both BIND and djbdns because they are problems in the zone data itself, not with the DNS server software.

One reasonably common problem in the DNS world is called a "lame" delegation. In this case, your zone file lists the IP addresses of DNS servers that supposedly serve your domain. However, one or more of the listed IP addresses is not serving your domain. Perhaps it is not running any DNS software at all, or the host is down or unreachable, or perhaps the IP address is mistyped. Most frequently the server is your slave server, but someone forgot to give it the zone information. In any case, the situation has two different impacts on your organization: it creates slightly slower performance on domain lookups, and it opens the opportunity for hijacking of your domain. If you list two domain servers in your zone and one of them is lame, then half the time people will try the lame IP address first. They wait for a response, often up to 30 seconds depending on their particular system and its settings. Eventually they give up and try the other nameserver, which works.

The other problem with lame delegations stems from the fact that every IP address belongs to someone. If you accidentally mistype an address in the zone file, then the person who controls that IP address can set up a DNS server that claims to serve your domains. Suddenly your customers might end up browsing a competitor's site, or your employees might end up connecting to a hacker's machine instead of your VPN gateway.

Missing zone information

Like bad zone data, missing zone data can create problems. The effects are the same with BIND or djbdns. There are a small variety of attacks that can be launched because of missing zone data.

In DNS terminology, "forward" zones are those that map a name to an IP address. The corresponding "reverse" zones map IP addresses to names. In order to be standards compliant and to resist some kinds of attacks, every machine that has a DNS entry should have both a forward and a reverse map. That is, if www.example.com is 12.34.56.78, then there should be an entry in the `56.34.12.in-addr.arpa` zone that maps 78 to www.example.com.

Matching forward and reverse records serves as a confidence indicator on the Internet. They imply that the IP address and name are under the same administrative control. Internet hosts tend to be suspicious of a server that does not have matching forward and reverse records in DNS. Some mail servers will refuse to take mail from a system that has no reverse record. All modern web browsers will warn their user if the browser makes an SSL/TLS connection to a web server that does not have matching reverse records. If you want to avoid casting doubts in the minds of your users, you should make sure that any secure web server has matching A and PTR records. This is true even for an intranet web server.

Risks Related to DNS and Mail

MX records in DNS are vital to today's email-dependent businesses. They determine where email for a given domain name goes. Typically, you have at least one MX record for your domain. Ideally, you have additional MX records for all the hosts in your externally published domains as well. To be safest, you have multiple MX records for all your hosts. Multiple MX records allow for fastest recovery when your primary mail server is unavailable.

When a standards-compliant mail transfer agent (MTA) wants to determine the correct mail server for a domain, it uses DNS. Consider the fragment of a BIND zone file shown in Example 5-1.

Example 5-1. MX records in a BIND zone file

```
$ORIGIN example.com.
$TTL            86400
example.com.
                A       12.34.56.78
                MX      10 mail-a.example.com.
                MX      20 mail-b.example.com.
www             A       12.34.56.78
                MX      10 mail-a.example.com.
                MX      20 mail-b.example.com.
mail-a          A       12.34.56.79
                MX      10 mail-a.example.com.
                MX      20 mail-b.example.com.
mail-b          A       12.34.56.80
                MX      10 mail-a.example.com.
                MX      20 mail-b.example.com.
```

In this example, an MTA trying deliver mail to an address ending in `@example.com` will try to connect to the server named `mail-a.example.com`, whose IP address is 12.34.56.79. If that server does not respond for some reason, the sending MTA will try `mail-b.example.com`. If the first server does respond, but rejects the email for some reason (e.g., an invalid destination address), the sending MTA does not try the other server.

Notice the additional numbers on the MX lines. They indicate a relative priority between the different possible mail servers. The lower the number (with zero being the lowest valid number), the higher the priority. That is, the lowest numbered server is tried first. Servers with equal numbers are tried in random order.

There are two security considerations involving MX records in DNS: all the records must match, and you should consider where your email might go.

Make sure that all your MX records, and their corresponding A and PTR records all match up. In an effort to crack down on unsolicited, bulk email ("spam"), some mail servers will categorically reject email from your mail server if all its DNS records do not match. Lost or significantly delayed email can be very costly or disruptive to your organization, or perhaps to another organization that is closely related to you.

As a redundancy measure, some businesses have backup mail servers. Because they are listed in your DNS zones, they receive your email when your primary server does not respond. Backup mail servers are most effective if they are on different networks and in different data centers than your primary server. If both the primary and backup are in the same data center, with the same connectivity to the Internet, then the Internet connectivity and the data center are single points of failure for email. If the one link to the Internet goes down or if the data center loses power, for example, both primary and backup mail servers become unavailable.

Backup mail service can create risks, however. Many small and medium-sized businesses cannot afford to operate mail servers in geographically distributed data centers. They often arrange for their Internet provider or another ISP to be their backup mail server. If the ISP that serves as a backup is less well protected than the organization's primary mail server, an attacker can try to compromise the backup mail server instead.

Given that DNS records of backup mail servers are public, the attacker can spend time analyzing your IP addresses and the backup mail server's susceptibility without ever probing your primary data center. It is absolutely critical, therefore, to consider how well protected any backup mail servers are when setting up your MX records in DNS.

Risks Related to DNS Attacks

Your DNS can be attacked by attacking the servers directly, by attacking servers you trust, or by attacking the domain registration, which seeds DNS. Each of these attacks can be mitigated or at least resisted through the best practices we describe in "Responding to DNS-Based Risks."

Cache poisoning

Cache poisoning is a DNS attack that was more popular a few years ago than it is today. Attackers maliciously configured DNS servers to send incorrect, superfluous records when responding to legitimate queries. This extra data is sent in the "additional" section of the DNS response. The additional section of a response is often used as a convenience for the server to provide relevant information that was not specifically requested but is related to the original query. For example, if I ask the authoritative example.com server for its MX record, it will send me the MX record. It will probably also put the A record (the IP address) of the mail server in the additional section, if the mail server is in the example.com domain.

The surprising thing is that older versions of BIND would store additional information as if it was authoritative. It did not matter that the bogus information did not come from the right server. The next time someone would query that BIND server (again, your organization's caching server), it would use the bogus data as if it were authoritative.

While this attack is no longer a major threat (it has been solved in BIND for years and was never a problem for djbdns), it highlights two important concerns. First, it demonstrates the value of running a secure DNS resolver for your organization.

Second, it shows how the utter lack of authentication between DNS servers creates a variety of trust problems that are hard to solve.

DNS spoofing

Some DNS abuse is possible because DNS uses User Datagram Protocol (UDP) datagrams for most messages. Simple UDP messages carry no authenticating information other than the IP address of the sender—which can easily be forged. Despite the fact that both BIND and djbdns guard against cache poisoning now, spoofing is harder to protect against. DNS needs to use UDP for a variety of reasons, efficiency being the most obvious. An unavoidable consequence of using UDP, however, is that spoofing is quite easy unless the DNS protocol itself adds authenticating information.

If any system on the Internet can monitor traffic between your caching server and the Internet, it can attempt to launch a spoofing attack against your users. It waits for a request for something like www.yahoo.com to be transmitted from your site to the Internet. Then it injects a response that looks legitimate. If the attacker knows in advance a certain set of sites (such as Yahoo!) that he will be attacking, he will craft his forged responses so that they even appear to originate from the correct IP addresses (i.e., yahoo.com's nameservers). Just like in the cache poisoning attack, the attacker has now inserted records into your server's cache. Your DNS server now believes his spoofed packet simply because it answered the question that was asked.

Monitoring a WAN line for such traffic, crafting the correct response on the fly, and injecting that response at the right time is tricky, but not impossible. There is a proof-of-concept program called the "Denver Project" (*http://www.ilionsecurity.ch*) that implements a simple LAN-based DNS spoofing tool.

Registration hijacking

There are a variety of ways that you can lose control of your domain altogether by losing control of its registration. Your domain expires from the Internet registry unless someone pays the renewal fees when they are due. There are professional scam artists who snap up lapsed domains and register them. They often demand high ransoms to return ownership. Although U.S. trademark law can help fight them off, the courts are slow and your organization can completely lose the use of your domain while the hijacking is sorted out in the courts.

Some attackers have successfully forged registration transfer agreements that convinced registrars to change ownership of domains. They forge documents, email messages, or whatever is necessary to persuade the registrar that they now control the domain. Then, they can control the NS records that appear in the root top-level domain (TLD) servers (e.g., the `.com`, `.org`, or `.net` nameservers). Suddenly the nameservers that serve your domain are not your nameservers, but are someone else's. Using an attack like this, an attacker can route all web traffic through transparent proxies at his site, or route all email through his own proxy mail server. He can monitor Internet communications by causing DNS lookups to resolve to his IP addresses instead of yours. Then he sets up proxy services that actually look up (using your nameservers) and connect to the correct real servers. Carefully done, this attack can proceed for a long time with few symptoms.

It is critical that you use a trustworthy domain registrar and that you stay up to date on all domain registration requirements. An occasional check with the registrar's web site is a good idea as well, to make sure nothing has unexpectedly changed. Be sure to treat the access codes (user ID, password) to the registrar's web site as confidential, as you would any other administrative password.

Responding to DNS-Based Risks

There are many different "best practices" that address various security concerns. They do not necessarily improve efficiency, maintainability, or manageability of your nameservers. They are worthwhile if you suspect your organization is exposed to some of the risks above. It is not usually a good methodology to simply invoke every possible security feature just because it exists. You should consider the threats that your organization faces, and which DNS features you use, and then apply the mitigations recommended below that make sense.

Depending on whether you use BIND or djbdns, you have different options for best practices. With djbdns you often get fewer choices with respect to security posture. The authors have chosen a specific stance on a particular risk, and that is the stance all djbdns users are forced to take. The default djbdns configuration will create a secure system that needs little or no tweaking. BIND, on the other hand, offers myriad security options. Virtually all BIND installations make use of several options to improve on the default security posture of a BIND configuration.

Limit recursion

A recursive query happens when a server looks up the answer to a client's query on the client's behalf. A client asks the server for a name that the server does not know and indicates that it would like the server to search for the answer if necessary. The server performs the various tasks of consulting the root domain servers, global top-level domain servers, or other servers as necessary to fulfill the client's request. If you run an externally facing DNS server whose only purpose is to answer authoritatively for your domain, it should not answer recursive queries. They consume unnecessary resources in CPU and bandwidth. More importantly, BIND has had several widely publicized bugs in its recursion algorithms, some of which completely compromised the server. This is a case where it is prudent to turn off a feature of BIND if you are not making use of it.

As with other BIND bugs, djbdns does not suffer this problem. Its authoritative server (`tinydns`) and its recursive server (`dnscache`) are different processes that usually run in different sandboxes, if not on different physical servers. It is hard to have unnecessary recursion on an authoritative djbdns server.

Limit zone transfers

There is no legitimate reason for anyone outside your organization to transfer your zones in bulk. A zone transfer request asks your DNS server to send all the zone information: hostnames, mail server records, nameserver records, etc. Although all this information is publicly available through your DNS server, there is no reason to make an attacker's life easier. Restricting zone transfers makes hackers' lives just a little harder and has absolutely no detrimental impact on legitimate use of DNS.

In BIND's *named.conf* file, you can create sets of trusted hosts who are allowed to transfer your zones, and then refer to that set of hosts later in each zone's configuration block. Example 5-2 shows an access control list (ACL) of two hosts that are allowed to transfer the zones in bulk.

Example 5-2. Restricting zone transfers with IP addresses in BIND

```
acl trusted-servers  {
        12.34.56.78;  // our name server
        23.45.67.89;  // our ISP
};
zone example.com  {
        type master;
        file "zones/example.com";
        allow-transfer { trusted-servers; };
};
```

Note that cryptography is far more difficult to spoof than IP addresses. To be even more careful about who can transfer zones, you can use transaction signatures (TSIG) to authorize zone transfers. (See "Transaction Signatures (TSIG)" for more information.)

Unauthorized zone transfers are primarily a BIND concern. If you use djbdns, you have to go to a lot of effort to enable even authorized zone transfers. The recommended way to synchronize zones in djbdns is to use `rsync(8)` and `ssh(1)` to copy the zone data from the master to the slaves. Clearly you will only enable such access between systems that you trust. It is highly unlikely that a host will be able to inadvertently download your zone information through `rsync` and `ssh`.

Maintain your own zones

One of the reasons that forward and reverse records often fail to match is because they are owned and distributed by different entities. You own your domain name (the forward mapping), but someone else owns the reverse map. Often that someone else is your upstream connectivity provider, but it may be ARIN, RIPE, or a carrier upstream from your immediate ISP. If your organization changes names frequently, or if you have many different public IP addresses to manage, you may find your upstream provider unwilling to make changes in the reverse maps as often as you would like. There is an elegant solution to this, but it may be too subtle for your upstream provider. They can delegate the name service responsibility for your chunk of addresses to your server. Consider Example 5-1, in BIND syntax, showing a chunk of our fictitious 12.34.56.X zone. Let's assume that our company `example.com` has been granted the IP addresses 12.34.56.72 through 12.34.56.80. The zone file in Example 5-3 shows how our upstream DNS provider can delegate the reverse PTR records to us for our IP addresses while maintaining direct control of the reverse records for other IP addresses.

Example 5-3. in-addr.arpa zone with delegations

```
$ORIGIN 56.34.12.in-addr.arpa.
$TTL 86400          ; 1 day.
...
70                  PTR         mail.othercustomer.com.
71                  PTR         www.othercustomer.com.
72                  CNAME       72.example-com.56.34.12.in-addr.arpa.
73                  CNAME       73.example-com.56.34.12.in-addr.arpa.
...
81                  PTR         mail.somebody.com.
...
example-com         NS          ns1.example.com.
                    NS          ns2.example.com.
```

In this situation, a client looking for the PTR record for `72.56.34.12.in-addr.arpa`, will not find it here. Instead, it finds CNAME records that point to a subdomain of `56.34.12.in-addr.arpa`. This subdomain, named `example-com` to help an administrator remember who it serves, is then delegated to the `example.com` nameservers. The client then queries the nameservers, either `ns1.example.com` or `ns2.example.com`, and finds the correct information from them. This technique is recommended and explained more fully in Chapter 6.5 of the *DNS and Bind Cookbook*, which is listed in the "Resources" section at the end of the chapter.

If you can get your upstream ISP to delegate the reverse records, then you gain a valuable measure of autonomy. You can update the reverse records as you need to without the intervention of your ISP. There are many advantages to such a situation. If a sudden problem causes you to switch to a backup data center where the IP addresses were different, you would want to be able to update the reverse records on your SSL-enabled web servers. Otherwise, visitors to your backup web servers would receive warnings about your SSL certificates. Likewise, when you bring new systems online with public IP addresses, or decommission old systems, you can trivially set the reverse records to be correct without having to interact with your upstream ISP.

ISPs may be reluctant to delegate the reverse records to you, however. You could use the reverse record to advertise your IP address as `www.yahoo.com` or some other domain that you don't own.

Run secure, organization-wide recursion servers

For resolution of domains other than your own, you should run all queries through one or more servers that perform recursive queries on behalf of internal workstations. They will live in your DMZ, and will need to talk to both internal and external hosts. This arrangement offers two kinds of security: it protects individual client systems inside your organization, and it limits the potential damage from malicious DNS attacks. This arrangement is depicted in Figure 5-1.

Centralized recursive queries allow the IT staff to direct all DNS traffic through just the authorized recursive, caching servers. This means that the firewall can prevent all DNS traffic flowing into or out of the organization, except for that going to the caching servers. Some Trojan programs use bogus DNS requests as a covert channel back to a controlling server. They install and lay dormant until the control system gives them a command. They send malformed DNS queries to their command server and receive responses that indicate what to do (such as participate in a DDoS attack). If DNS must pass through a central query server, then such covert back-channels are prevented or hindered.

Centralizing recursion usually means that queries will be faster because records will frequently be cached. Additionally, if there are recursion or cache-poisoning bugs in the resolvers of your internal workstations, those bugs will not be exploitable by an outside attacker. You have more time to get an effective patch tested and deployed because the buggy DNS functionality is not directly exposed.

Separate caches from authoritative servers

Even if you use BIND, which can run both caches and authoritative servers in the same process, you should separate them. It is not necessary to separate them onto different physical machines, however.

If you are using FreeBSD and want to keep both processes on the same system, you can run them in separate jails, each with its own IP address. Likewise, on OpenBSD, two processes can be run in different chroot environments, and each can be assigned a different IP address.

This separation of duties is a fundamental security principle. In this case, you are protecting your authoritative server from cache-oriented attacks. If an attacker sends a flood of queries or a series of poisoned responses to your cache server, you do not want them to affect your authoritative server.

Summary

You may have noticed a trend among the various security vulnerabilities and problems we cited above. Many problems exist with BIND that simply do not exist with djbdns. This is not surprising, however, since djbdns was written to solve them. Though djbdns explicitly addresses many of BIND's problems, it does not offer many of the usability features that BIND offers. Usability and security often find themselves at opposite ends of a functionality axis. BIND has chosen one point on the axis, and djbdns has chosen another. Deciding which one addresses the needs of your environment will be up to you.

DNS Software

BIND and djbdns are not the only two software packages that perform DNS services. In the context of FreeBSD and OpenBSD, however, they are the only realistic choices for production-quality, stable DNS services. They are independently developed systems that operate very differently, but ultimately achieve the same goal.

BIND 9

The first versions of BIND were originally written at the University of California at Berkeley many years ago. The Internet Software Consortium (*http://www.isc.org/*) maintains it now. In recent years, the ISC set aside the entire Version 8 code base and rewrote the software from scratch. The Version 9 rewrite is cleaner, more consistent, and is the reference implementation for the official DNS standards published by the IETF. Some early adopters of BIND 9 were left with an unpleasant taste in their mouths because the early versions were lacking many key features that were commonly used in BIND 8. You may find mailing list messages and web pages disparaging BIND 9 for various reasons. Be sure to consider the age of the documents before believing them completely. Features are now complete that were gradually phased in, and many issues have been corrected.

BIND is all things DNS rolled into one large, complex program. Everything mentioned in every official DNS standard is implemented—completely or incompletely—somewhere in BIND. It acts as master, slave, server, and client all at various times. Depending on what you want your nameserver to do, this can be a convenience, or a needless amalgamation of features.

BIND implements a number of security standards including TSIG and DNSSEC. It adds a remote management API with *rndc*. It also adds a few automation features such as dynamic DNS, *NOTIFY* messages, and incremental zone transfers. Several of these features will factor into our discussion of secure DNS operations.

djbdns

Daniel J. Bernstein wrote djbdns in reaction to BIND's overwhelming complexity, size, and history of problems. BIND's complexity can be daunting and error-prone and its security track record is spotty. Additionally, BIND uses a lot of memory in normal operations. The extant versions of BIND when Bernstein was first writing djbdns had a variety of well-known and significant vulnerabilities. Even since djbdns was written, significant vulnerabilities have been discovered in BIND—including in BIND 9.

Instead of being a monolithic super-server, djbdns is actually a series of small, specialized programs—in the best Unix tradition. Each program handles a very specific set of responsibilities according to a small, well-defined set of rules. Furthermore, each program can be used as a logical unit for encapsulation. Each one can be chrooted or jailed. Each can run as a different user or run on a different server.

Security is the first and foremost priority of djbdns. The code's simplicity, separation of duties, and small size are intentional efforts to keep the system focused and secure. Bernstein even offers a $500 bounty to the first person who identifies a verifiable security flaw in djbdns. This is an interesting gesture; however, being the first to document a hole in djbdns after so many years of operation is probably far more compelling than $500 in 2005. The fact remains that there are no documented djbdns-specific flaws. There has never been a bug so egregious as a root-level compromise through a buffer overflow.

Documentation and usability are low on the priority list for djbdns. The documentation is spotty and very task oriented. That is, if you want to know how to do a specific task, there will be one suggestion on a web page somewhere that merely lists the command to run. The meaning behind the command and the internal workings are left undescribed. There are practically no comments in the source code, either.

Typical Architecture

In order to discuss DNS we need to establish a vocabulary of the systems and services that are involved. Figure 5-1 shows a typical DNS installation for a small to mid-sized organization.

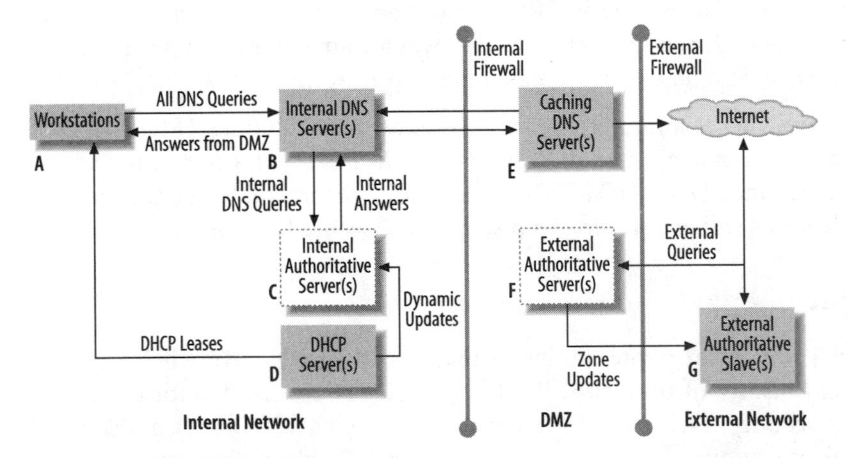

Figure 5-1. An example DNS configuration

- The caching DNS server (E) in the DMZ performs recursive queries, but only for queries that originate from the internal network.
- Inside the organization, all workstations (A) are set to query a single internal DNS server or set of servers (B). Those servers are the only hosts whose DNS queries are allowed to leave the internal network. They forward all queries to the caching DNS server (E) to have them serviced.
- There is an authoritative internal server (C) that is authoritative for internal host names and IP addresses. Depending on the software configuration, it might be the same system as (B).
- The internal DHCP server (D) might send updates to the authoritative internal server (C) every time a new lease is given out. For simplicity's sake, this DHCP server sometimes runs on the same system as C, though it does not have to.
- In the DMZ there is an authoritative server (F) that serves domain information for the organization. Typically, for robustness, there is some other server (G) at a different geographical location that acts as a slave to F and answers authoritatively for your zones. These servers are the means by which the rest of the world queries your zone information. Some organizations configure BIND so that E and F are the same server.

In an organization running djbdns, (B) and (C) must be different IP addresses. They might be two different jails on the same system, two different chroot environments, or two whole physically different machines. Likewise (E) and (F) must be on separate IP addresses. Regardless of how many physical systems there are, there are four distinct configurations to manage.

BIND Versus djbdns

There are many comparisons of the two programs on the Internet and in print. Be forewarned, however, that the opinions on both sides are strong and forcefully presented. We try to present only comparisons that are relevant in a security context, and we try to present them in an impartial way. Table 5-1 compares important functionality and how it is accomplished in djbdns and BIND.

Table 5-1. Functionality in BIND and djbdns

	BIND	djbdns
Authoritative server for zones	Built-in to named	`tinydns`
Caching nameserver	Built-in to named	`dnscache`
Zone transfers	Built-in to named	Manually configured `rsync` and ssh scripts
Remote management	`rndc`	Not possible
Dynamic update	`nsupdate`	Not possible

Table 5-1. Functionality in BIND and djbdns (continued)

	BIND	djbdns
Adding new data to zones	Manually edit zone files or nsupdate	add-* scripts or manually edit data file
Sanity checking of zone data	named-checkzone	add-* scripts
Memory usage	Usually high limited ability to tune it	Usually low easily tuned
Cryptographically signed records	TSIG built-in to named	Not possible
Integration with Microsoft Windows	Dynamic updates	Not possible

One process or many?

No matter what role your nameserver will play, BIND will always use the same configuration file. You will have to add configuration directives to enable or disable certain functionality to suit your particular application. BIND will always cache and it will always try to load zone information into RAM. This can cause resource constraints, especially if you are using a small system. On the other hand, hardware is cheap and FreeBSD and OpenBSD are also free. A few hundred dollars can obviate any RAM issues.

Compare this monolithic BIND process with the one or two processes that you run with djbdns. The simpler your needs, the fewer processes you will run, and the smaller they will be. If you need a complex system, however, you will find that you need multiple IP addresses and/or multiple systems to accomplish all the different tasks. If you plan to run all your DNS services (zone transfers, authoritative query responder, caching server) on a single system, djbdns will add some non-DNS complexity to your server. To help offset the additional complexity, Bernstein provides a set of tools, separate from djbdns, that manage the chroot requirements automatically.

Zone maintenance

With djbdns, you get a set of utility programs that do basic maintenance for you. They even check for some common errors. There are some uncommon configurations that are not easily supported by these scripts. There are also a few record types (e.g., DNAME) that djbdns does not support at all, even though they are defined in RFCs. Most sites either do not use these records, or can probably live without them.

In BIND, the zones are updated by hand by editing text files. In the past, the file format was not very robust and BIND was not helpful in diagnosing accidental mistakes. It was very easy, for example, to accidentally set your MX record to be *mail.example.com.example.com* by leaving out an important period on the MX line. Such errors are still easy to make in BIND zone files, but BIND 9 made the syntax far more strict and regular than BIND 8. This allows it to flag more errors than BIND 8 did. It also includes tools to check configuration files (named-checkconf) and to check zone files (named-checkzone).

Dynamic updates

BIND offers dynamic updates, a feature that djbdns does not implement. They allow you to send DNS records over the network that modify a zone as it runs. These updates are received by the `named` process and cause it to add, delete, or modify records. Once the update is processed, BIND updates the serial number automatically.

One common and very useful application of dynamic updates is the integration between the ISC's DHCP server and BIND. When the DHCP software issues a lease for an IP address, it can update the forward and reverse DNS maps in BIND automatically using dynamic DNS. When a lease is granted, the DNS zones get the new forward and reverse records. If a lease expires and is not renewed, the zones are updated with deletions of the corresponding records.

There is a dark side to dynamic updates. As Yoda said in *The Empire Strikes Back*: "Once you start down that path, forever will it dominate your destiny." To use dynamic updates, you essentially relinquish all manual control over the zone files. BIND takes over. You will no longer be able, for instance, to follow the convention of using the date for the zone serial number (e.g., 2004081600 for the first update on August 16, 2004). Each new update will increment the serial number by one. You cannot edit the zone file manually anymore. The next time BIND makes an automatic change, it will clobber any manual changes you might have made and it will completely rewrite the zone file. Lastly, BIND keeps a journal file for every dynamically updated zone. These journal files are binary and essentially unreadable. They record the changes from one serial number to the next, so that BIND can send the proper differences from any prior serial number to the current data. These files can be problematic, especially in active zones like those that are regularly updated by a DHCP server. The journal files grow without bound and are never truncated by normal BIND operations. To truncate them safely, you must stop the server gracefully, remove the journal files (not the zone files!), and restart the server.

If you want to integrate with a Microsoft Windows Active Directory environment, you can, using dynamic updates in the way that BIND implements them. It is possible to service all your DNS through BIND, even the dynamic updates that recent versions of Windows want to issue. Even though Windows Advanced Server 2003 and similar server products offer DNS services, there is no need to run multiple DNS servers on different platforms and architectures.

Incremental zone transfers and notify

When a zone has been changed, either manually or through a dynamic update, BIND can send *NOTIFY* messages to all the necessary name servers for that zone. If the other servers are also BIND servers, they can respond by sending zone transfer requests. This allows servers to receive updates as soon as they happen, without waiting for a TTL to expire and without any manual intervention by the administrator (other than making the change to the zone).

Incremental zone transfer (*IXFR*) requests, as opposed to zone transfer (*AXFR*) requests, are also unique to BIND. They allow a slave server to send the serial number of the zone information it currently has so that the master server will send only the changes to the zone that have happened since that serial number. If the difference is too large to fit in a single UDP datagram, the two servers negotiate a TCP connection to transfer the data.

Remote control

BIND additionally has the ability to perform various operations in response to commands received over the network. It can drop zones, reload zones, and create zones, among other things. There are definitely security implications to enabling this feature. It allows, however, for a separation of privileges whereby a junior administrator could be charged with managing routine zone data on a server where she does not normally have any sort of login access.

In order to manage djbdns, she would have to have permissions to log in on the DNS server, and run some commands as root, perhaps through a mechanism such as `sudo`. This is not to imply that it is impossible to arrange the same zone management structure in a djbdns system. The difference that we are pointing out is that, as with many things in djbdns, you are given some good tools, some sparse documentation, and then you are left to roll your own updating mechanism. With BIND, you get integrated support for this kind of remote maintenance—whether you want it or not.

Summary

Perhaps the most relevant way to summarize the differences between BIND and djbdns is to look at how they most affect your workload as the system administrator. BIND gives you many features, whether you need them or not. In order to use many of the features safely, you must configure cryptography support in BIND and understand how to create security keys. It is relatively easy—with nothing more than BIND and its accompanying tools—to set up a server, enable secure, automatic updating with another server, and remotely manage it. You must remain vigilant with BIND, however, given its history of vulnerabilities. There are many more resources, books, and web sites that give documentation and hints about how to run BIND than there are giving hints about djbdns.

With djbdns, you are likely to be able to sleep more easily in terms of security. There are no known vulnerabilities. Despite the fact that it implements less DNS functionality than BIND, you will probably only use a small subset of its features. The biggest drawback is that maintenance is all manual and must be automated by you, the administrator. Documentation is scarce, too. BIND is so large that it can hardly help but to contain vulnerabilities. On the other hand, djbdns is so small that it shifts a significant amount of the security burden to you. Djbdns leaves it up to you to implement secure replication, secure remote management, and to set up all the different servers on different systems or IP addresses. There are documents and example configurations to start from, but they must be customized to fit your environment, and you have to know what to customize. There is plenty of room for you to make mistakes in these ancillary tasks; you must be careful not to create non-DNS vulnerabilities on your servers.

Proponents of djbdns argue that the dynamic updates, *NOTIFY*, and *IXFR* features are either buggy, unnecessary, or less efficient than existing alternatives. There definitely were bugs in early versions of dynamic updates. They have improved to production quality now. Many companies rely on them. The djbdns alternative to *NOTIFY* and *IXFR* is to use a program like `rsync` (*http://rsync.samba.org/*) over a secure channel established through `ssh`. The cryptography is certainly strong, and it handles very large files efficiently. Of course, there have been errors in both `rsync` and OpenSSH over the years, too. Nothing is bulletproof.

We think that hardening BIND 9 is probably the best first step if you are making the transition from experienced administrator to experienced, security-minded administrator. If you look at the documentation for djbdns and you think "I can handle that," then you will probably be more secure for choosing djbdns. Remember, however, that security is measured relative to the hostility that you face; and no increased security posture comes for free.

Installing BIND

If you use OpenBSD 3.5, BIND 9.2.3 is included in the standard *base35.tgz* file, which is the best way to manage it. If you keep your system up to date with patches (as described in Chapter 4), then you can probably keep BIND 9 up to date with the rest of the operating system. The OpenBSD project staff are scrupulous about screening the software they bundle and are aggressive about updating software like BIND when vulnerabilities are announced. If you stay up to date, you will be in good shape. A reasonable version of BIND 9 is included with the base OpenBSD operating system, and it is configured well, so we will not discuss how to install a separate version from scratch on OpenBSD. There are few, if any good reasons to do that, and many good reasons to stay with the version that is provided by the installation.

Both FreeBSD 4.x-RELEASE and FreeBSD 5.x-RELEASE ship with BIND 8.3.4 by default. Though it is the opinion of the authors, rather than an objective fact, we believe BIND 9 is the better foundation for building your DNS infrastructure than BIND 8. The probability of new vulnerabilities being found in BIND 8 is considerably higher than in BIND 9. The discussion in this chapter, therefore, focuses on how to install, configure, and maintain BIND 9.

FreeBSD

With FreeBSD, you want to overwrite the default version of BIND by installing *ports/dns/bind9* from the ports tree. If you do not overwrite the original version, you will have duplicate copies of critical BIND components. You could inadvertently invoke the wrong one, or a script whose PATH was incorrectly set could invoke the wrong one. The command-line syntax of both `named` and `nsupdate` have changed significantly between Versions 8 and 9.

The FreeBSD ports system makes it easy to overwrite the installed version of BIND. There are two steps:

1. Insert **`NO_BIND=TRUE`** in */etc/make.conf*. This ensures that BIND 8 is not built and installed when you are upgrading your system using the buildworld/installworld paradigm as described in the *FreeBSD Handbook* and in Chapter 4 of this book.

   If you choose to use the `PORT_REPLACES_BASE_BIND9` option (described next), you will clobber your BIND 9 installation by running **`make installworld`** unless you use **`NO_BIND=TRUE`**.

2. Insert **`PORT_REPLACES_BASE_BIND9=TRUE`** in */etc/make.conf*. This causes the port version to overwrite */usr/sbin/named* and */etc/named* and other files in the base installation. This means that when you put **`named_enable="YES"`** in */etc/rc.conf*, it will launch BIND 9 that you compiled in ports.

If you accidentally overwrite a BIND 9 installation with BIND 8, you may have difficulty diagnosing it. BIND 8 will often accept much of the same syntax in the *named.conf* and zone files. It will gripe about what it does not understand, but it will probably run. In terms of serving zone information, it will probably run correctly. Your biggest clues will be functionality (like cryptography and dynamic updates) that suddenly stops working.

Note that the version tracked in *ports/dns/bind9* is not always the absolutely latest version. It is occasionally behind by a few minor revisions, unless there is a major security concern. Most sites can usually get along safely without being on the bleeding edge. DNS is such a critical function that the FreeBSD port maintainers are a little conservative about updating it.

Installing djbdns

Whether you are using FreeBSD or OpenBSD, djbdns is not included with the operating system. In FreeBSD, it is available as a port. Under OpenBSD, you must build from source following Bernstein's installation instructions. Documentation is not included by default with djbdns. It is available as a separate download online. You should probably download the documentation and familiarize yourself with it before installing.

Preliminaries

There is a little planning to do before installing djbdns. You will need more than just the djbdns software itself in order to run any of the djbdns programs. Two utility packages are required that provide functionality other than DNS service. Despite the fact that it is probably possible to run djbdns service in some other way, it is better to obey the convention and use these assistant programs.

Locating zone data

The installation instructions for djbdns suggest creating directories in */etc* for DNS-related services. In general, this is a fine idea. Both OpenBSD and FreeBSD are careful about how they handle */etc* when upgrading the operating system. There is one case, however, in which it might be undesirable to put your `tinydns` configuration in */etc*. All of your zone data will be stored wherever you create the *tinydns* directory. If you have a lot of zone data, you may not want all that zone data in your root partition. It might fill your root partition; it makes *fsck* take longer to run on your root partition in an emergency; or it might simply violate your conventions of separating data and configuration information. Some administrators use immutable filesystem flags or read-only mount points for configuration data (such as the */etc* directory or the */* partition). In such a case, you might want to put your DNS zone data elsewhere. The easy solution is to use */usr/local/etc/tinydns* or some other location that puts the data on a different, larger partition. Since the directory will be symbolically linked to */service* (or */var/service* on FreeBSD), it's true location is not very important.

Daemontools

Bernstein has written a series of tools, called "daemontools," that coordinate Unix services. Some of the tools orchestrate the starting, stopping, and signaling daemon processes. Other tools help run setuid and setgid programs safely and set environment variables for services. There is also a tool for managing logfiles. These are general-purpose tools for running all sorts of service processes in a Unix environment. You may find them useful for more than just djbdns.

Assuming that you follow the standard instructions for installing these programs, your root directory will have a directory called */service* in it. The subdirectories within it correspond to services that will be maintained by the daemontools `supervisor` process. Every five seconds or so, `supervisor` checks to be sure all the services are still running. Any that are not running are restarted using a standard launch script.

Unless you override the `SERVICEDIR` environment variable when you build them, the FreeBSD port of daemontools will use */var/service* instead of */service* for the services. Bear that in mind when you read documentation online. Also the FreeBSD ports will automatically fetch manpages and install them. No documentation is part of

Bernstein's distribution. While his site offers HTML documentation, the manpages are separate and are maintained by someone else. They are not normally part of an installation. If, for some reason, you do not want the manpages installed, you can set the `WITHOUT_MAN` environment variable when you build the port.

ucspi-tcp

The ucspi-tcp tools implement the Unix Client-Server Program Interface (UCSPI) over TCP. UCSPI is an interface standard Bernstein wrote to specify the interactions between programs and communications channels. They also provide a library of networking functions that are used by the djbdns programs.

Like the daemontools, the FreeBSD port of these tools will fetch the manpages unless you set the `WITHOUT_MAN` environment variable before you build.

FreeBSD

The DNS service itself can be installed from *ports/dns/djbdns*. Note that the *daemontools* and *ucspi-tcp* packages are also ports. The only dependencies are *ports/sysutils/daemontools*, and *ports/sysutils/ucspi-tcp*, so they will automatically be installed.

Installing on OpenBSD via source

The *ucspi-tcp* library and *daemontools* do not depend on each other or on any other software, so they can be installed in any order. Follow the straightforward instructions at *http://cr.yp.to/djbdns.html*.

Note that the installation process for daemontools will edit your */etc/rc.local* file, adding a command to your boot process.

Once you have installed the ucspi-tcp and daemontools, you can install djbdns from source following its instructions.

The instructions boil down to the same procedure for each package. For each package (*daemontools*, *ucspi-tcp*, and djbdns), do the following:

1. Download the source from *http://cr.yp.to/*.
2. Unzip and untar it (e.g., **`tar -zxf`** ***`packagename`*****`.tgz`**).
3. cd into the directory (e.g., **`cd`** ***`ucspi-tcp-0.88`***).
4. Run **`make`**.
5. Assuming everything went well, run **`sudo make setup check`** to install the software.

For `tinydns` or `dnscache`, there are more steps. These programs act as services, so they must be registered with the daemontools' `supervisor` process.

6. Run the configuration script for the program (**tinydns-conf** and **dnscache-conf**, respectively). The configuration script creates the directory structure necessary for the supervisor.
7. Create a symbolic link in */service* so that the supervisor will find the program and launch it.

Installing on OpenBSD via unofficial ports

Although the OpenBSD group does not distribute ports for djbdns in their official ports tree, Giacomo Cariello created a set of experimental ports at *http://experimental.bug.it/*. Ports for *daemontools*, *ucspi-tcp*, and djbdns are available there. These ports would make djbdns straightforward to install if they worked. Unfortunately, the latest version of these ports is for OpenBSD Version 3.2, which is several years old. These ports do not build with the OpenBSD ports system that shipped with OpenBSD 3.6. Before building from source, though, you may want to look at Cariello's site and search on Google a little to see if a new, working set of ports is available.

Operating BIND

Having read about the various attacks and risks associated with BIND, you may worry about the stability, security, or suitability of running BIND for a major enterprise. You should not. BIND is enterprise-class, production-quality software. Like all such software, whether open source or not, you must be aware of its weaknesses and guard against them. Consider that at least one of the .com nameservers runs BIND 9: if it can handle the load and stress of the .com zone, it can handle your zones.

Running BIND in chroot

BIND comes with the built-in ability to run in a chroot environment. You do not need to do much to configure a chroot environment properly for it. To make BIND run in a chroot environment, run it with the -u and -t options. The -u option indicates which user ID to assume while running. After doing the things that it must do as root (such as binding to port 53), BIND will then call setuid( ) to run as the given user ID. The -t option identifies the root of the chroot environment.

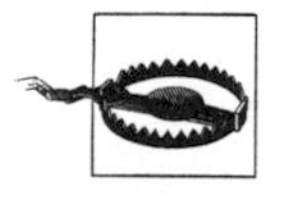

The instructions below work for the versions of FreeBSD and OpenBSD that we tested while writing. Be sure to check the BIND Administrator's Reference Manual (ARM) for the latest information when installing. It is distributed as part of the BIND 9 distribution.

FreeBSD stores its DNS zone data in */etc/namedb* but does not include a chroot environment there. OpenBSD comes preconfigured to run BIND in a chroot sandbox, and it uses */var/named* as its root. Because FreeBSD needs more configuration than OpenBSD to run its BIND in chroot, we will use */etc/namedb* as the root of our chroot environment in our examples. The same concerns about locating zone data in */etc* apply to BIND as to djbdns. See the discussion on "Locating zone data" to help decide if you ultimately want your zone data in */etc*.

Make a filesystem

The chroot filesystem typically needs three directories: */dev*, */etc*, and */var*. In this example, using */etc/namedb*, you need to create */etc/namedb/dev*, */etc/namedb/etc*, and */etc/namedb/var* directories. The *named.conf* file will tell named where to look for data and where to write its logfiles.

Three devices are needed in the */dev* directory: */dev/null*, */dev/zero*, and */dev/random*. You have to use the mknod command to do this. To create the devices properly, you must first use **ls -l**, as shown in Example 5-4, to determine the correct major and minor numbers for the devices.

Example 5-4. Using ls to determine major/minor numbers for device nodes

```
OpenBSD% ls -l /dev/null /dev/zero /dev/random
crw-rw-rw- 1 root  wheel    2,   2 Jan 15 01:30 /dev/null
crw-r--r-- 1 root  wheel   45,   0 Aug 19 16:24 /dev/random
crw-rw-rw- 1 root  wheel    2,  12 Aug 19 16:24 /dev/zero

FreeBSD% ls -l /dev/null /dev/zero /dev/random
crw-rw-rw- 1 root  wheel    2,   2 Jan 12 13:33 /dev/null
crw-rw-rw- 1 root  wheel  250,   0 Jan  9 11:13 /dev/random
crw-rw-rw- 1 root  wheel    2,  12 Jan  9 10:22 /dev/zero
```

Notice that the numbers are different for */dev/random* between FreeBSD and OpenBSD. FreeBSD 4.x uses still different numbers. Using sudo, create the device nodes as shown in Example 5-5.

Example 5-5. Making device nodes

```
FreeBSD$ sudo mknod /etc/namedb/dev/null c 2 2
FreeBSD$ sudo mknod /etc/namedb/dev/random c 250 0
FreeBSD$ sudo mknod /etc/namedb/dev/zero c 2 12
```

The virtual */etc* directory needs to contain a *named.conf* file. Note that if you are running FreeBSD, you will use */etc/namedb/named.conf*. That means you will create */etc/namedb/etc/namedb* in addition to */etc/namedb/etc*.

When running in chroot, using the -t option, all the filesystem paths are translated. That is, if named is compiled to use */etc/namedb/named.conf* (which is how FreeBSD compiles BIND by default), then it is really expecting */etc/namedb/etc/namedb/named.conf*. It is a good idea to remove or rename the */etc/namedb/named.conf* file that lives in the real */etc* directory. It might mislead you or another administrator who forgets that *named* runs in a chroot environment.

Alternatively, you can add -c /etc/namedb/named.conf to the named_flags option in */etc/rc.conf*. This will cause that file to be used as the configuration file instead of */etc/namedb/etc/namedb/named.conf*.

Launch BIND from /etc/rc.conf

To launch at named boot time, set the named_enable variable in */etc/rc.conf*. Set the named_flags variable to include the correct command-line options for your installation. For OpenBSD, there is a single line to add:

```
named_flags="-u named -t /var/named"
```

OpenBSD comes with a user called named already in the password file and a chroot environment already built in */var/named*. By virtue of the fact that named_flags is not the string NO, named is invoked at boot time. Note that the named command in */etc/rc* is run from the default PATH. That is, rather than invoking */usr/sbin/named* explicitly, the script just invokes named. The binary to execute is resolved using the PATH environment variable set at the beginning of the */etc/rc* script. If you want to override the named binary that is executed, you will have to manually edit the */etc/rc* script itself.

To enable named at boot time on FreeBSD, a very similar named_flags line needs to be added to */etc/rc.conf*. Notice that FreeBSD calls its DNS user bind instead of named. The named_enable variable must be set to **YES**. If you are running BIND 9, but chose not to overwrite the base installation, you have to define an additional variable, named_program, to specify which named binary to execute. A typical FreeBSD configuration looks like:

```
named_enable="YES"
named_flags="-u bind -t /etc/namedb"
```

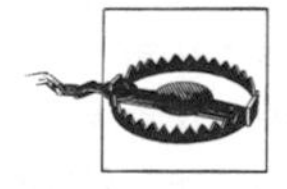

FreeBSD, beginning with the 5.X versions, now uses a more advanced */etc/rc* system for booting. The tasks for starting up BIND are in */etc/rc.d/named*. They include a special function that will automatically keep a chroot area up to date. If you set **named_chroot_autoupdate=yes** in */etc/rc.conf*, a series of commands will execute at boot time to make sure that some files are copied into the right place. Do not use this variable and functionality if you run BIND 9. It does not make all the devices that you will need (e.g., */dev/random*) and it tries to copy an obsolete program (*named-xfer*). The automatic chroot feature only works for BIND Version 8.

Configuration Ideas

There are a few standard techniques that DNS administrators use to make their servers more secure, more auditable, or both. They include the restricting access to certain features, restricting access to functionality, and obscuring the version number.

Security restrictions

All of the following options are applicable in both FreeBSD and OpenBSD contexts. They are useful for either defending against attacks or for preventing extraneous use of your server. All of these options are demonstrated in Example 5-6.

`allow-recursion`
: This also should be set to `none` if your server is authoritative. If your server is a caching server that is supposed to allow recursion, omit this directive from your default options section, and instead add it to the view that you define for recursion.

`allow-transfer`
: Set this to `none` to prevent anyone from performing zone transfers by default. For each zone that should have zone transfers enabled, specifically identify the proper servers through an access control list (ACL).

`controls`
: This line should always be present in the *named.conf* file, whether you intend to use `rndc`'s ability to control `named` or not. If you do not want to use `rndc` in any way at all, this line must still be present. It should read `controls {};`.

`query-source`
: Sometimes it is useful to have BIND use a specific source address and port. Perhaps the server is "multi-homed" (i.e., having more than one IP address assigned to it). Perhaps, in order to make the firewall rules maximally restrictive, the DNS responses must have both source and destination ports set to 53. The `query-source` line can accomplish these tasks.

`version`
: Set it to something other than the obvious. An attacker can try to probe your BIND version by querying for the TXT record "version.bind" in the Chaos class. Chaos is a vestigial class that is not used anymore. To try to query your own version, run **`dig @`*`servername`*` version.bind. chaos txt`**. Replace *servername* with the name of your BIND server. Realize that this is of very limited value. Only script kiddies will blindly trust the version that your server reports and base their attacks on it.

The configuration options in Example 5-6 are a recommended starting point. You will need to customize them for your own use.

Example 5-6. Several security-related BIND options

```
options {
        directory "/etc/namedb";         // inside our virtual root
        allow-recursion { none; };       // we are authoritative only
        allow-transfer  { none; };       // default deny; override in zones.
        query-source address * port 53; // for firewalls
        version "Undisclosed";           // obscure our version.bind
};
controls {
        inet 127.0.0.1 allow { localhost; } keys { rndc_key; };
};
key rndc_key {
        algorithm "hmac-md5";
        // This is just some randomness that I got by doing
        // dd if=/dev/random bs=32 count=1 | openssl base64
        secret "sQMUKllOIV1gUz6oUkIaxU1B5uQBioXFgAORoa+/OZA=";
};
include "example.com.zone";             // See Example 5-8
```

Logging

BIND 9 provides reasonably fine-grained logging options to allow you to sort through all the different events it might log and guide them to the right places. Example 5-7 shows one potential configuration for logging.

Example 5-7. Organizing BIND's logs

```
logging {
        channel my_default    { syslog local7; severity info; };
        channel my_security   { syslog local6; severity notice; };
        category security     { my_security; };
        category default      { my_default; };
        category config       { my_default; };
        category xfer-in      { my_default; };
        category xfer-out     { my_default; };
        category update       { null; };
        category lame-servers { null; };
        category queries      { null; };
};
```

In the example, we have created just three categories of messages. The usual messages that one might expect to accumulate in */var/log/messages* are directed to *syslog* using the *LOCAL7* service at severity *info*. Security-oriented messages (as defined by BIND's notion of "security") are sent to a different `syslog` service. This allows us to configure `syslog` to treat them differently. Perhaps we will log security messages off-system in addition to a special security logfile. Lastly, a few types of logged messages that are rarely useful are discarded. These tend to be useless messages that bloat logfiles, except in specific circumstances when you need forensic information. See the ARM for the full list of categories of events that can be logged.

There are a few good reasons, however, why you might temporarily watch the `update` or `xfer-out` categories more closely. If you suspect that someone is trying to misuse your DNS server, you may want to send these two categories to a special logfile for a little while. Sometimes performance for DNS can slow down because Windows systems are attempting many dynamic updates (a fundamental technique used in Active Directory). Turning on update logging will quickly show you if that is the case. Alternatively, you may find attempted updates from nonlocal networks. These may be symptomatic of an attack probe of some kind, or they may be the result of a simple misconfiguration somewhere at the foreign site. The `xfer-out` category will show you who is trying to transfer zones (using either *AXFR* or *IXFR* queries) from your server. A quick `grep` for "denied" will find the systems that are attempting and failing to transfer your zones. This might be useful information to correlate with firewall or intrusion detection logs to see if the failed transfers coincide with other unusual network activity.

Using includes to separate permissions

Some parts of the `named` configuration are more sensitive than others and should be protected differently. Logging options, for instance, are much less critical than the keys that allow updates or authenticate zone transfers. By using BIND's `include` directive, you can put sensitive material in separate files, and then protect those files more carefully. The fragment of *named.conf* shown in Example 5-6 demonstrates this by including a file named *example.com.zone*, which contains the zone configuration information shown in Example 5-8. Keys used for `rndc` or TSIG, for example, are good candidates to be included this way.

Managing BIND

BIND includes a program called `rndc` for managing the `named` daemon. In previous versions, this program was called `ndc` and was substantially limited in what it could really do. The `rndc` program, by contrast, can do many things that administrators have wanted for a long time. Zones can be added and deleted, updates can be sent to slave servers, and the server can be stopped and started.

In order to use `rndc`, it is important to configure it properly. If it is configured poorly, then a variety of vulnerabilities are introduced. Remote users could stop the server or even drop whole zones.

Example 5-6 included the two statements (**`controls`** and **`key rndc_key`**) that enable the control by `rndc`. BIND 9 includes a script called `rndc-confgen` that will create the key file and the corresponding *rndc.conf* file. By giving rndc-confgen the `-a` option to perform automatic configuration and the correct `-t` and `-u` options, like you would give named, it will create the files in the right locations. For example: `rndc-confgen -a -t /etc/namedb -u named`.

Transaction Signatures (TSIG)

One of the long-standing problems with DNS is the lack of authenticity for records in zones and the ability to establish trust relationships between servers. Some solutions could exist, using TCP connections that used application-level authentication. However, with DNS being as pervasive as it is, it has always benefited from being UDP-based. Individual packets, often no larger than 512 bytes, travel quickly across the net and create minimum burden on the network. To continue in this low-bandwidth tradition, DNS needs authentication that can still fit in UDP packets. Several different security mechanisms have been defined in DNS. These mechanisms are covered in more detail in *DNS and BIND* by Liu and Albitz. Of the various DNS security measures (typically considered together under the label DNSSEC), only TSIG has real practical value today.

Defined in RFC 2845, TSIG provides a mechanism for attaching a digital signature to a DNS request. Currently the signature is a message authentication code (MAC) using the MD5 hashing algorithm, thus the algorithm is called *hmac-md5*. Any request can be signed. It can be a simple request for an MX record, or it can be a dynamic update request. Responses can also be signed in the same way. Using TSIG, two DNS servers can authenticate their conversations.

Cautions about using TSIG

One of the significant drawbacks to TSIG is that it is based on a symmetric cryptography system. It requires both DNS servers to have the same shared secret established in advance. TSIG, therefore, is only used between systems that explicitly trust each other (for example, two servers operated by the same organization). It is only practical on a small scale. It might be scalable to perhaps a handful of organizations, or across a few dozen systems within a large organization. It also suffers another risk of symmetric cryptography: if the shared secret is compromised, then authentic messages can be forged without being detected.

TSIG is useful, so long as you maintain its key as carefully as you maintain other critical cryptographic keys. Most SSL-enabled web servers, for example, store a private key in a file that must be readable by the web server but must also be protected from prying eyes. The TSIG key for `named`, then, is very similar and must be handled appropriately. As an alternative to what is shown in Example 5-6, BIND 9 will also look in the file */etc/rndc.key* for the `rndc` key (or */etc/namedb/rndc.key* under FreeBSD). While this was primarily added to BIND as a migration aid for migrating from BIND 8 to BIND 9, it serves the additional purpose of allowing us to protect our key material differently than the *named.conf* file itself.

If you are using FreeBSD, the *rndc.key* and *rndc.conf* files are probably good candidates for ACLs (see Chapter 2). Using ACLs, the file access permissions can be set to permit only the *bind* user to access the file.

Practical uses for TSIG

There are two common, practical uses of TSIG: authenticating dynamic updates and authenticating zone transfers (either full or incremental). Example 5-8 shows a domain with both of these options enabled. The server will only respond to zone transfer requests if they are signed by a specific key. It will also accept dynamic updates to the zone, but only if they are signed. All of these directives could be put in a separate file called *example.com.inc* and then that file could be included using BIND's include syntax.

Example 5-8. Restricting access via TSIG

```
key "example.com.key." {
        algorithm hmac-md5;
        secret "WW91IGFjdHVhbGx5IGR1Y29kZWQgdGhpcz8=";
};

acl "tsig_example.com" {
        key example.com.key.;
};

zone    "example.com"  {
        type master;
        file "example.com";
        allow-update   { "tsig_example.com"; };
        allow-query    { any; };
        allow-transfer { "tsig_example.com"; };
};

server  12.34.56.78 {
        keys { "example.com.key."; };
};
```

The syntax demonstrated in Example 5-8 suggests ways that access can be controlled. There is no limit to the number of different access control list (ACL) statements that can be included in the configuration file. Furthermore, an ACL can combine TSIG-based authentication with IP-based authentication. That is, requests from certain IP addresses could be trusted without signatures, while the presence of a correct signature would cause requests to be honored regardless of the originating IP address.

The server line in Example 5-8 shows how to indicate which cryptographic keys your server shares with another server. There are several limitations to this scheme. You can only specify servers by IP address. If the server's IP changes, you must alter your *named.conf* file and restart `named`. All conversations with that server will be signed with TSIG signatures—even basic queries. This can increase the computational load on your server as it computes signatures and verifies the signatures on the responses. You cannot limit TSIG usage, for example, to just zone transfer requests. Lastly, though the syntax implies using multiple keys with a given server, it is actually not possible. BIND only supports exactly one key per server.

Keep in mind, when writing access control lists, that each ACL is an "or" list. Access is granted if any one of the characteristics in the ACL is satisfied. Likewise, the allow-transfer and allow-update lists work the same way. As long as the request satisfies one of the listed authorizers, the request is honored. More complex behavior is possible, but it makes the *named.conf* file dangerously complex.

Operating djbdns

There are two different functions you will most likely use in the djbdns suite. On a given machine, you will either run `dnscache` to act as a caching server, or you will run `tinydns` to be an authoritative server. If you use jails, you may run them both on the same system, but with different IP addresses. The operation of both services is largely the same. Most of this section discusses running `tinydns`, because it requires the most careful configuration and the most frequent updates to its configuration.

Generally speaking, once `dnscache` is configured correctly, it runs without much maintenance or change. This is one of the key advantages of djbdns' separation of duties. It mandates that the DNS cache for the organization must be independent of the authoritative server. The caching server, then, can be set up once and largely left alone while it does its job.

Running tinydns

The `tinydns` installation sets up its own chroot environment by default. It runs in that environment and *setuid* to a nonprivileged user by default. Assuming your `tinydns` configuration is located in */etc/tinydns* as the instructions suggest, then you will have a directory called */etc/tinydns/root* where all the DNS zone information lives. There is a file there named *data* that contains, in text form, all the zone information. There is also a *Makefile* that contains rules for turning the *data* file into the *data.cdb* file. The *data.cdb* file is an optimized binary file that is actually used by tinydns to serve the zone data.

Routine Maintenance

There are a number of common maintenance tasks with tinydns whose execution varies based on your individual environment. You often will have to manually manipulate the *data* file, which contains the source data for all your zones.

The tinydns data file

While it is true that some tasks are automated by the various `add-*` scripts, many tasks are not. It is highly likely that you will need to edit the *data* file from time to time to do all the things in your zone that you need to do. This file is primarily intended to be produced and parsed by programs, but it is straightforward enough that a human can read and manipulate it.

The *data* file represents zone records by listing them one per line. The first character indicates what kind of record is being created, and the remainder of the line is a series of colon-separated fields describing the record. Note well that, unlike a BIND zone file, a single line of a tinydns *data* file often expands into many DNS records, sometimes in multiple zones. The lines that create A records, for instance, can automatically create the corresponding reverse PTR records in the appropriate in-addr.arpa zone.

The following summary describes the lines that you might put in a tinydns *data* file.

`.` *(period)*
: This record sets a nameserver for the given domain. The domain is considered to be this domain, as opposed to a domain that we are delegating. The `tinydns` server will automatically generate a start of authority (SOA) record for this entry. In this example, the domain is example.com and the server that serves it is `ns.exampleisp.com`:

```
.example.com:12.34.56.78:ns.exampleisp.com
```

Note that all the fields that are part of an SOA record (such as the TTL, expiration time, refresh time and hostmaster email address), and all the nameserver entries are automatically filled in with default values. If you want to have control over the fields in the SOA record, you will have to look up the `Z` record in the djbdns documentation.

`&` *(ampersand)*
: This record is a delegation to another name server. It creates an NS record and corresponding A records (if they fall within the tinydns server's ken), but does not create an SOA record. For example:

```
&lab.example.com:12.34.60.4:ns.lab.example.com
```

`=` *(equals)*
: This entry creates a normal A record and corresponding reverse `PTR` record. The `PTR` record is of no use unless the reverse zone is delegated to your server. If it is, however, you do not need to do anything extra. The reverse records are always created automatically. For example:

```
=www.example.com:12.34.56.79
```

`+` *(plus)*
: Exactly like the equals record, except that the reverse PTR record is not created. For example:

```
+mail.example.com:12.34.56.80
```

`@` *(at)*
: As suggested by the `@` symbol, these records establish MX records. This example duplicates, in tinydns syntax, the same MX structure shown earlier in Example 5-1. For example:

```
@example.com:12.34.56.79:mail-a.example.com:10
@example.com:12.34.56.80:mail-b.example.com:20
```

`C`

CNAME records begin with the letter `C` as the first letter on the line. In this example, oldname.example.com is an alias for the true name server.example.com. The server.example.com name must have at least an A record associated with it. The name oldname.example.com cannot have any other records defined for it. For example:

```
Cserver.example.com:oldname.example.com
```

Putting several of these examples together, we create a *data* file that creates much of the same structure that is shown in Example 5-1, as shown in Example 5-9.

Example 5-9. tinydns configuration replicating Example 5-1

```
.example.com:12.34.56.81:ns.example.com
=example.com:12.34.56.78
@example.com:12.34.56.79:mail-a.example.com:10
@example.com:12.34.56.80:mail-b.example.com:20
=www.example.com:12.34.56.78
@www.example.com:12.34.56.79:mail-a.example.com:10
@www.example.com:12.34.56.80:mail-b.example.com:20
=mail-a.example.com:12.34.56.79
@mail-a.example.com:12.34.56.79:mail-a.example.com:10
@mail-a.example.com:12.34.56.80:mail-b.example.com:20
=mail-b.example.com:12.34.56.80
@mail-b.example.com:12.34.56.79:mail-a.example.com:10
@mail-b.example.com:12.34.56.80:mail-b.example.com:20
```

It is a little unusual to see so many MX records in a DNS zone. If it is your intention that all email goes to exactly one mail server (or one set of organizational servers), then this is necessary. The rules for delivering email include vestigial accommodations for systems that have only an A record and no MX record. Mail transfer agents (MTAs) will try to deliver email directly to a host if it has only an A record and no MX record. So, if something (a misconfigured daemon, for example) sends mail to *webmaster@www.example.com* (instead of *webmaster@example.com*) these MX records will route the mail to the correct mail server.

Load balancing

The standard documentation suggests that you should always use the various `add-*` scripts when adding hosts and records to your zones. This will break down when you need to do anything beyond using mundane records (A, MX, NS, CNAME) in mundane ways. If, for example, you want to balance load across multiple web servers, DNS can assist with that. The standard method for doing this is to return multiple A records (IP addresses) for a given name. Example 5-10 shows the result of querying for `www.google.com` using *dnsqr*, the recursive querying tool that comes as part of djbdns.

Example 5-10. Multiple A records for load balancing

```
$ dnsqr a www.google.com
1 www.google.com:
433 bytes, 1+4+9+9 records, response, noerror
query: 1 www.google.com
answer: www.google.com 2663 CNAME www.google.akadns.net
answer: www.google.akadns.net 269 A 216.239.39.99
answer: www.google.akadns.net 269 A 216.239.39.104
answer: www.google.akadns.net 269 A 216.239.39.147
```

In this case, the akadns.net nameserver returned three IP addresses. It turns out that each time you issue the same query, you will receive a set of three IP addresses, drawn randomly from the set of all valid IP addresses for www.google.com.

You can use tinydns to do this kind of load balancing, but it is not as simple as running the add-host script multiple times. The add-host script considers it an error if you try to define more than one IP address for a host, or if you try to define more than one host for an IP address. You must manually edit the *data* file to create multiple A records for a host name. There you can insert any valid combination of DNS records. Example 5-11 shows how to add three lines that assign three IP addresses to the name www.example.com.

Example 5-11. tinydns configuration file for load balancing

```
+www.example.com:12.34.56.78
+www.example.com:12.34.56.81
+www.example.com:12.34.56.82
```

If you have many IP addresses for a single machine, tinydns will return a randomly chosen set of eight IP addresses each time the name is queried. The number eight is not configurable, but is probably suitable for most applications.

Naming nameservers

Keep in mind that the `add-*` scripts with `tinydns` impose their own notion of machine naming on your zones. The `add-ns` script only takes a zone and an IP address as arguments. It will automatically name your nameservers without prompting you. If your zone is `example.com`, and your nameserver's IP address is 12.34.56.79, then the documentation recommends running **`add-ns example.com 12.34.56.79`** to create your nameserver record in your zone. This will create a nameserver named `a.ns.example.com`. If you want a different naming scheme for your nameservers, you will have to edit the *data* file by hand. You sidestep the error checking features associated with djbdns when you create all the NS and SOA records by hand. Be sure you know what you are doing, if you take that course.

Wrapping Up

DNS is a critical piece of any networking infrastructure. Unfortunately, its design makes it ripe for attack. FreeBSD and OpenBSD systems make excellent choices for DNS servers because of their inherent stability and additional security features, like ACLs, that can be used to secure the server. Depending on your security posture, you can choose from BIND 9 or djbdns to serve your domains. If you choose BIND, you will have a lot of management tasks automated for you. You may also need to turn off features that you are not using to improve its security. If you choose djbdns, you will not have so many features to turn off as you will have features to implement yourself. You will have to create a secure replication scheme, secure updating mechanism, and delegation procedures. You will worry less, however, about the DNS server software itself being a major source of risk for you.

Ultimately you need to consider the environment where you are using DNS. You need to consider the risks that are presented in this chapter and how your organzation might be affected by them. Then you can pick the right software and the right set of configuration options to make your DNS system fit your needs.

Resources

These are pointers to various DNS-oriented resources, grouped by DNS server software.

BIND Resources

BIND (Berkeley Internet Name Daemon)
: The main web site is *http://www.isc.org/*. It includes full documentation on installing, configuring, and operating BIND.

BIND Administrator's Reference Manual (ARM)
: This can be found at */usr/share/doc/bind9/arm/Bv9ARM.html* on an OpenBSD system or a FreeBSD system that has the BIND 9 software installed overwriting the base installation. It is also available online at *http://www.nominum.com/content/documents/bind9arm.pdf*.

DNS and BIND, Fourth Edition, Paul Albitz and Cricket Liu (O'Reilly), 2001
: This book includes some good overview material about how DNS works generally. But it is focused on BIND. If you are interested in djbdns, there is nothing in here about it.

DNS and BIND Cookbook, Cricket Liu (O'Reilly), 2002
: This is a more tactical book that covers a lot of common usage scenarios and installation issues.

DNS on Windows Server 2003, Robbie Allen, Matt Larson, and Cricket Liu (O'Reilly), 2004
: If you want to integrate BIND with a Windows environment and run it on a Windows server, this is a good reference for how to do that.

djbdns Resources

Daniel J. Bernstein's web site (http://cr.yp.to/)
: All of Daniel J. Bernstein's software can be found at this web site. The daemon tools are at *http://cr.yp.to/daemontools.html*, the ucspi-tcp tools are available at *http://cr.yp.to/ucspi-tcp.html*, and djbdns itself is at *http://cr.yp.to/djbdns.html*. The documentation, such as it is, is also there.

  Bernstein has written a number of other programs that strive to be secure replacements for notoriously insecure programs. His *qmail* replacement for *sendmail*, *tcpwrappers* replacement for *inetd*, and various other utilities are all here, also.

Building Secure Servers with Linux, Michael D. Bauer (O'Reilly), 2002
: While not specific to either BSD, this book includes a decent chapter on djbdns. It is one of the few substantive chapters in print on how to configure djbdns.

Manpages for djbdns (http://smarden.org/pape/djb/manpages/)
: If you like to keep documentation around in manpage format, Gerrit Pape has created manpages that can be installed for most of Bernstein's software.

Selected DNS-Related Requests for Comments (RFCs)

- RFC 1034: Domain Names—Concepts and Facilities
- RFC 1035: Domain Names—Implementation and Specification
- RFC 1183: New DNS RR Definitions
- RFC 1591: Domain Name System Structure and Delegation
- RFC 1886: DNS Extensions to support IP Version 6
- RFC 1995: Incremental Zone Transfer in DNS
- RFC 2065: Domain Name System Security Extensions
- RFC 2136: Dynamic Updates in the Domain Name System
- RFC 2137: Secure Domain Name System Dynamic Update
- RFC 2168: Resolution of Uniform Resource Identifiers using the Domain Name System
- RFC 2308: Negative Caching of DNS Queries
- RFC 2317: Classless IN-ADDR.ARPA Delegation
- RFC 2845: Secret Key Transaction Authentication for DNS (TSIG)

CHAPTER 6

Building Secure Mail Servers

Laugh-a while you can, monkey-boy.
—Lord John Whorfin
The Adventures of Buckaroo Banzai Across the 8th Dimension

Providing mail service can mean several things. When a user clicks Send, the message must be transported from their system through intervening mail servers to the destination machine. Mail Transport Agents, or MTAs, are responsible for getting mail from point A to point B. *Mail transport* is the backbone of mail service.

Of course, mail transport is not the whole story. Once on the destination system, the Mail Delivery Agent, or MDA, is responsible for placing the mail message into a user's inbox. No discussion of providing mail service can be complete without covering *mail delivery*.

Mail delivery is often taken for granted by users. From their perspective, mail consists of messages sitting in their inbox accessed through webmail or a mail client. We refer to such programs as Mail User Agents, or MUAs. These programs utilize mail access protocols like the Post Office Protocol (POP), the Internet Message Access Protocol (IMAP), and the Messaging Application Programming Interface (MAPI). *Mail access* is the third key component of mail service.

The single function of providing mail service is complex, but can be done in a secure fashion with a little planning and diligence. We begin by looking at risks associated with providing mail services. This motivates our discussion of mail architecture and subsequent software configuration as mitigation techniques. As mail service is an expansive topic, we focus on securing the MTA.

Email has become central to our online lives. For most people, it's the primary means of electronic communication. While those clever little email forwards used to make [some of] us chuckle, they're now just meaningless messages in a pile of ever-increasing virus-laden junk mail.

Despite this increase in unsolicited commercial email (UCE or spam) and inherent problems in the design of the Simple Mail Transfer Protocol (SMTP), few people relish the thought of giving up email altogether. Delays, corruptions, or interruptions can have major detrimental effects. The fact that people have come to rely on it so much makes them very sensitive to failures in email delivery. It's this dependence on the service in the face of adversity that makes email critical.

As security-minded system administrators, we must guarantee both the security and availability of the services required for mail access, transport, and delivery while at the same time mitigating the risks. By looking at the kinds of attacks levied against mail servers in general, we can begin to think about how to ensure that these attacks against our servers fail.

Mail Server Attacks

Mail servers are juicy targets just like DNS and web servers, and for similar reasons. These servers all provide important functionality for individuals outside of the organization. They are widely publicized, which makes them easy to find and attack.

Mail servers may be attacked to establish a foothold in an organization's network or merely to acquire a staging ground for other, unrelated attacks. Such attacks aren't specific to mail servers alone, and attackers in this case are generally seeking an exploitable condition that will provide access to the operating system. These attacks are typically the first thing system administrators worry about when deploying any service. A compromised operating system means a system rebuild and subsequent analysis. If the system was a staging ground for other attacks, other systems may need rebuilding as well.

Mail servers are also subject to attacks by individuals who wish to exploit the mail service itself. The most obvious example is the use of an organization's mail server to deliver unsolicited commercial email. This kind of attack can succeed when a mail server accepts all incoming messages and sends them to any destination—an "open relay" configuration. In this case, the operating system is not under direct threat, but being an open relay may lead to a denial of service (DoS) attack due to the volume of incoming mail or being blacklisted by other organizations. The side effects of being blacklisted may include angry customers, lost productivity, lost sales, and negative publicity.

Finally mail servers sometimes play the role of oblivious accomplice. Despite operating properly, mail servers assist in the delivery of computer viruses and worms that can wreak havoc on an organization's network, infrastructure, and client systems. "Experts" often quote dollar figures in the billions when referring to damages caused by viruses. This may or may not be accurate, but viruses have certainly brought massive organizations to a standstill for days. The Melissa virus in 1999 infected several Fortune 500 companies causing major damage. Hundreds of other companies disconnected from the Internet in fear. Building a virus-resistant mail infrastructure that allows for rapid response, even before antivirus vendors publish updates, should be a requirement for any security-minded system administrator.

Viruses and Worms

The terms virus and worm are often used interchangeably. While they both refer to malicious code, or malware, there is one key difference. Worms do not require any user action in order to propagate, whereas viruses often require that a user execute some program. RFC 1135, The Helminthiasis of the Internet, discusses the propagation of the Internet Worm of 1988 (The Morris Internet Worm). It defines the terms virus and worm as follows:

"A 'worm' is a program that can run independently, will consume the resources of its host from within in order to maintain itself, and can propagate a complete working version of itself on to other machines."

"A 'virus' is a piece of code that inserts itself into a host, including operating systems, to propagate. It cannot run independently. It requires that its host program be run to activate it."

Operating System Level Attacks

One of the most notorious operating system level exploits in networked computing came as a result of an SMTP-initiated `debug` mode built into an early version of `sendmail`. The Morris Internet worm was released on November 2, 1988 and proceeded to exploit `sendmail` and `fingerd` to gain access to systems. Sendmail has been the target of several other OS-level attacks for one key reason: it runs as root. Exploiting a vulnerability in the `sendmail` daemon listening on port 25 of any mail server may eventually lead to a root shell on a system.

While the debug code was stripped from `sendmail`, vulnerabilities continued to be published for years. A quick survey of the Bugtraq SecurityFocus mailing list turns up a variety of local privilege escalation, remote compromise, and denial of service attacks possible against Sendmail over the years. The techniques used fill the entire spectrum: buffer overflows, removing or hard linking to key files, exploiting poor configuration, passing in illegal arguments, and so on.

Of course Sendmail is not the only piece of mail software with vulnerabilities. A search on *http://www.securityfocus.com/* will quickly turn up a few Postfix and qmail advisories. Fortunately these are remote denial of service vulnerabilities and less severe than remote root compromises.

The good news is that the vulnerabilities in mail software that give rise to operating system level attacks can often be mitigated by small configuration changes, software patches, and/or upgrades.

Illegitimate Mail Relaying

Mail administrators appear to be particularly prone to deploying open relays, judging from the sheer volume of servers that match this description in blacklists. This is often due to uninformed, lazy, or sloppy configuration, but even conscientious administrators can accidentally create an open relay configuration.

In a multiple-server site in which one external mail server is responsible for communicating with the outside world and additional internal servers house mailboxes, the external server often implicitly trusts all internal hosts. The internal hosts for their part pay little attention to mail routing and merely pass all mail to the external server. If the internal servers also allow connections from external sources, anonymous external users may pass messages to an internal server that forwards the message to the external server, and the mail will be delivered. Despite diligence during server configuration, sloppy architecture can lead to open relays.

In 1995, Matt Wright wrote a small Perl script to be used as a backend for "contact us" pages on the Web. The script received certain variables from a web page in the form of an HTTP POST or GET request as shown in Example 6-1, and would create an email message to be delivered to a recipient configured in the HTML page.

Example 6-1. HTML "contact us" sample snippet using formmail.pl

```
<html><head><title>Contact Us</title></head><body>
Please fill out this form and we will get back to you shortly.<br />
<form name="contact" method="post" action="/cgi-bin/formmail.pl" />
 <input type="hidden" name="recipient" value="user@domain.com" /> <br />
 <input type="text" name="realname" /><br />
 <input type="text" name="e-mail" /><br />
 <textarea name="comments" rows="5" cols="4" wrap="virtual">
 Please enter your comments here...
 </textarea>
</body>
</html>
```

In 2001, web sites around the world were using Version 1.6 of this script, yet it contained little in the way of security checks. In fact by typing in the URL in Example 6-2 and providing known parameters in the URI, users could anonymously send mail anywhere.

Example 6-2. Exploiting formmail.pl Version 1.6

```
http://your.server.com/cgi-bin/formmail.pl?recipient=dest-addr@anywhere.
net&message=This%20is%20SPAM.&realname=Anyone&e-mail=bogus@sender.com
```

Early versions of `formmail.pl` did not attempt to verify that the request came from the local server and would quietly generate and send email. Subsequent fixes to the `formmail.pl` script to add REFERER checks were marginally effective but still exploitable.

The point here is that if you attempt to deploy your mail servers in a vacuum without considering the surrounding architecture, you may one day be surprised to find you're part of the problem.

Unwanted Mail

There are two categories of unwanted mail: common unsolicited commercial mail, and malware. Finding these kinds of messages doesn't indicate that your server is being attacked, they just utilize mail transport as a means of efficient delivery. However, unwanted mail consumes resources, reducing the amount of legitimate mail your servers are able to process and reducing the effectiveness of your organization's users. Don't pass by "consumes resources" without giving it serious consideration. Many organizations, after putting in place spam and virus blocking software, suddenly discover that they are rejecting three to ten times as much email as they are accepting. That's anything but a drop in the bucket.

Malware can be viruses, worms, or spyware hidden in email messages that exploits bugs in code (generally on client workstations) and is often propagated by users. While unwanted mail may lead users to point their fingers at poorly configured mail servers, the servers themselves are not particularly to blame for the propagation of unwanted mail. Nevertheless, when you need to stem the flow of spam and malware into your network and you know that mail is one of the key vectors that viruses and worms use to attack that software—improving your mail system's ability to stop unwanted mail becomes an appealing goal.

Mail Architecture

So far, we've discussed three classes of attacks against mail servers: those that exploit the application to gain access to the operating system, those that leverage poor configuration in the mail system to provide for arbitrary mail delivery, and those that use the mail delivery systems as a carrier for malware. In order to defend against these attacks, we must again abide by the defense-in-depth rule for systems security. What better place to start than with the architecture of the systems involved?

Protect the Operating System

Attacks seeking access to the operating system may use any piece of mail software that accepts input from users, either directly or indirectly. Architecturally, this is difficult to defend against. Your best bet is to tightly restrict who has access to the interfaces that expect direct user input. These include protecting the services that provide mail transport (Sendmail, Postfix, or qmail listening on port 25) and mail access (software that provides IMAP/POP).

Another avenue for direct user interaction is through a local or NFS mounted filesystem. Note that a mail server that allows user logins falls into the "Workgroup" class of system described in Chapter 3 and will be difficult to secure. If users demand mail delivery to local systems, consider using *.forward* files, *aliases*, or making them use `fetchmail` to redirect mail to workstations. This leaves critical mail servers with administrator-only access while providing users access to mail on their local workstations.

Let's start with a mail system consisting of one machine that listens for incoming connections on port 25 and also allows IMAP and POP mail access on ports 110 and 143 to mail content on local disks. What software is installed on this system is fairly important. Some organizations have little choice and must run Microsoft Exchange, Novell Groupwise, or some other groupware platform to satisfy external requirements. Other organizations are tightly bound to Sendmail or may have other legacy internal mail systems in place.

The easiest way to mitigate some of the risks associated with allowing users on the Internet open access to your mail system is to control mail flow and access, as shown in Figure 6-1.

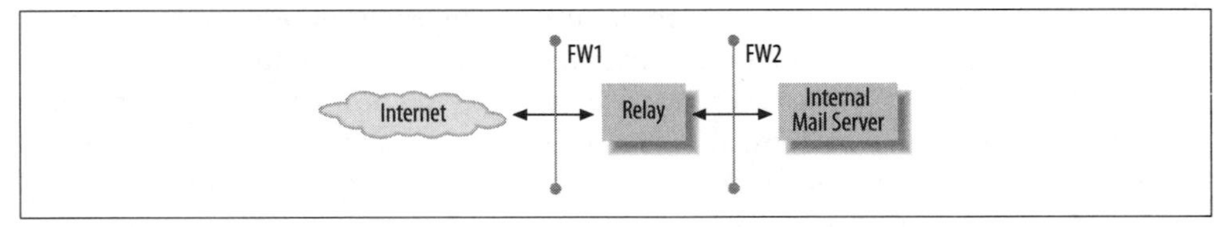

Figure 6-1. Simple mail architecture

This example outlines an internal mail server (or servers) and an external "relay" server, which does nothing more than accept inbound mail and pass it to the internal system. The relay provides a single point of interaction with outside users that can be tightly controlled and diligently maintained, thwarting attacks coming in from the Internet.

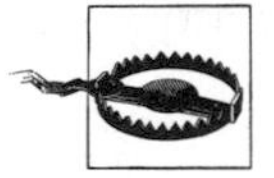

Of course, most *successful* attacks against systems in general *do not* come in from the Internet but from internal users. Keeping external interfaces up to date and patched is vital as the number of externally originating attacks will probably be higher. Forgetting the risk posed by internal users, however, will likely get you into trouble with the first attack.

Both the mail relay and the internal mail server now provide mail transport: they both listen on port 25 for incoming connections and do something with received messages. If you ensure both systems are running patched versions of mail transport software, attacks aimed at exploiting the service to gain access to the operating system are likely to fail.

Avoid Being an Open Relay

Any competent mail administrator would swear that he would never be caught administering an open relay. While he might not intentionally deploy such a system, accidents do happen. A simple mistake, or a series of configuration changes, may result in an open relay if you don't verify the effects of each change. With any combination of networked systems, it's nearly impossible to look at a single mail server and say, "I am not an open relay." You must look at the mail flow in your organization and periodically audit configuration to ensure mail can't flow from external senders to external recipients.

Three strategies can help you avoid an open relay configuration. A controlled and documented mail flow, as shown in Figure 6-2, is a good start. Strict change control procedures with regression testing reduce the likelihood of erroneous configuration. Regular auditing ensures compliance with the desired configuration.

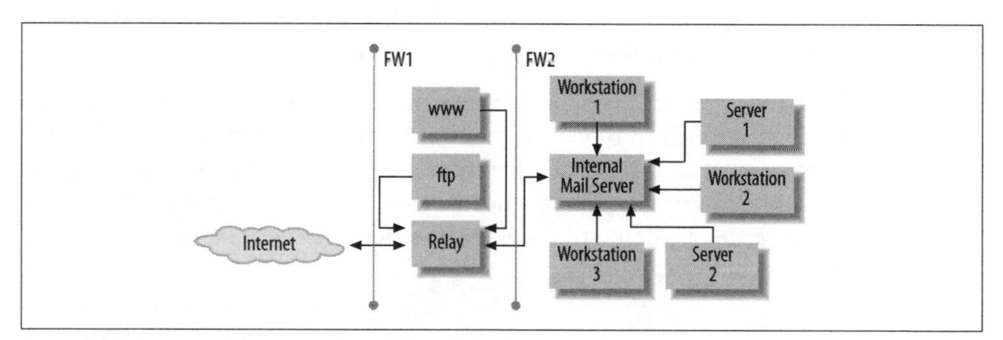

Figure 6-2. Strict enforcement of mail flow through key systems

When the time comes to audit, the following steps help reduce the risk of being an open relay:

1. Ensure all systems on your network send mail directly to a designated mail server. This means internal systems should send mail to the internal mail server, and systems on your DMZ should send mail to the mail relay.
2. Ensure firewall restrictions prevent any systems outside the organization or on the DMZ from reaching the internal workgroup mail server. Likewise, ensure the mail relay accepts inbound connections on port 25 from the Internet, and bi-directional communication on port 25 with internal mail server and nothing else!

3. Ensure your mail servers do not implicitly trust any messages that originate on other systems. Most mail transport software will accept a list of IP addresses or address/mask combination describing systems for which the server should automatically accept and relay mail. List no other addresses than those local to the mail server in question.
4. Ensure your mail servers are aware of which domain(s) are considered "internal," and mandate that either the recipient or the sender must be a part of this domain.

These steps work for the simple mail architecture shown in Figure 6-2. More complex configurations will of course require a different procedure, but the mail flow guidelines should apply universally. Still, open relays aren't the only possible problem. Any scripts on web sites that accept POST or GET data containing a recipient should be subjected to great scrutiny.

Stop Unwanted Mail

Spam, viruses, and worms are a bane to administrators and users alike. At best, these messages consume bandwidth and resources and at worst, they cause network outages and system failures. Most administrators who provide user support have to explain to users that no, in fact, their user account has not been hijacked to send spam—that there is no greater security in an email header than there is on the return address of a snail-mail envelope (more on this topic later).

Protecting your infrastructure from unwanted mail is tricky. You must configure carefully and set thresholds to block the greatest amount of illegitimate mail, while allowing legitimate mail to pass. The extent to which you can be authoritarian will depend on your organization's tolerance for lost (or bounced) legitimate mail from false positives. In general, there are three approaches you can take with unwanted mail:

Quarantine
: You may quarantine messages you feel are illegitimate or harmful into a malware repository. This repository needs periodic audits to delete existing messages or allow legitimate mail through. Alternately, you could set up a time-limited quarantine that automatically purges messages after a fixed period of time. This allows for more flexibility and requires less administration.

Reject
: One of the most popular ways of dealing with suspect mail is to reject it. This notifies the sender that the message did not look legitimate and therefore was returned. While this is easier on the administrator, the number of messages traveling back to nonexistent/fraudulent senders may start to clog your mail queue. What's worse, most mail users pay no attention to messages from `MAILER-DAEMON` saying `550 Content rejected. Contact postmaster@iblockyourmail.net for`

`assistance`. Instead, they call the intended recipient and accuse them of having broken mail servers.

Tag

Often used in combination with a rejection strategy, some organizations use software that *marks* or *tags* suspect messages letting users' MUAs filter based on the tags in the message header or body. This approach uses thresholds set by the administrator, the user, or both. In some cases, users are not willing to concern themselves with tuning their spam filter, thus combination approaches with "opt-in" user-configured filtering work well.

Content filtering with SpamAssassin

SpamAssassin uses a system of weighted rules to compute the likelihood that a particular message is spam. This provides a far more effective means of filtering mail content than by specifying "bad strings" or "suspicious headers" and so on in a flat text file. The key advantage is that the SpamAssassin rules are updated on a regular basis. Unless your full-time job is to observe new spam and update your personal rules file, SpamAssassin will probably provide more timely rule updates.

SpamAssassin is a fairly substantial and configurable mail filtering application. We don't cover the intricacies of installing and configuring SpamAssassin here. Visit the project home page at *http://spamassassin.apache.org/* to learn more.

SpamAssassin is easy to install on both FreeBSD and OpenBSD systems through the port in *mail/p5-Mail-SpamAssassin*. There are two main ways to make SpamAssassin parse incoming mail in conjunction with Sendmail: use `procmail` or use a SpamAssassin milter. Both are available in the ports tree on OpenBSD and FreeBSD systems. Postfix may be coupled with SpamAssassin in three main ways: using `procmail`, defining SpamAssassin as a content filter, or using amavisd-new (a high performance MTA and content checker interface).

Arbitrary content filtering

Arbitrary content filtering gives the administrator the ability to reject or drop mail by matching some string in the header or body of a message. While SpamAssassin does a decent job of tagging incoming spam, certain situations may arise where arbitrary filtering may be appropriate:

- Having set your SpamAssassin threshold to 5.0, you notice after a few months or a year that you have not seen any false positives above a 12.0 threshold. You need a way to block all messages SpamAssassin marks with a value greater than 12.

- A new piece of malware is announced on a mailing list to which you are subscribed. It's particularly insidious and spreads quickly but always has one of three subject lines. You need to make sure this virus does not get past your mail relay, and you need to do it yesterday.
- You want to block messages with certain attachments outright.

For these "quick and dirty" situations, content filtering based on administrator-configured pattern-matching is a good choice.

DNS real-time blacklists (RBLs)

In addition to rejecting based on headers or content, mail can be rejected based on the host from which the connection is being made. We have thrown around the word "blacklist" a few times in this chapter but have not yet described what it means. Blacklists, DNS blacklists, or real-time blacklists (RBLs), are essentially lists of systems known to be open relays or known to have sent spam in the past. These blacklists can be retrieved or accessed over the Internet through DNS. Mail servers are often configured to verify every incoming connection to ensure it is not from a blacklisted server—if it is, message transmission is denied. The original RBL site, *http://www.mail-abuse.com/*, offers a subscription-based service (it costs money) but is one of the more reputable blacklist services available. Other trustworthy RBL providers include: Spam Cop, the Open Relay Database, and RFC-ignorant.org. See the "Resources" section at the end of this chapter for links to these public service RBL providers.

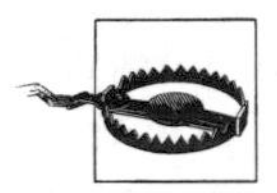

Do some research before you start using any RBL; they list sites for different reasons. RFC-ignorant, for instance, will list any site that fails to obey the rules defined by the mail-related RFCs. This may block more than you bargained for.

The facilities available to us on FreeBSD and OpenBSD systems to accomplish these tasks are diverse. We'll go through them in the final stages of mail software configuration. One important thing to remember is that you shouldn't rely on only one way of stopping unsolicited mail. These approaches complement each other, they aren't mutually exclusive.

Mail and DNS

Mail servers rely heavily on DNS. An improperly configured nameserver is sure to result in general mail flow problems including lengthy delays, mail loops, and mail rejections. It's imperative that you understand DNS records as they pertain to mail before deploying your mail server. If others are responsible for administering the DNS servers for your organization, you'll at least need to let them know what you need.

First and foremost, your mail server must have an address (A) record. This makes it possible to *resolve* the fully qualified domain name of your name server into an IP address. Second, and frequently omitted by lazy or uninformed mail and DNS administrators, your server should have a pointer (PTR) record. This allows you to *resolve* the IP address back into the hostname. Third, there must be a mail exchanger (MX) record configured for every domain for which your mail servers accept mail.

Each MX record in DNS has two important variables: a priority and the fully qualified domain name of your mail server. A snippet from a BIND zone configuration file might look something like Example 6-3:

Example 6-3. MX records

```
$ORIGIN mexicanfood.net.
                        MX    10    refried.mexicanfood.net.
                        MX    20    garbanzo.mexicanfood.net.
                        MX    30    bruchetta.italianfood.net.
```

The three `MX` records all reference servers that should be configured to accept mail for *mexicanfood.net*. Other mail servers will attempt to reach them in order of priority from lowest to highest. If any server is unreachable, the next server will be tried.

The server with the lowest priority is called the "preferred" MX, while the others are referred to as "backup" MXes. Backup MX servers are often configured to store-and-forward. When the preferred mail server becomes unreachable, the backup MX will accept the messages and hold them in a queue until the preferred server becomes available. In Example 6-3, both *refried* and *garbanzo* would have to be inaccessible for external systems to send mail to *bruchetta*.

One last thing to keep in mind is direct delivery. In a network of Unix systems, all running some mail daemon, you might end up sending mail from host to host, without needing MX records at all. If user paco on system *taco.mexicanfood.net* tries to send mail to user bruce on system *guacamole.mexicanfood.net*, how does it get there without an MX record for *guacamole.mexicanfood.net*? When there is no MX record for the latter half of the email address, mail servers will look for an A record. As long as *guacamole* resolves, *taco* will be able to connect directly to port 25 on *guacamole* and deliver the message.

Security Implications

The dependence SMTP has on name resolution should reemphasize the importance of deploying a secure DNS architecture. If name resolution for your domain is hijacked in one of the ways mentioned in the Chapter 5, rerouting your mail traffic (and web traffic, FTP traffic, etc.) becomes trivial. It is imperative that all systems involved in providing name services for your domain are tightly secured so they can be trusted.

This issue of trust exists with DNS servers and is also important with SMTP servers. Just as DNS slaves outside of your organization have to be systems you can trust, you also need to trust servers acting as backup mail exchangers. Admittedly, the risks are not quite as great:

- A compromised backup MX server may expose private or confidential queued mail, and an attacker might delete the messages altogether.
- A poorly configured backup MX may be more susceptible to a DoS attack. If timed correctly, it may be unavailable when you need it most.
- If the backup MX is not configured with the same spam-blocking mechanisms as your primary servers, the volume of spam that hits the backup when your primary servers go down may inadvertently create a DoS itself.

Ten years ago, backup MX servers were an imperative: systems were commonly intermittently connected. If you did not have one, momentary connectivity outages would likely result in the loss of mail. These days, most legitimate mail senders will patiently wait several days before giving up on your primary server altogether. Systems generally come back up quickly, and hard disks are a good deal larger.

Instead of seeking an extra-organizational backup MX, consider having a second onsite server or a server in an offsite co-location facility. The former provides decent protection against the loss of one system, the latter mitigates the risks associated with system failures and losses of connectivity at one location.

So far we've been looking at how mail servers are supposed to work using DNS and MX records. Bad guys don't always play by the rules, of course. Most spammers will download a list of MX records for the organization and either find the least protected one, or throw mail at all of them in some haphazard way. If you've configured one of your backup mail exchangers to simply pass mail to your internal mail server, you're going to be in trouble. They'll discover sooner or later that mail sent to your backup MX won't bounce spam and they'll start using it exclusively. Make sure all servers listed in your list of MXes are equally well protected.

SMTP

The Simple Mail Transfer Protocol, which governs mail flow, was not designed with security in mind. By default, SMTP servers will accept connections from anywhere and allow anyone to interact with the daemons providing service. What's worse, the daemons believe everything you tell them, as shown in Example 6-4. This conversation can be easily carried out by connecting to port 25 on a mail server via `telnet`. Lines starting with a number are mail server responses, highlighted lines are commands sent to the mail server.

Example 6-4. SMTP conversation

```
220 woot.home.korff.org ESMTP Sendmail 8.12.9/8.12.9; Sat, 11 Sep 2004 11:52:26 -0400
(EDT)
HELO im.your.father.luke
250 woot.home.korff.org Hello [172.16.0.2], pleased to meet you
MAIL FROM: <darth@vader.net>
250 2.1.0 <darth@vader.net>... Sender ok
RCPT TO: <yanek>
250 2.1.5 <yanek>... Recipient ok
DATA
354 Enter mail, end with "." on a line by itself
From: "Darth Vader" <darth@vader>
To: Nobody!
Date: Yesterday
Subject: Tomorrow

I'd give my right hand for an open relay.
.
250 2.0.0 i8BFqQwu008586 Message accepted for delivery
QUIT
221 2.0.0 woot.home.korff.org closing connection
Connection closed by foreign host.
```

It's important to know what's happening during this SMTP transaction, so let's take these lines one by one.

HELO

The HELO request allows the client to identify itself to the server. The server will attempt to do a reverse lookup on the IP address of the incoming connection. In this example, the reverse lookup failed, so the IP address of the client appears in the response. After the HELO, there is a new "envelope" ready for the coming mail message. These days, most mail clients use the extended hello command, EHLO, which is a way of simultaneously identifying yourself and asking the server, "What are your capabilities?"

HELO requires a client to claim an identity. It's then possible for the server to reject the claim under certain situations:

- When the IP address does not reverse resolve into the hostname provided as an argument to the HELO (DNS PTR record incorrect or missing)
- When the hostname provided as an argument to HELO does not resolve at all. (DNS A record missing)
- When the server has been configured to block the host, the domain in which the host resides, or the netblock in which the host resides

Unfortunately if you choose to configure your mail server in this way, you'll have throngs of unhappy users beating down your door because you're blocking a lot of legitimate mail. Too many administrators of mail servers know too little about DNS.

Envelope information

The subsequent `MAIL FROM:` and `RCPT TO:` commands are very much like writing your target and return address on the outside of a regular envelope. This SMTP envelope information governs where the mail is routed. Note that recipients do not always have access to this information after the message is delivered.

`DATA`

The `DATA` command tells the mail server that all subsequent input is going to be the mail message. The server will expect a series of lines to be considered the mail "header" followed by a blank line, followed by the message body. A period (`.`) on a line by itself marks the end of the message.

`QUIT`

As the name implies, this is used after the message has been sent to the mail server and the client wishes to terminate the connection.

Envelope Versus Header

Most ordinary users don't really understand that SMTP is very much like regular mail. There is an envelope that contains address information and determines how the message contained "within" is to be routed. One important difference is that with SMTP, the raw envelope information is often discarded after message delivery. You may look at a message and see that it was addressed to *myaccount@home.com*, but in fact you received it at *myaccount@work.com*.

The key here is that when you look at a message in your MUA, you are examining the partial contents of the message *header* and the message *body*, not the envelope. Worse, the partial header information typically shown by most MUAs is never verified and thus cannot be trusted. In order to fully understand where the message came from and how it was sent, you must look at the contents of the entire message (all headers and body), as seen in Example 6-5.

Example 6-5. Message from Darth Vader

```
From darth@vader.net Sat Sep 11 11:56:11 2004
Received: from im.your.father.luke ([172.16.0.2])
        by woot.home.korff.org (8.12.9/8.12.9) with SMTP id i8BFqQwu008586
        for <yanek>; Sat, 11 Sep 2004 11:54:00 -0400 (EDT)
Message-Id: <200409111554.i8BFqQwu008586@woot.home.korff.org>
From: "Darth Vader" <darth@vader>
To: Nobody!
Date: Yesterday
Subject: Tomorrow
Status: RO

I'd give my right hand for an open relay.
```

You'll notice three headers have been added: a `From` line, `Received` lines, and `Message-Id`. Carefully examining the `Received` message headers will help you trace how messages reached the target systems and what systems (not people!) were responsible for sending the message.

Security Implications

There is no native security here. As the acronym indicates, SMTP is simple. It provides a means for messages to get from point A to point B, and that's it. Senders are not verified in any way. There are no provisions to ensure that only the recipient is able to read the message. Messages are transported from the sender to the recipient across any number of mail servers in clear text. Fortunately, as security has become a greater concern in recent years, several add-on systems provide some of this functionality.

SMTP AUTH via SASL

The Simple Authentication and Security Layer (SASL) provides "authentication support to connection-based protocols" like SMTP. It's been built in accordance with RFC 2554 that defines how clients can authenticate themselves to an SMTP server. You'll often see the term "SMTP AUTH" used almost interchangeably with SASL. The former is the service extension to SMTP defined in the RFC to allow for authentication. The latter is the library that actually does the authentication.

SMTP AUTH lets administrators deploy mail servers that allow anyone to send mail, as long as they can authenticate. It doesn't help a recipient verify that a message sent from a particular address actually *came* from the person listed on the `To:` line. Nor does it guarantee that the message has not been modified in transit. Its most common use is to allow legitimate senders to use the organization's mail server even when they are coming from unknown and untrusted networks, like WiFi hotspots and hotels.

You might be thinking that you could configure your mail server to only send messages if the sender is from your domain, regardless of the IP from which the connection was made thus alleviating the need for SMTP AUTH. Think again. SMTP headers are trivially faked as we will discuss later, and this style of configuration makes your mail server an open relay.

TLS

Transport Layer Security (TLS), which supercedes Secure Sockets Layer (SSL), is a communications protocol that provides private and reliable communications by cryptographic means. TLS is often coupled with SASL to provide authentication over an encrypted connection so that usernames and passwords are not transmitted in clear text.

While SASL combined with TLS does provide a flexible and secure way for roaming users to send mail through your mail server, it is not the only option. Other approaches include "POP before SMTP," which uses the authentication in a POP session to create a window of time during which an SMTP session originating from the same client IP address will be permitted to relay through the system. Another alternative is client-based certificates that allow users who have certificates installed on their computer (wherever they are) to authenticate. While these options are both viable and used by various organizations, SASL combined with TLS is easy to implement, secure, and flexible. Thus it is this option that we cover in this chapter.

SPF

The neverending war against SPAM has given rise to the Sender Policy Framework (SPF). While SASL and TLS together allow responsible administrators to restrict who uses their servers to send mail, a plethora of uninformed administrators are still running open relays. SPF provides a mechanism for MTAs to verify that the server sending a message from a given domain is *authorized* to do so. In Example 6-4, if SPF guidelines were followed, the mail server *woot.home.korff.org* that received mail from *172.16.0.2* would look for a specially formulated TXT record for *vader.net* in order to determine whether *172.16.0.2* is allowed to send mail from that domain. If everyone created these specially formulated TXT records for their domains, mail servers could verify senders and reject mail if the server was not authorized to send mail from that domain. Of course if everyone ensured their servers weren't open relays, that would help, too. The trouble is, it's difficult to make *everyone* do *anything* in particular.

SPF continues to be a controversial "solution" to SPAM for a variety of reasons. For more information about this framework, see the SPF resources at the end of this chapter. One final piece of good news: SPF support, for those who want it, is available as a plug-in to SpamAssassin Version 3.0.0.

Message integrity, privacy, and non-repudiation

Another category of problems associated with sending and receiving email might be summarized as "message validation." First of all, without additional software, there's no way to guarantee that the message a recipient receives is the same message that the sender sent. In other words, there is no guaranteed message integrity. Second, because messages are not encrypted during transmission, a rogue intervening mail server could easily redirect unencrypted messages to another host. Thus there's no expected privacy. Finally, the recipient has no way to know for sure who sent the message; she can only see who's listed on the `From:` line. In other words, there is no ability to provide non-repudiation.

These problems are grouped together because they can be solved through cryptographic means. Products like Pretty Good Privacy (PGP), the GNU Privacy Guard (GPG), and the Secure MIME (S/MIME) standard are all capable of providing message integrity, privacy, and non-repudiation. Unfortunately, an appropriate treatment of these methodologies and the underlying concepts in cryptography are well beyond the scope of this chapter. It's important to be aware that these problems exist so that if you need to address them at some point, you'll know you have reading to do.

Mail Server Configurations

So far we've discussed some of the attacks possible against mail servers and brought up a number of additional security-related issues. We've also introduced several methodologies to protect servers from attack and stem the flow of unwanted mail. That is, we've discussed what the problems are, and to some extent, *what* solutions exist. We now turn our attention to where you can put some of these solutions into effect.

In order to examine specific "cases" of mail servers, we have to look at our infrastructure purely in the context of mail flow. We no longer care what a server is, only how it handles mail. Figure 6-3 shows four kinds of mail servers: the mail relay, the internal/external mail servers, and the null-client.

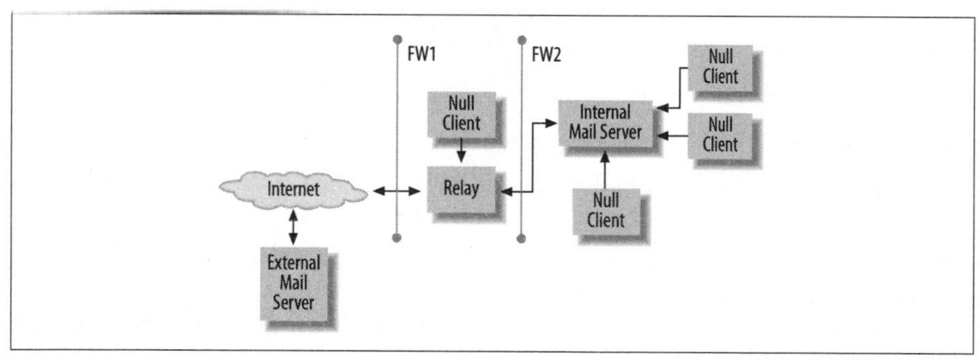

Figure 6-3. Four classes of servers

This is by no means the only possible mail architecture, merely one of the most commonly seen in small to medium sized companies with typical electronic messaging requirements. In particular, the flow of mail into and out of an organization may be handled by completely different sets of servers. There may be cases where flows need to be split so that inbound mail is processed by a different set of rules and restrictions than outbound mail. In most situations, however, single servers are capable of handling bidirectional flows.

Null Client

The null client is a workstation or server that performs no local delivery and accepts no mail from outside the system. Any mail generated from the system is immediately sent to one preconfigured server. Most servers that do not handle mail for a living fall into the null client category. Workstations that do not perform local delivery may also be null clients. Virtually all desktop systems, whether they run Windows, Mac OS, or some kind of Unix, should be configured as null clients.

Fortunately configuring null clients is simple:

- Disable any daemons listening for SMTP traffic, or restrict the daemon to the loopback interface.
- Configure the MTA to accept mail originating on the system and to send it to an upstream mail server.

No other mail "intelligence" is required for a null client. Generally, the configuration never changes throughout the life of the machine, even though the mail software will be periodically upgraded.

Internal Mail Server

The internal mail server is a particularly complex system. It not only houses an MTA, which accepts mail from the mail relay and local null clients, it also performs local delivery and provides mail access. Finally, it's responsible for taking any mail not destined for the organization and passing it on to the mail relay.

When configuring your internal mail server, keep in mind the following:

- Only administrators should be able to log in.
- The operating system should be locked down as much as possible. See Chapters 3 and 4 for more information on system hardening.
- All changes to configuration files (in general, but especially those pertaining to your mail software) should be tracked. Consider using `sudo` to control which administrators are allowed to make configuration changes. This will also help your audit trail.
- Any mail leaving this server should appear to come from your domain, not the hostname of your mail server. You should take pains to ensure all outgoing email addresses are valid. Some local accounts may be exceptions to this rule, for example root and cron.
- The administrator should know every program to which mail may be redirected through an alias, a *.forward* file, or an *:include:* mailing list. Configure your MTA software to restrict the programs which may be used as destinations in these files. You may even restrict it so that no programs may be used as destinations in these files.

- Disable any MTA functionality you don't need.
- Any message size limit you specify in an internal mail server will affect mail between organizational users. You should set a threshold, but it may be higher than similar limits on the mail relay.
- Virus protection may be useful. The virus protection on your relay helps keep viruses from entering or leaving your organization. Internal virus protection is also mandatory to keep viruses from spreading within your organization after having been brought in on a floppy or some other out-of-band mechanism. Use a different vendor than you do on your mail relay as the union of virus signatures from different vendors will be greater than if you only choose one vendor.
- Configure SpamAssassin with per-user controls, if possible.
- Provide secure access. This will include requiring authentication for both sending and receiving mail and protecting the communications channel using some form of encryption.

While this is not an exhaustive list of configuration possibilities on an internal mail server, you should give careful thought to each one.

Mail Relay

A mail relay can provide an excellent strategic opportunity to the mail administrator. Figure 6-3 shows a mail architecture where every message entering and leaving the organization passes through this system. This is the ideal system to make early accept/reject decisions for incoming and outgoing mail.

Some argue that mail originating from internal users is generally legitimate and should not be checked. However, internal users may repeatedly send large attachments outside the organization that bounce. Setting a message size limit ensures you aren't wasting resources. In addition, in a virus outbreak, you wouldn't want infected mail leaving your network and infecting others.

When configuring your mail relay, refer to the first six bullets in the checklist for your internal mail server. They apply here also. In addition, consider the following:

- Message size limits should be configured here and should be more stringent than on the internal server. Values under 10 megabytes are appropriate.
- Use content filtering effectively whether by blocking certain networks, hosts, addresses, domains, or blocking by substrings in message headers or the message body.
- Configure DNS blacklists.
- Virus protection may be useful. Use a different vendor than you do on your internal mail server.

- You may want to configure SpamAssassin on the mail relay with reasonable default settings that apply globally. This will help you, in combination with content filtering, to block all UCE rated above a certain threshold at the relay level.

While these options are not exhaustive, you should carefully evaluate each for your mail relay.

External Mail Server

Not all organizations have an "external mail server." This is the server that lets remote users send and receive mail directly—without the use of a webmail gateway or VPN. Sometimes these servers are placed along side a mail relay in the perimeter network. Other organizations choose to place them outside of any firewalls.

The external mail server should be configured just like an internal mail server. However, since these servers often need to relay mail for users from unknown networks, authenticated SMTP and encrypted sessions are mandatory.

In addition, external mail servers sometimes perform all mail duties for an organization, especially for organizations whose business it is to provide mail access to customers. In these cases, they may be strategically important just like the mail relay. You should evaluate all the configuration guidelines recommended for a mail relay on these systems also.

Now that we have covered problems and solutions in a general sense, it's time to get down to specifics. We now examine how to configure our mail servers to ensure they do what we need. To be able to answer these questions, let us first look at the relevant software.

Sendmail

Several pieces of software boast MTA capabilities, but Sendmail is probably the most well known. In its first incarnation, it was developed by Eric Allman in 1979, called Delivermail, and shipped with 4.0 and 4.1 BSD. In the early 1980s, it became known as Sendmail and is now the default mailer on most open and commercial Unix systems today.

As Sendmail was being developed, the "Internet" as we know it today was just beginning to form. TCP/IP had just been developed and communication standards were furiously being formulated to govern the ways computers should interact. It was in this wild-west environment that Sendmail was written. It was developed to implement a "general purpose internetwork mail routing facility," according to Allman's "Sendmail Installation and Operation Guide" (October 25, 1997, *http://www.sendmail.org/~ca/e-mail/doc8.8/op.html*) and to not rely on any one transport protocol. At the time of its development, the flexibility Sendmail offered was its greatest strength and translated directly into its rapid and widespread adoption.

In these days of ubiquitous TCP/IP networking and the universal reliance on the SMTP protocol, its flexibility (more specifically, the wealth of compiled code implementing this flexibility) is its greatest drawback.

While this bit of historical aside may seem unnecessary in a book about building OpenBSD and FreeBSD servers, bear in mind that Sendmail continues to be the default mailer on both operating systems. Cotemporary critics insist that Sendmail's long history has given rise to a massively complex mail transport system implementing a wealth of features rarely used. A system this complex is rarely fully understood by those who administer it and this lack of understanding during deployment can lead to a host of security problems. As evidence, critics offer Sendmail's long list of discovered vulnerabilities during the years.

Many administrators who eschew Sendmail in favor of alternate mailers do so without really assessing Sendmail's security posture today. In recent years, Sendmail has shown comparatively few vulnerabilities. The availability of commercial support for the product has made it a more attractive option for companies who have this as a requirement. These administrators often have little recent experience with Sendmail and choose to administer a different platform as a result of preconceived notions. As with any system, however, you should administer software you are comfortable with—if you know Sendmail, feel free to use it.

Installation and Configuration

Sendmail is installed as the default MTA on both OpenBSD and FreeBSD systems, thus there is little to do for installation. You may recall from Chapter 3 that Sendmail will be listening on `127.0.0.1:25` by default. In order for Sendmail to work properly, you must not use the `nosuid` option (in */etc/fstab*) when mounting the filesystems that contain your mail queue and the `sendmail` binary.

FreeBSD users may also choose to install Sendmail through ports instead of tracking updates to the daemon with the operating system.

If you try to install Sendmail through ports and override the `PREFIX` environment variable to convince the port to overwrite the base version, the installation will fail and you will be chastised. Instead, accept the default */usr/local* prefix and run **`make mailer.conf`** from the *mail/sendmail* directory in your ports hierarchy to update */etc/mail/mailer.conf* to point to the version of Sendmail installed through ports.

Whether or not your system has been recently built, your first priority in running any server should be to bring your system up to date. Because Sendmail is part of the base operating system, it will be upgraded with the rest of the system.

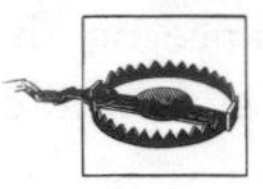

FreeBSD users who are tracking Sendmail through ports must not forget to upgrade that port in addition to performing a system upgrade. Be careful during the `mergemaster` step of the system upgrade not to overwrite the changes your port has made to */etc/mail/mailer.conf*. If you choose to set `NO_SENDMAIL=true` in */etc/make.conf* to speed up your system build, make sure you delete all existing Sendmail binaries. If you leave them behind, they will not be updated to account for vulnerabilities.

Follow the appropriate procedures to bring your system up to date; see Chapters 3 and 4 for more information. Ensuring that you are running an up-to-date version of Sendmail will go a long way toward protecting your operating system from compromise.

Root Background

The `sendmail` binary used to be a *setuid* root program. This means that regardless of which user was invoking the command, it would run as root. Allowing arbitrary users to run programs as root is, of course, fairly dangerous and the default was changed to a *setgid* binary as of Version 8.12. This allows `sendmail` to run as the user invoking the program, yet continue to transfer mail via SMTP or write to the client mail queue */var/spool/clientmqueue*.

Another important aspect of `sendmail` to remember is that when root access is not needed, the binary drops privileges. Certain aspects of handling mail, of course require root privileges, for instance:

- Listening on privileged port 25 for SMTP
- Reading *~/.forward* files restricted to user-only read/write access
- Writing out files owned by arbitrary users

For this kind of flexibility, `sendmail` must from time to time do things as root. When root privileges are not needed, `sendmail` will fork, drop privileges using `setreuid(3)`, `seteuid(3)`, or `setuid(3)` as available. When the child process has completed its non-root task, it exits, leaving behind the parent still running as root.

The Configuration Files

For administrators without years of experience configuring and tuning Sendmail, one of the keys to successful and sane configuration is to treat *.cf* files as binaries: don't modify them—to change the configuration, modify the corresponding *.mc* file. OpenBSD places the source *.mc* files in */usr/share/sendmail/cf*. Most importantly the *openbsd-localhost.mc* is the source of */etc/mail/localhost.cf*: the default configuration file used by `sendmail` on OpenBSD. FreeBSD users should instead use the *.mc* and *.cf* files in */etc/mail*. Additional example *.mc* files are located in */usr/share/sendmail/cf/cf*.

Details on how to modify *.mc* files, a background on the `m4` macro language processor, etc., are beyond the scope of this book. However, these details are fully covered by the *README* found under */usr/share/sendmail* on your FreeBSD or OpenBSD system.

Overall Sendmail Security

At the beginning of this chapter, we talked about three types of situations you should look out for when deploying a mail server: attacks that threaten the operating system, illegitimate mail relaying, and blocking unwanted mail. While architecture and software updates mitigate the risks, there is more work to be done in the configuration of your mail software. This section delves into some of the configuration options available to you with Sendmail. As we point out how each option mitigates risks, you can decide whether it's worth using on your servers.

File and directory permissions

It is imperative that Sendmail's binaries and configuration files have appropriate permissions. Weak permissions on files and directories can easily result in system compromise. For instance:

- Everyone who has write access to your *sendmail.cf* can use the program form of the `F` command combined with setting the `DefaultUser` to `0:0` to cause `sendmail` to execute an arbitrary script as root. If that script happens to make one of your installed shells (or a copy of a shell in */tmp*, for instance) a *setuid* binary, anyone with local access can get root access.
- Attackers may also exploit group-writable *.forward* and *:include:* files to gain system access as the file owner.
- Protecting the *aliases* file alone is not sufficient as that is merely a source file to generate the alias database, a `db3(3)` format file called *aliases.db* in */etc/mail*.
- Improper directory ownership can result in root-owned files being overwritten or directory owners being replaced.

To help prevent these situations, `sendmail` will check the permissions of all `sendmail`-related binaries, configuration files, and directories on the system. You can force an audit with the following command:

```
% sudo sendmail -v -d44.4 -bv postmaster
```

Observe the output closely and ensure your system does not fall prey to weak permissions. Once you have solidified the desired permissions on your system, you may want to employ some combination of file immutability and permissions auditing software like Tripwire, Osiris, or `mtree(8)`.

Beware recipient programs

Most sendmail configuration files, including *.forward* files, *:include:* mailing lists, aliases, and the *sendmail.cf* configuration file itself, support the execution of arbitrary programs. We mentioned earlier that *.forward* and *:include:* mailing list files are parsed and acted upon in the user context. If you've been diligent, these files will be writable only by the owner, ensuring that the execution of programs is intentional. If you've not been careful, users could easily start running programs as other users.

Still, just the fact that these files point to arbitrary programs means you've got another problem to deal with. All of these programs have suddenly become a part of your mail system, and you'll have to audit them, too. Be especially wary of the aliases file: sendmail will take actions on this file in the daemon user context.

You might want to consider restricting users from passing incoming mail to programs by ensuring their shell as specified in the *passwd* files is not in */etc/shells*. You may still allow login by specifying a valid shell that is not in */etc/shells*: you could, perhaps, create a */bin/allow-login* shell, which is a copy of */bin/tcsh*, and ensure */bin/allow-login* is not listed in */etc/shells*.

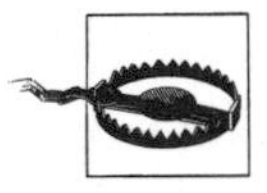

Beware of letting users log into your mail server. Keeping an administrator-only machine secure is certainly easier than securing a system with a variety of local accounts. Consider enforcing the use of mail retrieval protocols instead of direct mail access as described previously.

There are, of course, a variety of other Sendmail-specific configuration options to consider also. One of these can help restrict what programs sendmail will execute on behalf of users.

Security-Related Configuration Options

Arbitrary program restriction

Sendmail comes with a variety of helper programs including smrsh(8). This "sendmail restricted shell" is meant to replace */bin/sh* as the shell used by sendmail to execute programs specified in configuration files in the *|/path/to/program* syntax. In fact, smrsh will only execute programs located in */usr/libexec/sm.bin* (by default) in addition to the shell built-in commands echo, exec, and exit.

To configure sendmail to use smrsh, thus tightly restricting users' ability to execute arbitrary programs (a good thing!), use a stanza similar to the following in your *.mc* file before your **MAILER(`local')** stanza:

```
FEATURE(`smrsh',`/usr/libexec/smrsh')
```

You will then need to link to programs that should be allowed to run. For example, to grant users the ability to pass mail into vacation(1) and procmail(1), issue these commands:

```
% sudo ln -s /usr/bin/vacation /usr/libexec/sm.bin/vacation
% sudo ln -s /usr/bin/procmail /usr/libexec/sm.bin/procmail
```

Don't blame Sendmail

As of Version 8.9 of Sendmail, the daemon is more careful about overall file and directory permissions making it more difficult for the careless administrator to deploy Sendmail with weak file and directory permissions. If you're adamant about supporting permissions that sendmail does not want to tolerate, you can use the appropriately named DontBlameSendmail option. So, if your configuration changes result in an insecure installation, and your host is compromised, blame yourself instead.

If you find you have a legitimate need to loosen the restrictions sendmail imposes on file ad directory permissions, review the documentation on this option at *http://www.sendmail.org/tips/DontBlameSendmail.html*. Remember, instead of making configuration files group writable, use sudo(8) to tightly control and audit who makes changes to what files. This will keep you from making configuration mistakes with DontBlameSendmail, and the strong audit trail will help deter or detect would-be saboteurs.

If you must use this option, it may be compiled into your configuration file with a statement similar to the following in your *.mc* file:

```
define(`confDONT_BLAME_SENDMAIL',`GroupWritableAliasFile,
IncludeFileInGroupWritableDirPath')
```

Masquerade your domain

Many organizations send mail internally and retain full hostnames for host-to-host mail. When the mail leaves the organization, however, these internal hostnames are no longer resolvable. In order to ensure that mail reaches the destination (because the sender's domain must resolve), it's usually a good idea to masquerade all hosts and subdomains within a domain to the top level domain.

That is, mail sent from two internal hosts *taco.mexicanfood.net* and *salsa.condiments.mexicanfood.net* should reach their destination and appear to have come from *@mexicanfood.net*. This configuration option is a appropriate for a mail relay and may be configured using a stanza similar to the following in your *.mc* file:

```
MASQUERDADE_AS(`mexicanfood.net')
MASQUERDADE_DOMAIN(`mexicanfood.net')
FEATURE(`masquerade_envelope')
```

These three lines ensure (in order) that mail sent from the local host is masqueraded, mail relayed through this machine from other hosts is masqueraded, and envelope information (in addition to header information) is masqueraded.

Note that usernames will be preserved and you may run into mail routing problems by collapsing your internal namespace. Thus, many organizations enforce organization-wide usernames and masquerade on the internal mail server also. If you choose to masquerade on your internal server, you will likely want to retain host information for system and service users like root and cron. To do this, use one of the following methods in your *.mc* file:

```
EXPOSED_USER(`root cron')
EXPOSED_USER_FILE(`/etc/mail/masquerade-user-exceptions')
```

Obfuscate greeting

It is of marginal value to obfuscate the greeting (for example, the first line of Example 6-4) `sendmail` displays when client programs or attackers connect to port 25 on your host. Most attacks you face come from scripts, iterating through open ports looking for daemons to exploit. These scripts rarely care about what mail server you happen to be running, they will attempt the exploit regardless.

Still, some administrators prefer to give away as little information as possible. A laudable goal and if you have secured your system and Sendmail in every other conceivable way and have time left over, by all means configure an obfuscated greeting by adding a stanza similar to the following in your *.mc* file:

```
define(`confSMTP_LOGIN_MSG',`$j MexiMail Server')
```

Permissions of transient files

As a consequence of normal operations, `sendmail` will create and delete a variety of files. These files fall into two categories: temporary files and queue files. The permissions of these transient files are controlled by the `TempFileMode` and `QueueFileMode` options. Ensure that if you compile new values into the *.cf* files provided with the base operating system, you do so with great care.

The values of these options may be changed from the *.mc* file using stanzas similar to the following:

```
define(`confTEMP_FILE_MODE',`0600')
define(`confQUEUE_FILE_MODE',`0600')
```

Privacy options

`sendmail` can be configured to be a little less helpful and a little more paranoid with the `PrivacyOptions` option in the `sendmail` configuration file. This is a particularly useful configuration item and we examine its possible values below.

`authwarnings`
: When specified, `authwarnings` tells `sendmail` to include `X-Authentication-Warning` headers into mail messages when certain situations arise that are cause for suspicion. Some examples of this include: when someone used the `-C` switch to use an alternate configuration file, use of the `-f` switch to replace the sender, hostname mismatches like the one in Example 6-4, not specifying `HELO/EHLO`, etc. These headers are fairly unobtrusive and you may find value in looking for them with your content filters as described later in this chapter.

`goaway`
: Shorthand specification for the following values: `authwarnings`, `noexpn`, `novrfy`, `noverb`, `needmailhelo`, `needexpnhelo`, `needvrfyhelo`, and `nobodyreturn`.

`nobodyreturn`
: This is "no body return," not "nobody return." That is, do not return the body of the message as part of a bounce. This can be especially useful if you have to deal with a lot of spam and returning the volume of illegitimate mail is chewing up your bandwidth.

`noetrn`
: Don't allow the SMTP `ETRN` command. If you are MX for an organization that has intermittent network capability and will only be able to receive mail at certain times, they may need a way to tell you to process your queue for them. These organizations could contact your mail server and issue, for instance, `ETRN` *`smtp.onlinesometimes.net`*. This will tell your server to process all messages in the queue that could not be delivered to *smtp.onlinesomtimes.net* due to network problems at last attempt. If this does not describe a situation you face, enable `noetrn`.

`needexpnhelo`
: The `EXPN` command is a handy, but often unnecessary information disclosure, as described later in this section. The `needexpnhelo` option causes `sendmail` to reject `EXPN` commands unless preceded by a `HELO/EHLO`. There is little real security value in this option alone, and `EXPN` should be disabled anyway.

`needmailhelo`
: Like the `needexpnhelo` option, `needmailhelo` requires a `HELO/EHLO` before the `MAIL FROM` command. From a security standpoint, `HELO` is weak and requiring it adds a little network traffic, no more.

`needvrfyhelo`
: At this point you can surely guess what this means. Make `sendmail` require a `HELO` before honoring a `VRFY`. Like `EXPN`, `VRFY` is nothing but unnecessary information disclosure and should be disabled anyway.

`noexpn`
: The `EXPN` command will expand local addresses. This will cause any relevant entries from a user's *~/.forward* file to be printed out, or list the addresses to

which the message will be delivered if the argument is an alias. The noexpn option also implies the noverb option. Use noexpn.

noreceipts
: The noreceipts option primarily turns off sendmail's ability to send return receipts. In fact, this option disables delivery status notifications (DSNs) altogether. DSN is what allows sendmail to notify senders when there are problems with mail delivery and be discriminating by tailoring status notifications based on specific errors. Many users rely heavily on return receipts and administrators rely on DSNs (users seem never to read DSNs), we recommend that you do not specify this option.

noverb
: This option turns on verbose processing of mail and should only be used when debugging.

novrfy
: The VRFY command is another source of unnecessary information disclosure. When used, sendmail will determine whether or not the argument specified to the VRFY command represents a valid account on the system. Frankly, there are other ways of getting this information, if a little slower. Still, VRFY is not a particularly useful feature and may be safely disabled.

public
: This turns off all PrivacyOptions.

restrictexpand
: Think of restrictexpand as noexpn in the command-line context. This option causes sendmail to run in nonprivileged mode when run with the -bv command-line argument so that attempts to expand contents of other users' *~/.forward* and *:include:* files fail. The restrictexpand option also disables the verbose -v command-line argument. Using this option is a good idea.

restrictmailq
: When specified, this restricts the use of the mailq command so that users who wish to view the mail queue must be in the same group as the group ownership of the queue directory. This can be valuable if non-administrators have access to the server.

restrictqrun
: Ensures that only root (specifically, the owner of */var/spool/mqueue*, which is root unless you changed it) is able to process the mail queue with the -q command-line argument to sendmail. While this alone does not provide much greater security, forcing administrators/users to use sudo to process the mail queue will provide better auditing.

Define privacy options in your *.mc* file with a statement similar to the following:

```
define(`confPRIVACY_FLAGS', `authwarnings,noexpn,novrfy')
```

Running sendmail as nonprivileged users

In certain situations, sendmail should run as another user for security reasons, but there is no obvious user to choose, for example, when sendmail is executing programs or writing files specified through *aliases*. In this case, sendmail drops privileges and changes to the user specified in the configuration file as the DefaultUser. On FreeBSD and OpenBSD systems, this user is mailnull. This user should not be a member of any groups (other than the mailnull group) on the system, should not have a valid home directory or shell, and should be used for nothing but this purpose.

In addition, sendmail can run in a variety of different modes including a listening server on *:25, 127.0.0.1:25, or purely to de-queue messages in either the outbound queue */var/spool/mqueue* or the locally submitted outbound queue */var/spool/clientmqueue*. In this last case, sendmail is run with the -Ac command-line argument, which causes it to start up and use the available *submit.cf* as its configuration file. By default, this file specifies the option RunAsUser=smmsp. The reason for this is that the daemon only needs to process files in */var/spool/clientmqueue* and send them outbound (and the *clientmqueue* is owned by smmsp:smmsp), so there is no reason to run as root.

Note that DefaultUser tells sendmail to use a specified non-root account when it needs to drop privilege but cannot decide which user to change to. RunAsUser, on the other hand, tells sendmail to run as the alternate user instead of root altogether. These two options may be configured from corresponding *.mc* files with statements similar to the following:

```
define(`confDEF_USER_ID', `user:group')
define(`confRUN_AS_USER', `user:group')
```

Safe file environment

As we have discussed, sendmail is able to deliver mail to both files and programs. In fact, it can deliver mail to anything that you can specify as a path: this includes items in */dev*, sockets, etc., provided it's running with the appropriate permissions. Using the SafeFileEnvironment option, you're able to simultaneously restrict sendmail from being able to write to anything other than regular files and specify a path under which all writing must be done. Obviously specifying a path of / will not restrict where on the filesystem sendmail may write, but will keep it from writing to non-regular files.

The safe file environment may be specified in your *.mc* file using the following stanza:

```
define(`confSAFE_FILE_ENV',`/home')
```

Trusted user

Sendmail's notion of a trusted user, specified as an argument to the `TrustedUser` option, allows a non-root user to manage Sendmail. This includes managing the various maps Sendmail uses and stopping (not starting!) and restarting `sendmail`. While this may be convenient in certain situations, the same behavior would be better achieved through the careful configuration and use of `sudo` to manage access rights. By default on FreeBSD and OpenBSD platforms, smmsp is the `TrustedUser` when `sendmail` is processing the *clientmqueue* (specified in *submit.cf*) and root is the `TrustedUser` otherwise.

Trusted users may be configured in an *.mc* file with using a stanza similar to the following:

```
define(`confTRUSTED_USER',`username')
```

Trusted users

Believe it or not, Sendmail has both trusted user and trusted users settings and they mean completely different things. Be careful when making configuration changes to either of these options. Whereas the `TrustedUser` is able to perform some Sendmail administration, the trusted users are only able to change the sender of a message by using the `-f` command-line argument. This can be useful when local mailing lists need to specify alternate sender addresses. Since SMTP has no particular restrictions on declaring From addresses, there is little real value in restricting trusted users. Still, the restrictive default is probably fine in most situations. The root, daemon, and uucp users are always listed as trusted users.

Trusted users, specified in the T class may be configured in one of the two following ways:

```
define(`confTRUSTED_USERS',`user1 user2 user3')
define(`confCT_FILE',`/path/to/trusted-user-file')
```

Limiting Denial of Service Attacks

By default, Sendmail is not very resistant to denial of service attacks. To help mitigate the risks of these kinds of attacks, several rate-limiting options exist.

`confCONNECTION_RATE_THROTTLE`
: Although it is difficult to devise a "reasonable" value for the number of connections `sendmail` should accept per second, this threshold nevertheless exists and is tunable. Fairly idle servers may make effective use of this by limiting connections to one every second. Mail administrators of servers that handle large volumes of mail will want to avoid defining this option.

`confMAX_DAEMON_CHILDREN`
: This configuration item limits the number of children the parent `sendmail` process can have running at any given time. This is a more useful configuration

parameter, but its value will depend on the resources available on your system. Once this limit is reached, other pending connections will be delayed.

`confMIN_FREE_BLOCKS`
: When this threshold is reached, `sendmail` will cease accepting messages. The default is 100 free blocks, though you may want to increase this value to leave room for other data on the filesystem (if there is any). Remember to always monitor system disk space closely.

`confMAXRCPTSPERMESSAGE`
: This configuration option defines the maximum number of recipients to which a message may be addressed. You may want to tune this value to a reasonable number to mitigate the risks of attacks that attempt to brute-force hundreds or thousands of usernames in one given message. Bear in mind, this is not common from spammers: UCE is usually sent with only a few recipients at most.

`confMAX_MESSAGE_SIZE`
: The maximum size of any given message that `sendmail` will handle. Keep this value under 10 megabytes if you can (even as little as two or three), and provide alternatives for transporting large files to your users.

Define these options in your *sendmail.mc* file, rebuild your `sendmail` configuration files and restart `sendmail`.

Blocking Unwanted Mail

As of Version 8.9, Sendmail refuses to relay mail by default. In order for messages to pass through your mail server, they must either be destined for a domain you handle, or the sending host must be a member of one of the domains listed in */etc/mail/relay-domains*. This can be further restricted by using `` FEATURE(`relay_hosts_only') `` in your *.mc* file requiring that the sending host itself be listed in the *relay-domains* file. Avoid other `FEATURE`s that open up relaying, as they are generally more permissive than you really want.

Access database

Sendmail supports an access database (usually */etc/mail/access*) that describes actions to take with mail based on hosts, domain, email addresses, network specification, or *tagged* connection and envelope information. Values of these keys must be `REJECT`, `DISCARD`, `OK`, `RELAY`, or an arbitrary error message. This can be useful to ensure mail from local networks and hosts is not blocked. Some also use access databases to list domains or addresses from which a lot of spam originates. Unfortunately this is an uphill battle: as soon as you list a sending location, the same message can appear from other sources.

DNS blacklists

Sendmail can easily be configured to reject mail from sites listed in real-time blacklists (RBLs) using the `FEATURE(`dnsbl')`. Alone, this `FEATURE` will use the original RBL at *http://www.mail-abuse.com/*. The other services mentioned previously may also be used when supplied as arguments to this `FEATURE`. Instructions for setting up blacklists for Sendmail may be found at each RBL provider site.

Milters

The Mail Filter API (milter) provides a way to hook third-party content filtering tools into Sendmail. A huge variety of plug-ins that use this milter functionality already exist and more appear regularly. We refer to these plug-ins colloquially as "milters" themselves, and describe a few key milters next.

Milter capability is built into Sendmail on FreeBSD by default. In order to get milter support with your Sendmail installation on OpenBSD, perform the following steps:

```
# echo WANT_LIBMILTER=YES >> /etc/mk.conf
% cd /usr/src/gnu/usr.sbin/sendmail
% make clean obj depend && make && sudo make install
% sudo mkdir /usr/include/libmilter
% sudo cp include/libmilter/*.h /usr/include/libmilter
```

One important thing to remember about milters is that they execute inline and are not post-processing options. Thus, they have the capability to reject messages during the SMTP conversation, obviating the need to store messages on disk. Traditionally, mail post-processing had been done after delivery to a delivery agent like `procmail(1)`.

Arbitrary content filtering

The *milter-regex* port in the *mail* directory of your ports hierarchy is your solution for "quick and dirty" content filtering. Installing this milter is as simple as a **`make install`** for both FreeBSD and OpenBSD systems. To activate this milter, add the following line to your *.mc* file and regenerate your *.cf*.

```
INPUT_MAIL_FILTER(`milter-regex',`S=unix:/var/spool/milters/regex.sock,
T=S:30s;R:2m')
```

In order for this milter to work, of course, the `milter-regex` daemon must be running so that */var/spool/milter-regex/sock* will exist when `sendmail` tries to send messages there. Create a startup script *milter.sh* and place it in */usr/local/etc/rc.d* to start `milter-regex` on boot with the `-c` argument specifying the configuration file (perhaps in */usr/local/etc/milter-regex*). Place expressions in this configuration file describing the kinds of messages you'd like to block. For instance, to block all messages SpamAssassin marks with a score of 12.0 or higher, use the following expression in your *milter-regex* file:

```
reject "This really, really looks like spam to me."
header /^X-Spam-Level: \*\*\*\*\*\*\*\*\*\*\*\*/
```

See the milter-regex(8) manual page for more configuration details and examples.

Virus protection

Virus protection is essential to stop the flow of malware through your servers to more vulnerable client workstations and servers running Windows. Viruses and worms that exploit vulnerabilities in Unix software are uncommon, but not unheard of. A variety of commercial and noncommercial options exist including McAffee Virus Scan, Kaspersky Anti-Virus, and Clam Anti-virus (ClamAV). Perhaps the most popular choice, and the one chosen by SourceForge, is ClamAV.

Installation of ClamAV as a milter on FreeBSD is as simple as running **make WITH_MILTER=YES install** from the *security/clamav* directory in the ports tree. OpenBSD users do not have an available *clamav* port on the system, but an unofficial *clamav* port is available at *http://www.fatbsd.com/openbsd/clamav/*. Once installed, the *clamav-milter* can be started using a command similar to the following:

```
% sudo clamav-milter -lo /var/spool/milters/clamav.sock
```

Of course, you may want to adjust where you put the socket. As with the regex milter, edit your *.mc* file and add a line similar to the following, and then regenerate your *.cf*.

```
INPUT_MAIL_FILTER(`clmilter',`S=local:/var/spool/milters/clamav.sock, F=,
T=S:4m;R:4m')
```

FreeBSD users can take advantage of the installed startup scripts in */usr/local/etc/rc.d* by configuring the following options in */etc/rc.conf*:

```
clamav_clamd_enable="YES"
clamav_milter_enable="YES"
clamav_milter_flags="--local --outgoing --max-children=50 --quarantine-dir=/var/
quarantine --dont-log-clean --headers --postmaster-only"
freshclam_flags="--daemon --checks=12"
freshclam_enable="YES"
```

OpenBSD users may want to ensure that clamd and clamav_milter start automatically when the system boots, that the added _clamd user is aliased to a human being's mail address in the aliases file, and that the freshclam virus database update program is run periodically through cron.

Before restarting sendmail to enable ClamAV support, be sure to edit the *clamav* configuration file. That's */usr/local/etc/clamav.conf* on FreeBSD. OpenBSD users may want to copy */usr/local/share/examples/clamav.conf* to */etc/clamav.conf* and edit that.

Authentication and Encryption

We discussed earlier that SMTP is an authentication-free protocol. By design, anyone can connect to an SMTP server and send mail that travels in clear text to the server. Certain organizations, however, who must accept and relay mail from known users on unknown and untrusted networks, need some means to verify that a user is who he says he is. One solution is the Simple Authentication and Security Layer (SASL).

Of course, authentication without encryption should send a shiver up the spine of any security-minded system administrator. Providing an encrypted channel over which authentication can occur for the SMTP exchange is handled by Transport Layer Security (TLS).

Installing Sendmail+SASL+TLS on FreeBSD

FreeBSD provides a *sendmail-sasl* port in *mail/sendmail-sasl*. A simple **make install** in the port directory will install the binaries in */usr/local/sbin*. You will also need to **make mailer.conf** to activate the version of sendmail from ports.

All that is left is a little configuration.

Installing Sendmail+SASL+TLS on OpenBSD

OpenBSD administrators should first install the Cyrus-SASL port from *security/cyrus-sasl2*, or if you prefer, retrieve the binary package and install it using pkg_add(1). Once installed, adjust the name of the shared object in */usr/local/lib* as follows:

```
% cd /usr/local/lib
% sudo ln -s libsasl2.so.2.11 libsasl2.so
```

The exact name of the library to which you must create a *libsasl2.so* symlink will vary based on the exact version of SASL you install on your system.

Once this is done, rebuild sendmail with SASL support as follows:

```
# echo WANT_SMTPAUTH=YES >> /etc/mk.conf
% cd /usr/src/gnu/usr.sbin/sendmail
% make clean obj depend && make && sudo make install
```

This will replace the Sendmail-related binaries on your system with those with SASL support, but you must still configure sendmail to use SASL and TLS.

Configuring Sendmail with SASL+TLS

To configure Sendmail to use SASL and to activate TLS support, edit the *.mc* source configuration file and add the following options:

```
define(`confCACERT_PATH',`/etc/mail/certs')
define(`confCACERT',`/etc/mail/certs/CA.cert.pem')
define(`confSERVER_CERT',`/etc/mail/certs/cert.pem')
define(`confSERVER_KEY',`/etc/mail/certs/key.pem')
define(`confAUTH_MECHANISMS',`PLAIN LOGIN CRAM-MD5 DIGEST-MD5')dnl
TRUST_AUTH_MECH(`PLAIN LOGIN CRAM-MD5 DIGEST-MD5')dnl
define(`confAUTH_OPTIONS',`p,y')dnl
```

Note that this allows "plain" logins where the users' passwords are transmitted in clear text over the network; with TLS, these clear-text passwords will be sent over an encrypted channel. Some MUAs do not properly handle any form of authentication other than plain text. If you find yourself in this position, use the PLAIN parameters, otherwise omit it. The exact location of your certificates may vary, but having at least these four certificate options defined in your *.mc* file will enable TLS support.

After you have modified your *.mc* file, rebuild your *.cf* file and install it. Once this is done, you must configure SASL to authenticate users in some way. Users may be authenticated against the local password file, an OpenLDAP server, a MySQL or PostgreSQL database, and so on. The details of configuring SASL are beyond the scope of this document, but a number of online HOWTOs for these topics exist.

To test SASL functionality, it may be worthwhile to use saslpasswd2(8) to create a separate authentication database and configure saslauthd(8) accordingly.

```
# echo "pwcheck_method: saslauthd" > /usr/local/lib/sasl2/Sendmail.conf
% sudo /usr/local/sbin/saslpasswd2 testuser
(follow prompts)
% sudo /usr/local/sbin/saslauthd -a getpwent
```

You will then need to restart sendmail for SASL authentication over TLS. Note that in order for saslauthd to start at boot, OpenBSD administrators need to add appropriate lines to their */etc/rc.local* script.

Postfix

Given the dissatisfaction with Sendmail's complexity, code bloat, and track record, it was only a matter of time before people started developing alternatives. One of these is a drop-in replacement for Sendmail and is called Postfix. Weitse Venema wrote a program called VMailer in 1997, and in early 2001, this software was released as Postfix Version 1.0. Postfix was designed from the ground up to be safe and robust, modular, to perform well, and to be compatible with Sendmail to make it easy for those familiar but unhappy with Sendmail to switch.

One significant difference between Postfix and Sendmail is its carefully crafted architecture. Postfix consists of a small suite of service binaries that each performs a simple task. The master binary, appropriately named master(8), runs as root and listens for incoming connections. When a connection is made, master spawns smtpd(8), which can run chrooted and handles SMTP transactions. When a message has been completely received by smtpd, it is passed on to the cleanup(8) daemon and eventually ends up in the incoming queue directory on the filesystem. This is just the beginning of how Postfix handles mail but should give you an idea of how Postfix was designed. Small programs handle simple tasks and handle them well in the best Unix tradition.

While understanding what all of the Postfix programs do is no easy task, configuring Postfix generally is. As mentioned earlier, Postfix was designed as a drop-in replacement for Sendmail. Most administrators familiar with Sendmail will be able to understand the terminology and architecture of Postfix without a great deal of effort. This makes configuring Postfix simple. Assisting with this endeavor are the comprehensive manpages and easy-to-read documentation and tutorials available at *http://www.postfix.org/*. For more information, consider the O'Reilly book *Postfix* by Kyle D. Dent.

Installation and Configuration: FreeBSD

To replace the base Sendmail installation on your FreeBSD system, change into *ports/mail/postfix* and run **make install**. You are provided a configuration menu similar to the one in Figure 6-4. You probably recognize some of these items as we briefly touched on them earlier in this chapter.

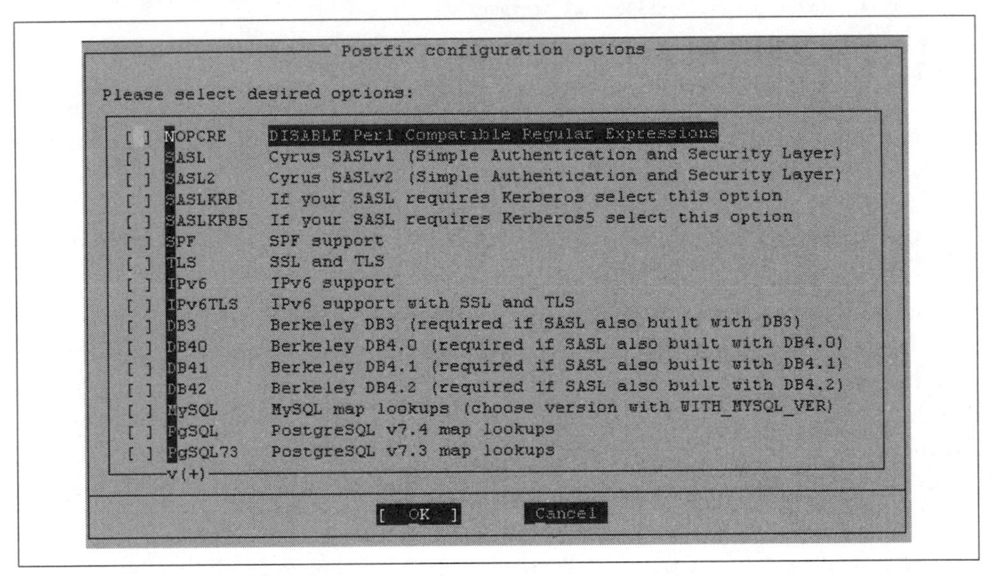

Figure 6-4. Postfix install options

Most of these options are self-explanatory, but as a reminder, we present this brief summary.

SASL2
: Install SASL2 if you need to provide SMTP authentication, that is, you require that users authenticate before they are allowed to send mail through your servers. This is useful when your users will connect to your mail server from untrusted networks in order to send mail. If you select SASL2, you will have another set of options to choose from that determines how SASL authenticates users. In many cases, the `SASLAUTHD` option will be appropriate; see the SASL

resources at the end of this chapter for links to more information about this topic.

SPF
: Install SPF support if you plan to implement the Sender Policy Framework as described earlier in this chapter. To jog your memory, SPF provides a means to verify that a given message was sent from an approved mail server by querying the responsible nameserver from the message originator's domain.

TLS
: This installs Transport Layer Security and provides for encrypted SMTP sessions. This is vital if you plan to use SASL. Otherwise, you probably don't need it.

DBx/MySQL/PgSQL/OpenLDAP
: Postfix is capable of querying several kinds of databases for map files such as aliases, virtuals, transport maps, and so on. If you have a need for this in your environment, select the appropriate option. We do not cover database-backed map lookups in this chapter.

Once you have selected the options appropriate for you environment, Postfix will install itself. At the end of the install process, you will be prompted to create one user (postfix) and two groups (postfix and maildrop). Do so. As mentioned earlier, the Postfix suite is composed of several daemons and many of them run as nonprivileged users. It is these users that are created at the end of the install process.

You are then prompted to activate Postfix in */etc/mail/mailer.conf*. Doing so will effectively replace Sendmail on your system. Although, binaries will not be overwritten, the `mailwrapper(8)` program, which acts as an intermediary between MUA software on the system, and the installed MTA will be told which binaries to execute for key MTA functionality.

Finally, additional steps may be required to complete your Postfix installation. These steps will be clearly stated in the output caused by your **`make install`** command. At the time of this writing, the port prompts you to modify */etc/rc.conf* and */etc/periodic.conf* to complete the Sendmail replacement. We will not go over these details as they are known to change from time to time and are clearly stated during the install process.

Installation and Configuration: OpenBSD

Installing Postfix on your OpenBSD system is fairly straightforward. However, before diving in, you have to make a few decisions in order to set the install *flavor* properly. Specifically, if you need to authenticate users before sending mail, you need SASL. If you're accepting usernames and passwords during the SMTP session, it makes sense to encrypt. For this, you need TLS. In other cases, it will not be necessary to set a *flavor*. Example 6-6 outlines the basic steps for installing Postfix and replacing Sendmail on your OpenBSD system.

Example 6-6. Installing Postfix on OpenBSD with SASL/TLS

```
% setenv FLAVOR "sasl2 tls pcre"
% make && sudo make install
% unsetenv FLAVOR
% sudo /usr/local/sbin/postfix-enable
```

If you don't need SASL or TLS support, merely remove them from your *flavor*. The `pcre` entry provides Perl compatible regular expressions support, which is helpful should you need to perform arbitrary content filtering later.

Running */usr/local/sbin/postfix-enable* activates Postfix in */etc/mailer.conf*. This causes MUA software on the system to use Postfix binaries instead of Sendmail ones without deleting or overwriting any Sendmail software. You may switch back to Sendmail at any time by running */usr/local/sbin/postfix-disable*. The enable script will also inform you of a few additional steps required to wrap up your Postfix installation. We will not cover these steps here as they have been known to change and are clearly stated during the execution of this script.

Postfix is now installed, and configuration files are stored in */etc/postfix*. Postfix is configured to run most of its processes from a chroot, including `smtpd(8)`: the master daemon process that listens on port 25 for incoming connections and accepts mail. Thus, as with any chrooted daemon, you need to create a logging socket within the chroot so that the process can send messages to syslogd. To do this, add the following line to */etc/rc.conf.local*:

```
syslogd_flags="-a /var/spool/postfix/dev/log"
```

If you already have a *syslogd_flags* configuration entry, merely append this argument pair to it.

Postfix Security Foundation

We have casually mentioned several times in this chapter that Postfix gains much if its security by design. Let's take a look at why and how this is so.

Do one thing, do it well

Doug McIlroy, the inventor of Unix pipes, had a vision for building Unix software. He believed programs should be built to do one thing, and to do it well. Programs should be written to accomplish discrete tasks and with interoperability in mind. Postfix is built with this philosophy in mind. The Postfix suite of programs "do mail." Postfix can act as a daemon, accept mail, check the content of mail, rewrite messages, deliver messages to other hosts, to the local filesystem, and so on.

As you might have guessed, "doing mail" is far more than one discrete task. Instead of trying to do everything in one program, Postfix employs several binaries, which handle each of these responsibilities. Communication is either handled directly through pipes, or by merely leaving files on the filesystem for another program to deal with. This has several consequences:

- Each program is easier to write, less complicated, and the program writer is less likely to overlook problems in the code.
- Most programs may run in a nonprivileged context but the `smtpd` daemon that listens on privileged port 25 must run as root.
- Programs not needed in a given environment may be easily disabled making exploitation of that program impossible.

Moreover, each program is able to perform operations on mail messages and leave the resultant message behind for another program to deal with. This lack of direct inter-process communication helps alleviate some security risks.

Understanding logging

As is often the case, increased security can bring with it a decrease in convenience. The programs that make up Postfix are unable to pass data directly to others, so as messages move through a series of these programs, logging is handled independently.

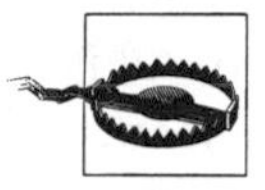

If you have data showing up in your Postfix logs, but some logs you expected to see are conspicuously missing, ensure you are getting logs from all Postfix programs. Chrooted programs need special provisions if `syslogd` is to be expected to capture relevant messages.

In a simple case, you might see a series of logs as follows:

```
Oct  5 00:04:50 woot postfix/smtpd[3199]:
 connect from dreadnaught.home.korff.org[172.16.0.2]
Oct  5 00:04:56 woot postfix/smtpd[3199]:
 AA22369: client=dreadnaught.home.korff.org[172.16.0.2]
Oct  5 00:05:02 woot postfix/cleanup[14647]:
 AA22369: message-id=<20041005040456.AA22369@woot.home.korff.org>
Oct  5 00:05:02 woot postfix/qmgr[11900]:
 AA22369: from=<root@dreadnaught.home.korff.org>, size=431, nrcpt=1
 (queue active)
Oct  5 00:05:02 woot postfix/local[29887]:
 AA22369: to=<root@woot.home.korff.org>, relay=local, delay=6,
 status=sent (mailbox)
Oct  5 00:05:03 woot postfix/smtpd[3199]:
  disconnect from dreadnaught.home.korff.org[172.16.0.2]
```

Six log entries for local delivery, and this is a simple case! On a busy mail server, it is not uncommon for log entries to be interspersed with one another: connections mixed with mail delays and errant spam rejections in the mix. Mail forwarding through *virtual* maps or *aliases* are even more complicated as the incoming and outgoing message are assigned separate queue IDs (`AA22369` is the queue ID above). It gets worse. With content filtering programs like SpamAssassin and amavisd-new, messages leave the Postfix system and are subsequently re-injected and assigned a new queue ID.

Deciphering Postfix logs can be challenging, but if you follow these guidelines, you should be able to avoid getting lost:

- The queue ID assigned by Postfix will describe any given message entering and leaving the Postfix system.
- In some cases, a message that leaves returns as a result of a forwarding map or an external content filter. In this case, `qmgr` will see the message twice and assign a new queue ID the second time. You can determine the newly assigned queue ID by looking at the second `qmgr` log entry containing the message ID (i.e., New queue ID, same message ID).

This should get you through the intricacies of Postfix logging.

Chroot

Postfix is able to chroot easily. OpenBSD administrators gain an advantage as the installation of Postfix through ports results in a chrooted configuration by default.

FreeBSD users should adjust the `chroot` column in the *master.cf* Postfix configuration file and change the `n` to a `y` for every process that should run chrooted. All Postfix processes may be chrooted with the exception of the *pipe*, *virtual*, *local*, and *proxymap* services. In almost all cases, it will be necessary to copy */etc/localtime*, */etc/resolv.conf*, and */etc/services* into */var/spool/postfix/etc*. Finally, create a log socket in Postfix's queue directory per the following:

```
syslogd_flags="-l /var/spool/postfix/var/run/log"
```

Of course, you must create */var/spool/postfix/var/run* before this will work.

If you are using SASL authentication, your dependence on configuration files, password databases, and libraries increases exponentially. Running a chrooted `smtpd` daemon with SASL is likely more trouble than it's worth.

Configuration files

Postfix requires only two main configuration files: *main.cf* and *master.cf*. Both are located in the Postfix configuration directory: */usr/local/etc/postfix* on FreeBSD and */etc/postfix* on OpenBSD.

The *master.cf* file controls the behavior of the various Postfix programs. You will likely make small modifications to this file (perhaps to chroot certain services) and then forget it exists, except in some border cases.

The *main.cf* file controls the behavior of Postfix and you will likely spend a fair bit of time working with this file. Fortunately, the *main.cf* file is easy to read and understand following a simple *parameter = value* syntax. This makes configuration easy, and mistakes less likely.

Whenever you make a change to either of these files, you must restart Postfix by running **postfix reload**.

Security-Related Configuration Options

As you configure your Postfix installation, remember that the fewer configuration changes you make, the more likely you are to have a reliable and secure installation. One of the most common mistakes made by administrators used to administering Sendmail is overconfiguration. Nevertheless, there are a few things to keep in mind.

Arbitrary program restriction

One of the dangers inherent in mail delivery is the power to pass mail to arbitrary programs. This can be done through *aliases*, *.forward* files, and *:include:* mailing lists. It may be worth your while to restrict exactly *which* programs may be executed through these facilities. One of the helper programs installed by default on your system was designed to do exactly this. It's called `smrsh(8)` and it only allows programs to execute if they are listed in */usr/libexec/sm.bin* (by default).

To configure Postfix to use `smrsh` to intercept mail sent to local commands, use the following configuration in your *main.cf* file:

```
local_command_shell = /usr/libexec/smrsh
```

Then link to programs that should be allowed to run. For example, to grant users the ability to pass mail into `vacation(1)` and `procmail(1)`, issue these commands:

```
% sudo ln -s /usr/bin/vacation /usr/libexec/sm.bin/vacation
% sudo ln -s /usr/bin/procmail /usr/libexec/sm.bin/procmail
```

Masquerade your domain

Many organizations send mail internally and retain full hostnames for host-to-host mail. When the mail leaves the organization, however, these internal hostnames are no longer resolvable. In order to ensure that mail reaches the destination (because the sender's domain must resolve), it's usually a good idea to masquerade all hosts and subdomains within a domain to the top level domain.

That is, mail sent from two internal hosts *taco.mexicanfood.net* and *salsa.condiments.mexicanfood.net*, should reach its destination and appear to have come from *@mexicanfood.net*. This configuration option is a appropriate for a mail relay and may be configured using a pair of stanzas similar to the following in your *main.cf* file:

```
myorigin = $mydomain
masquerade_domains = $mydomain
```

This assumes you want your mail to come from *$mydomain*. If your mail server's hostname is *fajita.dmz.mexicanfood.net*, *$mydomain* will be *dmz.mexicanfood.net*. To change this behavior, explicitly set *$mydomain* to something else:

```
mydomain = mexicanfood.net
```

You may run into mail routing problems by collapsing your entire user-namespace. Thus, many organizations enforce organization-wide usernames and masquerade on the internal mail server also. Finally, as you will invariably receive mail from the root account (and perhaps several other accounts) of this machine, you probably want to retain host information for system and service users so you can avoid looking at message headers to find out where the message came from. To do this, use:

```
masquerade_exceptions = root cron
```

Obfuscate smtpd banner

It is of marginal value to obfuscate the `smtpd` banner (for example, see the first line of Example 6-4) `smtpd` displays when client programs or attackers connect to port 25 on your host. Most attacks you will face come from scripts, iterating through open ports looking for daemons to exploit. These scripts rarely care about what mail server you happen to be running, they attempt the exploit regardless.

Still, some administrators prefer to give away as little information as possible. A laudable goal and if you have secured your system and Postfix in every other conceivable way and have time left over, by all means configure an alternative `smtpd` banner by adding a stanza similar to the following in your *main.cf* file:

```
smtpd_banner = $myhostname MexiMail Server
```

Disable unneeded commands

Restricting certain SMTP commands is of moderate value. Postfix's implementation of these commands is well tested and not known to cause significant problems, but you may want to consider turning them off.

`etrn`
: If you are MX for an organization that has intermittent network capability and will only be able to receive mail at certain times, they may need a way to tell you to process your queue for them. These organizations could contact your mail server and issue, for instance, **`ETRN`** ***`smtp.onlinesometimes.net`***. This will tell your server to process all messages in the queue that could not be delivered to *smtp.onlinesomtimes.net* due to network problems at last attempt. By default Postfix will only allow `ETRN` for domains to which the server is configured to relay mail. If the situation described above does not apply to you, you may disable `etrn` altogether by setting `smtpd_etrn_restrictions` to `reject` in your *main.cf*.

vrfy
: By default Postfix will allow VRFY command which is supposed to let clients determine whether or not a user exists without sending mail. Postfix, however, will always return a 252 code informing the client to "go send mail and find out. " VRFY may be disabled altogether by setting disable_vrfy_command to yes; there's little justification for or against.

Limiting Denial of Service Attacks

Postfix ships with a good default configuration for limiting the risk of being affected by a denial of service attack. This includes reasonable concurrency limits for daemons, maximum SMTP syntax errors before disconnection, minimum free disk space, and so on. Most of these variables will not need tuning unless you observe problems in the behavior of your Postfix installation.

bounce_size_limit
: This limits the size of mail bounces. Messages are truncated to this size, allowing you to see the bounce, without having to deal with the entire content of the message. This may be worth lowering from the default of 50,000 to keep spam bounces from clogging your mailbox.

default_process_limit
: Postfix limits the number of any given subprocesses that may be concurrently running. The default of 100 may be excessive in your environment and you might want to choose a lower number. This will affect every Postfix subprocess. To use different thresholds for different subprocesses, you may specify limits on a per-process basis in the maxproc column in your *master.cf*.

mailbox_size_limit
: This configuration parameter controls the maximum size of a given user's mailbox. Of course this only makes sense on a system where Postfix is performing local delivery.

message_size_limit
: As you might guess, this limits the size of messages. The default of 10 MB is not unreasonable, but if you can lower it, do so. Make sure you provide alternatives for transporting large files to your users.

smtpd_error_sleep_time *and* error_limits
: Postfix has two error thresholds that control when the smtpd daemon starts delaying responses. The daemon accepts the number of errors specified in smtpd_soft_error_limit before instituting delays (of 1 second, by default) to all subsequent responses. When the error count reaches the number specified by smtpd_soft_error_limit, the connection is terminated. While this provides an effective means of slowing down spammers, setting this value too high could allow a determined attacker to initiate connections with jibberish data resulting in more and more daemon processes. Eventually the daemon limit will be reached and

legitimate connections will have to wait, or be denied altogether. It is important to be aware of these configuration options so that you avoid inadvertently changing them without fully understanding the ramifications.

`smtpd_recipient_limit`
: This parameter controls the maximum number of recipients a mail message can have. The generous default of 1000 is in place as a sanity check. You may wish to reduce this value in your environment.

Although these configuration parameters are by no means a comprehensive list of tunable limits within the Postfix system, they are some of the most important. Consider reading the *TUNING_README* (distributed with the Postfix source) and the manual page for `postconf(5)` for information about additional limits, when to use them, and when to avoid changing them.

Blocking Unwanted Mail

There are myriad ways of blocking unwanted mail through Postfix. We cover a few of these options and point out when they are appropriate for use.

Access table

The *access(5)* table allows you to configure your server to accept or reject mail based on hostnames, domain names, networks, or mail addresses. An access table will generally have entries similar to Example 6-7.

Example 6-7. A basic access file

```
1.2.3                   REJECT I don't like your network
peruvianfood.net        REDIRECT intrigue@mexicanfood.net
joe@                    DISCARD # silently throw away, dangerous!
```

Many other options are possible, see the *access* manpage for more possibilities. The access database can be use in conjunction with a variety of checks including:

- `check_client_access`
- `check_helo_access`
- `check_recipient_access`
- `check_sender_access`

In turn, these checks are tied to specific restriction parameters. For instance, to control which clients are allowed to use your mail server, you would specify:

```
smtpd_client_restrictions =
    check_client_access hash:.../postfix/client-access
```

Then, in your client-access table, you could specify networks or hostnames that should be denied access.

Likewise check_helo_access may be listed as a value to smtpd_helo_restrictions. We point out these two configuration possibilities not because they are of tremendous use, but because you could waste a lot of valuable time trying to figure out how to set them properly. Spammers use ever-changing source networks and specify different values for HELO all the time. There is little use in trying to block UCE with manual updates to these maps.

The latter two configuration options may be listed in smtpd_recipient_restrictions as they are both relevant during the same stage of an SMTP transaction. So, you might want to configure the following:

```
smtpd_recipient_restrictions = permit_mynetworks ...
    check_sender_access hash:.../postfix/sender-access
    check_recipient_access hash:.../postfix/recipient-access
    ... reject_unauth_destination
```

Sender and recipient access maps can be more useful for configuring mail addresses to which and from whence messages should be rejected. For instance, you may want to block mail sent from offers@ or sales@ globally, depending on your organizational mail policy. Likewise, you might want to block mail being sent from the outside world to any of your internal mailing lists at the mail-relay level.

Finally, in general, access maps do not provide the kind of flexibility required to deal with spam, but they can be useful in globally rejecting or discarding certain kinds of messages or when problem accounts, networks, or domains arise.

Arbitrary content filtering

Postfix is capable of performing arbitrary content filtering through header and body checks by defining the following in your *main.cf*:

```
header_checks = pcre:.../postfix/header-checks
body_checks = pcre:.../postfix/body-checks
```

These let you define substrings that, when found in the header or body of messages, should result in message rejection or the message being silently discarded. Header and body checks are useful in blocking mail with certain attachments, sent from certain parts of the world with which your organization traditionally has no contact, containing key phrases containing marketing buzzwords or indicating pornographic content, etc.

For example, you may want to block all mail tagged greater than 12 by SpamAssassin. For this, you would need the following entry in your header checks.

```
/^X-Spam-Level:\s\*\*\*\*\*\*\*\*\*\*\*\*/          REJECT
```

Elaborating on the diverse opportunities available in content filtering is not worthwhile here. Instead, visit the resources listed at the end of this chapter for more information on this topic.

DNS blacklists

Postfix can be easily configured to reject mail from sites listed in real-time blacklists (RBLs) using the `reject_rbl_clcient` directives under your `smtpd_recipient_restrictions` in *main.cf*. To configure RBLs in your Postfix installation, add stanzas similar to the following under your recipient restrictions:

```
reject_rbl_client relays.ordb.org
```

See the specific RBL provider's site to determine exactly which host to list.

Virus protection

Virus protection is essential to stop the flow of malware through your servers to more vulnerable client workstations and servers running Windows. Viruses and worms that exploit vulnerabilities in Unix software are uncommon but not unheard of. A variety of commercial and noncommercial options exist including McAffee Virus Scan, Kaspersky Anti-Virus, and Clam AntiVirus (ClamAV). Perhaps the most popular choice, and the one chosen by SourceForge, is ClamAV.

Postfix and ClamAV are generally connected through an intermediary piece of software called amavisd-new. Postfix is configured to use amavisd-new as a content filter, and amavisd-new in turn passes mail to the ClamAV (you may also want to use SpamAssassin through amavisd-new if you are using virus protection).

ClamAV and amavisd-new are available as FreeBSD ports, but OpenBSD users must download the source, compile, and install it in the traditional GNU fashion (though an unofficial ClamAV port may be retrieved from *http://www.fatbsd.com/openbsd/clamav/*).

After amavisd-new and ClamAV are configured, Postfix should be configured to accept mail as usual, pass it to the amavisd-new content filter listening on another port (specified in *amavisd.conf*), which will in turn pass mail back to Postfix on yet another port (also specified in *amavisd.conf*) for re-injection into the mail queue.

First, Postfix should be configured to send mail to amavisd-new by adding the following to your *main.cf*:

```
content_filter = smtp-amavis:[127.0.0.1]:amavisd_port
```

Then adjust your *master.cf* so that amavisd-new can send mail back to Postfix:

```
smtp-amavis unix -       -       n       -       3  smtp
    -o smtp_data_done_timeout=1200
    -o disable_dns_lookups=yes
127.0.0.1:reinjection_port inet n - n - - smtpd
   -o content_filter=
   -o smtpd_recipient_restrictions=permit_mynetworks,reject
   -o mynetworks=127.0.0.0/8
   -o strict_rfc821_envelopes=yes
```

This allows any content filters attached to amavsid-new to parse messages before they are returned to the Postfix system for delivery.

Authentication and Encryption

We discussed earlier that SMTP is an authentication-free protocol. By design, anyone can connect to an SMTP server and send mail, and this mail will travel over clear text to the server. Certain organizations, however, who must accept and relay mail from known users on unknown and untrusted networks need some means to verify that a user is who she says she is. One solution is the Simple Authentication and Security Layer (SASL).

Of course, authentication without encryption should send a shiver up the spine of any security-minded system administrator. Providing an encrypted channel over which authentication can occur for the SMTP exchange is handled by Transport Layer security (TLS).

Verifying Postfix+SASL+TLS installation

If you followed the directions earlier in this chapter and installed Postfix with SASL and TLS support as described, you should be ready for configuration. It's a still a good idea to verify that your Postfix installation was in fact built with the requisite support. This is easily achieved by using `ldd(1)`:

```
% ldd `which postfix`
/usr/local/sbin/postfix:
        Start    End      Type Ref Name
        00000000 00000000 exe   1  /usr/local/sbin/postfix
        05444000 25449000 rlib  1  /usr/local/lib/libpcre.so.0.1
        00755000 2075b000 rlib  1  /usr/local/lib/libsasl2.so.2.13
        08965000 28971000 rlib  1  /usr/lib/libssl.so.8.0
        08b9c000 28bcd000 rlib  1  /usr/lib/libcrypto.so.10.3
        050d0000 25109000 rlib  1  /usr/lib/libc.so.30.3
        04867000 04867000 rtld  1  /usr/libexec/ld.so
```

This transcript is from an OpenBSD 3.5 system and your output may differ slightly. Nevertheless, if your Postfix installation supports SASL, TLS, and PCRE, you should see corresponding libraries listed in this output as `libsasl2`, `libssl`, and `libpcre`.

Configuring Postfix with SASL+TLS

After you have verified that your `postfix` binary supports the requisite functionality, you may turn your attention to configuration. Enabling SASL in Postfix is easy, merely add relevant lines from the options below to your *main.cf*:

```
smtpd_sasl_auth_enable = yes
broken_sasl_auth_clients = yes
smtpd_sasl_security_options = noanonymous
```

The first option enables SASL. The second allows some older Microsoft clients to authenticate. You may be able to omit this option depending on the MUAs you need to support. The third option looks innocuous but in fact is a deviation from the default of noplaintext, noanonymous. What this option does is to enable plain text authentication where the users' password is transmitted in clear text over the network; with TLS, these clear-text passwords will be sent over an encrypted channel. Some MUAs do not properly handle any form of authentication other than plain text. If you find yourself in this position, omit the noplaintext this configuration entry, otherwise specify it.

While the smtpd_sasl_auth_enable option tells Postfix use to use SASL, it does not specify how. Specifically, you will want your mail server to relay mail for those users who can authenticate. To do this, adjust your existing smtpd_recipient_restrictions as follows:

```
smtpd_recipient_restrictions = permit_mynetworks
    permit_sasl_authenticated
    ... reject_unauth_destination
```

Order is important, and the permit_sasl_authenticated directive should be listed early to ensure mail from your authenticated users is not excessively tested. Once this is done, it is time to configure TLS. This is achieved by adding lines similar to the following to your *main.cf*:

```
smtpd_use_tls = yes
smtp_use_tls = yes
smtp_tls_note_starttls_offer = yes
smtpd_tls_key_file = .../postfix/ssl/smtpd.pem
smtpd_tls_cert_file = .../postfix/ssl/smtpd.pem
smtpd_tls_CAfile = .../postfix/ssl/smtpd.pem
smtpd_tls_loglevel = 1
smtpd_tls_received_header = yes
tls_random_source = dev:/dev/urandom
```

Of course, you need to have created the relevant PEM files. After these configuration changes have been made, we must configure SASL to authenticate users in some way. Users may be authenticated against the local password file, an OpenLDAP server, a MySQL or PostgreSQL database, and so on. The details of configuring SASL are beyond the scope of this document, but a number of online HOWTOs for these topics exist.

To test SASL functionality, it may be worthwhile to use saslpasswd2(8) to create a separate authentication database and configure saslauthd(8) accordingly.

```
# echo "pwcheck_method: saslauthd" > /usr/local/lib/sasl2/smtpd.conf
% sudo /usr/local/sbin/saslpasswd2 testuser
(follow prompts)
% sudo /usr/local/sbin/saslauthd -a getpwent
```

You will then need to restart Postfix for SASL authentication over TLS. Note that in order for `saslauthd` to start at boot, OpenBSD administrators need to add appropriate lines to their */etc/rc.local* script.

qmail

Yet another drop-in Sendmail replacement is qmail. Like Postfix, qmail was designed to be secure, to perform well, to be reliable, and simple. Designed by Dan Bernstein (author of djbdns), and first released in 1997, it also follows the Unix tradition of using small, simple programs to accomplish small tasks and linking these programs together to perform more complex tasks. However, much like the *http://cr.yp.to/qmail.html* and *http://www.qmail.org/* web sites, the software is "not designed to be easy to use," writes Russell Nelson on the (unofficial) qmail home page (August 13, 2004, *http://www.qmail.org/*). Qmail implements exceptionally fast and secure MTA functionality, but was designed to be different from most other mailers. If you are primarily familiar with Sendmail or Postfix but do not yet have experience with qmail, you will be at a disadvantage when trying to effectively deploy and administer a server running qmail.

In this chapter, we focus on Sendmail and Postfix because their similarities allow us to address security concerns instead of the mail software itself. If you are deploying a mail server running qmail on OpenBSD or FreeBSD, you are likely to find the information in this chapter generally useful but not specific to your situation. Also consider resources such as the qmail web sites mentioned above, *http://www.lifewithqmail.org/*, and the O'Reilly book *qmail* by John Levine.

Mail Access

After you have built a mail architecture to send and receive mail, you need to provide a way for users to access it. Securing mail access has already been partially addressed by architecture: if you place your mail storage within a protected internal network, external attackers are unable to access it directly. Nevertheless, because most successful attacks originate from within, you must take steps to secure the software that provides this service.

Guidelines for Securing Mail Access—Internally

The key protocols involved in mail access are POP and IMAP. The former allows users to download and (by default) remove mail from the mail server, and the latter allows users to view and manipulate messages on the server. The most popular software suites that provide this functionality include Courier, WU-IMAP, Qpopper, Cyrus-IMAP, and Binc IMAP. While we cannot explore in detail the installation, configuration and security options of each of these pieces of software, there are some general configuration guidelines which apply.

Authentication and logging
: Ensure that all mail access sessions with your mail server are authenticated and that connections, and subsequent authentication attempts (successes and failures), are logged. Try to avoid using plain-text authentication if you do not need to support MUAs that require it. Enforce strong password policies so that users have good passwords that rotate frequently enough to keep from having stale passwords but infrequently enough to keep users from writing their passwords down on a Post-It note attached to their keyboards.

Encryption
: Most mail access software supports encryption and you should enable it wherever possible. This helps ensure that passwords are not exposed and potentially sensitive information in mail messages is not being transmitted in the clear over the local network.

Software security
: Like all server software, mail access suites are prone to attack and vulnerabilities are disclosed with some regularity. Before choosing a software suite, examine its track record and determine whether you have the time required to keep your software up to date and patched.

Following these three guidelines will accomplish most of what is required in securing access to your message store. Additional security may be possible but will vary on the mail access software suite you have chosen to deploy.

Guidelines for Securing Mail Access—Externally

So far, we have assumed that mail access originates on the internal network. Invariably organizations need to provide mail access to users outside the network, whether they are at home, at alternate work sites, or roaming. This problem is typically solved in one of two ways: VPNs and webmail. These two options are not mutually exclusive, and both are shown deployed in Figure 6-5.

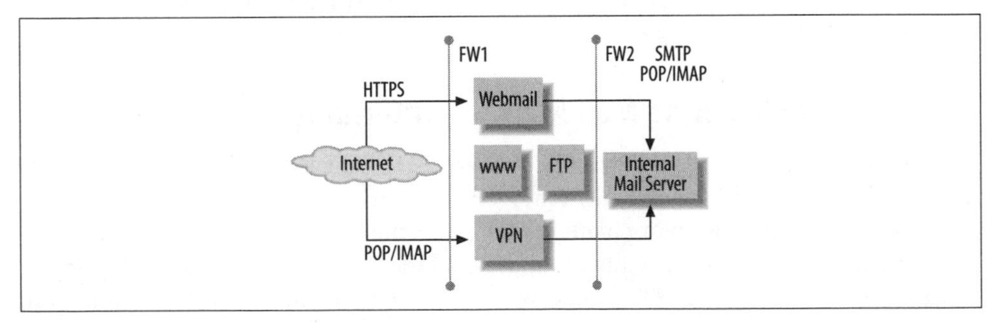

Figure 6-5. VPN and webmail access

Virtual private networks (VPN)

Providing VPN access (as depicted in Figure 6-5) to your internal network for roaming users not only provides for secure mail access, but may generally provide secure access to whatever resources you wish to make available. VPN installations can be nontrivial to set up, but many support two-factor authentication, making them viable as a secure external access method. Once a user has connected to the local network over the VPN, he may check mail as he normally would. One major drawback is that VPNs often require the installation of client software, which makes their use from nonorganizationally owned systems more challenging.

Webmail

Many organizations provide some form of access to the internal mail storage using a webmail frontend. As shown in Figure 6-5, systems that provide webmail access often reside on a perimeter network and allow only HTTPS traffic to the server. The webmail server itself communicates with the internal mail server using traditional POP and IMAP protocols for mail retrieval. Mail is also submitted over HTTPS and sent to the internal mail server via SMTP. The options for providing webmail access are as diverse as for providing direct mail access: SquirrelMail, Imp, Open Webmail, and so on. Of course, general security guidelines apply. Remember that attacks against a webmail server can attempt to either exploit the webmail software and gain access to the webmail system, or use the webmail server as a means to attack the internal mail server.

Protect the server
: Ensure the server on which your webmail application is running is locked down as much as possible. Traffic to the machine should be restricted to HTTPS and authentication should be mandatory and logged.

Encryption
: Enforce the use of HTTPS, not HTTP, for access to the webmail application. All authentication should also happen over HTTPS. Of course, you may want to enable HTTP access to the server for the sole purpose of redirecting traffic to the HTTPS URL to make things easier for your users.

Software security
: Remember that your webmail application is going to be some collection of scripts and/or binaries. Ensure that all software on which your webmail application relies is up to date. SquirrelMail for instance relies heavily on PHP, thus you should ensure that you have secured your PHP installation and that your PHP libraries are patched against all disclosed vulnerabilities.

Following these guidelines, and making effective use of webmail and VPN will go a long way to securing external access to internal mail.

Wrapping Up

If there is one thing that you take away from this chapter, let it be an appreciation for the complexity of building a mail infrastructure. There are a myriad of software choices at every level: from message transfer agents to message delivery agents, from mail access software to mail user agents. Each of these pieces of software in turn generally relies on other software to provide key functionality. This makes providing truly secure mail access a very difficult goal to achieve, but as long as you take things step by step while maintaining an understanding of the risks involved and how your architecture is designed to mitigate those risks, you will be in a much better position.

Resources

A list of resources follows.

MTA Software

- Sendmail.org: *http://www.sendmail.org/*
- Sendmail Installation and Operations Guide (distributed with Sendmail source)
- *sendmail*, Third Edition, Bryan Costales (O'Reilly), 2002
- *sendmail Cookbook*, Craig Hunt (O'Reilly), 2003
- *sendmail 8.13 Companion*, Bryan Costales et al. (O'Reilly), 2004
- Postfix.org: *http://www.postfix.org/*
- *Postfix: The Definitive Guide*, Kyle D. Dent (O'Reilly), 2003

Spam Defense and Antivirus

- Clam AntiVirus: *http://www.clamav.net/*
- MAPS (RBL): *http://www.mail-abuse.com/*
- Open Relay Database (RBL): *http://www.ordb.org/*
- RFC-Ignorant.org (RBL): *http://www.rfc-ignorant.org/*
- SpamAssassin: *http://spamassassin.apache.org/*
- SpamCop (RBL): *http://www.spamcop.net/*
- SPF: *http://spf.pobox.com/*
- SPF Wikipedia entry: *http://en.wikipedia.org/wiki/Sender_Policy_Framework*

SMTP Security

- OpenSSL: *http://www.openssl.org/*
- SASL at Carnegie Mellon: *http://asg.web.cmu.edu/sasl/*

Mail Access Software

- Courier IMAP: *http://www.courier-mta.org/imap/*
- Cyrus IMAP Server: *http://asg.web.cmu.edu/cyrus/imapd/*
- Fetchmail: *http://catb.org/~esr/fetchmail/*
- IMP (Webmail): *http://www.horde.org/imp/*
- Qpopper: *http://qpopper.sourceforge.net/*
- SquirrelMail (Webmail): *http://www.squirrelmail.org/*
- UW IMAP information center: *http://www.washington.edu/imap/*

Selected Mail-Related Request for Comments (RFCs)

- RFC 753: Internet Message Protocol
- RFC 974: Mail Routing and the Domain System
- RFC 1225: Post Office Protocol—Version 3
- RFC 1869: SMTP Service Extensions
- RFC 1893: Enhanced Mail System Status Codes
- RFC 1991: PGP Message Exchange Formats
- RFC 2033: Local Mail Transfer Protocol
- RFC 2060: Internet Message Access Protocol—Version 4, rev 1
- RFC 2246: The TLS Protocol Version 1.0
- RFC 2076: Common Internet Message Headers
- RFC 2476: Message Submission
- RFC 2487: SMTP Service Extension for Secure SMTP over TLS
- RFC 2821: Simple Mail Transfer Protocol (Supercedes RFC 821)

CHAPTER 7

Building a Secure Web Server

What he trusts in is fragile;
what he relies on is a spider's web.
—Job 8:14, Holy Bible,
New International Version

The World Wide Web: to many people, it *is* the Internet. Few machines in your network are so blatantly visible if they are compromised. Your router might be weak, your mail server might be compromised, but it is hard for the average person to see that. If your web server is compromised, however, all manner of things go very wrong very fast. Your organization might be publically humiliated, it might lose money or sales, or your server might be commandeered to attack another site. Additionally, it is a core server in your network that probably has many non-administrators working on it. You know that if your mail server suddenly breaks or if the firewall starts denying everything, it was either an administrator or a hacker who did it. With web servers, you have any number of sources of code and configurations that are managed by a wide variety of people with varying skill sets. The potential for inadvertent problems is high. The system is critical and there are a lot of sources for problems, both inside and outside your organization. Fortunately, with FreeBSD and OpenBSD, you have an outstanding tool chest full of diverse tools for securing your web servers.

In this chapter, we focus on Internet-facing web servers, because FreeBSD and OpenBSD systems thrive there, despite the hostile environment. First, we cover a variety of topics related to running a secure web server, starting with the importance of web server security and the kinds of attacks web servers face. Next, we describe a general web architecture that puts the operating system and the web server software in context. Having established why you care about security and which defenses the operating systems can offer, we describe how to install and configure two popular web server packages: Apache and the Tiny HTTP daemon (`thttpd`). Apache is the best known and most commonly used web server on the Internet and it can do just about everything. Because of its Swiss-army-knife capabilities and the potential to misconfigure it, we focus on a variety of pitfalls and best practices for configuring it. The thttpd server is less well known but is often used by people with very demanding web sites. It has a variety of very specific, performance-oriented features, but fewer settings to configure, so its configuration is necessarily simpler.

Web Server Attacks

Sometimes your web server is the specific target of an attack because of who your organization is or what it represents. Sometimes people hack your web server for the same reason they climb a mountain: because it's there. Web server attackers often want:

- To embarrass or discredit an organization
- To earn respect among hackers by indiscriminately vandalizing a site
- To gain a foothold in the organization's network for deeper penetration at a later time
- To leverage the server in malicious activity against another network
- To try to obtain sensitive or confidential data
- To simply deny your server the ability to serve its pages

Web site defacement has obvious repercussions. It is easy to imagine the embarrassment of a high-profile company when their web site is defaced. Sometimes hackers hack a web site to express an opposing viewpoint right from the site they oppose. Such vandalism is only likely on your site if your organization is associated with one side of a controversial issue. Of course, there are innumerable electronic vandals who vandalize for the sake of vandalizing.

Some hackers will attack your web server with a goal of using it illicitly in some other activity. They may want to put their cracked, illegal copies of software there for people to download. They may want to set your web server up as a node in a distributed denial of service (DDoS) attack. They might even be so lucky (and you might be so unlucky) that they get interactive access (i.e., shell access) on your web server. Then they may merely pass through, using you as one more hop in a long chain of logins that help obscure their origins.

Web servers are often located in the network's DMZ, making them natural first steps for breaking into an organization's network. Broken routers or firewalls would be even better entry points, but they tend to be more tightly controlled than the web server. An attacker knows he will always have access to port 80 on the target system.

Why You Care

The direct effects of hacking a web server may seem benign. In actuality, they can have a surprisingly abrupt and negative impact. Hackers who put illegal software on your web site and then share the location among their friends may suddenly and completely consume available resources on both your system and your network. Your server may fail under the load, or your organization may receive a surprisingly large bill for excess bandwidth usage. If your Internet service provider (ISP) is notified that your server is a participant in a DDoS attack, they may choose to "shoot first, ask questions later" and remove your server's connectivity to the Internet. If your web server shares your organization's primary (or only) link to the Internet, you may find your whole company unceremoniously disconnected while you and the ISP sort out what is wrong. Lastly, some sites that are the targets of DDoS attacks respond with "counterattacks." Your web server or network could be targeted by some form of electronic retribution.

Many web servers perform one or more e-commerce functions. Perhaps they handle the storefront; maybe they're the shopping cart server; or they might allow customers to get shipping information on orders they've already placed. Even if all the web site's transaction processing is ultimately handled in a secure data center, the web server stores the data momentarily. A hacker who can break in and monitor communications or data flow has an opportunity to capture personal information, user IDs and passwords, or perhaps even credit card information. If you are running a commercial web server, these risks are probably foremost in your mind. The only thing more fearsome than a CIO asking about an enormous bandwidth bill is a CEO who must notify customers that their credit card information is now in the hands of Eastern European hackers.

The recently passed Notice of Security Breach sections of the California Civil Code (California Civil Code Sections 1798.29 and 1798.82–1798.84, *http://www.privacy.ca.gov/code/cc1798.291798.82.htm*) have broad effects for organizations handling personal information in the United States. If "unencrypted personal information was, or is reasonably believed to have been, acquired by an unauthorized person," then the person must be notified. This law is very new and has not yet been vigorously tested in the courts. It probably applies to organizations incorporated in California. It may apply to organizations that merely do business in California. While there remains a lot of uncertainty about how broadly it applies, it certainly creates legal fear and uncertainty for web sites that deal with personal information. Even though your web site only deals in name and addresses, you could find yourself being compelled by law to notify users that their names and addresses were possibly compromised. No organization wants to be compelled to broadcast the fact that they have successfully been hacked.

Specific Threats to Web Servers

The kinds of general risks we've described typically materialize through specific technical mechanisms. These include file or data disclosure, file uploads or storage, program execution, operating system vulnerability exploitation (e.g., privilege escalation), and web server vulnerability exploitation (e.g., buffer overflow).

File and data disclosure

File and data disclosure were among the earliest kinds of attacks on web servers. Both Apache and Microsoft's Internet Information Server (IIS) were subject to a variety of directory traversal attacks. Two standard encodings, HTML entity encoding and HTTP URL encoding, are often combined in unexpected ways to cause the web server to do unusual things. You've probably seen ampersands (&) encoded in HTML as `&`. That's HTML entity encoding, and it represents characters with an ampersand, their decimal (or hexadecimal) ASCII value, and then a semicolon. It can represent the whole character set, though, including 2-byte UNICODE characters. For example, the letter "A" can be represented `A`. Similarly, you've probably seen spaces encoded in URLs as `%20`. That's an example of a totally different encoding: HTTP URL encoding. It allows web pages to encode non-alphanumeric characters in URLs using a percent sign and the character's 2-digit ASCII hexadecimal value. Again, you can represent more than just punctuation. The letter "A" can be encoded as `%41`. These encodings were intended to handle non-alphanumeric characters such as those with accents or whitespace such as spaces and tabs. Hackers exploit these encodings in a variety of ways to construct obscured paths that bypass security checks. For instance, they can encode */etc/passwd* as `%2F%65%74%63%2F%70%61%73%73%77%64`. The earliest versions of many web servers would fail to notice, after decoding the string, that the file requested lived outside the web server's document root. Even today complex variations on this theme crop up from time to time as part of attacks on modern web applications.

File downloads are not the only problem you will face. Uploads can be a problem when they allow hackers to store data on your server that they, or someone else, will come retrieve later. Hackers probably won't fill your hard disk with junk. They might, however, upload a few gigabytes of MP3s, a few hundred megabytes of software whose licensing protections have been disabled, or perhaps some illegal pornography. You might find your web server suddenly attracting a lot of unwanted attention, both from hackers and from law enforcement.

File uploads can also destroy useful data. If a hacker can upload and overwrite important files, such as web orders that have not been transmitted to the fulfillment system yet, it may also cause your organization to lose money or information.

Lastly, uploads can be a critical step in compromising the server's security. If a hacker can upload a program to your web server and somehow trick the web server into executing it, she can go a long way toward defeating security measures.

Arbitrary program execution

Arbitrary program execution is the ultimate vulnerability in any server software. If a hacker can find a way to execute a program of his choosing on your web server and control some of the arguments to that program, then he can usually escalate into a variety of other attacks. He might use a CGI script or some PHP code, for example, to upload a program onto your server that is subsequently executed. He might merely abuse a program that already lives on your server but has vulnerabilities. Suddenly, a locally exploitable vulnerability in the line printer spooler daemon (`lpd(8)`) that seemed inconsequential is suddenly a very important threat. It can allow an intruder to escalate privileges and gain access to your web server without having direct local access.

Application abuse

There are a variety of other attacks against web servers that cannot be mitigated at the operating system level. Attacks such as SQL code injection, HTML injection, and cross-site scripting (XSS) are critical attacks to prevent. This is an important point that we cannot stress enough: the network and the operating system cannot fully compensate for bad applications. They can help, but they cannot obviate the need for careful, security-conscious programming. Despite being important, these attacks are outside the scope of this book because they exploit neither the web server software nor the host operating system. An example will help illustrate this point, and then we will move on.

Web sites often offer a form where a person can type a message, enter his email address, and click a button to send a message to someone associated with the web site. These "contact us" pages are usually for submitting feedback on the web site, contacting the sales department, or reporting a problem with a product. There are a variety of freeware and shareware CGI programs available for downloading that will do the necessary web-to-email processing. One notorious example, `formmail.pl`, has been repeatedly abused to send email from arbitrary senders to arbitrary recipients with arbitrary message content. If you aren't using this script but still see errors in your web server's log where someone has requested */cgi-bin/formmail.pl*, you're probably looking at an exploit attempt. Spammers love to find vulnerable applications like this one.

For a more detailed example of these `formmail.pl` vulnerabilities and exploits, see the "Illegitimate Mail Relaying" section in Chapter 6.

As an administrator there are only so many things you can harden and configure to prevent abuse of your server. The firewalls, routers, web server software, and operating system are all very important. All is for naught, however, if badly written applications are blindly allowed to run on the web server.

Web Architecture

A web server that does any significant work usually consists of many pieces. Figure 7-1 depicts a simplified architecture showing the multiple layers that make up a modern web server.

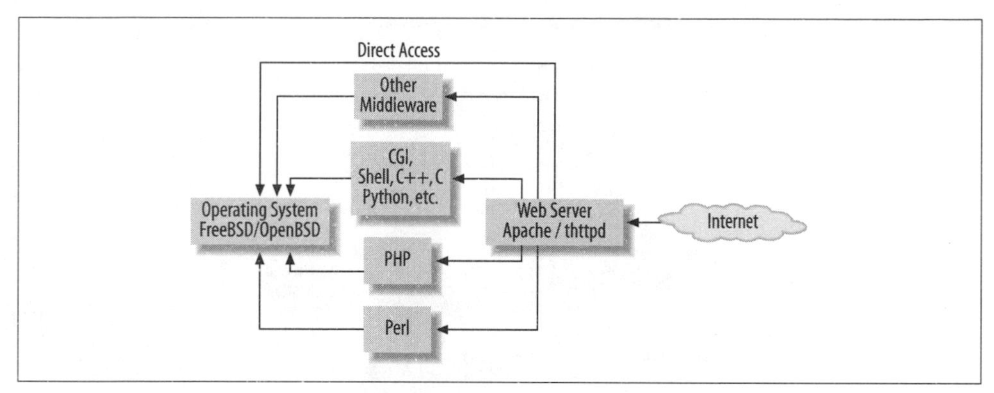

Figure 7-1. Simplified web server architecture

The most important relationship implied in Figure 7-1 is the transitivity of security. Users on the Internet make requests that invoke one or more other programs that ultimately access resources in the operating system. Depending on your configuration, you may be able to eliminate many of the alternate paths from the Internet to your operating system.

It may be surprising that no firewall or router is depicted in this diagram. Surely your firewall helps protect your web server, right? Only to a point. Many significant attacks that have severe impacts on your organization pass unmodified through proxies, firewalls, routers, and network-based "intrusion prevention systems." They use requests that are well-formed from a protocol point of view but that tickle bugs in the underlying application software. Exploitation of these bugs can yield access to the operating system, all passing happily beneath the radar of the network-based security controls. Third-generation firewalls are only aware of source and target ports—incoming traffic to HTTP ports 80 and 443 are usually not restricted. Even fourth-generation firewalls, which can analyze and understand HTTP requests, are not 100% effective in stopping well-formed attacks.

One of the goals of securing a web server is to prevent Internet-based users from having unintended interactions with the operating system. Figure 7-2 shows many layers where some sort of protection can be built. The operating system is at the bottom, and the network-based protections are at the top. This chapter focuses on configuring the operating system to protect itself, and making the web server safer than its default configuration.

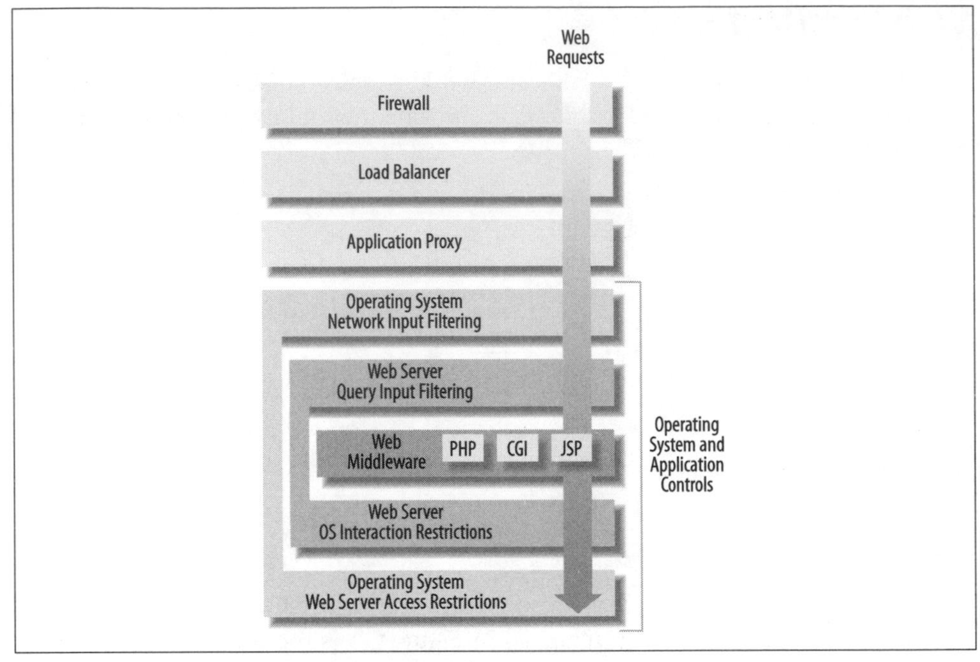

Figure 7-2. Layers of security relevant to a web server

Server Software Choices

Figure 7-3 shows the Netcraft web server survey from June 2004 ("Nearly 2.5 Million Active Sites Running FreeBSD," Netcraft, Inc., *http://news.netcraft.com/archives/2004/06/07/nearly_25_million_active_sites_running_freebsd.html*. Similar data for OpenBSD was not available.) At that time, there were 2.5 million active sites running FreeBSD. FreeBSD has consistently been increasing in usage since January 2002. OpenBSD, while not represented in the graph, is equally strong as a reliable and efficient host operating system for a web server.

There are really only a handful of production-quality web servers that see a lot of use on the Internet. Apache dominates, accounting for approximately two thirds of all web servers, according to Netcraft LTD (*http://www.netcraft.com/*). The other products that rank behind Apache do not run on FreeBSD or OpenBSD: SunONE and Microsoft's IIS.

Apache is an excellent choice for almost any web application. It is the most flexible, well-documented, and best supported web server available. If you have a need with a web server, chances are that a good solution already exists using Apache (and perhaps one or more modules).

We also discuss thttpd, a compact, no-frills web server that's easy to configure and manage. It doesn't offer all the complex APIs and integrated middleware that Apache

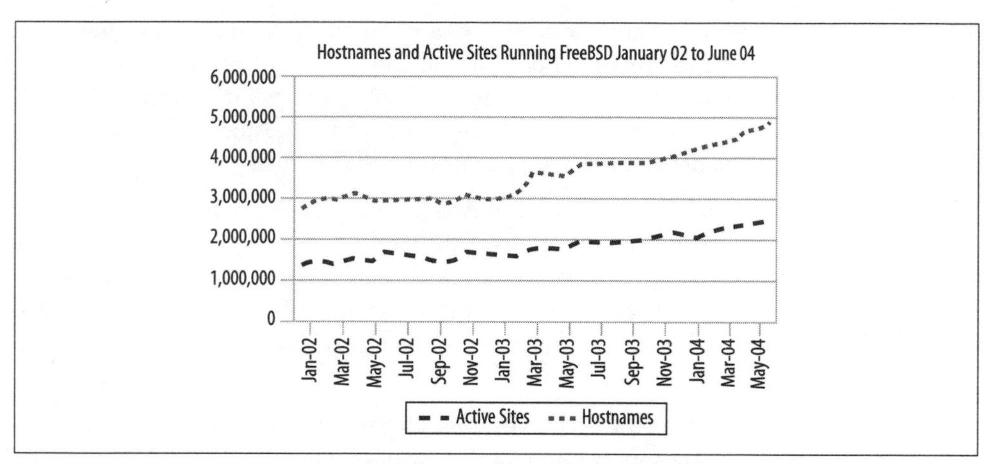

Figure 7-3. Hostnames and active sites running FreeBSD, January 2002 to June 2004

does, but it can serve static pages very quickly and perform a remarkable job of throttling and bandwidth smoothing functions over its traffic.

The Zeus web server is a commercial product that does not run natively on either operating system we consider here. Although it ranks fourth in popularity on the Internet, according to Netcraft LTD, that's with only a 1.5% representation among web servers.

Apache

Apache is the workhorse of the Internet. More sites run Apache than all other web server software packages combined—by a margin of two to one. Its popularity stems from its maturity (it was one of the first production quality web servers ever), its price (it is released under a free license similar to the GNU General Public License), and its flexibility. Apache's near-infinite configurability, like BIND and Sendmail, however, cuts both ways. It creates a variety of opportunities for security issues. The standard Apache configuration probably releases more information about your system than you would like. It also makes it easy to inadvertently make files available that you did not intend to expose. It is the most commonly used web server, so hackers are well versed in the default configuration, know its weak spots, and know how to leverage them to learn about your system.

There are two versions of Apache available, Version 1 and Version 2. Version 1 is mature and stable, and has been under development for almost as long as the World Wide Web has existed. Version 2 began development in 1998 and saw its first beta release in 2000. Despite the years of opportunity to migrate to Version 2, most web servers that run Apache still run version 1.3. If you have an existing infrastructure based on Version 1.3, there is no urgent reason to upgrade to Version 2.

If you are starting from scratch, version 2 is a good place to start. You may find, though that you want the functionality that you can only get from modules written to the 1.3 API. You should strongly consider whether you want to use such modules, though, since their authors are not keeping up with the Apache product. Eventually Version 1 will be deprecated and its support will diminish.

The threading and performance aspects of Apache have been reworked significantly in Version 2. In particular, the multiprocessing modules (MPMs) allow you to take advantage of your operating system and your particular kind of traffic patterns. If your traffic is steady and heavy, then the multithreading features of the threaded MPM will help you. Additionally, several modules (such as the all-important SSL module) are included by default.

Configuring Version 2 is also easier than configuring Version 1. Enabling and disabling modules is done by simply commenting or uncommenting a single line. Modules do not have to be listed in a specific order or more than once in a Version 2 configuration file. The syntax of some popular directives associated with server aliasing and multi-homing have been made simpler as well.

Installing Apache

As with most FreeBSD installations, you will want to install Apache on FreeBSD using the ports collection so that you have maximum control at build time. There are way too many build options to cover them all, so we discuss the most security-relevant ones.

Apache 2 is not included in the OpenBSD ports collection, nor is it bundled with OpenBSD. You must retrieve the sources, configure, compile, and install by hand. Even so, consider reading the section on FreeBSD installation—you'll be faced with many of the same choices and set many of the same options. You'll just use the `configure` script to make your choices.

FreeBSD

Apache 2 may be installed from *ports/www/apache2*. Before diving into the familiar **`make`** and **`make install`**, there are a number of options to consider. Note that, if you plan to use Apache in a *jail(2)* or *chroot(2)* environment (as described later in "Using Jail or Chroot"), you can choose between using the ports system to build or building from source.

Makefile options. The *Makefile* in *ports/www/apache2* contains many options you can set at build time. If you run **`make show-options`**, you may peruse them. A subset of these options, mainly those that have security ramifications, are shown in Table 7-1.

Table 7-1. Apache 2 port options

Option	Meaning	Default
WITHOUT_SSL	Disables SSL support. Only enable this if, for some reason, you do not want SSL support.	Not set
WITH_SUEXEC	Enables *suexec(1)* support. See "mod_suexec" later in this chapter for more details.	Not set
SUEXEC_DOCROOT	The DocumentRoot for *suexec*.	*/usr/local/www/data*
SUEXEC_USERDIR	The directory where users put their personal, per-user HTML files and CGI files.	*public_html*
SUEXEC_SAFEPATH	The initial value for the PATH environment for CGIs executed through *suexec*.	*/usr/local/bin:/usr/bin:/bin*
SUEXEC_LOGFILE	By default, *suexec* will log here directly (not via *syslogd*).	*/var/log/httpd-suexec.log*
SUEXEC_UIDMIN	Minimal allowed UID. Users whose numeric UID is less than this can never use CGIs via *suexec*. Examples are root and operator.	1000
SUEXEC_GIDMIN	CGIs whose group ID is lower than this will never execute via *suexec*. Examples include wheel and operator.	1000
SUEXEC_CALLER	The user allowed to call *suexec*. This should be the user ID under which the web server runs.	*www*
SUEXEC_UMASK	Defines a *umask(2)* for CGIs launched by *suexec*.	Not Set

You will control which modules you run and how they are configured by setting these options to `make`. Even if you're not going to use SSL (or you think you're not going to use it), there is no harm in building it. Simply comment it out in the *httpd.conf* file and you'll be safe. Even if a vulnerability is reported in *mod_ssl* and you built a vulnerable version of it, you won't be vulnerable if that module isn't loaded.

Example 7-1 shows how to build Apache with a few more restrictive options. Often user IDs and group IDs for privileged users are below 500. Neither FreeBSD nor OpenBSD ship with a standard user ID higher than 100, except *nobody* on OpenBSD, who is 32767 for historical reasons.

Example 7-1. Making Apache with non-default options

```
% cd ports/www/apache2
% make SUEXEC_UIDMIN=500 SUEXEC_GIDMIN=500 \
    SUEXEC_CALLER=www SUEXEC_UMASK=0027
```

Recording your use of Apache 2. Having installed Apache version 2, take a moment to tell your ports system, that you use Apache Version 2 instead of Version 1. Most web-related ports will assume Apache 1 unless they find `WITH_APACHE2=YES` in your */etc/make.conf(5)* file. When you build web-related ports, they will recognize that you use Apache 2 and configure themselves accordingly. At the time this was written, there were about 40 ports that recognized the `WITH_APACHE2` flag.

OpenBSD

It's worth mentioning that OpenBSD 3.6 distributes Apache 1.3.29 already integrated into the base operating system and there are some compelling reasons to use it. As with all software integrated into the OpenBSD platform, it has been audited by project team members looking for security issues. They've not only audited it but they've also created a *chroot* environment for Apache! You'll see when we get to "Advanced Web Servers with Jails" that this is no small effort. In short, they have dotted a lot of i's and crossed a lot of t's for you, and they have a very good track record of doing things securely. Since OpenBSD's ports system does not have the `portupgrade` facility, tracking the version that is in the operating system is also one of the most reliable ways to stay up to date and take advantage of the team's efforts at securing the software.

The bulk of the work for Apache 1 has been taken care of by the OpenBSD team, so we will cover installing, configuring, and securing Apache 2. Download the latest stable version of Apache from *http://httpd.apache.org/*, extract it using `tar`, and run the included `configure` script. This process should be familiar and routine to most system administrators.

Configure parameters. You will specify to the `configure` program the same sorts of parameters for your build process that the FreeBSD ports *Makefile* uses—just in a different format. Table 7-2 shows the FreeBSD port option and shows how to set the equivalent `configure` option to the same default value.

`configure` accepts other options, we're just focusing on a consistent set across operating systems. For a list of other options, run `configure` with the `--help` argument.

Table 7-2. Apache 2 configure options

FreeBSD ports option	Option for configure
WITHOUT_SSL	SSL is disabled already in the default Apache configuration. You need to add **--enable-ssl** to the configure line.
WITH_SUEXEC	**--enable-suexec**
SUEXEC_DOCROOT	**--with-suexec-docroot=/usr/local/www/data**
SUEXEC_USERDIR	**--with-suexec-userdir=public_html**
SUEXEC_SAFEPATH	**--with-suexec-safepath=/usr/local/bin:/usr/bin:/bin**
SUEXEC_LOGFILE	**--with-suexec-logfile=/var/log/httpd-suexec.log**
SUEXEC_UIDMIN	**--with-suexec-uidmin=500**
SUEXEC_GIDMIN	**--with-suexec-gidmin=500**
SUEXEC_CALLER	**--with-suexec-caller=_httpd**
SUEXEC_UMASK	**--with-suexec-umask=0022** (Note that this is normally not set)

At this point you can **make** and **install** Apache 2. Once installed, the security concerns for FreeBSD and OpenBSD are largely the same.

Configuring Apache

A few options and configuration issues apply generally. By default, your end users can influence an awful lot of Apache's behavior. Following the principle of least privilege, you should curtail their capabilities to just the minimum needed to achieve their goals.

User overrides

Many configuration parameters for Apache can be overridden by your users if you aren't careful. To keep most of the behavior controlled by *httpd.conf*, you should disable functionality globally and re-enable it at the `VirtualHost` level and disable users' abilities to override *httpd.conf* settings with *.htaccess* files. As a rule you should be aware of which virtual servers or locations use specific features, and you should only enable the features each virtual server needs.

The snippet of *httpd.conf* in Example 7-2 shows how you can generally disable PHP, enable it for a given `VirtualHost`, and then prevent users from overriding your settings.

Example 7-2. Example httpd.conf fragment selectively enabling PHP

```
# disable PHP generally
php_flag  engine  off

<VirtualHost  www.example.com>
    DocumentRoot      /usr/local/www/data/example
    # Enable PHP in this virtual server
    php_flag  engine  on
    Options  IncludesNOEXEC
    AllowOverride  None
</VirtualHost>
```

An important side effect of this configuration is that it disables the users' ability to override all options, PHP-related or otherwise. This is usually not a problem, because only a handful of options are ever overridden, and you can probably work those out on a case-by-case basis. Giving users the liberty to override arbitrary options in their *.htaccess* files will let them override decisions you have made in the *httpd.conf* file.

Protecting critical files

There are several files that are worth protecting on most web servers. If you have interactive users logging into the server, it's obvious that you need to keep them away from these files. However, you should protect the files anyways as an application of "defense in depth."

If you're using SSL (and most secure web servers do, these days), then you have a pair of very important files: your private key and your public key certificate. The process for generating a private key and a public key certificate, and then having it signed by a certificate authority (CA), is somewhat involved and beyond the scope of this chapter. If you need guidance on how to generate these keys, look at Chapter 17 of *Web Security, Privacy, and Commerce* by Garfinkel. It has more step-by-step instructions and some explanations. From this point on, we will assume you have a private key in a file named *server.key* and a public key certificate in *server.crt*.

As you might guess, your private key needs very strict permissions all around. Your certificate may be more loosely protected since it is a public key, but placing it under the same protections isn't a bad idea. Since Apache is run as root and changes identity to some other user after loading these files, only root needs to read these files at all. If an attacker or malicious user is able to compromise these files, then she can defeat the primary protections of SSL. By knowing your private key she can decrypt the transmissions sent to your web server. If she finds a way to intercept traffic, he wins.

The public key certificate and private key files are good candidates both for ACLs and/or filesystem flags, as described in Chapter 2. The default path to your public key certificate file is */usr/local/etc/apache2/ssl.crt/server.crt* and the default path to your private key file is */usr/local/etc/apache2/ssl.key/server.key*. Example 7-3 shows a series of commands that significantly restrict the permissions on these two files.

Example 7-3. Restricting access to SSL certificate and key files

```
% CERTDIR=/usr/local/etc/apache2/ssl.crt      # create some variables
% PKEYDIR=/usr/local/etc/apache2/ssl.key      # to make the other commands
% CERT=${CERTDIR}/server.crt                  # shorter
% PKEY=${PKEYDIR}/server.key

% setfacl -b ${CERT} ${PKEY} ${CERTDIR} ${PKEYDIR} # erase any existing ACLs
% setfacl -m u:root:r ${CERT} ${PKEY}         # root can only read the files
% setfacl -m g:: ${CERT} ${PKEY}              # group gets no permissions
% setfacl -m o:: ${CERT} ${PKEY}              # no one else gets permissions

% setfacl -d u:root:r ${CERTDIR} ${PKEYDIR}   # Make these ACLs the
% setfacl -d g:: ${CERTDIR} ${PKEYDIR}        # defaults in these directories
% setfacl -d o:: ${CERTDIR} ${PKEYDIR}

% chflags schg -R ${CERTDIR} ${PKEYDIR}       # system immutable flag, too
```

Example 7-3 is a good example of using ACLs and filesystem flags in harmony. The ACLs set the overriding permissions on the files, and then the `chflags(1)` command keeps those permissions from changing as long as the system remains at a *securelevel* greater than 0.

Remember that you will periodically renew your certificate. Most Certificate Authorities (CAs) issue web server certificates that expire every year or two. You will have to undo all of these protections on the *server.crt* file in order to update it. If it's immutable, that means a reboot! You should never have to alter the *server.key* file, though, as long as you continue to have the same public key certificate reissued each year.

If your Apache server configuration is rarely updated, you can gain additional security by setting the system immutable flag on the *httpd.conf* file. This will help prevent an attacker from being able to overwrite your configuration. If you add a lot of `VirtualHosts` or make changes to your configuration file regularly, consider breaking the volatile configuration elements out of the main *httpd.conf* file using the `Include` directive. You might then be able to use the user immutable flag on these files. This will probably thwart a variety of attacks, but it will not require you to reboot in order to make a change to your configuration.

Resisting denial of service

Apache's default configuration tries to keep serving web pages as long as it possibly can. Unlike Sendmail, which has various ways of degrading its service if it detects the load creeping up, Apache blithely keeps accepting requests up to the point that some critical resource is exhausted and imposes a hard limit. To help resist denial of service attacks related to resource exhaustion, you can tune your `MaxClients` in your *httpd.conf* file.

`MaxClients` is the maximum number of child processes the master `httpd` will allow to run at a given time. It is not dynamic and it has no knowledge of what your server's capabilities are. You have to size it statically based on your best knowledge of your server's capabilities and its usage patterns. To tune `MaxClients`, you should start by looking at the size of a typical `httpd` process and consider how much RAM you have installed in your server. Using the tool `top(8)`, you can see the size (both virtual and resident) of a process. Example 7-4 shows an `httpd` process in `top`'s output.

Example 7-4. Viewing process information with top(8)

```
  PID USERNAME PRI NICE  SIZE    RES STATE    TIME   WCPU    CPU COMMAND
25682 nobody     2    0 23212K 11512K poll    0:04  4.00%  4.00% httpd
```

The `httpd` process in our example is 23 megabytes in virtual size, and is using 11.5 megabytes of actual RAM. It's normal for the virtual size to be much larger than the resident size, because the virtual size takes into account shared libraries and other areas of memory (e.g., memory mapped regions of device driver memory) that a process has available. Assuming the server in question has 512 megabytes of RAM, and we need to leave some available for processes other than Apache, we might choose

450 megabytes as our maximum memory allotment for Apache. Dividing 450 by 11.5 suggests that we should set `MaxClients` to be 39 or 40. After that, we are likely to start thrashing.

This calculated number could still be high or low, depending on the complexity of the web pages that are being served. If every web page access requires a CGI program to run a query on a database, we might find that 40 concurrent accesses are not sustainable. If we have a single dynamic page that can cause the server to consume up to 100 megabytes of memory, we'll want to take that into consideration also. If after your calculations your `MaxClients` value results in serious performance problems, perhaps a memory or CPU upgrade is in order.

Module Overview

There are a variety of modules that come with Apache. Each provides specific functionality; however, many of them also have specific security concerns. As a general principle, you should only enable modules for which you can identify a specific functional requirement. You should also periodically audit, or at least informally review, your use of Apache to see if modules are enabled that are not being used. In the following sections, we consider eight of the approximately 35 common modules. These eight either have the most significant security risks, are the most commonly used, or both.

The CGI, PHP, and Perl modules are the biggest, most complicated, and most dangerous modules that most people run. We discuss how to build, install, configure, and run them safely. The other modules we discuss, while not trivial, are easier to configure properly and have fewer options to worry about.

mod_cgi

The CGI module is a critical part of Apache that allows programs to be executed and have their output served as the response to a web query. It is installed and enabled by default. Example 7-5 shows the default settings in *httpd.conf* for the CGI module, which are pretty reasonable.

Example 7-5. Default CGI permissions in httpd.conf

```
ScriptAlias /cgi-bin/ "/usr/local/www/cgi-bin/"
<Directory  "/usr/local/www/cgi-bin">
    AllowOverride None
    Options None
    Order allow,deny
    Allow from all
</Directory>
```

The most important features here are `AllowOveride None` and `Options None`. They make it impossible to list the contents of the CGI directory or to do anything other than execute the scripts that live in */usr/local/www/cgi-bin/*.

Ideally, there should be very few CGI programs that actually live in the *ScriptAlias* directory. Instead, use a method of running CGI programs as specific users. The *mod_suexec* and `cgiwrap` mechanisms are both good ways to contain the potential damage from a poorly written CGI program. The section "Run CGI programs as normal users" describes how to install, configure, and run them.

mod_php

PHP is one of the most maligned web technologies available to run in Apache. It is an interpreted programming language, with a syntax similar somewhat to C++ or Perl. It can either execute as a standalone language, or embedded in web pages through *mod_php*. Most the dangers of PHP can be chalked up to its Perl-like tolerance of sloppy programming constructs, and the readily available mass of poorly written free PHP programs. You need to carefully consider what scripts you run, what privileges you give them, and how much you can contain potential damage.

PHP and permissions. PHP scripts execute as the web server's user ID (e.g., www) and group (again often www). This is problematic for a variety of reasons. If the script can be controlled through a code injection attack, it could conceivably kill the web server process (thus acting as a denial of service). Alternatively it could invoke shell scripts, and do virtually anything the www user could do on the system.

The unprivileged web user, www, is not usually allowed to write in any part of the filesystem. This means that PHP-based programs will store data in a database, a specific directory that is writable to the www user, or a world-writable directory such as */tmp*. A database is the preferable option, but it's not always an option if PHP is built without database support or the PHP applications themselves do not offer that option. This will tempt non-root users to create world-writable directories in the parts of the filesystem they control, so that their scripts can read and write data to permanent storage. World-writable directories are generally a bad idea, but even more so when accessed through PHP scripts of dubious quality. Try to stay aware of the ways your web developers use PHP, and make sure they have appropriate, permissions-regulated places to store their data. A database server like MySQL is probably ideal.

Although we are focusing on *mod_php*, it is possible to build a PHP interpreter as a standalone executable and then invoke it as a CGI. This is not desirable from a performance point of view, but it can be useful on low-bandwidth sites where security is more important than performance. By making the PHP interpreter its own binary, you can use techniques like *suexec* or `cgiwrap` to have it execute in its own user context. Users could then run their own PHP code as their own user ID, reducing the potential damage from poorly written code.

mod_php Apache configuration. To secure the PHP runtime environment, configure it well and make sure that your users cannot circumvent your efforts. The PHP runtime environment is controlled in three places: the *php.ini* file, the *httpd.conf* file, and *.htaccess* files in individual directories. These files control the same set of options, but settings in the *httpd.conf* file override those in the *php.ini* file. Any *.htaccess* files in web content directories can override the *httpd.conf* options. This order of precedence is shown in Figure 7-4.

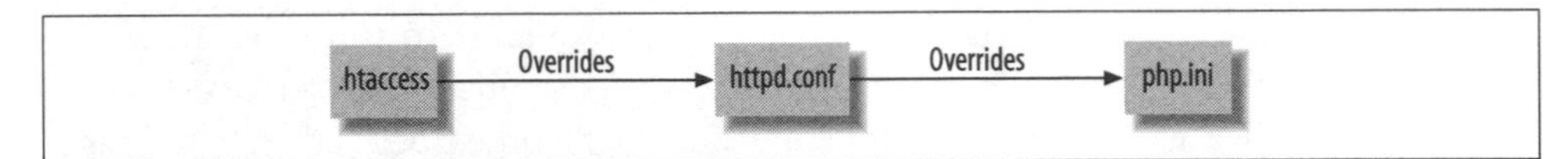

Figure 7-4. Order of precedence of PHP configuration files

What is important to note is that end users have the ability to create *.htaccess* files anywhere they can create web content. Thus, they can override your server-wide security choices if PHP options in *.htaccess* files are honored. If `AllowOverride` includes either `Options` or `All`, then users can override the *httpd.conf* file. Unfortunately, this is a binary option: users have full access to override all PHP settings, or no PHP settings.

PHP configuration. While you can configure PHP in a variety of places, it makes the most sense to configure it in the *php.ini* file. Then, as long as you prevent users from creating their own configurations, you can rest assured that your PHP configuration is in a protected location associated with PHP, rather than commingled with your Apache configuration or distributed across user directories.

PHP installs two example files: *php.ini-dist* and *php.ini-recommended*. Both of these will be found in */usr/local/etc* on a default FreeBSD or OpenBSD ports installation of *mod_php*. The *php.ini-dist* file is not intended for use, but instead shows you what the default values are for all the options. It is heavily commented and a good source of information. The *php.ini-recommended* file lists settings that the PHP team thinks make for an efficient, secure configuration. The following settings help improve the security posture of PHP.

`register_globals = Off`
: In early versions of PHP, if someone invoked a PHP script through a URL like *http://www.example.com/info.php?test=true*, then the PHP script named `info.php` would set the variable `$test` to the value `true` in its global namespace. This is the effect when `register_globals` is `On`. Beginning with PHP 4.3.0, `register_globals` is `Off` by default. This is always a good practice, however you may find particular PHP scripts that require `register_globals` set to `On`. Be careful about enabling it. Such scripts are probably susceptible to various input-validation attacks.

`display_errors = Off`
: It is a good idea to minimize the amount of error information an attacker might glean from your PHP scripts, misconfigurations, or other system problems. If `display_errors` is enabled, then PHP generates pretty, informative messages that help you track down the problem. They may, however, leak information about the names of script files, hosts that your script is trying to contact, or permissions on resources that should be hidden from an attacker. Error output is only sent to the web server's error log and not sent with the HTTP response when `display_errors` is `Off`.

`variables_order = "GPCS"`
: The letters in this setting stand for *GET*, *POST*, cookie, and server. An additional letter is allowed here: `E` for environment. `variables_order` determines whether variables defined in one of these five places will be predefined in the PHP namespace, and, if so, the order of precedence. The order of precedence is lowest to highest. For example, there is an environment variable `PATH` that is initialized to */usr/local/bin:/usr/bin:/bin* when Apache launches. If a web browser requests *http://www.example.com/?PATH=/tmp* and sends a cookie `PATH=/var`, then the `variables_order` setting determines what the ultimate value of `PATH` will be when a PHP script tries to read it. In this case, the environment is not considered because `E` does not appear in `variables_order`. Because `C` comes after `G` in `GPCS`, the value passed in the cookie (*/var*) takes precedence over the value passed in the URL (*/tmp*).

  If your web site uses PHP, and it does not expect parameters from GET requests at all, a better value for this would be `PCS`. Generally speaking, the variables inherited from outside your script should come from as few places as possible.

mod_perl

Perl is a well-known scripting language that is extremely well-suited for writing CGI programs. Its built-in support for parsing strings and matching patterns makes it a powerful tool for web development tasks. Like PHP, Perl is modular, allowing developers to draw on the work of others.

Perl's problems in a web context are similar to PHP's. Perl allows many dangerous syntactic structures like the backtick (`). Like PHP, many modules are written partially or totally in C or C++. This means that, even though Perl is a garbage collected language with automatic memory allocation, there may be commands and modules that can be invoked with bad arguments to exploit buffer overflows and the other vulnerabilities caused by poor programming in the underlying C or C++.

If you operate a web server of any significance, you probably will be using one or more Perl scripts. It is one of the most popular languages for CGI programming. Like other standalone programs and scripts, Perl scripts can be executed as CGI programs without any special configuration just by placing the scripts in `ScriptAliased` directories. There is a distinct disadvantage to running Perl as a CGI if you are looking for performance. Each time a script executes, the entire Perl interpreter must be loaded into memory, perform significant runtime initialization, and then run your script. If your script is small and optimized, the time spent in this initialization probably dwarfs the time spent actually doing anything useful. If your web site is not popular, or the script is rarely run, this probably does not matter.

The answer to running the interpreter as a CGI is *mod_perl*. The *mod_perl* module was created to load one instance of the Perl runtime environment into memory when the server starts. Then, all scripts can execute in this prepared environment. This provides major performance improvements.

As an additional measure of security, add the line `PerlTaintCheck On` to your *httpd.conf* file. This requires Perl code that is executing under *mod_perl* to obey Perl's *taint* rules. This is the same as invoking **`perl -t`** to run the script. These rules effectively force developers to perform (at least trivial) input filtering. They must perform some transformation on any data that comes from outside the program (e.g., an environment variable, a web form input, and so on) before they can subsequently use that data in certain contexts. For example, a value that was provided to the script by a form element on a web page cannot subsequently be passed unmodified as an argument to an `eval` statement; some string replacement must be performed first. See the *perlsec* manpage for documentation on Perl's *taint* mode.

While `PerlTaintCheck` is not bulletproof, it causes all *mod_perl* programmers to at least perform a few input checks on their code. In particular, because it is systematic and automatic, it helps programmers find places where they need input filtering. Good programmers will welcome the assistance and use it to help them harden their programs.

mod_include

The *mod_include* module provides server-side-include (SSI) functionality. It's most often used to provide very simple and straightforward inclusion of one file within another. It can also execute commands on the server and insert the results of the command's execution into the file, before the file is sent to the web browser. It also provides a variety of convenience routines such as the ability to determine and print file modification times, file sizes, and the server's current time.

HTML files are only parsed for SSI directives if *mod_include* and parsing are both enabled in the *httpd.conf* configuration file. Typically this means establishing the `server-parsed` handler for files ending in *.shtml* and enabling the `Includes` option on a web-visible directory. Some administrators also like to use the `XBitHack` directive so that any HTML files marked executable on the filesystem will also be server parsed. This is especially useful when taking existing sites and adding SSI functionality. You won't have to rename pages, so you don't have to update cross-references.

The HTML fragment in Example 7-6 demonstrates several different *mod_include* directives. We discuss several security implications using it as a reference. The scenarios are ordered from least risky to most risky, with the final scenario effectively offering an attacker a variety of ways to totally compromise the web server.

Example 7-6. HTML file using mod_include directives

```
<h1>Server Information Page</h1>

<p>This is our standard disclaimer:</p>
<p><!--#include  file="disclaimer.html" --></p>

<p>Here is a dubious way to retrieve the date:</p>
<p><!--#exec cgi="/cgi-bin/my-date" --></p>

<p>Show the user what query string they used:</p>
<p>You typed
<!--#exec cmd="/bin/echo $QUERY_STRING" --></p>
```

The first #include directive in Example 7-6 is the classic example of how SSI can be used simply and safely. Apache merely opens the file *disclaimer.html* (which, by the syntax in the example, must exist in the same directory as our example file) and inserts its contents directly into that part of the file before it is sent. The file *disclaimer.html* does not need, therefore, to be a complete HTML file. In fact, it need not contain any HTML tags at all in our example. It can, however, include SSI directives; and if it does, they will be parsed. The *mod_include* module can be used recursively and will continue to parse directives that it finds in each included file. Unless a dangerous use of SSI directives exists in *disclaimer.html*, this is a simple and safe use of SSI.

For security reasons, the file specified in the #include directive may not be absolute: it may not begin with / nor may it contain ../ or any encoding of that string. Untrusted users are often allowed to create web pages on web servers, so this prevents directives such as <!--#include file="/etc/passwd" --> from divulging the contents of sensitive files.

The next lines in Example 7-6 execute a CGI program called my-date from the server-wide */cgi-bin* directory. This looks like CGI, but it is actually different. The output of the CGI command will be inserted unmodified into the middle of the body of the web page. Thus, if the output of the CGI program's output is not plain text or HTML, it is likely to look very bad when rendered in the web browser. Outside the context of *mod_include*, CGI programs can return any kind of data. They can send images, spreadsheets, movies, or any other MIME* content type. When executed by a

* MIME is "Multipurpose Internet Media Encoding" and is described in RFC 1341 and many other follow-on RFCs. It defines special "content-type" designators that allow web browsers, email programs, and other Internet-enabled software to invoke appropriate other software to handle certain kinds of documents.

server-side include, however, their data will be embedded inside a document, so it only makes sense to send text or HTML.

When invoking a CGI through *mod_include*, an attacker can influence the environment in which the CGI executes through the query string and the user agent identifier. When a user requests a web page, he can specify a query string, even though the page does not process queries. For example, he can access the page via a URL like *http://www.example.com/index.html?ATTACK=true*. Despite the fact that *index.html* is a plain HTML file, this is legal syntax. If *index.html* invokes a CGI program through the #exec directive, the `QUERY_STRING` environment variable for that CGI program will be set to `ATTACK=true`. If the CGI program parses the `QUERY_STRING` variable, then an attacker can try to insert, for example, shellcode to make the CGI misbehave. Thus, a file that appears to be pretty safe at first glance can actually incorporate CGI code that is vulnerable.

Lastly, Example 7-6 demonstrates how to execute a shell command directly from inside an HTML file. This a very bad practice, especially in our example, because we pass `QUERY_STRING` as an argument to a shell command. This gives an attacker the opportunity to craft query strings that can be passed directly to programs executing on the host system. A specially crafted URL such as *http://www.example.com/?foo;/bin/date* will show `foo`, followed by the output of running `/bin/date`. Imagine the consequences if `/bin/date` were replaced with `rm -rf /*`! It wouldn't remove the whole filesystem, but it would remove everything the www user could remove.

The availability of *mod_include* functionality can be limited on a system-wide, per-`VirtualHost`, or per-directory basis. Additionally, given how dangerous the #exec option can be, it can be restricted separately as shown in Example 7-7.

Example 7-7. Permitting SSI while denying #exec

```
<VirtualHost www.example.com>
    DocumentRoot /data/www/www.example.com
    Options None
    AllowOverride IncludesNOEXEC
</VirtualHost>
```

Unless you have a specific use for SSI, disable it. If you do have a specific need for it, enable it without enabling #exec.

mod_dav

The DAV module was created to offer compatibility with the Distributed Authoring and Versioning (DAV) protocol, defined by the Internet Engineering Task Force (IETF) in RFC 2518. Microsoft created the DAV standard, which defines a variety of methods within HTTP. In addition to the usual GET, POST (and other less well-known methods) defined in RFCs 1945 and 2068, DAV defines methods like SEARCH and PROPFIND. In this way, products like Microsoft Outlook Web Access can use the same shared calendar and other shared resources that the proprietary clients like Outlook use.

Unfortunately, Apache's *mod_dav* implements a free-for-all security model. Though you can restrict access to it in a robust manner, once a user is authenticated she is authorized to do anything. There is currently no way to map the authentication at the HTTP level to Unix authorization on the filesystem.

If you cannot use digest authentication, at least protect the DAV traffic by using SSL. All the DAV directives work within SSL-enabled sessions. This will protect your user IDs, passwords, and the actual web content as it passes from the user's client application to your server. You may find performance suffers in such a situation, however. DAV sessions use many very small HTTP requests—more than a normal web browsing session. Add the overhead of cryptography, and it may not be acceptable under heavy load.

Enable *mod_dav* at your own risk. The primitive authentication/authorization capabilities create a situation where all users who have any access have full access to the data stored there. Such a permissions structure does not work for many organizations. Furthermore, if you accidentally fail to apply any restrictions to the DAV-enabled filesystem, then anyone who notices that DAV is enabled will be able to store arbitrary data there. You will quickly become a hot spot for trading illegal software.

mod_autoindex

Apache includes an automatic file and directory indexing module called *mod_autoindex*. It is helpful for people who just want to make files available through the Web with minimal effort. The module can be configured to understand a variety of file types, decorate the file listings with appropriate icons, and to display any *README* files that happen to be in the directory. *mod_autoindex* is also the module that determines what names of files will be displayed (and an order of precedence) when a URL is requested that does not correspond to a file. For example, the main web page for most web sites is usually named either *index.htm* or *index.html*. The contents of *index.html* are sent when the URL *http://www.example.com/* is requested. When no index page is available, *mod_autoindex* sends a directory listing.

It is often the case that novice web developers, or their web-authoring software, will choose a default filename for a web page that is something other than the traditional *index.html*. For example, if the directory is *marketing*, then the software or the developer will sometimes name the main file *marketing.html*. This would be accessible via a URL such as *http://www.example.com/marketing/marketing.html*. The novice developer might not realize he could have a prettier URL such as *http://www.example.com/marketing/* by naming the file *index.html*. Imagine that the rest of that directory contains marketing materials that should not be downloaded directly; instead, they should only be available to someone after he fills out the form in *marketing.html*. If a visitor strips *marketing.html* off the end of the URL, however, he will see the directory listing, and can bypass the form altogether.

Administrators should make an effort to educate their users in the minimal value provided by security-through-obscurity. In this case, placing documents in a directly accessible directory with a web page frontend is of little security value. Instead, the documents should have been placed outside the `DocumentRoot` and delivered via download to the requestor.

The worst impact of *mod_autoindex*, then, is that it sometimes makes it easy to bypass security-through-obscurity mechanisms on the server. It is not exploitable to gain unauthorized access to the system or cause any other major problem. Like other modules, it should be disabled unless you have a specific use for it. Also like other modules, it can be disabled by default and only enabled on specific areas.

mod_info and mod_status

Two modules, *mod_info* and *mod_status*, provide information to an administrator about the running configuration. They can help you troubleshoot problems or just give you a current snapshot of the runtime status of your server. However, without any constraints, they are the next best thing to posting your *httpd.conf* file on your web site, which is probably something you do not want to do. Your security cannot realistically depend on obscurity, but there is no need to casually divulge configuration information.

In the interest of keeping your server's configuration hidden from prying eyes, you should carefully consider whether you need to use *mod_info* and *mod_status* at all. If you do need to use them, you should consider how tightly you can control access to them. They are marvelous diagnostic tools for understanding how your server is configured. If an attacker can reach them, however, she can learn a great deal of information.

It is tempting to simply restrict access to these modules to the local loopback address (e.g., 127.0.0.1 or *localhost*). After all, you are the administrator and only you can generate requests to the web server that originate on the web server, right? Consider the case where a user can put the following string in a web page and use server side include processing: `<!--#include virtual="/server-info/" -->`. The request for the *server-info* web page embedded in their HTML will originate from the local system. Remarkably, this request will succeed and the user will be able to embed your server's information in his own web page, which he can peruse.

In general, you should disable these two modules except during times when you are specifically troubleshooting a problem. When they are enabled, only enable them in a `VirtualHost` that you control for system administration purposes. You should use some sort of username and password-based security, on top of IP address–based security. Instead of restricting access to *localhost*, allow connections only from your workstation, or an administrative host or subnet.

mod_userdir

On large, multiuser systems the average non-root user needs a mechanism for making web pages and displaying them. Apache offers this functionality through *mod_userdir*. A user can have a directory and files in a well-known location (a directory named *public_html* in her home directory by default), and Apache associates that directory with a URL based on her login name. For example, user *jsmith* might have a home directory */home/jsmith*. The file */home/jsmith/public_html/index.html*, then, would correspond to the URL *http://www.example.com/~jsmith/*.

By itself, this module does not create any noteworthy security concerns. However, it can be combined with server-side includes, PHP, CGI, or *suexec*, for example, to create security risks. The primary risk is that it gives every user a place where he can install his own *.htaccess* file and bypass (inadvertently or intentionally) restrictions you placed in the system-wide *httpd.conf* file. This is where users can create their own PHP configuration options, for example, that may differ from your site-wide defaults and create more risks.

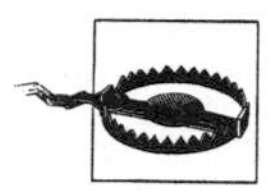

You probably don't want to enable `UserDir` at a global level. Instead, enable it only on `VirtualHosts` that need it, and even then, specify which users are enabled if that's practical. Careless configuration can lead to some embarassing results. For instance, if you're an ISP hosting a local church and a pornography site on the same system, you don't want */~pastor/* to be evaluated for both the church web site and the porn site.

If you have users who need this style of web page access, be careful what other options you provide and what you allow them to override in their *.htaccess* files.

Apache Best Practices

There are a few specific recommendations for running an Apache server that can help you run it more securely. Some of them are operating system tuning parameters, while others are configurations of Apache itself. If you consider applying these practices, be sure to consider your specific situation. It is not necessarily true that you should turn on every security option and every optimization possible. In general you should enable only the modules you need, and the optimizations that address specific problems you face.

Enable only modules you need

As mentioned previously, instead of disabling modules you do not think you need, disable all modules. Then enable only those you know you will need. If you run into problems, you should be able to figure out which additional modules you need to enable.

Apache provides a small set of example configuration files. One of them, typically named *highperformance.conf* has a minimum number of modules enabled. Although it also has a variety of other options tuned for performance, the `LoadModule` commands are the most relevant to consider in terms of minimizing modules.

Modules are enabled and disabled in the *httpd.conf* file by commenting out the corresponding `LoadModule` directive in the *httpd.conf* file. In Apache 1.3, there is an additional `AddModule` directive that must also be commented out. Failure to disable both lines in an Apache 1.3 will result in a syntax error. Furthermore, for Apache 1.3, the `AddModule` and `LoadModule` directives must list the modules in the same order. Apache must be restarted for these changes to take effect.

Minimize information leaks

Unless Apache is configured otherwise, the web server will provide its version (e.g., `Apache/2.0.52`), which modules it has (e.g., *mod_perl*, *mod_php*), and even the module version numbers (e.g., `PHP/4.3.2`). It sends this information not only in the environment available to CGI programs and SSI pages, but also in the headers of every HTTP response. For example, a fully loaded web server with no special configuration might send the following in every HTTP response:

```
Server: Apache/2.0.52 (UNIX) PHP/4.3.2 mod_perl/1.26 mod_ssl/2.8.16 OpenSSL/0.9.7b
```

That is a wealth of information for an attacker. OpenSSL has had known exploits in the past, including a timing attack that could divulge the server's private key. By offering up version information so willingly, you only help potential attackers. You certainly do not benefit in any way from including this information.

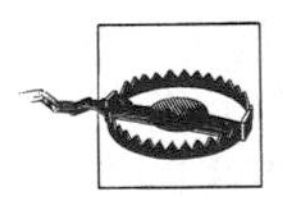

Remember that most web server attacks are scripted. Scripts may not care about what versions of software you are running and may attempt exploits regardless. Obfuscating your header information so that you can "safely" run vulnerable software is folly.

By default, Apache will also append a tag line to the bottom of any pages it generates for you (such as those created by *mod_autoindex* and error documents). That tag line indicates that the web server is Apache and it often includes the version number. Again, this is information that you, as an administrator, have no need for; however, it may prove useful for attackers.

Unlike BIND and Sendmail, there is no trivial way to cause Apache to report a fake version identifier. A little obfuscation to confuse the script kiddies never hurts. The most you can do, without modifying source code, is to make Apache simply report itself as "Apache." This is easy to configure, as shown in Example 7-8.

Example 7-8. Disabling extraneous version information in httpd.conf

```
ServerTokens      ProductOnly
ServerSignature   Off
```

Always separate HTML and CGI locations

Apache tries to protect the CGI directory from being browsed to prevent the programs from being downloaded instead of executed. However, if the CGI directory (almost always called */cgi-bin/*) is within the `DocumentRoot` of a virtual server (or within a user's *~/public_html* directory), then there is a chance that the programs can be downloaded. All too often programs such as Perl scripts will embed sensitive information like database usernames and passwords in the source code of the script. If the script is downloaded, an attacker learns something valuable (and perhaps directly exploitable) about your systems.

On a related note, watch out for lingering artifacts from development and test. Developers and administrators frequently create scripts like *test.sh* or *phpinfo.php* within the `DocumentRoot` in the course of developing or debugging a web application. It is critical that these sorts of scripts be removed or made nonexecutable when they are not actively being used. Better yet, restrict these kinds of activities to a development or test environment that is not directly exposed to external visitors. Tools exist that crawl through web sites and check for long lists of commonly named debugging scripts. Use them, before they're used against you.

Protect sensitive configuration files

Another way attackers probe system security is by trying to download *.htaccess* files. In order to have their desired effect, these files must live in web-accessible directories. However, they also give clues to the security of the system. For instance, they may identify resources that are protected, thereby giving an attacker a roadmap for future attacks. Rules such as the one in Example 7-9 are typical in the outermost scope of an *httpd.conf* file.

Example 7-9. Protecting .htaccess files in httpd.conf

```
<Files ~ "^\.ht">
    Order allow,deny
    Deny from all
    Satisfy All
</Files>
```

This rule is provided in most example *httpd.conf* files. It protects any file beginning with *.ht* like password-based access files, commonly named *.htpasswd* and *.htgroup*. There is no reason that the files need to be named *.htaccess*, *.htpasswd*, or *.htgroup*. In fact, as a security precaution, you should probably choose other names for these files and don't store password and group files within the `DocumentRoot`. But just in case your system users fail to heed this advice, protect them from being downloaded by implementing a configuration similar to Example 7-9.

Run CGI programs as normal users

Web server administrators often find themselves performing a variety of security gymnastics to make all the UIDs of all the processes match their requirements. The `httpd` process must run as root, initially, in order to listen for connections on ports less than 1024. Once a connection is made, the server process immediately switches to the unprivileged www user to minimize the risk of doing bad things as root. In addition to root and www, you have users who generally do not login to the web server either as root or as the www user: they must also be accommodated by the web server configuration.

Since the script running as the www user cannot normally write files into directories owned by a normal user, novice users often create world-writable directories and files for their CGI program ouput and scratch space. Clearly this is not very desirable from a security point of view.

Both *suexec* and `cgiwrap` allow users' CGI scripts to run under their individual UIDs. Their scripts can read and write files anywhere in their home directories, and damage from any poorly programmed scripts they might write will be contained. While undesirable, it is better to put one user's data at risk than many users' data.

cgiwrap. On FreeBSD, `cgiwrap` can be installed from *ports/www/cgiwrap*. It is not available in the OpenBSD ports tree, but it is not complicated and it has no dependencies. Retrieving the source, configuring, and installing it manually under OpenBSD is not difficult. In either case, the net result is a pair of *setuid* root binary files named `cgiwrap` and `cgiwrapd`, which may be placed in your CGI directory (e.g., */usr/local/www/cgi-bin*). They should be executable, but not readable, by all users. There are no changes necessary to Apache's configuration.

`cgiwrap` examines its PATH and execution environment, determines dynamically which user's permissions to adopt, and then invokes CGI programs with that user's permissions. Its purpose is to perform critical safety checks, and then switch users in a way that is safe and does not create new exploit possibilities. One advantage to `cgiwrap` is that it supports lots of different users, all using their own sets of CGI programs. You can install `cgiwrap` once, in one location, and then all users' web sites can take advantage of it.

cgiwrap also includes a very useful debugging binary called cgiwrapd that can be installed in the CGI directory. When it is invoked, instead of cgiwrap, the output of the CGI program is turned into plain text and sent along with a report of the execution environment. Normally, when a CGI program exits prematurely and produces bad output or no output, the Apache server simply sends a generic Error 500: Internal Server Error web page to the browser. This makes debugging problems very difficult without access to error logs. With cgiwrapd, developers can point to a debugging URL like *http://www.example.com/cgi-bin/cgiwrapd/user/myscript* and get more useful output.

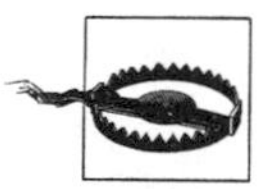

Be careful with cgiwrapd. It exposes a wealth of information about the internal execution environment of your web server. If possible, enable it only when a user needs it. Since it is *setuid* root, however, only an administrator can enable or disable it.

One of the primary disadvantages to cgiwrap is its complexity. Users put their scripts in an obvious filesystem location, such as */home/user/cgi-bin/myscript*, but the URL for the script will be something unintuitive like *http://www.example.com/cgi-bin/cgiwrap/user/myscript*. If you download CGI programs that someone else wrote, you may find it difficult to configure them to run in a cgiwrap environment.

mod_suexec. The *suexec* module comes with Apache and uses a slightly different approach to running CGI programs under users' own IDs. The Apache httpd documentation describes 20 checks that *suexec* performs before actually executing code as a user other than the unprivileged www user. Although we can't cover all 20 checks, two of the most useful include making sure that the file to be executed is owned by the target user and is not writable by anyone else or *setuid*. Ultimately, however, these checks merely determine whether the program is allowed to run and if it may be run with the privileges of the designated user.

The primary advantage of *mod_suexec* is its tight integration with the Apache web server. It can operate in ways cgiwrap cannot, because it can intercept requests for CGI programs before they are dispatched. With *mod_suexec* installed, two new directives, User and Group, can be used in VirtualHost definitions. These directives, as you may suspect, define the user and group under which CGIs must run. Additionally, *mod_suexec* can be used with *mod_userdir* style directories (e.g., *http://www.example.com/~jsmith/*), executing CGIs with the appropriate user's permissions. Example 7-10 is analogous to Example 7-7 where the CGI programs in this example server all execute as user *jsmith*.

Example 7-10. Enabling mod_suexec in httpd.conf

```
# This expands the configuration from Example 7-7
<VirtualHost www.example.com>
    DocumentRoot      /data/www/www.example.com
```

Example 7-10. Enabling mod_suexec in httpd.conf (continued)

```
    Options             None
    AllowOverride       IncludesNOEXEC
    User                jsmith
    Group               webusers
</VirtualHost>
```

There is one small disadvantage with *mod_suexec*. It is not as simple to enable or disable as `cgiwrap`. Enabling it, disabling it, or reconfiguring it, requires changing the Apache configuration file and restarting the server. It also does not offer the debugging aid that `cgiwrapd` offers.

On the other hand, a *mod_suexec*-based server is slightly easier to delegate to a junior administrator than one that uses `cgiwrap`. While restarting the server is an unfortunate requirement, it is a task that can be easily done using `apachectl(8)` via `sudo(8)`. Likewise, editing the *httpd.conf* file can also easily be delegated to junior administrators. `cgiwrap`, on the other hand, requires the authority to manipulate files that are *setuid* root.

Summary

Remember that no runtime environment can ensure that CGI programs have no errors or vulnerabilities. These two programs are simply privilege containment systems. They enable users' CGI programs to read and write into the filesystem safely, and they help control damage from poorly written programs. It is still vitally important that your CGI programs be well written.

Encrypting Web Traffic

By default, web traffic is sent in plain text, so if someone can eavesdrop anywhere in the network between a client and a server, she can see everything that goes by. Encryption helps to protect sensitive data when it is transmitted over the Internet.

RFC 2246 defines a protocol called Transport Layer Security (TLS). This is the standardized version of a protocol originally developed by Netscape called the Secure Sockets Layer (SSL). Despite the fact that virtually all encrypted web traffic uses the modern TLS protocol, the vast majority of people still refer to encrypted web traffic as SSL. We follow this convention as well.

SSL is a transport layer protocol, just above the HTTP level, encrypting what would normally be clear-text HTTP traffic. Figure 7-5 shows most of the OSI reference model network layers, with the ones relevant to our discussion in black. The web browser in this example transmits the password "mozart" to the transport layer. At the transport layer, the password is encrypted using a session key that has been pre-established between the web browser and web server.

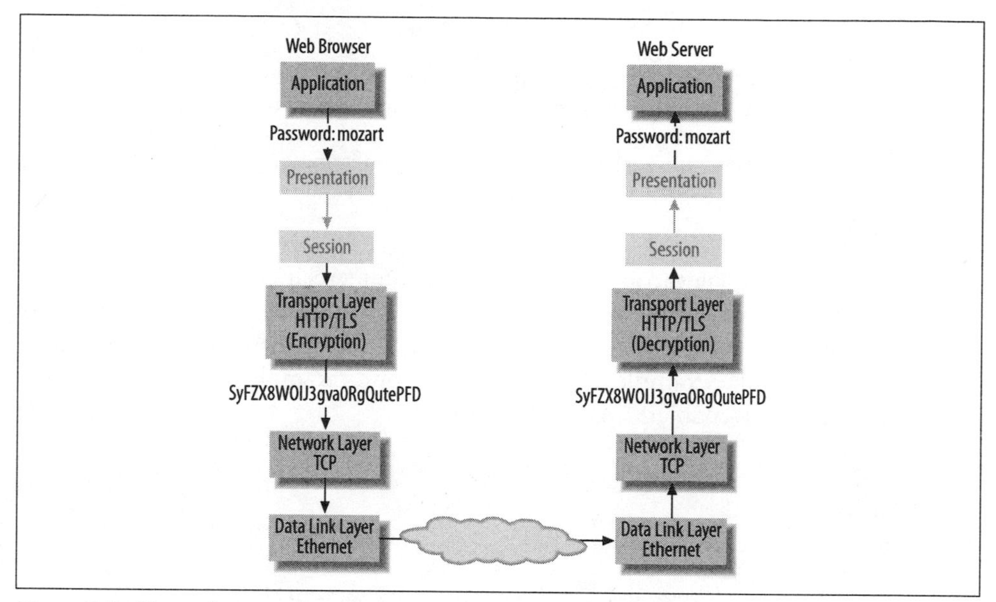

Figure 7-5. Network protocol stack showing SSL encryption

SSL generally gives you two assurances: (1) the data is encrypted as it is transmitted over the Internet; (2) your browser really is communicating with the site you think it is. There are a variety of ways to undermine the fundamental assumptions that make these two assurances strong. Your operating system, however, can only do a little to prevent SSL from being subverted. We will mention what you can do, but some of the concepts required to fully discuss the risks (certificates, authority and trust, and DNS integrity) are too big to cover here.

SSL and certificates

Before you can SSL-enable your web server, you must generate a private key and get a signed certificate as described previously. For detailed instructions and to purchase a certificate, visit either a low-end retailer like InstantSSL (*http://www.instantssl.com/*) or a high-end retailer like Verisign (*http://www.verisign.com/*). They have complete instructions on what you must do and can walk you through the process.

You can also create your own certificate independent of any certificate authority. The problem with self-signed and issued certificates, however, is that your users will see many ugly warnings from their web browsers. You have to tell your users to dismiss these warnings about untrusted certificates. If they ever are the victim of a man-in-the-middle attack, though, they will blithely dismiss the warning that is their only clue that their session has been hijacked. For the sake of your users' trust, you should purchase a commercial certificate.

You may also choose to distribute your own CA certificate—the one you use to sign your certificates—to your users in some out of band fashion. This may work in some cases, but you have to educate users about installing custom certificates and field additional help-desk requests stemming from difficulties or misconfigurations.

Enabling SSL

Assuming you have gone through some process, commercial or otherwise, to obtain a signed certificate, you have two files: a public key certificate and a private key. We will call the public key certificate *server.crt* and the private key *server.key*. This naming largely follows the examples Apache has laid out. Example 7-11 shows a minimally configured SSL-enabled Apache `VirtualHost`.

Example 7-11. Apache SSL configuration

```
<VirtualHost *:443>
    DocumentRoot /usr/local/www/data/secure
    SSLEngine On
    SSLCertificateFile    /usr/local/etc/apache2/ssl.crt/server.crt
    SSLCertificateKeyFile /usr/local/etc/apache2/ssl.key/server.key
</VirtualHost>
```

At this point, your web server will listen on port 443 (the officially designated port for HTTPS) and will communicate over SSL.

SSL, TLS, and cipher choice

As an HTTPS connection is established, the two sides—browser and server—each send a list of their cryptographic capabilities. Each identifies which ciphers it understands and what parameters it supports with those ciphers. For example, a browser with export-grade cryptography might identify itself as supporting DES, but only with 56-bit keys. During this handshake, the strongest algorithm that both browser and server support will be chosen. If a web browser connects and only offers the weak encryption, your Apache server has two choices: continue the connection with weak protection over the data, or close the connection telling the browser that they have no satisfactory algorithms in common. There are a number of ciphers that are common and well-known, but are also cryptographically weak. RC2, RC4, and export-grade DES should be avoided if possible, especially by e-commerce and financial sites.

Restricting ciphers at the server

You can restrict which ciphers your server is willing to use to ensure that only clients capable of high-grade cryptography can connect with the `SSLCipherSuite` directive. If you restrict which ciphers you are willing to use, realize that you will restrict which web browsers can connect. Older versions of Microsoft Internet Explorer and

Netscape, especially those that shipped with export-grade cryptography, will have a limited set of ciphers available.

The SSLCipherSuite directive in your *httpd.conf* file is a very complicated directive with a dense syntax. It controls which algorithms are accepted by your server and your server's order of preference. By default, Apache is configured with a pretty generous set of algorithms. The default SSLCipherSuite directive is:

```
ALL:!ADH:RC4+RSA:+HIGH:+MEDIUM:+LOW:+SSLv2:+EXP
```

The Apache *mod_ssl* documentation describes what this cipher suite includes quite clearly:

> [F]irst, remove from consideration any ciphers that do not authenticate, i.e., for SSL only the Anonymous Diffie-Hellman ciphers. Next, use ciphers using RC4 and RSA. Next include the high, medium and then the low security ciphers. Finally pull all SSLv2 and export ciphers to the end of the list.

If you want to create a more secure configuration, consider the following cipher specification:

```
TLSv1:!ADH:!EXP:!NULL:!MD5:!LOW:+HIGH:+MEDIUM
```

This favors TLS ciphers, without any anonymous Diffie-Hellman, no export-grade ciphers, no NULL ciphers (i.e., those that don't actually encrypt), no algorithms that use MD5 for their hash, and none of the weak algorithms (such as RC2) that have been classified as "low" grade. It favors the "high" grade algorithms (such as AES with 256-bit keys) over the "medium" algorithms (such as RC4). You can find out what the aliases "high," "medium," and "low" refer to by looking at the manpage for *ciphers(1)* on FreeBSD or openssl(1) on OpenBSD.

If you are too draconian in your selection of ciphers, you should be aware that some users will utterly fail to connect to your server, and you will have no opportunity to send a nice error message when that happens. The web browser will issue an error message that is probably opaque and incomprehensible to the user. Internet Explorer gives its general-purpose (and wrong) Cannot find server or DNS Error message. Mozilla Firefox says, Firefox and www.example.com cannot communicate securely because they have no common encryption algorithms. To make matters worse, since the browser and server never properly communicated, there will be no trace of this failed attempt in your server logs. An IDS system might be able to detect and log such failures, but Apache cannot. A good solution is to support one or two low-grade ciphers and, using some JavaScript, PHP, or SSI, redirect users to a page that handles their request. The page could recommend that they upgrade their browser, or warn them that they are using low-grade cryptography, or redirect them to a server where low-grade cryptography is acceptable.

CPU usage

When enabling SSL, you will find that the computational load on your server increases. The cryptography involved in SSL is nontrivial. Busy sites will quickly discover that the CPU cannot keep up with nearly the same number of connections over SSL as it can over vanilla HTTP. There are two solutions to this problem: add more redundant servers or install hardware cryptographic accelerators. You might be tempted to add redundant servers to meet demand, but there is probably a more cost-effective method that more fully exploits the power of OpenBSD and FreeBSD.

A hardware cryptographic accelerator can offload the computation involved in performing cryptography. They also often provide hardware random number generators, which are better than any software-based pseudorandom number generators, making your transactions more secure. This is an area where OpenBSD excels, and FreeBSD does almost as well. You only have to purchase and install a compatible hardware cryptographic accelerator card and OpenBSD will detect it and use it by default. The list of compatible cards is constantly growing, and can be found in the release notes for whichever version of OpenBSD or FreeBSD you install. What makes it so easy to use is the fact that the hooks for using acceleration are already built into the kernel and all devices that are supported register themselves at boot time. Simply by plugging a card into a PCI slot, the system will detect the card at boot and begin to perform hardware-accelerated cryptography. See Chapter 2 for more information on hardware-accelerated cryptography in the BSDs.

thttpd

The `thttpd` server, from Jef Poskanzer (*http://www.acme.com/software/thttpd/*), is a throttling, simple web server with a small footprint. The first "t" in `thttpd` stands for "tiny," "turbo," or "throttling," depending on whom you ask. It is a very simple, carefully programmed HTTP server that provides basic services and can execute CGI programs. It does not have a plug-in API like Apache. There is a commercial version (Premium `thttpd`) that incorporates FastCGI support. To the extent that most programming of dynamic content can be done through CGI, most dynamic content can be done with `thttpd`. However, PHP and some Perl programs running as CGI programs may perform poorly. In high security situations, its limited feature set and its built-in ability to do complex throttling on web traffic are invaluable. Some sites even use a combination of Apache and `thttpd` to distribute their dynamic and static content, respectively. For example, the interactive web pages that require executing complex Perl or PHP or Java will be served by the Apache server, but the images and other static content is served via `thttpd`. This has the advantage of speeding up the access to images and other static content, but also gives the ability to throttle bandwidth usage in the event of a sudden burst of heavy traffic.

The thttpd server is often the right answer if your needs are characterized by serving static web pages and running straightforward CGI programs. It can also be the right answer if you want to limit your bandwidth using well-formulated throttling rules. Finally, it is very useful for its small footprint, both on disk and in RAM. If you're resource-constrained (e.g., an embedded environment), then thttpd is probably a better fit than Apache. If, however, you need SSL, thttpd is probably the wrong choice. While there are ways to make it work, they are poorly documented and not directly supported by the web server software itself.

Installing thttpd

thttpd is easily built and installed from ports on both OpenBSD and FreeBSD from *ports/www/thttpd*.

On FreeBSD the port will install a */usr/local/etc/rc.d/thttpd.sh* startup script that is responsible for starting thttpd. This script actually launches a wrapper named *thttpd_wrapper*, which restarts the thttpd daemon should it die for some reason, and sends a mail message to root. Note that this could be a mail bomb waiting to happen. If you should accidentally misconfigure your *thttpd.conf* file, you could find the wrapper program sending mail to root every 10 seconds until you have it fixed.

The OpenBSD version of the port installs nothing more than a */usr/local/sbin/thttpd* binary. You have to create your own process for launching *thttpd* at boot time. Fortunately, the *thttpd.sh* script and the *thttpd_wrapper* script can be found in the source tree where you built the port (*ports/www/thttpd/w-thttpd-2.25b/thttpd-2.25b/scripts/* at the time of this writing). You can easily install them manually.

Note that if you already have Apache installed and active, thttpd will probably fail to run. Apache comes before thttpd alphabetically, so *apache2.sh* will execute before *thttpd.sh* at boot time. It will bind to port 80 and thttpd will quit because it cannot acquire the already bound port. Either configure Apache so it does not listen on port 80, or disable it if you are not using it.

Configuring thttpd

Unlike Apache, thttpd does not come with a default configuration file, and the ports maintainer has not chosen to offer one. Example 7-12 shows a basic *thttpd.conf* file that tries to emulate a similar layout to that provided by a default Apache installation.

Example 7-12. Sample thttpd.conf file

```
dir=/usr/local/www/data
cgipat=/cgi-bin/*
logfile=/var/log/httpd-access.log
pidfile=/var/run/httpd.pid
index_names=index.html index.htm
```

No fully fleshed-out examples of *thttpd.conf* files ship with thttpd, but you can find a few on the Internet. However, there really are very few options to specify. The normal options that you need are so few in number, in fact, that you can often specify a working configuration right from the command line.

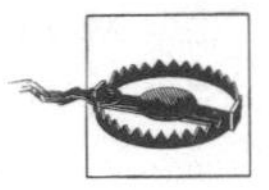

> Just because you can specify a configuration on the command line does not mean you should. We are merely trying to illustrate the simplicity of thttpd configuration. After all, configuration files can be version controlled. The command-line interface exists, however, to be used for quick-and-dirty testing.

The configuration in Example 7-12 is really the minimum set of options that you need to set to make a functional web site. CGI programs necessarily *must* live under *dir*. Because of thttpd's design, however, there is no danger that the source of a script will be sent instead of the script.

There is also a convenient program called makeweb that is distributed with thttpd. When invoked, it will create a directory named */usr/local/www/user* and create a symbolic link from */home/user/public_html* to */usr/local/www/user*. This allows the Apache style per-user URLs (provided by *mod_userdir*) to work, and it provides the familiar *public_html* directory for users.

Resisting Denial of Service

The throttling parameters in thttpd are completely different from those in Apache. With thttpd, each bandwidth allocation is given a minimum (implied as zero if not specified) and a maximum. The server tracks moving averages for all URLs that it processes, and it matches them against the throttling parameters. If the given URL is exceeding its bandwidth allocation, thttpd imposes a delay between transmitting blocks of data for the connections that are requesting that URL. It also guarantees a minimum bandwidth allocation to make sure that requests actually complete.

The thttpd server does not implement a means of limiting the total number of concurrent connections to the server like Apache's MaxClients directive. However, this kind of limit *can* be enforced by the operating system. To impose a limit on it, limit the total available file handles for the process. Each network connection requires a file handle, so limiting the total number of open file handles an easy way to limit the number of concurrent connections. Add a line to the thttpd.sh script like **ulimit -n 80**, to limit the thttpd daemon to 80 open file handles. Each daemon probably has at least two file handles open at any given instant: the web page it's reading off the disk and the network port it is connected to. It may open other files briefly as a side-effect of normal execution (e.g., */dev/null* or */etc/malloc.conf*). If you're going to limit httpd this way, you should probably start with a number about twice as large as the total number of daemons you want, and then tune according to your observations.

OpenBSD limits the number of available file handles to 128 by default for root and daemon processes through a setting in */etc/login.conf*. FreeBSD has the same capability of limiting file descriptors in */etc/login.conf*, but does not impose any limits by default.

Advanced Web Servers with Jails

Administrators rarely get to have the final say in what technologies their web servers must support. The web team will come to you with a demand for the latest, greatest PHPNuke-MySQL-ImageMagick-XML technology, and management will decree that it must be supported. Running Apache in a *jail* or *chroot* environment will help limit your server's exposure to vulnerabilities in the web applications. There have been vulnerabilities in Apache's `httpd` itself, too, and this will help protect you if you fall prey to an exploited vulnerability.

Using Jail or Chroot

Unfortunately, Apache does not support jail or chroot easily the way BIND does. It takes work. So, before we launch into configuring Apache in a jail, we have some planning to do.

Remember the difference between *jail* and *chroot* from Chapter 2. For convenience in this chapter we often say "jail" to refer equally to both environments. It means "jail" for FreeBSD administrators and "chroot" for OpenBSD administrators since only FreeBSD has jail. The instructions here only differ in the syntax of the command that launches the environment.

How many instances?

If you are hosting a single web server for an organization, you may only be concerned about one user group and one set of requirements. In that case you only need to jail your single instance of Apache. If you work for an ISP, or if you work in the IT department of a large organization, you may have many user populations to support. You might have to protect your server from the users and the user populations from each other. You might even have conflicting requirements; for example one user set might require PHP Version 4 while another requires PHP Version 5. In these kinds of situations you can create multiple instances in different jails. Just use different IP addresses for each server instance and they can stay separated.

It's decidedly simpler to chroot or jail a single instance of Apache, but if we do it well enough once, we should be able to repeat it. Many variables affect your decision about whether or not to chroot or jail and, if so, how many instances to run; so we will focus on how to chroot or jail a single instance. When there are problems that you will have to overcome in order to run multiple instances, we'll point them out and describe some potential solutions.

Building and installing into a jail

There are two ways to build: using the ports system and directly from the source. In Chapter 2, we discuss how to make a feature-rich *jail* that we build packages in, so that we can then install those packages in a minimal *jail* for execution. If your configuration is easily supported by the configuration options in the ports system and you're using FreeBSD, this is probably the best way to go. Building from source is also viable, and is necessary on OpenBSD. Chapter 2 contains an example of building Apache in a jail, so we will describe how to build Apache from source here.

There are dozens of ways that you can choose to configure Apache to run in a jail. We have picked one way that is effective and clear. Vary it according to your needs and preferences.

We will use */jail* as our jail directory for our examples in this section. Recall from Chapter 2 that if Apache is looking for a file */etc/pwd.db*, for example, then we will need to create */jail/etc/pwd.db*.

We will give Apache's `configure` script a different base directory instead of */usr/local*. Since we have to run `make install` during this process, we don't want our jail-friendly Apache to be installed on top of our real Apache that runs out of */usr/local*. We will run Apache out of a */web* directory. You will need to create a real */web*—at least temporarily—in order to let the binaries install. If you want to create a symbolic link from */web* to some other location in the filesystem, that will work. To configure Apache, then, we run a command like:

```
./configure --prefix=/web --enable-ssl
```

Your actual command will probably vary, based on what modules you need.

Now that it's configured, you can run **make** to perform the build, and **make install** to install into our */web* staging environment. After the installation is complete, pare down the directory to eliminate detritus that comes from a general-purpose Apache installation. In */web* you will find a *man* directory with manual pages, as well as a *manual* HTML documentation directory. You can probably delete these. You may also find the standard *icons* directory unnecessary unless you are using *mod_autoindex* as described later in this chapter. After you have removed all the files and directories you don't want from */web*, copy what's left to */jail/web* using a command like **cp -pr /web/* /jail/web**.

You will also see *build*, *lib*, and *include* directories in */web*. At first glance, you might think they are superfluous, since you will only be running a server here. While you're right in thinking that they're not used at runtime, they are necessary if you plan on building Apache modules (e.g., *mod_php*, *mod_perl*, etc.). Though you may not need them in your */jail/web* runtime environment, you will want them in your */web* staging environment so you can use them later to build compatible modules.

Finding and adding support files

Apache needs additional files, present in your operating system, but not yet in your *jail*. Table 7-3 lists the files that you will need and indicates whether they are needed in FreeBSD, OpenBSD, or both. Note that the only part of the entire process that needs to be done as root is the making of the */dev/null* device in */jail/dev/null*. You can (and should) configure, build, and install Apache as an unprivileged normal user. For example, if you are creating multiple jails, you can have each jail's files owned by a different user.

Table 7-3. Files used in Apache jails

File	Location
Null device	*dev/null*
Maps UIDs to user IDs	*etc/pwd.db*
C runtime library	*usr/lib/libc.so.34.1* (OpenBSD)
	lib/libc.so.5 (FreeBSD)
Math library	*usr/lib/libm.so.2.0* (OpenBSD)
	usr/lib/libm.so.2 (FreeBSD)
Threading library	*usr/lib/libpthread.so.6.0* (OpenBSD)
The runtime dynamic loader	*usr/libexec/ld.so* (OpenBSD)
	libexec/ld-elf.so.1 (FreeBSD)
Cryptography library	*usr/lib/libcrypto.so.11.0* (OpenBSD)
	usr/lib/libssl.so.9.0 (OpenBSD)
	lib/libcrypt.so.2 (FreeBSD)

By the time you try this, it is possible that something will have changed in either FreeBSD or OpenBSD or Apache to make these instructions incomplete. If, after installing these files, the server will not launch, it will probably tell you what library it needs. For example, you may see `/libexec/ld-elf.so.1: Shared object "libdb4.so.0" not found`. In that case, run **`ldd /web/bin/httpd`** and look for the library in the output. You will see output like: `libdb4.so.0 => /usr/local/lib/libdb4.so.0 (0x280fc000)`. This means that you need to copy */usr/local/lib/libdb4.so.0* to a location in the jail, such as */jail/lib*.

You may also want some files such as */etc/localtime*, */etc/resolv.conf*, and */etc/hosts*. The */etc/localtime* file will let Apache log entries in the correct time zone. The */etc/resolv.conf* and */etc/hosts* files influence how the processes in the jail resolve hostnames. However, if */etc/resolv.conf* and */etc/hosts* are omitted, they will resolve names using the default resolution in the regular (non-jailed) operating system. Refer to Table 2-4 for other files that you might want or need in your jail.

Launching httpd in chroot(8) on OpenBSD or FreeBSD

Before launching your chrooted `httpd`, ensure the IP address on which your Apache server will be listening is correct. With a single chrooted installation like this, the specification of IP address is unimportant. On systems with multiple instances of chrooted Apache servers, however, running them on separate IP addresses is imperative. You may even need to configure multiple IP addresses per chroot. This is certainly possible—just make sure not to allow one chrooted instance to use another's IP.

IP specification boils down to adding a line such as **`Listen 12.34.56.78:80`** to your *httpd.conf* file. See the Apache documentation for more information about the Listen directive. Once this has been done, you can launch the chrooted Apache process by running **`chroot /jail /web/bin/httpd -DSSL`** as root (either interactively, or in a script that is run by root at boot time).

While it's always easiest to have SSL-enabled Apache servers start automatically, you pay a small price in security to enable it. Ideally, the server's private key should be stored encrypted on the filesystem and should require a passphrase to decrypt it. Apache cannot start (even the non-SSL functions will not start) until it is decrypted. Your alternative, to enable automatic startup, is to leave your private key unencrypted in the filesystem. No one will need to be around to start the service, but your key can be compromised more easily.

Launching httpd in jail(8) on FreeBSD

If you are using Apache on FreeBSD, use *jail* instead of *chroot* whenever you can. *Jails* take the same amount of work to set up, but their security is more robust and thorough than *chroot*. As we mentioned in Chapter 2, `jail` requires quite a few arguments.

```
jail -u root /jail www.example.com 12.34.56.78 /web/bin/httpd  -DSSL
```

In this case we have explicitly said the jail will have to run as root. Apache needs to bind to port 80, and it can only do that if it starts off running as root. The next argument is the root of the jail filesystem, */jail*. The next two arguments, the hostname and IP address, distinguish `jail` from `chroot`.

No process, not Apache, a CGI program, a PHP web page, or a malicious hacker's program that accidentally gets installed in the jail, can perform any network activity with any IP address other than the one assigned to this *jail*. Normally, if an attacker injected the right code into a vulnerable *chroot* or non-chrooted system, he could use raw sockets to spoof the source address of malicious packets. Or, he could try to sniff packets by opening the network device in promiscuous mode. None of these things are possible in a `jail`. We know that any mischievous activity will have the *jail*'s IP address on it, so our network detection systems will have an accurate picture of the traffic (malicious or otherwise) going in and out of the *jail*ed process. We also know that someone who compromises the *jail* thoroughly will still be significantly limited in what he can do, especially since we didn't install `/bin/sh` or any other shell in our `jail` filesystem. That step by itself dramatically limits an attacker's capabilities.

A Two-Tiered Architecture

For a powerful way to enforce separation of privileges and web site isolation, we propose a combination of Apache's *mod_proxy* with FreeBSD's jails or either operating system's chroot. If you run many web sites on a single host and you have many different users managing those sites (a situation that begs for FreeBSD and Apache), you can achieve a level of separation that will allow your users to have unprecedented control over their web configuration, yet will keep their mistakes from affecting other users.

Pictures are worth a thousand words, so let's start off our architectural discussion with Figure 7-6. It shows a general overview of the architecture, and will serve as a reference for sections to come.

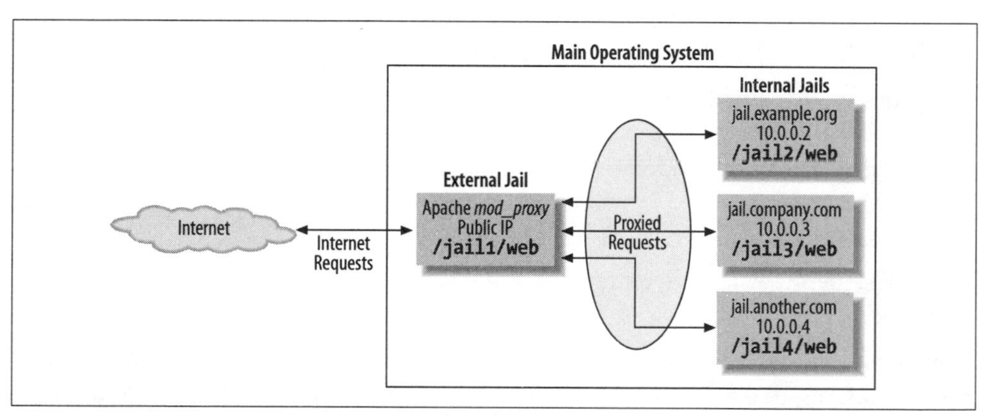

Figure 7-6. General architecture of a multiple jail system

This architecture uses a frontend *jail*ed Apache instance that exposes a single IP address to the Internet. This external *jail* uses *mod_proxy* behind the scenes to redirect traffic to *internal jail*ed web server instances. Each of these internal *jails* is assigned a distinct RFC 1918 private IP address and is accessible only through Apache. Finally, in our example, each internal *jail* handles the web needs for a given organization. This makes our proxy rules easier to differentiate, but bear in mind that more complex configurations are certainly possible.

The rest of this section is devoted to a structured walkthrough of setting up exactly this configuration. Once you can handle this specific example, you should be able to carry the lessons you've learned onto more interesting scenarios.

Configure the internal jails

First off, create a *jail* for each organization as described in "Using Jail or Chroot." These *jails* should be configured with whatever modules and options they need—but remember, enable only the modules you need. For example we set the ServerName in the two *jails* to *jail.example.org* and *jail.company.com*. Aside from setting this directive to something other than the one you really want to publish, configure everything else normally.

In order for Apache to access each jailed site, you'll want to assign names to them. Jailed web sites are configured with local, unroutable IP addresses (e.g., 10.0.0.2 or 192.168.0.5). You can either give each *jail* a name in DNS that maps to the associated IP address, or add an appropriate entry to */etc/hosts*. In this example, we assign the name *jail.example.org* to IP address, 10.0.0.2 and *jail.company.com* to 10.0.0.3.

If you've been reading carefully, you'll note that we have not mentioned what web server is running within the *jail*. In fact, there is no reason why the jailed web site cannot run thttpd or some other web server software. Since the jailed web server does not know that it is jailed, any web server software should work just fine.

Now, in order for Apache to access the *jail*, you need to add aliases to your network interface. On FreeBSD, we insert two lines like this in */etc/rc.conf*:

```
ifconfig_xl0_alias0="inet 10.0.0.2 netmask 255.255.255.255
ifconfig_xl0_alias0="inet 10.0.0.3 netmask 255.255.255.255
```

On OpenBSD, append the following two lines to */etc/hostname.xl0*:

```
inet alias 10.0.0.2 255.255.255.255
inet alias 10.0.0.3 255.255.255.255
```

Of course, you will need to replace *xl0* above with the name of your network interface.

Your host is now accessible not only on the primary public IP address, but also on the two aliases 10.0.0.2 and 10.0.0.3. This may not be what you want. If your host is in a DMZ, you can use your local or network-based firewall to restrict access to these IP addresses so that no one in the outside world can connect directly to them. You might be wondering why you didn't just use the loopback (lo0) interface. By assigning routable IP addresses to your *jails*, you have created a convenient mechanism for expansion. You can move a jail from one host to another by migrating the jail's private IP to a new host. See "Modularity" for a little more information about moving internal jails.

Configuring the external jail

The external jail contains an instance of Apache that is essentially just a big dumb proxy. It blindly accepts and proxies traffic to the internal jailed web sites. For this external jail, you need Apache with *mod_proxy*, and probably very few other modules. The externally facing web server can run out of a *jail* or *chroot* as well. It's like creating a firewall/DMZ architecture in the middle of your host. For every web site you want to proxy, add a configuration block as shown in Example 7-13 to your *httpd.conf*. This tells Apache to proxy the requests to the internal jails.

Example 7-13. Proxying for two jails

```
<VirtualHost www.example.org>
        ProxyPass         / http://jail. example.org/
        ProxyPassReverse  / http://jail. example.org/
        ProxyVia          On
</VirtualHost>

<VirtualHost www.company.com>
        ProxyPass         / http://jail.company.com/
        ProxyPassReverse  / http://jail.company.com/
        ProxyVia          On
</VirtualHost>
```

Jail versus chroot

We've used the term *jail* throughout this section, even though you might only have chroot available to you. If you have FreeBSD and can use jails, do. They are safer and harder to escape. Aside from the syntax of the command that launches the internal web server, however, the concepts are the same. The jail will need the same support files as a chroot environment will.

Advantages and Disadvantages

There are a lot of great advantages to this system, but it does create some management and maintenance concerns, too.

Ultimate separation

This scheme creates a great separation between different user bases. Now, if one set of users completely corrupts their web configuration or their pages, they will not affect the other users or the external proxy that handles routing requests.

WebDAV might be secure enough to use if each site's users are segregated into their own jails. Each jail will have its own filesystem, permissions, and configuration for authorization. Although all the users in a given jail have equal permissions on that jail's files, they do not have any access to the files in other jails. The users are partitioned from each other, and they get to use a protocol that integrates nicely with their development tools.

The separation is so complete that you might consider allowing advanced power users to control the *httpd.conf* file for their jailed server. After all, if they corrupt the file, only their site will fail.

Performance

It is clear that there might be a performance penalty to this architecture. Two servers, the external proxy and the jailed internal server, might handle every request. You can mitigate this problem somewhat by turning on caching at the external proxy. Then, static content such as stylesheets, images, and JavaScript files will be handled by the external proxy most of the time. Dynamic content can still be generated by the internal server, and it will suffer the small penalty of being handled by two servers.

Modularity

Each individual site is easy to migrate to new host hardware, when needed because it is completely self-contained in a *jail*. If a site gets too much traffic and needs to be migrated to a beefier host system, its *jail* can be copied wholesale to the new host, and that new host can be given the IP address associated with the *jail*. If you're using DNS for name resolution of this private address space, you're done!

It's easy to run different versions of web server software this way, too. Perhaps you want to try out Apache 2. Maybe your customers want significantly different module sets. Completely segregating configurations can turn very complex single Apache installations into several very simple ones. Since simplicity is easier to administer, you might prefer this route.

Wrapping Up

Almost every system administrator has responsibility for at least one web server, and web servers are some of the most visible machines on the Internet. Taking precautions with you web server is both prudent and necessary. If you need complex functionality, Apache is probably the best server to choose. If you need low overhead, a small footprint, or bandwidth limitations, `thttpd` is a good choice.

Regardless of which operating system you choose (both FreeBSD and OpenBSD make excellent web servers), the single most important lesson in running a web server securely is to enable only the functionality you need. Not only can a feature unexpectedly create a security risk by itself, it might create a security risk when it unexpectedly combines with another feature (as *mod_include* can trick *mod_access* by issuing requests from *localhost*). Consider how you segregate the permissions of your web services. You can run perl and PHP scripts as CGIs so that you can use *suexec* or `cgiwrap` to map their privileges onto a specific userid. You can instead run them in *mod_perl* and *mod_php* and use various OS techniques like `ulimit` to limit the web server's ability to access operating system resources. Likewise, you should limit your users' abilities to override configuration settings. Understand their needs and grant just the permissions they need to achieve their goals.

Resources

These are pointers to various web-based resources, grouped by web server platform.

Apache Resources

The Apache Web Server
: The main web site is *http://httpd.apache.org/*, which includes full documentation on installing, configuring, and operating.

  Apache: The Definitive Guide, Third Edition, by Ben and Peter Laurie (O'Reilly), 2002.

mod_perl
: This module is also managed by The Apache Group. *http://perl.apache.org/*.

thttpd Resources

The `thttpd` *Web Server*
: This is the original free version of thttpd. *http://www.acme.com/software/thttpd/*.

The Premium `thttpd` *Web Server*
: This version of `thttpd` is maintained and sold by Sascha Schumann. It claims to include a variety of performance enhancements, and to support the FastCGI API. *http://schumann.cx/premium-thttpd/*.

General Resources

`cgiwrap`
: The software that runs setuid to allow CGI programs to run as normal users. *http://cgiwrap.sourceforge.net/*.

FastCGI
: This software creates an API that is language independent and allows faster execution of CGI programs. It can work with either Apache or Premium thttpd. *http://www.fastcgi.com/*.

PHP
: The main web site is *http://www.php.net/*. Also, see *Programming PHP*, Rasmus Lerdorf and Kevin Tatroe (O'Reilly), 2002.

SSL
: *Network Security with OpenSSL*, John Viega, Matt Messier, and Pravir Chandra (O'Reilly), 2002.

  SSL and TLS: Designing and Building Secure Systems, Eric Rescorla (Addison Wesley), 2000.

Apache: The Definitive Guide, Third Edition, Ben Laurie and Peter Laurie (O'Reilly), 2002. The Apache guide focuses more on the web server than SSL, but it has several chapters of good information that is especially relevant for web service.

Selected Web-Related RFCs

- RFC 1341: MIME (Multipurpose Internet Mail Extensions): Mechanisms for Specifying and Describing the Format of Internet Message Bodies
- RFC 1945: Hypertext Transfer Protocol, HTTP/1.0
- RFC 2616: Hypertext Transfer Protocol, HTTP/1.1
- RFC 2518: HTTP Extensions for Distributed Authoring, WEBDAV
- RFC 2246: The TLS Protocol Version 1.0

CHAPTER 8

Firewalls

Firewalls are a network response to
a software engineering problem.
—Steve Bellovin

Firewalls are a key part of any security infrastructure. Once viewed as a choke point at the very front end of a network, they are now liberally sprinkled around enterprises allowing for security administrators to enforce fine-grained access control to any asset. They are viewed as an enabling technology assisting businesses and individuals in performing activities in a secure and reliable fashion.

FreeBSD and OpenBSD make great platforms for firewall deployments. Through their stable development process, the BSDs can be configured in a very secure fashion. This is key, as a firewall is the nexus for many network-borne attacks and an insecure firewall makes for an insecure network. Further, the BSDs provide high performance networking that is fundamental to the scalability of a firewall. Firewalls can control access to many different networks at once, so it is critically important for a firewall to maintain low latency even under heavy load.

This chapter discusses configuration, deployment, and administration of FreeBSD and OpenBSD-based firewalls. It compares and contrasts the features available under each operating system as well as provides example configurations for common firewall scenarios. Finally, this chapter provides a solution for high availability architectures with these open source solutions.

Firewall Architectures

Firewalls are not a "one size fits all" device. The policy they enforce on a network varies from organization to organization. Also, the manner in which they are used, maintained, and integrated into a network can vary wildly.

The first step in successfully deploying and using firewalls is proper placement of the firewalling devices. This requires understanding the existing network, the services running over the network, and the user requirements of the network. A good firewall administrator is also a good systems and network administrator. Multiple talents must be brought to bear to ensure that a firewall serves to enable secure data transactions while not hindering the operations of the users and systems.

Improper firewall architecture can cause a security problem even if the ruleset on the firewall is technically "correct." Attackers may be able to bypass the firewall due to improper placement. Or you may not be able to enforce the desired security policy due to the firewall's location. For example, if you're attempting to control access between the accounting network and administrative network in Figure 8-1, the existing firewall will be of no use.

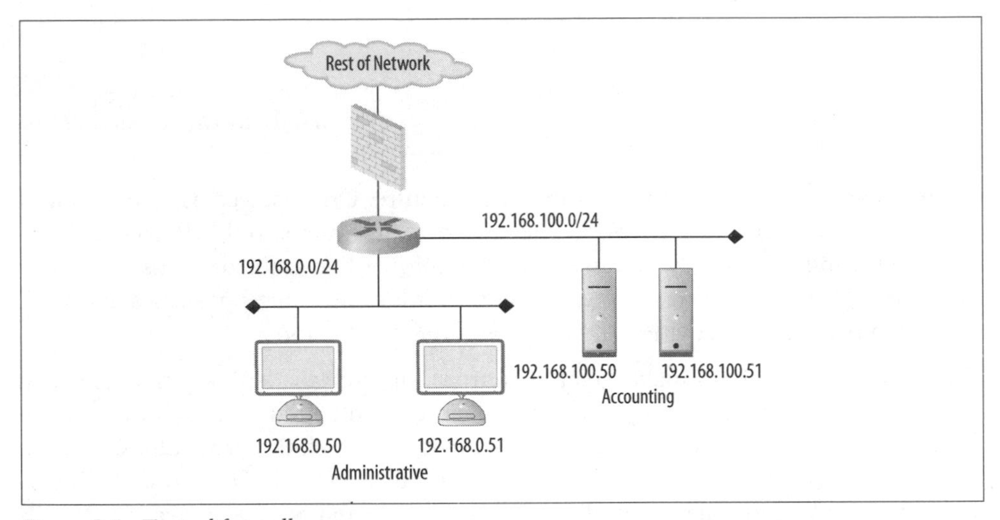

Figure 8-1. Typical firewall setup

Further, if a firewall is overly intrusive in a network, there will be a tendency to place relaxed rules on the firewall to compensate. This is a difficult, yet common, situation for many security services; security is compromised for the sake of functionality. In order to ensure that your network is as secure as it can be, you must understand the options you have with respect to firewall architectures and deploy your systems accordingly.

Bump in the Wire

The simplest firewall architecture, termed *bump in the wire*, is shown in Figure 8-2. In this setup, the firewall is a choke point for all traffic coming into and leaving a network. This is a common configuration, as it provides a single point of administration and policy enforcement. It also requires only one firewalling device making this architecture relatively inexpensive to deploy.

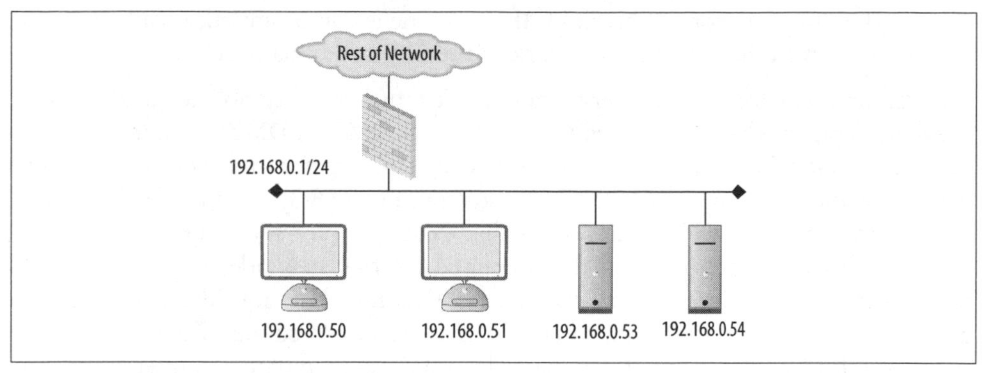

Figure 8-2. Bump in the wire firewall architecture

However, in larger networks, such as that in Figure 8-1, there may not be fine-grained enough control over traffic on the network. Traffic between the accounting and administrative networks cannot be controlled. For this reason, the bump in the wire architecture is commonly used in small networks such as those found in home offices and small server farms. Commodity firewalls, such as those found embedded in DSL routers and wireless access points, are typically this kind of "one network in, one network out" device.

Still, a bump in the wire firewall may be useful at the very front of a large enterprise. While unable to enforce fine-grained access control, a perimeter firewall can filter out overtly malicious traffic from external sources. For instance, you may want to filter out all Windows NetBIOS traffic from entering your network. A bump in the wire firewall at the ingress point to your enterprise can ensure that NetBIOS traffic is completely stopped at your network edge. This setup allows the frontend firewall to handle the "low hanging fruit" while pushing finer-grained decisions to internal firewalls. This flies in the face of the security principle of denying all traffic except that traffic that is explicitly allowed. However, this principle can be difficult to enforce at busy border networks where what is and is not allowed is difficult to determine.

DMZ

Many networks, especially those in smaller organizations, are composed of two basic types of systems: workstations and servers. Workstations are used by staff to access internal resources, surf the Net, send instant messages, and so on. Workstations are generally clients and almost never require connections initiated from outside networks.

Servers are machines accessed by clients. In the case of a small office, a web and mail server may need to be accessed from both internal workstations and other clients on the Internet. Servers require different security policies: their services must be made available through a firewall rather than blocked. However, with this access comes risk. Opening up Internet connectivity for servers makes it possible for attackers outside the office network to break in. If a machine is compromised, ideally it can be quarantined from the rest of the network to prevent further damage.

The requirement for different server and workstation security policies leads us to a firewall architecture called a *demilitarized zone*, or DMZ. A DMZ is a line of demarcation; a region between an area controlled by one organization and an area controlled by another. A network DMZ, as shown in Figure 8-3, has a network segment that contains the external facing servers that exists between the "wild" external network (such as the Internet) and the protected internal network. Sometimes this is referred to as a three-legged firewall. This architecture allows for different policies to be applied to each network. It also enables the firewall to contain the servers in the event of a break-in. In general, the servers should never initiate a connection to the internal workstations. Adhering to the concept of default deny, the firewall policies can be configured to deny all connections from the server network to the workstation network. While an attacker may still be able to jump from one server to another (there is no firewall control between the servers on the server network in Figure 8-3), it's unlikely she will be able to directly compromise a host on the workstation network.

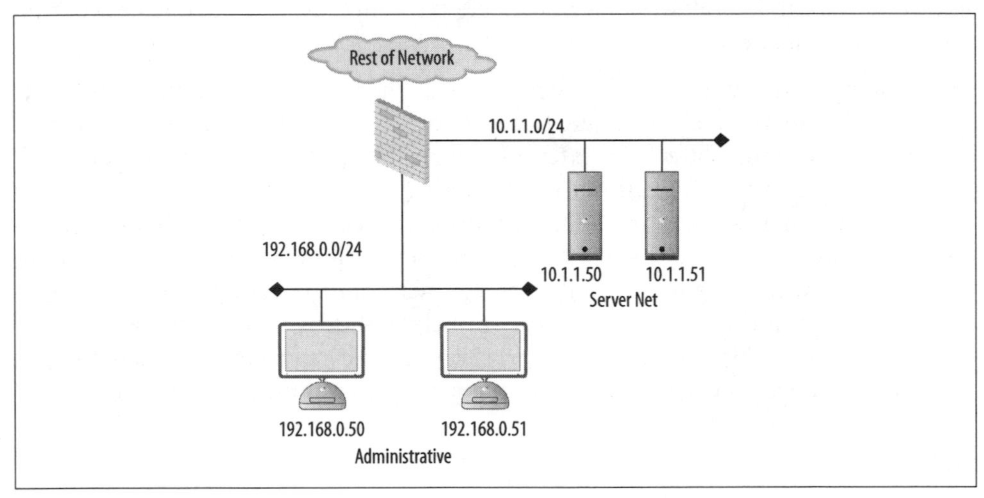

Figure 8-3. DMZ firewall architecture

Spider

The DMZ architecture is driven by the need to enforce different policies and quarantine one network from another. This idea can be extended to encompass multiple networks connected to one firewall. A *spider* architecture allows one firewall to control traffic between many directly connected networks. In Figure 8-4, the firewall can control traffic between the accounting, administration, server, and wireless networks. Note the difference between this setup and the one in Figure 8-1. In a bump in the wire network, these internal systems would form a soft chewy center; all traffic between internal hosts would be allowed due to the lack of a firewall. In a spider architecture, access control decisions can be made on a much more local basis.

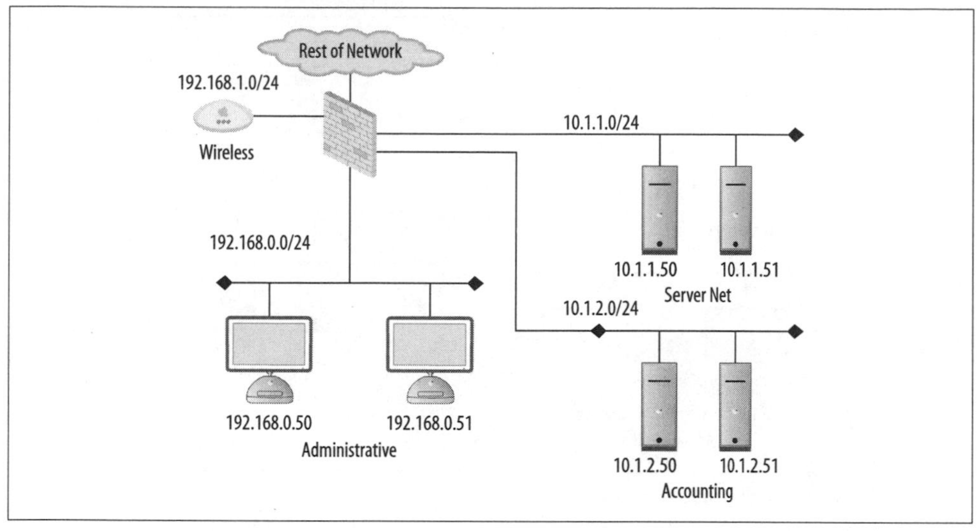

Figure 8-4. Spider firewall architecture

Conceptually, a spider architecture is not really different from a DMZ network with one physical firewall. It allows multiple network connections to be terminated into a single host. This allows an economy of scale where only one firewall is needed for multiple networks. The spider network in Figure 8-4 can be broken down and implemented in several firewalls as shown in Figure 8-5. This architecture obviously involves many more firewalls, to keep track of that can cause administrative overhead and very complicated routing tables and rulesets. However, be aware that a spider architecture may put all of your security and availability eggs in one basket. A single breach in security or a single hardware failure can cause dramatic problems. Also, on networks with large amounts of traffic, a firewall in a spider architecture will have to inspect a great deal of traffic. This could cause performance problems for the network.

Transparent

There are times when, for various reasons, a firewall cannot be inserted in a standard way. Up until this point, the firewalls in each architecture have been on a layer 3 (i.e., subnet) boundary. That is, each interface on the firewall is on a different IP subnet. A firewall can actually be deployed so that it bridges between two interfaces and does not act as a gateway for the hosts on the network. This is known as a *transparent* firewall and is shown in Figure 8-6.

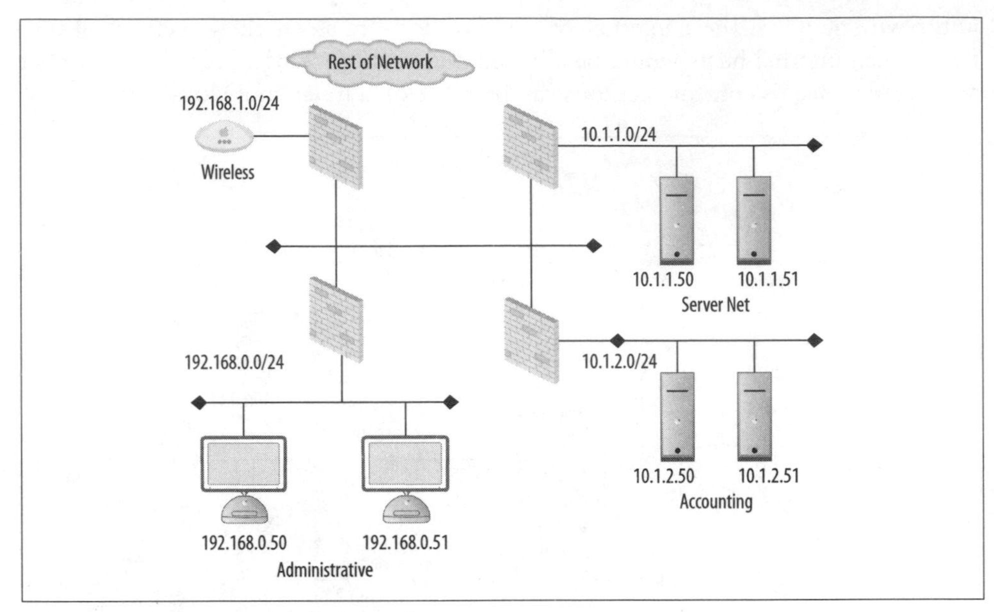

Figure 8-5. Broken apart spider network

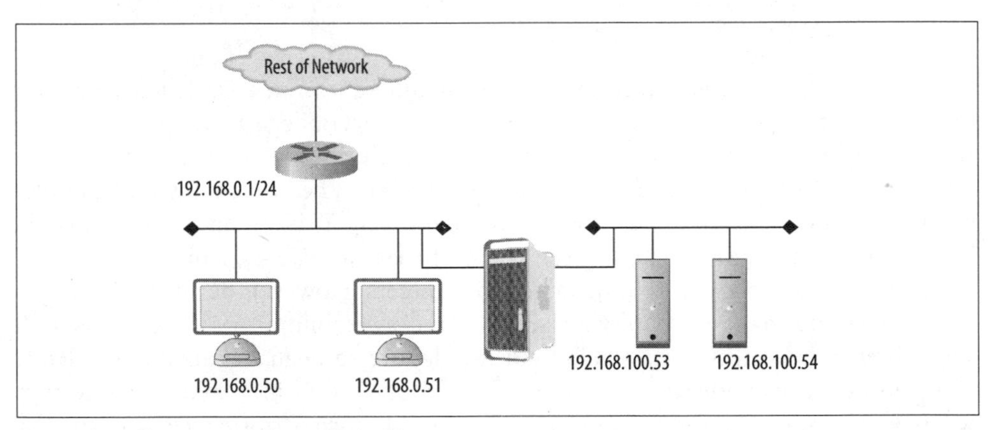

Figure 8-6. Transparent Firewall Architecture

Transparent firewalls are not often used; however, there are circumstances that arise where this architecture is a silver bullet. Transparent firewalls are common when it is necessary to maintain the existing network architecture (so as not to break a routing protocol or addressing scheme). They are also useful when a network has a very limited number of addresses but needs to perform firewalling between two types of hosts. In general, you'll know if you are in a situation that requires transparent firewalling.

Host

Firewalls have historically been a standalone network device. However, as attackers have become more sophisticated and users have become more mobile, standalone firewalls no longer fulfill users' security needs. A laptop may be protected from attacks when it is plugged directly into a corporate network and resides behind the corporate firewall. However, when the user goes to lunch with the laptop and uses a public WiFi hotspot, the corporate firewall is of no use whatsoever. In order to be protected, the laptop should run a *host-based* firewall.

Host-based firewalls run directly on an endpoint machine and come in many flavors. Windows XP has native firewalling capabilities. There are many third-party firewalls available such as ZoneAlarm and Checkpoint's personal firewall solutions. Of course, FreeBSD and OpenBSD's firewalls can be configured at both the network and the host level.

Host-based firewalls are great because they protect the host even when a network firewall is not available. They allow for extraordinarily fine-grained access control. However, running firewalls on every host can be administratively difficult. All the machines would have to have firewall policies pushed to them, and troubleshooting a problem would always involve checking the firewall configuration. Because of the operational expense of using host-based firewalls, many organizations limit their use to road-warriors, critical datacenter servers, and other machines with explicit need.

High Availability

So far, discussion has been limited to a single firewall at a given location within a network. While this is great for the purposes of outlining concepts, in reality, a single firewall creates a single point of failure for the connected networks. Firewalls can (and do) stop working due to hardware or software problems. Also, due to the nature of a firewall, a misconfiguration can cause a firewall to become unreachable. It's common to hear a firewall administrator blurt out an expletive after making a firewall rule change because she inadvertently locked herself out due to a ruleset problem.

Maintenance needs to be periodically performed on firewalls just like any other IT asset. Hardware needs to be upgraded, operating systems need to be patched, etc. Sometimes maintenance outages are overlooked and treated as a cost of doing business. However, these outages and general system failures don't need to result in a service disruption for networks attached to the firewall.

High availability (HA) is a concept in which critical systems are designed, configured, and managed in a way to attempt to minimize downtime. In the scope of firewalls, this means having multiple firewalls, usually two, in a firewall deployment. For instance, Figure 8-7 is Figure 8-2 implemented with a highly available architecture.

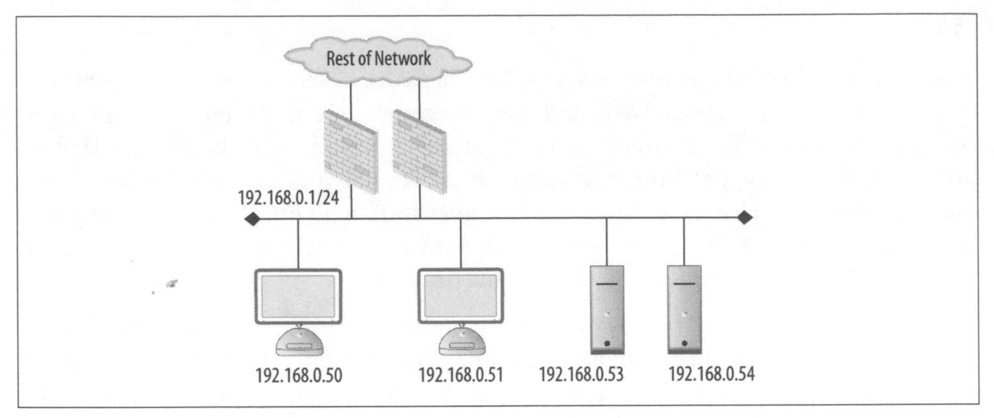

Figure 8-7. HA firewall architecture

There are several modes of operation for highly available firewalls:

Hot-Cold
: An HA firewall pair in Hot-Cold mode is the simplest HA setup. The hot machine acts as the primary firewall, actively passing and filtering packets. The cold machine has an initial configuration similar to the hot machine, but it has no ability to detect failure in the hot machine or even the configuration of the hot machine before it fails. An administrator must interact with a cold host to configure it and then place it in service. Hot-Cold can be thought of as "keeping a spare machine in the closet in case something breaks." From the author's experience, the time to return to normal operations in a Hot-Cold architecture can vary 15 minutes to 24 hours depending on how prepared an organization is to bring the cold host online.

Hot-Warm
: Slightly more complex, a Hot-Warm architecture reduces the amount of time needed to bring the second machine online. The hot host is actively passing and filtering traffic. The warm host has a synchronized configuration with the hot host. This allows for an administrator to switch the warm host to primary firewall duties in 5 to 30 minutes. Still, a Hot-Warm setup does not automatically detect and handle failure.

Hot-Standby
: In a Hot-Standby implementation, the second firewall is able to automatically take over in the event of a system failure. Configuration information is synchronized between the hot and standby hosts. Further, information regarding the health of each system is transmitted between them to allow the standby host to automatically bring itself online. Also, in more advanced setups, the firewalls exchange information regarding traffic going through the hot host. That way, if the standby host needs to take over, existing connections are maintained transparently.

Hot-Hot

Hot-Hot is the most advanced HA firewall architecture. In this mode, both firewalls are actively passing and filtering traffic utilizing synchronized configurations and traffic data. An external load balancer must be used to route a particular connection through one host or another. In the event of failure, all traffic is automatically rerouted to the other hot firewall.

The concept of high availability firewalling has been around for a number of years. However, until recently (OpenBSD 3.5 and FreeBSD 5.2.1), the open source BSD-based operating systems were not useable in a Hot-Standby or Hot-Hot firewall setups. Companies such as Nokia use BSDs for their core operating system and wrote their own high-availability code for use in their commercially available firewall appliances. Now, using publicly available software, administrators can deploy HA firewalls on both OpenBSD and FreeBSD.

Firewalls and Routing Protocols

A firewall is a network device. Historically, network devices have taken the form of routers and switches. These layer 3 (router) and layer 2 (Ethernet switch) devices often exchange information that is vital for a robust and available network. Routers will use routing protocols such as OSPF, RIP, and ISIS to pass routing information and handle link failure. Switches used protocols such as spanning trees to stop loops from forming.

A firewall is generally a layer 3 device. It takes the place a router would normally occupy. As such, firewalls tend to cause problems for network engineers. Where a router would normally participate in an OSPF network, for instance, a firewall is likely to not understand OSPF natively. This creates network boundaries that may result in large routing tables on the firewall and static routes having to be placed in routers pointing traffic through the firewalls.

Organizations constantly struggle with whether or not to allow firewalls to run routing protocols. It is possible to run `routed` or `zebra` to handle RIP, OSPF, and other routing protocols. The question becomes whether you *should*.

On one hand, it makes the network much easier to maintain if every layer 3 gateway is running a routing protocol. It minimizes outages due to link failure and does not require static routes to constantly be updated manually. On the other hand, a firewall as a security device should be relatively static and run as few services as possible. A routing protocol is one more thing to go wrong and one more service for an attacker to compromise.

At the end of the day, it's a decision that only you and your organization can make. Be realistic about the impact that not running a routing protocol will have on your day-to-day operations. Also, understand the risks your firewalls face and determine if you are willing to amplify your risk by running a routing daemon.

Host Lockdown

This may be obvious, but it needs stating. A firewall is a security device, and as such, needs to be configured as securely as possible. This book is filled with information regarding securing FreeBSD and OpenBSD hosts, so we will not bore you with repetition here.

However, we will offer some advice. If at all possible, make sure that the host performing firewall duties is not supplying other services such as those of a web or DNS server. A firewall is a target on the network, and by minimizing the services running on it, you will have a much better chance of standing up to attack.

As a challenge, one of the authors competed with friends to see who could configure a functional firewall with the fewest running services. At one point in a FreeBSD 4 release, he was able to have a functioning and remotely administrable firewall using only eight processes. While this idea may seem extreme, it serves as an example of how stripped down a BSD-based firewall can be.

The Options: IPFW Versus PF

The BSD-based operating systems make great platforms for firewalls. However as we have seen already, there are usually important differences between FreeBSD and OpenBSD that will affect your decision regarding which one to choose. Firewalls are no different.

IPFW

FreeBSD's primary firewall is called IPFW (Internet Protocol Firewall). IPFW is composed of two parts: a kernel-level packet filter engine and a userland utility for controlling firewall functionality. IPFW has been part of FreeBSD since FreeBSD 2.0. During the summer of 2002, however, IPFW went through a major overhaul as part of FreeBSD 5 development. This "new" IPFW became known as IPFW2. However, for the sake of sanity, we will refer to IPFW2 simply as IPFW.

PF

OpenBSD utilizes a firewall mechanism called PF (packet filter). Like FreeBSD's IPFW, PF is made up of a kernel-level packet filter and a userland utility for control of the firewall functionality. Unlike FreeBSD, PF is exposed via a device node, `/dev/pf`.

PF is a newcomer to the OpenBSD world. For a number of years, OpenBSD utilized a firewall called IPFilter. In 2001, however, the author of IPFilter had a licensing dispute with the maintainers of OpenBSD. The end result was that IPFilter was removed from OpenBSD, and a new packet filter had to be developed. PF was created to fill the void left by IPFilter. PF has been designed from day one to integrate cleanly into OpenBSD, and as such, is very usable and flexible.

There is also a port of PF to FreeBSD for those that prefer PF functionality to that offered in IPFW. However, like OpenSSH, PF is an OpenBSD project primarily and ports to other operating systems are a secondary concern. Therefore some PF functionality available in the latest release of OpenBSD may not exist yet in the FreeBSD PF. Prior to FreeBSD 5.2.1, PF was available in the ports tree. With the release of FreeBSD 5.3, PF is included in the core operating system.

Differences

There are major differences between IPFW and PF. From an administration perspective, the first thing you'll notice is that IPFW is list-based while PF is much more object-oriented. A PF configuration is broken into many different parts, while IPFW configurations are generally shell scripts with rules processed in order. Both firewalls support stateful and stateless processing of connections.

In IPFW, the first rule in a ruleset that matches a packet "wins." That means, if a ruleset has a rule to allow traffic to port 80 before a rule that denies all traffic, the packet destined to port 80 will be allowed. In PF, the exact opposite is true; the last rule that matches "wins." In the same example, the packet to port 80 would be denied by the firewall. While counterintuitive at first, this functionality actually lends itself to very complex yet readable configurations. If you really need to have a packet match a rule and then be processed in PF, you can use the `quick` keyword to force the issue.

In IPFW, denied packets are logged through the syslog facility. In PF, denied packets are logged to a special interface called `pflog0`. This interface is actually a BPF (Berkeley Packet Filter) interface that allows utilities like `tcpdump(8)` to sniff logged packets directly. This feature can be used by IDS engines and monitoring tools to analyze the firewall's activity without having to directly interact or affect the firewall processing.

PF implements Network Address Translation (NAT) and Quality of Service (QoS) directly into the firewall. In IPFW, these features are provided by userland programs. There are pros and cons to each approach, but in general, there is no functional difference. The integration in PF makes administration a bit easier as all configuration is done in one file.

Under the hood, PF performs more aggressive optimization than IPFW. In PF, large lists of rules are compressed into a table. So while the configuration file for PF may still have list-like properties, the core processing engine of PF treats the rules in a more efficient manner. This ultimately results in a tree data-structure for the rules making even huge rulesets rapidly searchable.

> **Network Address Translation**
>
> Network Address Translation is a mechanism for many IP addresses behind a network device to share a smaller number of addresses (usually one) on the other side. NAT was originally created as a mechanism for IP address conservation. For instance, your ISP would give you only one IP address, but using NAT you can have many hosts online behind your router going to the ISP. All the internal IP addresses get translated to the one IP address on the other side, and the router or firewall keeps track of whose traffic belongs to whom.
>
> Over the years, NAT has also taken on a security slant. NAT allows security engineers to "hide" a network behind one IP address, nearly completely limiting an external attacker's ability to connect to internal hosts. While some would argue the security advantages versus a normal, non-NATing firewall, the utility of NAT has proven itself over the years.

Finally, PF has the capability to force reassembly and normalization of fragmented packets before sending them through the firewall. This prevents fragmentation attacks behind the firewall. This is a very convenient feature, as it prevents other applications on the firewall (such as an IDS sensor) from having to deal with fragments.

It may seem that PF is the weapon of choice when building a firewall. If you need the flexibility and scalability that PF offers, it is definitely a worthy firewall. However, for smaller-scale deployments, such as a small or home office, IFPW's simple interface and straightforward administration may be a better bet.

Basic IPFW Configuration

So, assuming you have chosen to build a FreeBSD-based firewall, where do you start? Well, first you need a machine to run the firewall on. The horsepower you require will depend on how much data you send through the firewall, what you do to the data, and any other activities you have the host perform. You could easily run a FreeBSD firewall with a DSL connection, and internal connection, and a wireless network connection on a 200MHZ Pentium with 64 megabytes of RAM. This is definitely not a state of the art machine, but for a simple home firewall, it doesn't break a sweat.

Obviously, you need enough network interfaces to suit your needs. Your setup will vary depending on the architecture you have chosen. For the basic IPFW setup here in this chapter, we will be using a bump in the wire architecture, unless otherwise specified.

Kernel Configuration

The first step in creating an IPFW firewall is to compile IPFW support into the kernel. The following kernel configurations control the functionality of IPFW.

`options IPFIREWALL`
: This kernel option enables the firewalling capability. It is the only kernel option required by IPFW. The other firewall kernel options are optional.

`options IPFIREWALL_VERBOSE`
: This kernel option enables IPFW to log packets to the syslog utility.

`options IPFIREWALL_VERBOSE_LIMIT=N`
: This kernel option controls how many packets are logged per entry in the ruleset. For example, if you are logging all denied SMB traffic, the firewall will stop sending messages to syslog after *N* packets. This option prevents a rule from logging so much as to fill up the logging filesystem.

`options IPFIREWALL_DEFAULT_TO_ACCEPT`
: This kernel option changes the default behavior of the firewall. Normally traffic is denied if it does not match any firewall rules. This inverts that logic and allows packets through that do not match any firewall rules.

The only option absolutely required for IPFW to function is `IPFIREWALL`. The others can be enabled if you need them. If you enable logging, we recommend that you compile in the logging limit because you never know when a rule will run away from you.

Startup Configuration

Since IPFW is not a process, it does not need to be started as a daemon would. However, it does need to be activated when the machine boots. Add **`firewall_enable="YES"`** to your */etc/rc.conf*, to enable firewall capabilities at boot. However, if you need to turn the firewall off and on by hand (for instance, when you're testing) you can set the `sysctl` variable `net.inet.ip.fw.enable` to `1` or `0` depending on if you are turning the firewall on or off. If you are in secure level 3, once the firewall is enabled, it cannot be disabled.

By default, IPFW will use the */etc/rc.firewall* shell script for its firewall configuration file. This stock firewall configuration file ships with FreeBSD and contains several different firewall behaviors. You can specify one of the following `firewall_types` in your *rc.conf* to use these canned rulesets:

`open`
: Allows all traffic in and out of the firewall.

`client`
: Basic ruleset for a *host-based* firewall architecture. Outbound connections are allowed, only a few select connections are allowed in.

`simple`
: A bump in the wire firewall configuration for firewalls with one internal and one external network interface. It allows a few services through to the internal network and permits all outbound traffic.

`closed`
: All traffic is denied.

/path/to/file
: Use this alternate file or script as the firewall ruleset.

You will need to modify *rc.firewall* to for the right IP addresses and netmasks for your network.

Firewall Configuration

The default firewall configuration in *rc.firewall* will likely not be exactly what you want. You can choose to modify the existing *rc.firewall*, create your own, or configure the runtime firewall by hand. However if you choose to configure the runtime firewall by hand, you must understand the `ipfw` utility and the things you can make the firewall do.

The basic syntax for any `ipfw` command is the following:

```
ipfw [-N] command [index] action [log] protocol addresses [options]
```

Optional arguments

First, let's look at the optional parts of the `ipfw` command. The `-N` flag instructs `ipfw` to resolve IP addresses and services to names when displaying them to the user. This has no effect on the way the firewall works, however it may slow display down as the host needs to look up hostnames through DNS.

The `index` option specifies where in the firewall rules this action will be inserted. The index values range from 1 to 65534. Rules are processed in order of their index (starting at 1). Using an index lets you insert a rule into the middle of an already existing and running ruleset. The last rule, 65535, is the default rule for the firewall, generally denying all traffic.

The `log` option indicates that `ipfw` should send a message to syslog whenever this rule is matched. Be careful to use this only for rules that match infrequently or in conjunction with the firewall kernel logging limit. Without the limit, a rule with a lot of matches can easily fill up the logging filesystem.

`ipfw` has the capability to track the state of TCP and UDP streams. For TCP, it is a relatively straightforward process. The firewall, upon detecting a new TCP session via a SYN packet, will set up a dynamic rule that allows all other packets within that TCP session to be allowed. UDP does not have the same session construct as TCP, so the firewall must guess what packets are part of a UDP flow. For most installations, this guess works just fine.

Finally, the `options` control extra abilities to some `ipfw` commands. The following are some of the more important options.

`in`
: Matches inbound packets.

`out`
: Matches outbound packets.

`via` *`interface`*
: Matches packets passing through a specified interface.

`keep-state`
: If a packet matches this rule, the firewall creates a state entry for this session. Any time a packet from this session (inbound or outbound) arrives at the firewall, the state entry will allow the packet through the firewall without having to run the packet through the ruleset again.

`setup`
: This will match a TCP packet that only has the SYN bit set, for instance, the first TCP packet of a TCP connection.

There are many other options that are documented in the `ipfw(8)` manpage.

Required arguments

`ipfw` accepts the following commands:

`add`
: Adds a rule to the existing ruleset. If an `index` is specified, the rule is inserted appropriately; otherwise, it is appended to the list.

`delete`
: Deletes a rule from the existing ruleset.

There are many actions `ipfw` can take on a packet. Chances are, if there's something you want to do based on matching a specific packet, there is an existing `ipfw` action that will do it. Here are some of the common actions.

`allow/accept/pass/permit`
: The packet is permitted to pass through the firewall.

`deny/drop`
: The packet is blocked by the firewall.

`reset`
: This action is only valid on TCP packets. The packet is blocked by the firewall. Further, the firewall sends a RST packet to the originating host in an attempt to stop further packets.

`skipto` *`number`*
: When a packet matches a `skipto` rule, `ipfw` jumps to the rule at index *`number`*.

`divert` *`port`*
: This action causes the packet to be diverted to the specified local port. This is often used for NAT support.

For the sake of simplicity, we will examine a simple small office firewall as shown in Figure 8-8. This is a DMZ architecture with a web and mail server running on the server network. The clients on the internal network are standard office workstations. The rules presented in this section could be used as a replacement for the *rc.firewall* in the default install.

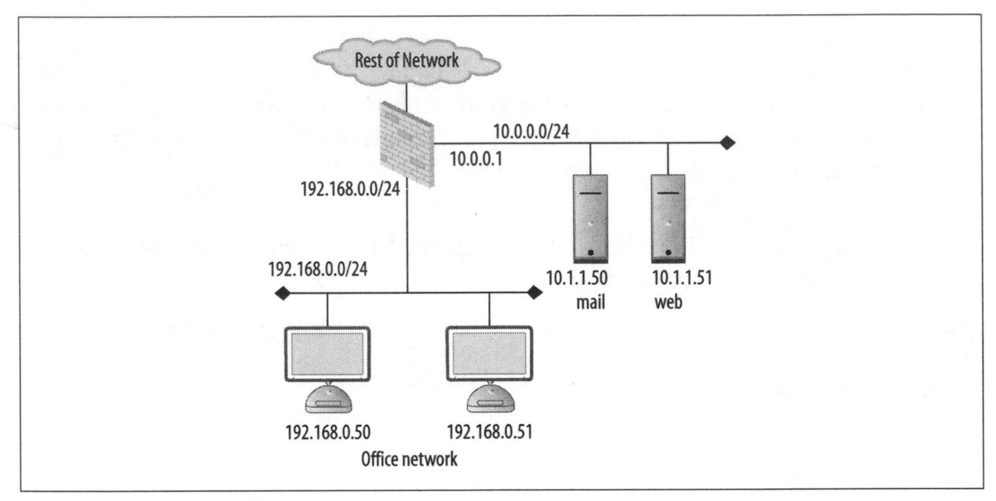

Figure 8-8. Example DMZ network

There are many philosophies on how a firewall should be configured. Some believe the absolute minimum traffic that can be allowed should be allowed. Others feel that this idea makes administration difficult and there is no reason to be that restrictive. The rules in this chapter are designed with the default deny principle in mind and are meant to be illustrative. Your firewall rules should be constructed in a way that makes sense for your environment.

First, to make the rules readable, define each network, network mask, interface, and firewall IP address as a variable in *rc.firewall*. Servers and other machines that will have specific rules should have variables assigned to them as well. For instance, the DMZ interface can be defined as follows:

```
dmz_if="xl0"
dmz_net="10.0.0.0"
dmz_mask="255.255.255.0"
dmz_ip="10.0.0.1"
```

To further simplify maintenance, a variable should be defined for the `ipfw` command itself. This allows you to manipulate the command used on all rules by only making one change (for instance, to use the –q flag for quiet output).

```
fwcmd="/sbin/ipfw"
```

For the first rule, make sure that traffic across the loopback interface is allowed. Further, make sure that traffic destined for localhost does not arrive on any external interface. Traffic to 127.0.0.0/8 should *always* go through the loopback interface. By definition, this is what the loopback interface is for. Anything addressed to the localhost subnet received on a physical interface is completely bogus.

```
${fwcmd} add pass all from any to any via lo0
${fwcmd} add deny all from any to 127.0.0.0/8
```

If a rule indicates that state should be tracked, then a dynamic rule is created for each session. Normally, these dynamic rules aren't checked until a packet reaches the first `keep-state` rule. However, if you'd like the firewall to check the dynamic rules first (that is, if you are going to have many state-aware sessions), then specify the `check-state` action early in the ruleset. In this case, we will be using state checking for the servers on the DMZ. Since we assume a fair bit of traffic to these servers, we utilize `check-state`.

```
${fwcmd} add check-state
```

Next, we need to prevent spoofing attacks and packets that should never be seen on the Internet. Traffic from the netblocks specified in RFC 1918: Address Allocation of Private Internets should never be received on the public Internet interface:

```
# anti-spoofing
${fwcmd} add deny all from ${int_net}:${int_mask} to any via ${dmz_if}
${fwcmd} add deny all from ${ext_net}:${ext_mask} to any via ${dmz_if}
${fwcmd} add deny all from ${dmz_net}:${dmz_mask} to any via ${int_if}
${fwcmd} add deny all from ${ext_net}:${ext_mask} to any via ${int_if}
# RFC 1918 address
${fwcmd} add deny all from any to 10.0.0.0/8 via ${ext_if}
${fwcmd} add deny all from any to 172.16.0.0/12via ${ext_if}
${fwcmd} add deny all from any to 192.168.0.0/16via ${ext_if}
```

These anti-spoofing rules are not perfect. Ideally, the rule would state "allow traffic through an interface if and only if its source IP address belongs to a network that exists on that interface." However, with ipfw, this logic can be difficult to enforce. Using the `skipto` command, rules can be created that enforce proper anti-spoofing logic. This, unfortunately, can make the rules difficult to understand and maintain, so generally the above construct is used.

There are many more networks that can be blocked from entering the public interface. For instance, there are many netblocks that are not currently allocated for use in the global routing table. These networks can be added to your ipfw ruleset and logged. Hits against the rules are interesting because these packets should never occur on the Internet in normal situations. They are almost always signs of an attack. A good starting point to build a list of networks to deny traffic from is RFC 3330, Special Use IPv4 Addresses, and IANA's list of allocated address space at *http://www.iana.org/assignments/ipv4-address-space*.

Traffic to the servers on the DMZ should be allowed from anywhere. Regardless of whether the client is on the internal network or on the Internet, the web server should be reachable. Also, the SMTP port of the mail server should be reachable from everywhere while the IMAP port should only be accessible from the internal network. In this case, we will use state tracking to make the firewall more efficient.

```
# Server rules
${fwcmd} add pass tcp from any to ${websrv} http keep-state
${fwcmd} add pass tcp from any to ${mailsrv} smtp keep-state
${fwcmd} add pass tcp from ${int_net}:${int_mask} to ${mailsrv} imap keep-state
```

We use protocol names for readability here. You could also specify ports 80, 25, and 143, respectively. As long as the service is listed in the file */etc/services*, however, the name and the port number are interchangeable.

Now for the internal clients, we allow all outbound TCP and UDP connections from our internal network. Whether or not this is an acceptable ruleset is a matter of your local policy. However, for the sake of maintainability and minimizing user impact in our relatively low security environment, these rules are reasonable.

```
${fwcmd} add pass ip from ${int_net}:${int_mask} to any
```

Next, the firewall itself should be protected. There's generally no reason for anyone except for administrators to communicate directly with the firewall. The exception is traffic used for network troubleshooting such as `ping` and `traceroute`. Allowing `ping` and `traceroute` packets in your firewall ruleset is another one of those religious wars that firewall administrators and security experts like to wage. Some say that allowing this traffic provides attackers with critical information that can be leveraged for an attack. Others feel that `ping` and tracerouting is a key part of maintaining a network. The authors, who have been responsible for running networks in the past, feel that concise troubleshooting ability outweighs the security consideration.

```
${fwcmd} add pass tcp from ${admin_host} to ${int_if} ssh keep-state
${fwcmd} add pass icmp from any to any
```

Finally, we explicitly deny all other traffic and log it.

```
${fwcmd} add deny ip from any to any log
```

The idea of logging all denied traffic may sound good, but in reality, this is really unworkable. Depending on your network, you may find you have certain types of traffic constantly being dropped by your firewall. For instance, the router to which you are attached may be constantly probing the firewall. By examining your logs, you're able to determine the types of benign traffic that will do nothing but fill your logs. You can then create specific rules before your deny all rule that silently drops this annoying traffic.

This basic set of rules should be enough to get you up and running with a few site-specific modifications. As with any active open source project, the features and operation of IPFW will change periodically. Further, IPFW is very feature rich, and much of it's functionality is out of the scope of this book. For the latest news and complete configuration options, see the FreeBSD web site and the `ipfw(8)` manpage.

Using the Firewall

Now that the firewall has rules, there is still the pesky aspect of actually running the firewall. Turing the firewall on and off, viewing and modifying the active ruleset, and resetting the log counters are all key administrative activities for any firewall. IPFW makes these processes intuitive and easy.

First, as was stated before, the firewall can be turned on and off by setting the `sysctl` variable *net.inet.ip.fw.enable* to **1** or **0** respectively. Depending on your setup, especially if you have NAT running, turning the firewall off can completely isolate the internal network. If NAT isn't running and forwarding is enabled (*net.inet.ip.forwarding* is set to 1), then your firewall just became a router and the internal network is completely exposed. Be aware of what you're doing if you turn your firewall off.

To see the currently running firewall rules, issue the **show** command to `ipfw`. For example:

```
% sudo ipfw show
00100      36       1986 allow ip from any to any via lo0
00200       0          0 deny ip from any to 127.0.0.0/8
...
```

This list has been cut short for the sake of example, but all your firewall rules will be listed. The first column is the rule number of a particular rule. By default, `ipfw` will increment the rule number by 100 from the previous rule. So, a basic ruleset will iterate as follows: 100, 200, 300, 400, etc.

The next column indicates how many packets have matched the rule and the following column shows the number of bytes. For instance, the first rule has been matched 36 times for a total of 1986 bytes. The final column is the rule itself.

If you're using `keep-state` to track connections, `ipfw` is creating dynamic rules in the background to handle state-based traffic. To see what dynamic rules have been created through stateful sessions, use the `–d` flag:

```
% sudo ipfw -d show
...
## Dynamic rules (3):
00400  172  24784 (296s) STATE tcp 192.168.0.78 49783 <-> 192.168.0.10 22
00400   16   1456 (1s) STATE tcp 192.168.0.78 49761 <-> 192.168.0.10 22
```

The first column is the rule number to which this dynamic rule is associated. The number in parenthesis specifies how long that dynamic rule has until it is aged out of the state table. The rest is similar to standard `show` output.

Rules can also be added to the ruleset on the fly. For instance, if you wanted to put a rule allowing all UDP port 53 traffic immediately following the loopback rules, you could do the following:

```
% sudo ipfw add 250 pass udp from any to any 53
```

We've chosen 250 arbitrarily; the important thing is that the number you specify must fall in between the two adjacent rule numbers.

Rules can also be deleted on the fly as well. If we realized that inserting a rule to allow all UDP port 53 traffic before our anti-spoofing rules was a really bad idea, we could do the following.

```
% sudo ipfw delete 250
```

Voìla, the rule is gone.

The ability to add and delete rules on the fly is a great administrative feature. However, it's critical to update the static ruleset with the rule as well. That way, if the firewall were to reboot for some reason, the new rule would be read out of your firewall configuration file automatically at boot time. Rebuilding the "correct" ruleset can be a time consuming process.

Also, be careful when modifying rulesets remotely. One typo, and you can lock yourself out of the host completely. Direct console access is now the only way to change the firewall configuration. There are various tricks to prevent a typo from causing this problem. One solution is to have the first rule in your firewall ruleset explicitly allowing traffic from your workstation to the firewall. Another trick is to schedule a reboot at some point in the future using the `at(1)` command (**`echo reboot | at now + 10 minutes`**) and then modify the firewall. If things go badly, the firewall will reboot automatically. If things go well, you can use `atrm(1)` to cancel the reboot.

Finally, you may find that you've reached your logging (verbose) limit on a rule. Either through inspection of **`ipfw show`** output (hey, I see my rule has more hits than my limit) or through syslog output (messages about the log limit being exceeded showing up in syslog), you discover that the rule is no longer logging. The counter on a rule can be reset by using the `zero` command and the rule number.

```
% sudo ipfw zero 100
Entry 100 cleared
```

Now all of rule 100's accounting as been cleared:

```
% sudo ipfw show 100
00100   0       0 allow ip from any to any via lo0
```

If you would rather get a clean slate for the entire ruleset, you can zero out all statistics by leaving off the rule number.

Basic PF Configuration

While IFPW and PF provide the same basic firewall services, they are dramatically different to configure and maintain. Some users find the list-based mechanism that IPFW uses easy to understand and use. Others find that the PF provides more flexibility and agility. PF's configuration may be non-intuitive at first, but once you get the hang of it, it can be immensely powerful; especially as rulesets grow.

From a hardware perspective, PF has about the same performance ramifications as IPFW. A simple home PF firewall can run on a Pentium-class machine. More sophisticated setups will require more hardware; however, there is generally no performance-related reason to buy the latest and greatest server for a PF firewall. Considering the criticality of the job, though, you probably want a machine under warranty or to consider an HA architecture.

Kernel and Startup Configuration

As with most OpenBSD features, there is no need to compile in any special kernel options. The default kernel has firewall support built in natively, so all you need to do is enable it. PF can be enabled by adding **pf=YES** to */etc/rc.conf.local*.

By default, PF reads firewall rules and information out of */etc/pf.conf*. Unfortunately the default ruleset will not be of much use. You will have to modify *pf.conf(5)* prior to using the firewall.

The structure of the rules in PF are dramatically different than those in IPFW. IPFW uses a simple list for firewall control. PF, on the other hand, breaks the configuration into sections that allow for greater flexibility. *pf.conf* has the following sections:

Macros
: Variables that can be used elsewhere in the configuration. For instance, the term *ext_interface* can be assigned the IP address of the external interface on the firewall.

Tables
: Variables that represent one or more IP addresses or networks. This allows multiple networks to be grouped together for the sake of simplicity.

Options
: Tunable firewall parameters such as TCP timeout values and logging information.

Scrub
: Controls the process of defragmenting and normalizing packets.

Queuing
: Controls the rate limiting and QoS features of the firewall.

Translation
: Rules that control address and port translation go here.

Filters
: Core logic of your firewall ruleset.

PF in FreeBSD

Even though PF is maintained as part of OpenBSD, it is available as a port in FreeBSD in the security ports directory for 5.2.1 and before, and its part of the core operating system starting with 5.3.

The port of PF is well maintained and installation should be seamless. You will need to have `device bpf`, `options INET`, `options PFIL_HOOKS`, and `options RANDOM_IP_ID` enabled in your kernel to get PF to working. And, by default, the configuration information of the ports tree version is stored in */usr/local/etc/pf.conf* rather than */etc/pf.conf*.

For PF in 5.3 and beyond, using PF instead of IPFW is a bit different. Your kernel must be configured with `device pf`. For logging capability, your kernel must have `device pflog` and for high availability synchronization your kernel must have `device pfsync`. Futher, you need to enable PF in your `rc.conf`. To stop using IPFW and start using PF, change **`firewall_enable="NO"`** and set **`pf_enable="YES"`**. The `pf_rules` configuration option allows you to set where the configuration file is stored and `pflog_enable` turns on logging for PF.

If you are using PF under FreeBSD, this section will still apply; you just need to be careful of where your configuration files are.

Firewall Configuration

Configuring PF can be a complex task. However, a basic firewall ruleset can be created in little time by focusing on the important parts of the ruleset. The rules presented in this section are meant as an example of a common setup. The default *pf.conf* has many commented out features that you should examine beyond what is in this text. Further, PF examples found in */usr/share/pf* can be very useful in understanding the detailed capability of PF.

First, start off by defining the networks and interfaces on the firewall as well as any important hosts on the connected networks. By setting these up as macros in the beginning, the resulting ruleset is more readable and maintainable. For instance, the DMZ network in Figure 8-8 can be defined as follows:

```
dmz_if="xl0"
dmz_net="10.0.0.0/24"
dmz_ip="10.0.0.1"
```

For groups of networks or hosts, tables are a more efficient way for PF to do ruleset matching. Any site specific network groups, such as all internal networks, should go in a table. Also the bogus and RFC 1918 networks that should never be routed across the public Internet should be defined as one table.

```
table <bogus> {10/8, 172.16/12, 192.168/16}
```

The options section of *pf.conf* will vary depending on your site needs. In a standard small office situation, the default options should be fine. However, for firewalls passing much more data such as those in a datacenter, the options section can be used to tune the memory used by the firewall and various timeout values.

Tuning memory and protocol options can be more art than science. For instance, on a firewall with many connections, you may want to force the firewall to expire connections more rapidly than normal to conserve resources. Unfortunately this can have dire consequences on long-term connections such as those with backend servers like databases or legacy systems.

Let's say database replication breaks due to the tuning done for the shorter connections. You have to fix it so you allow longer-lived connections but end up installing more memory to compensate. As you can see, firewall tuning can be like a game of Whack-A-Mole; hit one problem on the head and another pops up. When tuning memory and protocol options, be aware of other changes in your environment that may result.

PF can automatically reassemble and normalize packets before allowing them through the firewall. This feature can stop fragmentation-based attacks dead and prevent attacks against end hosts based on low level packet trickery. However, reassembling packets can use a great deal of memory, especially if you are under attack. In general, all traffic arriving on the external interface of a firewall should be reassembled. If you face a memory problem, it's preferable to buy more memory rather than turn this feature off.

```
scrub in on $ext_if all fragment reassemble
```

Finally, it's time to actually enter the rules for the firewall. The logic of the rules is the complete opposite of IPFW. As you recall, in IPFW, the first matching rule "wins" and the packet is handled by that rule. In PF, the last matching rule "wins."

So, for the first rule, all traffic should be denied and logged. That way, traffic that does not match any other rule in the ruleset will be blocked.

```
block in log all
```

Packets that transit the localhost interface are rarely (if ever) illegitimate. There are many processes on an BSD machine that expect to be able to communicate through the localhost interface. Traffic should be allowed through localhost using the `quick` keyword. Using the `quick` keyword, a rule can force a "win" and act immediately on the packet. There is no reason to continue processing localhost traffic.

```
pass quick on lo0 all
```

Next, spoofed packets should be denied. Spoofed packets are bad regardless of the targeted service. PF has the ability to automatically create anti-spoofing rules given the network that is configured on an interface. For instance:

```
antispoof quick for $int_if inet
anitspoof quick for $dmz_if inet
```

Further, the bogus networks should be dropped early in the ruleset as well. Packets sourced from bogus networks are interesting because they should never occur for non-malicious traffic. Using the `log` keyword, PF will log these packets to the logging interface, `pflog0`.

```
block in log quick on $ext_if from <bogus> to any
```

Finally, rules can be added for the DMZ and internal hosts. For the DMZ, traffic should be allowed from anywhere to the public services. As in the IPFW example, state-tracking should be used to increase the efficiency of the firewall.

```
pass in on $ext_if proto tcp from any to $websrv http keep-state
pass in on $ext_if proto tcp from any to $mailsrv smtp keep-state
pass in on $ext_if proto tcp from $int_net to $mailsrv imap keep-state
```

We use protocol names for readability here. You could also specify ports 80, 25, and 143 respectively. As long as the service is listed in the file */etc/services*, however, the name and the port number are interchangeable.

Obviously these rules need to be customized for your network. When initially setting up the firewall, you may want to have your first network allow and log all traffic. That way you have less opportunity of locking yourself out of the host and you can view the logs to determine what other rules need to be created.

Using the Firewall

Like IPFW, PF provides functionality for managing a running firewall. From stopping and starting the firewall functionality to flushing rules to viewing statistics from the firewall, the `pfctl(8)` utility is the administrative interface to PF.

The firewall can be enabled and disabled by passing pfctl the -e and -d flags, respectively. This can be useful for troubleshooting a firewall problem, especially when you are unsure as to whether the problem is really the firewall or not.

There are a series of statistics and information pfctl can present via the -s flag. The following common keywords can be used with pfctl -s.

rules
: Shows the currently loaded firewall ruleset. Can be used with -v for more detailed information.

state
: Shows all currently active states. This is very useful if your rules extensively use the keep-state pragma.

info
: Shows statistics and counters relevant to the entire firewall.

all
: Displays all available information pfctl has. This is a useful debugging tool that can be croned once a night to output to a file or email for review.

For instance, to see verbose output on the currently loaded ruleset, you would do the following:

```
% sudo pfctl -s rules -v
scrub in on sis0 all fragment reassemble
  [ Evaluations: 283        Packets: 111        Bytes: 0          States: 0     ]
block drop in log all
  [ Evaluations: 6          Packets: 1          Bytes: 229        States: 0     ]
pass in quick on lo0 all
  [ Evaluations: 3          Packets: 0          Bytes: 0          States: 0     ]
block drop in on ! sis0 inet from 192.168.0.0/24 to any
...
```

This output goes on for all your rules. After a while, the statistics associated with your rules may become so large as to become useless. You can zero out the statistics by issuing **pfctl -z**.

If you make a change to your *pf.conf*, you can validate the ruleset before you install it by using **pfctl -n**.

```
% sudo pfctl -ng -f /etc/pf.conf
/etc/pf.conf:68: syntax error
```

While this is not the most verbose parsing information you could hope for, it's much better than making a mistake and locking yourself out of your firewall.

Once you've cleaned up the ruleset and validated it, pfctl allows you to flush all existing rules and load rules from a file.

```
% sudo pfctl -Fa -f /etc/pf.conf
rules cleared
nat cleared
```

```
altq cleared
states cleared
pf: statistics cleared
0 tables deleted.
```

The -F flag flushes information from the firewall. The a modifier, used here, flushes all the rules. The s flag will flush just the active states in the firewall, a useful debugging tool. Be careful when flushing and reloading rules over the network as you can lock yourself out of the firewall.

Logging

The logging capability of PF is quite different than IPFW. PF logs denied packets to a pseudo network interface called pflog0. Data sent to pflog0 is in a *pcap* data structure. In a nutshell, this means that utilities like tcpdump can sniff pflog0 and interpret the traffic just as they would a normal interface.

However, running tcpdump all the time and watching the output is not exactly a scalable way to run your firewalls. The pflogd(8) daemon solves this problem by writing packets from pflog0 to a logfile (*/var/log/pflog* by default). Again, the data is written to disk in *pcap* format so any *pcap*-aware application can read the logfiles.

pflogd can be passed flags through *rc.conf.local* (or *rc.conf* for FreeBSD) at boot time. The most interesting flag is -s, which dictates how much of each packet is captured. By default, only the first 96 bytes are logged. This is generally enough data to capture all the headers. However, if you're interested in the entire payload, set the capture length much higher. For Ethernet networks, the maximum packet size is 1500, so a capture length of 1600 is guaranteed to capture all data in every logged packet.

The logs can be viewed using tcpdump. The tcpdump utility that ships with OpenBSD can understand and display the extra information PF puts into each packet regarding the rule that denied the packet. This information is contained in the link layer information of each packet and can be displayed with the -e flag.

```
% sudo tcpdump -e -r /var/log/pflog
16:49:28.195569 rule 0/0(match): block in on sis0: 192.168.0.67.50394 > 192.168.0.11.
80: S 3529314353:3529314353(0) win 65535 <mss 1460,nop,wscale 0,nop,nop,timestamp
3683841540 0> (DF) [tos 0x10]
16:49:30.819388 rule 0/0(match): block in on sis0: 192.168.0.67.50394 > 192.168.0.11.
80: S 3529314353:3529314353(0) win 65535 <mss 1460,nop,wscale 0,nop,nop,timestamp
3683841545 0> (DF) [tos 0x10]
```

Here, for instance, two SYN packets to port 80 were dropped by the 0th (first) rule. tcpdump is a very powerful utility, and a complete description of how to use it to analyze packets is outside the scope of this text. Read the tcpdump(8) man page for a good introduction to packet analysis.

The pfctl(8) and *pf.conf(5)* manpages are also good sources of information.

Handling Failure

Firewalls, like any other computer application, can fail. The cost of failure can vary depending on the role the firewall is serving. The failure of a firewall used in a SOHO environment can mean lost productivity for a handful of users. The failure of a firewall that protects an e-commerce web site can mean thousands of dollars in lost revenue.

For a number of years, commercial routers and firewalls have had the capability to provide high availability in the face of device failure. Various vendors support various architectures as described earlier in the "High Availability" section. For those who chose to use open source firewalls, however, the options have been extremely limited. Most of the solutions we authors have seen were based on homemade scripts and `cron` jobs. Thankfully options are emerging in the FreeBSD and OpenBSD arenas that begin to give network engineers high availability options using the firewalls they know and love.

In order to have a highly available firewall cluster, two services must be provided. First, the firewalls need to have the ability to share an IP and MAC address between multiple hosts. This link and network layer redundancy ensures that the failure of a firewall is handled transparently on the local network. The other service required is to synchronize state information between firewalls to keep active sessions alive even when one of the firewalls fails. This makes firewall failures transparent to the hosts that are communicating end-to-end through the firewalls. Without synchronization, all active sessions through the firewall would need to be reestablished.

CARP

Sharing IP and MAC addresses is key to providing seamless access to hosts directly connected to the firewall. Sharing the IP address is relatively easy. However, sharing the MAC address is the hard part. If each firewall in the cluster used its own MAC address for a shared IP address, failure of the primary firewall would cause problems for directly connected hosts. These hosts would have to expire their ARP entry for the old IP/MAC address pair and acquire the new pair via a new ARP request. This expiration and renewal process can take an extended period of time (on the order of minutes), which is generally not acceptable in a highly available architecture.

The solution is to create a virtual MAC address that is shared between multiple firewalls. Cisco originally developed and patented the Hot Standby Router Protocol (HSRP) to accomplish this feat on their routers. After some time, the IETF worked on creating the Virtual Routing Redundancy Protocol (VRRP) to do basically the same thing. In fact, VRRP was so similar that Cisco and the IETF became embroiled in a patent dispute that eventually led to developers having to pay a license fee to Cisco if they wished to use VRRP. For the open source development community, this meant that the current standard for sharing an IP/MAC address pair was unusable.

The Common Address Redundancy Protocol (CARP) is a patent-free mechanism for sharing an IP/MAC address pair and handling failure between devices in a cluster. It originally was released in OpenBSD 3.5 and has since been ported to FreeBSD. CARP is substantially different from VRRP and should prevent it from being the target of patent disputes. CARP allows the open source community to finally begin to create real clustering capabilities, not just for firewalls but any clustered service such as web or mail servers.

CARP Configuration

CARP is included in the default OpenBSD distribution. However, as of this writing, there is only a placeholder in the FreeBSD source tree for CARP. To obtain CARP functionality in FreeBSD, you must apply the patch at *http://people.freebsd.org/~mlaier/CARP/* and follow the directions in the patch for installation.

The configuration of CARP is basically the same for OpenBSD and FreeBSD. In this example, we will provide configuration guidance for a hot-standby architecture on OpenBSD. However, these commands and configurations are similar in intent in FreeBSD. This example is based on the example network topology in Figure 8-9.

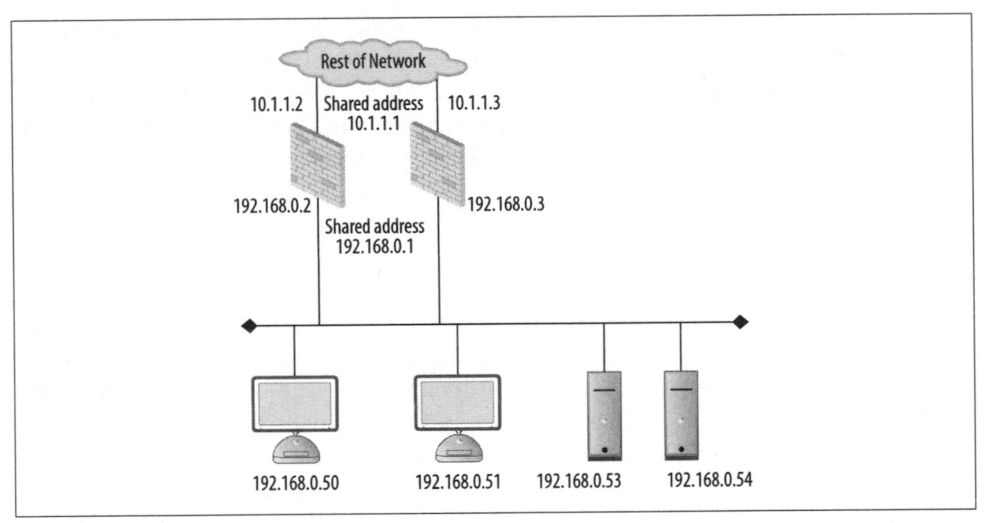

Figure 8-9. Example CARP network

First ensure CARP is enabled. By default, *net.inet.carp.allow* should be enabled, however it doesn't hurt to check to prevent troubleshooting problems later. Also, you will need to enable *net.inet.carp.preempt*. This variable allows you to force one host, if it is online, to always be primary in the Hot-Standby architecture. Without preemption, the first CARP host that is put on the network is the master. From an administration standpoint, this is not ideal as you are never sure why one host is master and not the other. With preemption, if the secondary host is the CARP master, than you know the primary firewall has failed.

CARP interfaces are treated similarly to any other network interface, meaning they can be controlled via hostname files or `ifconfig(8)`. The IP address that is shared between two hosts must be in the same IP subnet as the IP address on that interface. For instance, the 192.168.0.1 address is shared on the 192.168.0.0/24 network in this example. Two CARP interfaces need to be created; one for the front and one for the back of the cluster. */etc/hostname.carp0* on the primary firewall should have the following:

```
inet 192.168.0.1  255.255.255.0 192.168.0.255 vhid 1 pass password
```

While */etc/hostname.carp1* should have:

```
inet 10.1.1.1 255.255.255.0 10.1.1.255 vhid 2 pass password
```

The `vhid` variable is the virtual host ID. It must be the same on both CARP hosts for a given shared IP address. The `pass` variable is a password used to validate the CARP traffic between the hosts. Unlike HSRP where passwords are sent in the clear, CARP uses SHA-1 to hash the update with the password to ensure the integrity of the updates.

On the secondary firewall, */etc/hostname.carp0* should look like this:

```
inet 192.168.0.1  255.255.255.0 192.168.0.255 vhid 1 advskew 100 pass password
```

The `advskew` variable modifies the CARP announcements from the secondary host to ensure that if the primary host is online, it preempts the secondary. */ect/hostname.carp1* should also have an `advskew` value of 100.

The firewalls on both hosts must be configured to allow CARP traffic between them. CARP uses a unique IP protocol identifier, 112, which `pf` knows by the `carp` keyword. CARP is also state based so you can configure the firewall to keep state for greater efficiency.

```
pass on { interface1 interface 2 } proto carp keep state
```

Upon rebooting, the systems will share 192.168.0.1 and 10.1.1.1. At this point a host will only take over when the primary host stops sending CARP traffic on all interfaces. Hopefully in the future, CARP will allow failover to occur if any interfaces go down.

pfsync

Once a firewall cluster is sharing IP addresses, there is still the issue of transferring state information between the two machines. If one firewall fails over to the other without sharing state information, any existing sessions transiting the firewall cluster will be dropped. This is not ideal.

OpenBSD has the capability through pfsync to exchange state information between firewalls. While there is no native pfsync-like capability in IPFW, pfsync is available if you use the FreeBSD PF port rather than IPFW.

pfsync passes state information between multiple firewalls. When a state is created, updated, or removed on one firewall, pfsync will notify the other firewall. If one firewall fails, the other will be able to seamlessly handle traffic that was in state on the primary firewall.

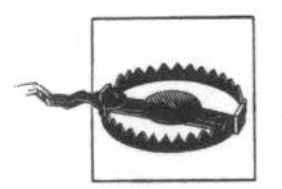

pfsync traffic sent between firewalls is not authenticated. Therefore, it is advisable to create a private network, such as a cross-over cable, between the two hosts to prevent attackers from injecting *pfsync* traffic into the firewalls. This has the added advantage of not burdening an existing network interface with the extra load of *pfsync* traffic, which can be quite large on busy firewalls.

On both hosts, create an */etc/hostname.pfsync0* file with the following:

```
up syncif interface
```

The *interface* should be whatever interface you want the *pfsync* data to go across. *pfsync* uses its own IP identifier (240) for traffic between the firewalls. pf knows this IP ID as the keyword *pfsync*. Add the following to your firewall rules.

```
pass quick on { interface } proto pfsync
```

Reboot the machine to get all the changes to take effect. Now, with CARP and *pfsync*, your firewall cluster is running in a Hot-Standby architecture. You should test the firewall cluster by shutting down the primary host and verifying that the secondary host takes over.

Wrapping Up

Firewalls are a key part of any network security architecture. OpenBSD and FreeBSD have long been known for their effectiveness as a network device and basic firewall. Now, with even more robust networking stacks and advanced capabilities like state synchronization and packet normalization, the BSDs are becoming enterprise-capable firewall platforms. With some forethought with respect to firewall placement and security policies, your BSD-based firewall will help keep intruders at the doorstep and away from your internal resources.

Resources

FreeBSD Handbook, Chapter 24, Firewalls

The *FreeBSD Handbook* has a summary of the firewalling options available under FreeBSD. It includes examples as well as configuration guidance and can be accessed at *http://www.freebsd.org/doc/en_US.ISO8859-1/books/handbook/firewalls.html*.

PF: The OpenBSD Packet Filter

This handbook is a great resource for detailed, up to date information on the PF firewall. There are several mirrors on the Net, including *http://openbsd.mirrors.pair.com/doc/pf-faq.pdf*.

FreeBSD Packet Filter (pf)

This site, *http://pf4freebsd.love2party.net*, is maintained by the team that has ported PF to FreeBSD. There are mailing lists, a TODO file, and the source code for the port.

CHAPTER 9

Intrusion Detection

This is the greatest case of false advertising I've seen since I sued the movie The Never Ending Story.
—Lionel Hutz
The Simpsons

Your network is firewalled, your servers are locked down, and you feel good about the defensive posture of your environment. However, you do not yet have any idea about the actual attacks being launched against your systems. Are evil hackers using automated tools to scan your network and inventory all your services? Are malicious internal users attempting to break into your severs using known vulnerabilities to commit insider fraud? If they are, are they succeeding?

In order to find out the answers to these questions, you may turn to an Intrusion Detection System (IDS). An IDS is, at its most basic level, a program or host that looks for signs that a resource is being attacked.

No Magic Bullets

While deploying an IDS may seem like a good idea, there are some pitfalls that you should be aware of. It's common to set up an IDS within an environment only to find out that its not as useful or efficient as you imagined it would be.

Monitoring an IDS

An IDS is no good in a vacuum. It's a passive system that monitors traffic and can alert a user when an attack is detected. Unlike a firewall that actively drops or rejects traffic, an IDS only analyzes the traffic it receives. At some point, a human needs to be involved in the monitoring activities of an IDS to make it useful. It's a bit like the old adage "if a tree falls in the woods and no one is around to hear it, does it make a noise?" If an IDS detects an attack and no one is monitoring it, does it do any good?

An IDS can generate an amazing number of alerts. From portscans to odd packets to actual attacks, an IDS requires sufficient horsepower and storage to operate. It is common for administrators to deploy old or second-hand equipment to run an IDS infrastructure. Unfortunately this may cause more harm than good as the admin will have to constantly fight with overloaded IDS sensors and central management hosts short on disk space. Keeping an IDS infrastructure up and running is a full-time job.

Responding to IDS Events

Once an event is detected by the IDS and an administrator is alerted, there should be some sort of reaction. The reaction could vary depending on what was detected by the IDS and the concerns of the IDS administrator. Some administrators ignore portscans, while others try to find the attack source and attempt to get the perpetrator taken off the network. For more serious and sustained attacks, such as a prolonged and invasive assault against a web server farm, the response may need to be more severe. Hosts may need to be taken off the network to be patched or rebuilt. Further, you may need to coordinate with other ISPs and law enforcement officials to pursue the attackers after the attack has stopped.

Ideally successful attacks against your systems will be relatively few and far between. If you have reasonable firewall rules, and you properly patch and configure your COTS and open source software, adhere to secure administration techniques, and your internally developed software is reasonably well built, most attacks from the public Internet will simply bounce off your hull. Whether or not you choose to respond to unsuccessful attacks is entirely up to you. While tracking down attackers may make the Internet as a whole a safer place, it may not make your own network demonstrably more secure. As you read the rest of this chapter and learn how to deploy a BSD-based IDS, you should consider where your threshold for reaction to IDS events will be. Maybe portscans are okay but vulnerability scans are too much. Make this a conscious decision before you go any further.

At the end of the day, your IDS should help make your network a safer place. A general way to think about this is a pyramid of needs similar to Maslow's pyramid of human needs. Maslow's pyramid postulates that humans must have basic needs met before they can perform more advanced social functions. For instance, if you do not have food and shelter, you will not be able to love and be a selfless part of society. With respect to security, maintaining and responding to an IDS event is toward the top of an IT security needs pyramid. At the base of the pyramid is secure configuration and patching practices. A bit further up the IT security pyramid is maintaining a firewall and secure system administration procedures. The next step on the pyramid is IDS and similar technologies. While useful for maintaining a secure environment, an IDS may not be necessary. And if the IDS is taking you away from fulfilling your more basic IT security needs, you may want to reconsider your decision to deploy an IDS. In fact, for many small to mid-size organizations, IDS may not make economic sense. Figure 9-1 shows a notional IT security pyramid. While the exact details of what is at each level of the pyramid may vary from enterprise to enterprise, the concept of having a solid security foundation before pondering IDS deployment is imperative.

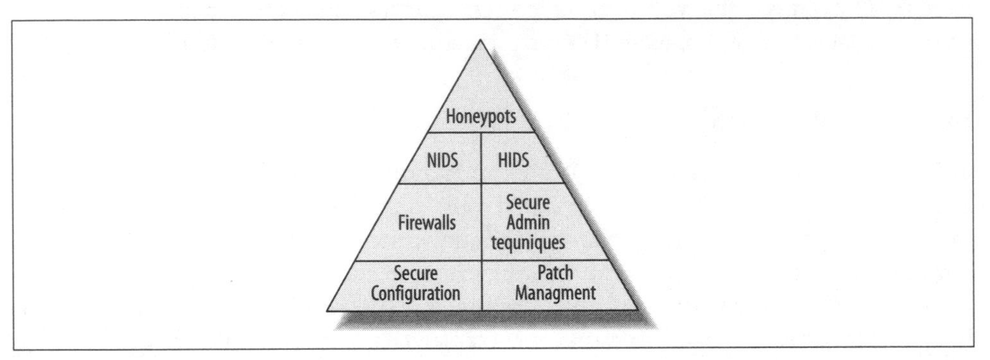

Figure 9-1. Notional IT security needs pyramid

IDS Architectures

Just as there are many types of networks and environments, there are many types of IDS. Understanding your IDS options is key to ensuring that your IDS infrastructure is a valuable addition to your security architecture and not simply wasted processing power.

Host-Based IDS

Host-based IDS (HIDS) monitors activities on a single host looking for signs of attack. HIDS may look for changes in important files such as password files and network configuration. Some HIDS actively monitor syscall activity to determine when a process is attempting to access a resource to which it normally would not have access. Further, some HIDS are geared towards protecting databases by observing queries and other transactions. Figure 9-2 shows HIDS processes running on multiple hosts. Notice that each host needs to have its own HIDS capability.

HIDS have the advantage of being able to detect a wide variety of attacks across diverse interfaces. HIDS can watch activity not only from the network, but also from the console or other interfaces. HIDS can also be highly customized to a particular host. For instance, syscall auditing can be highly accurate on hosts like mail and DNS servers that do the same thing day in and day out.

Unfortunately, HIDS can have a large management overhead. The HIDS software must be installed on every host that is to be monitored. For free software, this is merely administrative overhead. However, when HIDS software is licensed per installation, costs can skyrocket. This, of course, needs to be balanced with the

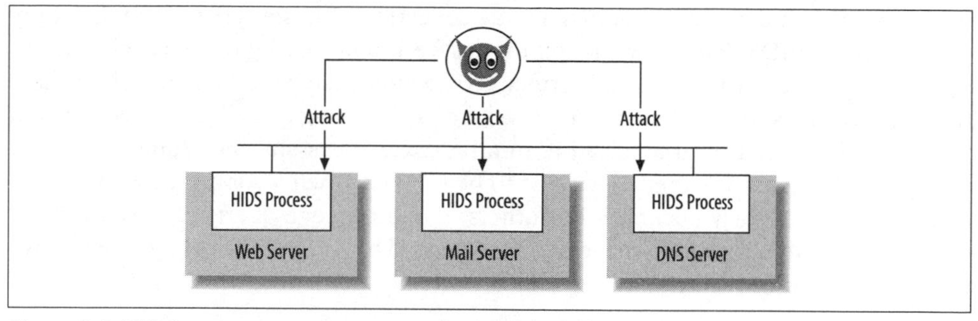

Figure 9-2. HIDS processes monitoring attacks on multiple hosts

potential Total Cost of Ownership (TCO) of a HIDS. While the open source solution may be license free, it may be ultimately more difficult to administer and use, costing you more money in the long run. Commonly HIDS are installed on servers that are higher value targets and may be worth the administrative and cost overhead.

Further, the audit logs from each HIDS installation have to be aggregated and examined. For networks with thousands of hosts, this can be quite difficult and may outweigh the advantages HIDS offer.

Network-Based IDS

Network-based IDS (NIDS) are intrusion detection systems that monitor network traffic for many hosts at a time. NIDS promiscuously sniff network traffic and look for signs of attack. Figure 9-3 shows a NIDS on the same LAN seeing an attack launched against the web server.

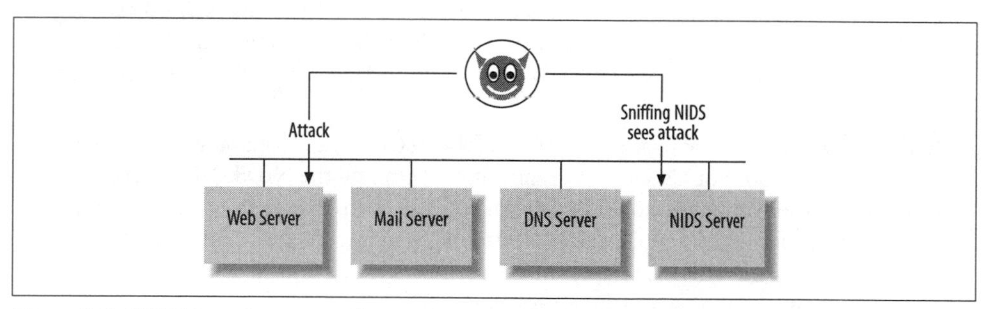

Figure 9-3. NIDS detecting an attack

NIDS tend to be made up of sensors located throughout a network and a centralized management server. The sensors are responsible for actively sniffing traffic and detecting attacks. Once an attack is sensed, these sensors send their data to the central management server. The central management host is also usually responsible for configuring and updating attack signatures on the sensors. This server may have a database to store the sensor events for rapid correlation and analysis by a security administrator.

NIDS excel at finding attacks across a wide collection of hosts. There is an economy of scale with NIDS that allow many hosts to be monitored by one special purpose sensor. However, there is also a sacrifice. NIDS don't have the view into each host that a HIDS does. NIDS alerts are a bit more of a "guessing game" in the sense that a NIDS will likely not be able to tell if an attack was successful. For some, this is an important distinction as they only want to be notified when a compromise or service disruption has actually occurred. For others, the knowledge of attacks, even if compromise was not achieved, is critically important. This is a debate that you will have to weigh in your own enterprise.

False Positives and False Negatives

There are many metrics that people try to use to quantify NIDS. Packets per second, total number of signatures, and number of concurrent sessions are all tangible quantities that NIDS vendors can measure in a lab. However, the rate of *false positives* and *false negatives* is not so measurable. Basically, false positives are events that a NIDS will identify as an intrusion but are actually not successful compromises of a system. This gets to a core issue with modern-day NIDS systems. Many of them are signature based, and when they alarm, they are really providing you notification that some traffic matched a known malicious signature. They do not actually detect intrusions, rather they detect signs of intrusions. Unfortunately that fine point is often lost on security administrators, making false positives a real problem.

False positives cause security administrators to waste their time tracking down intrusions that never actually happened. Or worse, false positives can desensitize administrators to alerts generated by a NIDS and cause them to ignore future alerts.

False negatives are successful intrusions that were not caught by the NIDS. False negatives are what people typically think of as an "IDS failure" because an administrator viewing IDS alerts thinks everything is fine, when in reality an attacker is inside the system.

Reducing the numbers of false positives and false negatives is an ongoing activity of not just the IDS vendor but also by the organizations running the NIDS. NIDS need to be tuned to their environment to minimize both values. Tuning is performed by manipulating settings for when a NIDS issues alerts and changing the traffic that can generate an alert. Tuning a NIDS can be a laborious process, but it's critical if you want to have a realistic view of ongoing attacks on your network.

One of the challenges of NIDS is placement of sensors. Sensors must be able to sniff traffic destined to hosts you want to monitor. In theory, you could place a sensor in front of each host. Figure 9-4 shows this extreme NIDS implementation. However, this would likely be prohibitively expensive to deploy and maintain. This architecture has all the management problems of HIDS architectures with none of the advantages of HIDS.

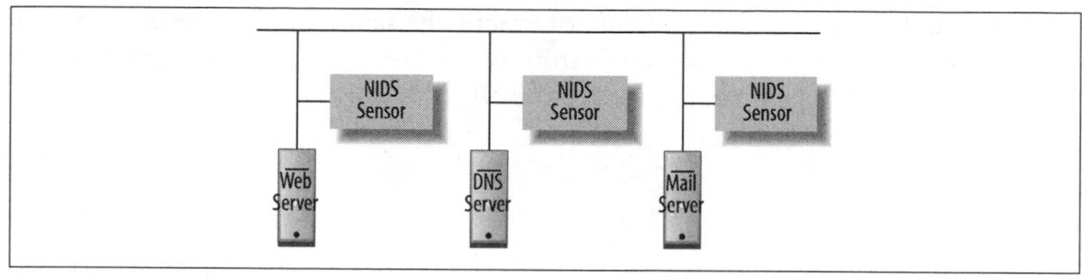

Figure 9-4. A NIDS sensor per host

So, sensor placement can be pushed farther away from the host in a network to be able to intercept traffic at subnet boundaries. However, this may still be expensive to deploy and difficult to implement on complex network infrastructures. Ultimately, sensors may be pushed to the core of a network. However, at the core, target traffic may bypass the sensor completely. Figure 9-5 shows attacks at the edge of a network being missed by a central core sensor.

Further, the amount of data being passed through the core of a network may exceed the capacity of the sensor. Ultimately, sensor placement in your network must be a balance between the economy of running fewer sensors and the advantages of having deeper sensor penetration.

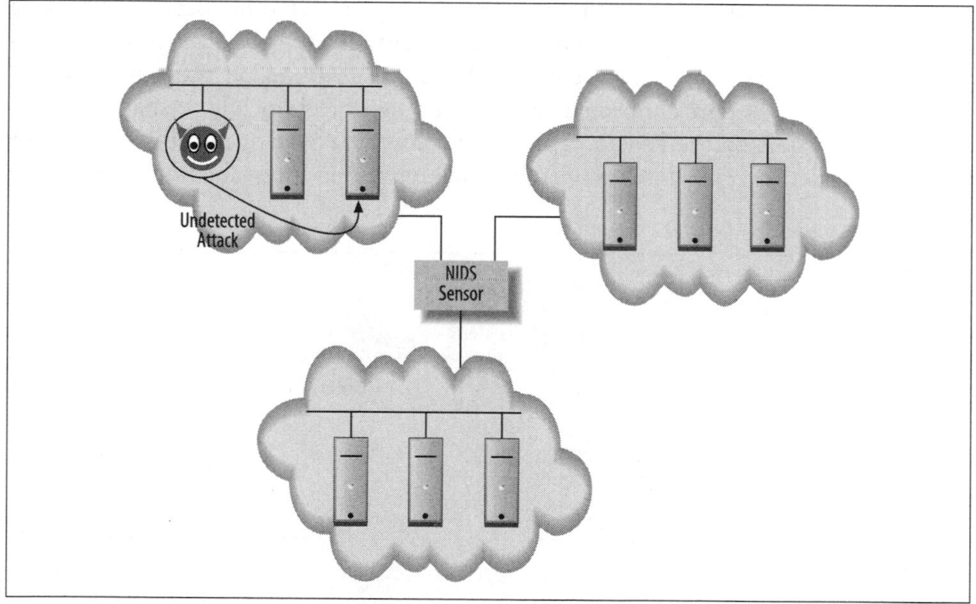

Figure 9-5. A NIDS sensor at a network core

There are a variety of ways to get traffic to a sensor. One option is a *tap*. A tap is a specialized device that splits traffic off of a physical wire into two streams. Think of it in the same way a phone line is tapped. One stream goes to the endpoint just as it was original destined. The other stream of exactly the same data goes to the IDS sensor. Figure 9-6 shows a network tap in front of a server. All traffic going to the web server is duplicated by the tap and sent to the NIDS sensor.

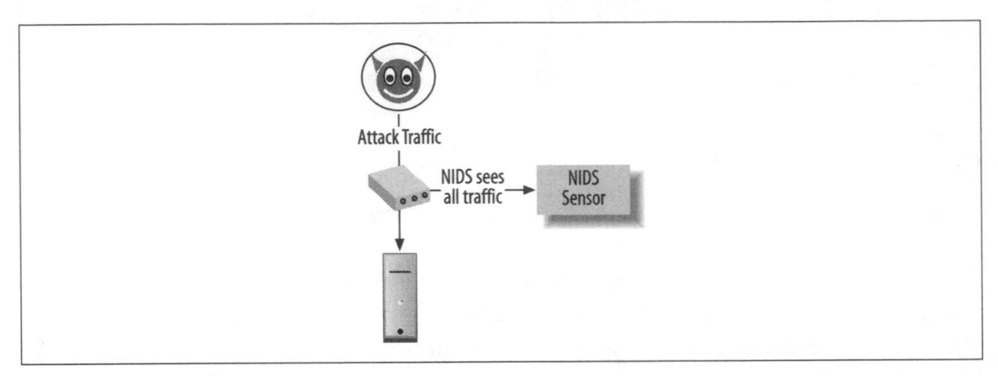

Figure 9-6. Network tap

However, a tap may be infeasible due to network architecture. There may not be a single wire that can be tapped that provides the proper view of your network. Another option is to utilize the potential capability that your Ethernet switches may have. Some switches can flood traffic from multiple ports or VLANs to a single port. For instance, on a Cisco switch, this is called a *span* port. On other devices, it may be called a mirror port. Span ports serve as virtual network taps and may be more flexible than a network tap. In Figure 9-7, traffic from all ports on the switch is forwarded to the span port connected to the NIDS sensor. Typically, a span port is a transmit-only port on the switch. That means any data sent from the NIDS sensor will be dropped by the switch, effectively making a one-way cable attached to the sensor.

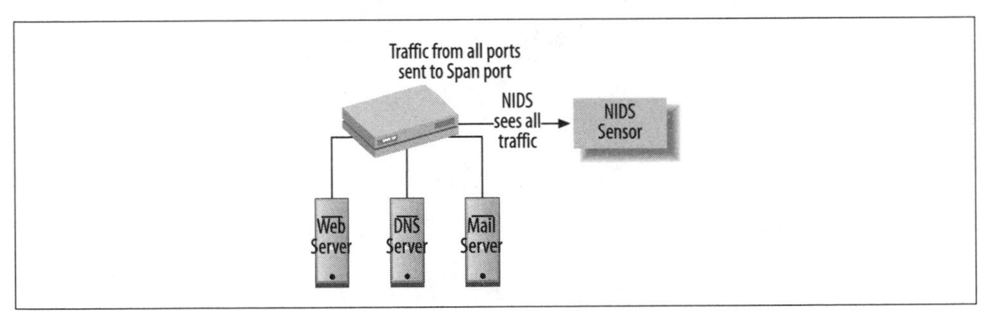

Figure 9-7. Span port on a switch

Another issue with respect to placement is whether your IDS sensor should be in front of or behind your firewall. Firewalls should be stopping the majority of random scans and attacks that target your network. If an attack doesn't make it past the firewall, then there is no chance of it successfully compromising a host. By placing your IDS sensors behind the firewall, you only watch traffic destined for internal hosts.

Internal placement can be good or bad, depending on how you look at it. Since many attacks are blocked by the firewall, you should receive fewer alerts from the IDS. However, the firewall may block precursor events, such as port scans, that may signal a broader attack at a later date. To overcome this, you can always put a sensor on the inside and a sensor on the outside of your firewall. Conversely, you can rely on your firewall logs to provide the detailed information about dropped packets. Again, the placement will be based on your particular environment.

Log Analysis Versus IDS

The term Intrusion Detection System tends to imply a specialized piece of software or hardware designed to detect attacks against a system. Some IDS products are highly sophisticated, enterprise-level systems. Other intrusion detection techniques may have security value, but ultimately may not be considered mainstream intrusion detection. Analysis of logfiles is such a technique.

By analyzing logfiles, an administrator may be able to find traces of an attack. However, logfiles are used for many other purposes besides intrusion detection. Although as it may not be necessary to draw a dark line around what is and what is not IDS, the term "IDS" tends to be associated with a specialized security product. Log analysis, while potentially part of determining if an intrusion has occurred, is more of a general purpose system administration technique. Some tools, like `swatch`, can be configured to monitor logfiles for security specific events such as password failures. These tools, however, are best incorporated into a holistic monitoring view rather than pigeonholed as an IDS solution.

Honeypots Versus IDS

As the old saying goes, "you attract more bees with honey than with vinegar." Similarly, you attract more hackers with an extremely vulnerable system than you do with a well secured system. That's the basic idea behind a honeypot. A honeypot is a host that entices an attacker. It may have active services with perceived vulnerabilities within these services (e.g., a version of OpenSSH that looks vulnerable).

However, the trick with a honeypot is that this "exploitable" host is not what it seems. A honeypot is really a collection of tools designed to fool an attacker into believing he has compromised a live host. However, no compromise has really occurred. Rather, the honeypot is logging the activities of the attacker, attempting to gain insight into his tools, methods, and potentially uncovering his motives for exploiting a host. For instance, a honeypot that is compromised by an automated script may indicate that an attacker was simply looking for a target of opportunity. However, a honeypot where an attacker interactively works with the host and attempts to learn about the services and how to exploit trust relationships may indicate a targeted attack upon your organization.

Honeypots are not IDS hosts. Their purpose in life is to be intruded upon, not detect intrusions. While you can infer activities on the rest of your network from the activities on a honeypot, it is not really a tool that gets integrated into your operations. Honeypots require a great deal of care to ensure they are not used in a manner you do not intend. Further, decomposing what has happened on a honeypot after an intrusion can be very time consuming. Honeypots make great research tools, however for an active enterprise with limited resources, they can be a tremendous waste of time.

More information on honeypots and lessons learned from them can be found at the Honeynet Project's homepage, *http://www.honeynet.org/*. The Honeynet Project is an organization dedicated to the study of how hackers operate and to assisting the community in understanding the ever-changing blackhat landscape.

Intrusion Prevention Systems

An IDS is a passive system. While the information an IDS generates may be useful for detection and responding to intrusions, responses are usually out of band and often involve a human. A recent trend has been for IDS vendors to create Intrusion Prevention Systems (IPS) that place IDS technology in the critical path to an application.

An IPS is an active version of an IDS. Rather than simply reporting an attack, an IPS will actively block the malicious traffic. The core logic is the same as an IDS, however the IPS sits in the network like a firewall and can control access to internal hosts. Figure 9-8 shows an IPS blocking an attack. Compare this to Figure 9-6 where the NIDS sensor is just a leg on the network and cannot do anything to prevent the attack from occurring.

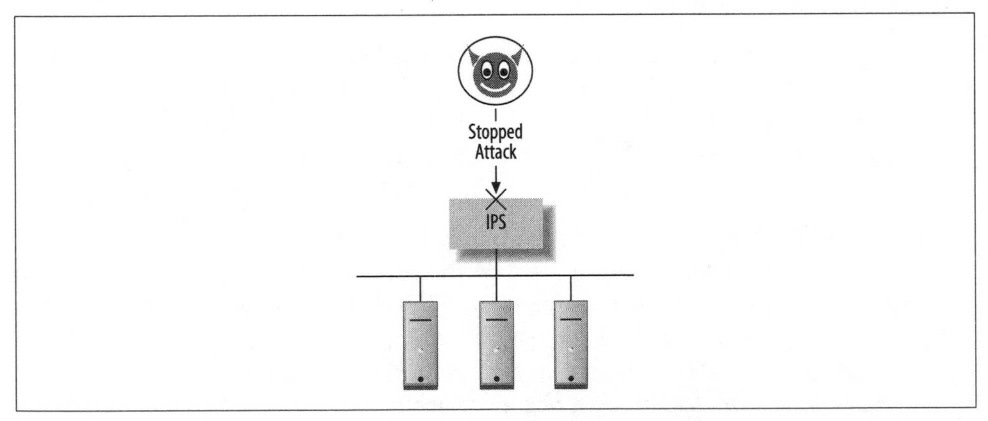

Figure 9-8. Intrusion Prevention System

The danger of an IPS is that legitimate traffic may be blocked by the device. IDSes have a history of excessive false positives. In the case of an IDS, a false positive only results in an alert being generated.

Although we're passing off false positive alerts from an IDS as innocuous, this is done purely for illustrative purposes. Remember the boy who cried "Wolf!" Never underestimate the desensitization that comes with gratuitous alerting.

In an IPS, the false positive can result in valid traffic being denied. In fact, an attacker may exploit this capability by spoofing traffic from a victim host to deny service through the IPS. For some networks, this is completely unacceptable. In the case of an e-commerce web site, denied traffic may be directly tied to loss of revenue. The risk of blocking valid traffic may outweigh the need to protect the network.

NIDS on BSD

If you finally decide to deploy NIDS, the next natural set of questions involve choosing the right IDS software or hardware capable of handing the traffic, and the core operating system to run. If you are reading this book, you may be considering an OpenBSD or FreeBSD-based IDS. Some commercial NIDS are based on a BSD operating system but are not available directly for FreeBSD or OpenBSD. For instance, Real Secure's Network Sensor runs under Windows, RedHat, Solaris, or Nokia's IPSO operating system. Nokia's IPSO is really a BSD-based operating system that looks a great deal like FreeBSD under the hood. However, Network Sensor is not available directly for FreeBSD.

A NIDS sensor is a security device. As such, it needs to be configured with security in mind and to withstand potential attacks. If an attacker discovers an IDS sensor on a network she is attempting to exploit, she will likely attempt to either subvert or disable the sensor. Therefore, the overall security of the sensor itself is crucial. A natural choice when security is a key motivator is OpenBSD. OpenBSD is commonly deployed as an IDS sensor and there is a large amount of community support.

FreeBSD is also a good choice for a NIDS sensor. While FreeBSD does not have the serious security overtones that OpenBSD does, FreeBSD's focus on performance and stability make it attractive for NIDS use. A NIDS may become a mission critical part of your security infrastructure. As such, the network performance, advanced hardware support, and maintainability make FreeBSD a solid choice for more advanced enterprises with more diverse NIDS needs.

Snort

The most popular open source NIDS is Snort. Snort has been around as an open source project for years. In 2002 Marty Roesch, the primary maintainer for Snort, started a for-profit company called Sourcefire. Sourcefire is a commercial IDS vendor that sells sensors and services based on Snort. Several Sourcefire employees still directly contribute to the Snort code base, and the public at large can still contribute to the Snort code as well. Sourcefire has value-added, proprietary software that goes beyond the "stock" Snort.

Snort has grown in popularity over the years. And as it has become more popular, it has also changed to fit the current NIDS needs. Originally a monolithic piece of software, Snort is now modular and adapts to suit different environments. Snort now makes use of preprocessors to speed up packet decoding and make the NIDS harder to evade. Snort also has different output options including flat files, various databases, and custom backends that allow high-speed sensors to operate more efficiently.

Sensor Hardware

The first step in setting up an NIDS sensor is choosing the right hardware. You will need to use a machine with enough horsepower to handle the amount of traffic you believe the sensor will handle, the size of the IDS signature set, the number of attacks you expect to see, as well as your tolerance for risk when it comes to potentially overdriving the host. As you can guess, there is no magic formula that says "use X processor with Y RAM and Z disk space" for an IDS sensor. In general, the more processor, memory, and disk, the better you will be. However, on a lightly loaded DSL-based network a Pentium-II class machine with 256MB of memory and a 10GB drive should be more than enough to run a NIDS sensor.

Your sensor will need at least two NIC cards. One card will connect to the network to be monitored and another to connect to for administrative connections. The network card used on the monitoring interface should be a high quality NIC capable of handling the amount of traffic on the sensor. For instance, the Intel NICs that use the `fxp` drivers are a good choice because the drivers are stable and the cards use hardware for much of the packet handling.

Host Lockdown

The next step in setting up an IDS sensor is to start with a secure initial build as described in Chapter 3. We emphasize, however, that an IDS host is a frontline security device. If it is compromised or made ineffective through a DoS attack, it's useless. An IDS needs to be secured just as a firewall or any other security-critical device would be.

Ideally, the only processes running on a Snort sensor are the core operating system components (such as init(8) and cron(8)), Snort, and some remote management capability like sshd(8). Further, the host should be firewalled to prevent any inbound traffic except ssh-based management traffic. To someone portscanning an IDS from an untrusted host, the sensor should look like a black hole. For extra security, you should consider not assigning an IP address to the interface on the monitored network. Without an IP address, an attacker has nothing to direct an attack against and serves as further security for the sensor.

Installing and Configuring Snort

Snort can be installed directly from the ports tree on both FreeBSD and OpenBSD. If you would rather install Snort by hand, the latest version can be downloaded from *http://www.snort.org/*. The Snort installation documents are largely self-explanatory and the port installs painlessly. One of the more important switches at compile time involves how you want to store alerts. By default, Snort stores attack information in flat files. It also has the ability to log to a database such as MySQL or MS-SQL. So, if you want to store alert information in a MySQL database, then use the **--with-mysql** flag at compile time.

Intrusion detection systems can generate huge logfiles. In fact, a common trick an attacker may play is to send a huge amount of traffic designed to trigger IDS events in an effort to obscure what is really going on. However, even on a good day, IDS logs can build rapidly. Ideally, you should dedicate a separate filesystem, */var/snort* for example, to store Snort logfiles. This will isolate problems caused by runaway Snort logfiles.

There are several important configuration files for Snort. First, the *snort.conf* file controls all the core functionality of Snort including input and output mechanisms, information on local networks, and location of other configuration files. Within *snort.conf* you can indicate what networks are local (HOME_NET) and which ones are not (EXTERNAL_NET). This allows Snort to determine when traffic is originating from within your networks and when traffic originates from outside. By default, the local and external networks are set to any as shown below to indicate Snort really should not care what networks are where.

```
var HOME_NET any
var EXTERNAL_NET any
```

You should set the HOME_NET variable to point to your internal networks. You can specify multiple (comma-separated) networks, but be sure you do not have any space in the variable. If your internal networks are 192.168.0.0/24 and 172.16.0.0/14, for instance, your HOME_NET variable would look like the following:

```
var HOME_NET [192.168.0.0/24,172.16.0.0/24]
```

The *snort.conf* file is well commented and contains more information on all the configuration options available to you. Similarly, the *threshold.conf* file allows for tuning the IDS to make it a bit quieter in the face of excessive alerts. Thresholds can be set to either limit the number of alerts, or completely suppress certain alerts or IP addresses. The *threshold.conf* file has a number of comments that will assist you in setting thresholds. However, for your first attempt, it's best to leave this file untouched.

Snort is a signature-based IDS system, meaning that it compares each packet against a set of rules to determine if that packet matches known malicious patterns. As is the nature of the security world, the definition of a "bad packet" changes from day to day. New attacks are discovered and new mechanisms for detecting attacks are created. Just as it is important to keep your anti-virus definitions up to date, you should keep your Snort rules current too. New Snort rules can be downloaded from *http://www.snort.org/dl/rules/*. Be sure to check the MD5 sum on the web site against the ruleset you've downloaded. You can then place the new rules files in your rules directory and restart Snort.

Containing Snort

As a front line security device, a NIDS sensor can be a target of attack. The obvious lockdown activities may not be sufficient to protect a Snort host from malicious code. There have been several vulnerabilities in Snort where a host could be compromised by traffic not even destined for it. Notably the CERT CA-2003-13 advisory discusses two vulnerabilities in Snort; one in the stream4 preprocessor and one in the RPC preprocessor. From the advisory:

> [The vulnerabilities] allow remote attackers to execute arbitrary code with the privileges of the user running Snort, typically root. Please note that it is not necessary for the attacker to know the IP address of the Snort device they wish to attack; merely sending malicious traffic where it can be observed by an affected Snort sensor is sufficient to exploit these vulnerabilities.

While this vulnerability has been fixed in current versions of Snort, the prospect of this type of attack is troubling. So, what can be done to protect Snort?

First and foremost, Snort can drop privileges to an unprivileged user once it has started. To utilize this capability, create a *snort* user with attributes similar to the following:

```
Username   : snort
Password   : <locked>
Full Name  : Snort User
Uid        : <next>
Class      :
Groups     : snort
Home       : /home/snort
Shell      : /sbin/nologin
Locked     : yes
```

Note that the password should be a * in the password file, just like the other system accounts on the host. This ensures that the account is completely locked out. When starting `snort`, use the **–u *user*** flag to force it to drop privileges. Be sure that the directory in which you are storing your alerts (such as */var/log/snort*) is writable by the snort user and group.

For even more security, Snort can be chrooted to prevent a successful attack from compromising the entire system. `snort` makes this easy by simply providing the `-t` flag at start time and specifying the root of the *chroot(2)*. This kind of chroot is a bit of a poor man's chroot. Rather than running Snort explicitly through the `chroot(8)` utility, Snort chroots itself once it has started. Because of this, the easiest place to chroot it to is the log directory, by default */var/log/snort*. If you attempt to *chroot* somewhere else, Snort has a hard time dealing with it. So, to *chroot* Snort in */var/log/snort* and run as user snort, you would start Snort in the following manner:

```
% sudo snort -u snort -t /var/log/snort
```

With FreeBSD, Snort can be contained in a jail instead. FreeBSD jails were discussed thoroughly in Chapter 2.

Storing Events in Flat Files

By default, Snort stores alerts in flat files on a local filesystem, usually in */var/log/snort*. This makes alerts easy to view and helps the administrator understand what is occurring on a host. In this mode, there is no real central host in the NIDS environment. The Snort sensor is really a standalone device that requires direct interaction to monitor. In small environments, this may be okay, but for larger installations, other capabilities are needed.

Snort makes a single *alerts* file that contains information on all traffic that tripped a rule in the Snort ruleset. To view the alerts in real time, you can use **`tail -f`** to watch the file as it grows. Here is a sample alert from an attack against an IIS server.

```
[**] [119:2:1] (http_inspect) DOUBLE DECODING ATTACK [**]
[Classification: Web Application Attack] [Priority: 1]
11/01-20:29:19.163907 192.168.0.99:52571 -> 192.168.0.10:80
TCP TTL:64 TOS:0x0 ID:5115 IpLen:20 DgmLen:212 DF
***AP*** Seq: 0x71850B78  Ack: 0xCBB1AFB1  Win: 0xFFFF  TcpLen: 32
TCP Options (3) => NOP NOP TS: 549495890 43275571
```

The first line indicates the type of attack this alert was for. In this case, the attack was a double decoding attack that attempts to exploit a weakness in IIS's *Unicode* decoder. The second line indicates that this is a web application attack and it is of the highest priority. Priority 1 means that the attack, if successful, would likely result in compromise of the host. The third line indicates the time the attack occurred and the source and destination IP addresses. The final group of lines provides low level information about the packet. This can be useful if you are doing low-level analysis of an attack. But in the case of a web attack such as this one, the extra packet information is not all that helpful.

Beyond the monolithic *alerts* file, Snort also creates a directory for each source host that generates an alert. Within that directory, Snort will create a file for each flow between the source and destination host. Here we see that three different hosts have been sending attacks through our network.

```
% ls -al /var/log/snort
total 76
drwxr-xr-x  3 snort  snort    512 Nov  1 02:16 .
drwxr-xr-x  3 root   snort   1536 Nov  1 03:02 ..
drwx------  2 snort  snort    512 Nov  1 20:54 10.0.0.1
drwx------  2 snort  snort    512 Nov  1 20:54 192.168.0.56
drwx------  2 snort  snort    512 Nov  1 20:54 192.168.0.99
-rw-------  1 snort  snort  70646 Nov  1 20:55 alert
```

Within the *192.168.0.99* directory we see the files corresponding to each flow.

```
% sudo ls -al /var/log/snort/192.168.0.99/
total 16
drwx------  2 snort  snort   512 Nov  1 20:54 .
drwxr-xr-x  3 snort  snort   512 Nov  1 02:16 ..
-rw-------  1 snort  snort  1044 Nov  1 02:16 TCP:49455-80
-rw-------  1 snort  snort  1044 Nov  1 02:16 TCP:49536-80
-rw-------  1 snort  snort  1041 Nov  1 20:54 TCP:52571-80
-rw-------  1 snort  snort  1041 Nov  1 20:54 TCP:52600-80
-rw-------  1 snort  snort  1038 Nov  1 20:54 TCP:52601-80
-rw-------  1 snort  snort  1041 Nov  1 20:54 TCP:52610-80
```

In this case, we can see there have been six different attacks the Snort sensor has detected. The filenames indicate the protocol (in this case TCP), the source port, and the destination port. All of these attacks target the web server on port 80.

Storing Events in MySQL

If you are looking to deploy more than one sensor, you should look beyond the default flat file capability of Snort. By using a database server connected to an internal network, multiple IDS can log alert information to a single source giving you a one-stop shop to examine alerts and monitor your network. Using a database server also has a security benefit. By running the server on a host inside your network (i.e., not running it on a sensor itself) and protecting it from the outside world, you no longer have to interact directly with the IDS sensors to analyze events. This allows for the sensors to be locked down to a greater extent and further limits your external exposure.

The first step is to install a database like MySQL. MySQL is an open source and mature database used for a variety of applications. It is widely supported and has a number of different options in the ports tree. You can install the appropriate MySQL port or build MySQL by hand. Installation instructions are plentiful online.

Properly installing MySQL and securely configuring it is a complex topic and beyond the scope of this chapter. However it is important that your database server, like any other host and application in your network, be configured and deployed securely. For more information on MySQL database security see *http://dev.mysql.com/doc/mysql/en/Security.html.*

After MySQL is installed, configured, and running on your system, you must create a database to hold the Snort alerts.

```
% echo "CREATE DATABASE snort;" | mysql -u root -p
```

The database needs to be have tables created to match the schema Snort is expecting. The Snort distribution contains SQL statements that will automatically create all the proper tables. If you installed Snort from ports, the MySQL-specific SQL statements will be in a file called *create_mysql* within the ports directory tree.

```
% mysql -D snort -u root -p < /usr/ports/security/snort/work/snort-XX/contrib/create_
mysql
```

Next, we will want to access the MySQL database as a user other than root. Note that a database user is not the same as an operating system user. However, it is convenient to have the usernames for the operating system be the same as the database to make things more consistent. When you grant a user access to a table in MySQL, a database user with the same name is automatically created. So first we will configure MySQL to allow a Snort user to INSERT and SELECT on the entire Snort database and UPDATE on the sensor table. UPDATE is required so sensors can be brought online automatically.

```
% mysql
> grant INSERT,SELECT on snort.* to snort@localhost;
> grant INSERT,SELECT,UPDATE on snort.sensor to snort@localhost;
> exit;
% mysqladmin -u snort password password
```

Finally, the remote Snort sensor needs to be configured to export the alerts to the MySQL database host. In the *snort.conf* file, look for a series of commented-out `output database` directives. Add the following line in that area of the configuration file.

```
output database: log, mysql, user=snort password=snort dbname=snort host=remotehost
```

Restart the Snort sensor process and you should be all set. If there is a firewall between your Snort sensor and your database, you will need to open up the MySQL port (TCP 3306) between the sensor and the database server. Snort is now logging to the remote database. The *README.database* has much more information about using snort with database backends. Further, there are a whole series of README files in the Snort distribution that provide valuable insight on a variety of topics including optimization, alternate operating systems, and HTTP inspection.

There are downsides to logging your IDS events to a central database server. Now, rather than having events logged locally, they are going over the network. With busy IDS sensors, this may result in excessive amounts of network traffic. Or, it may result in overtaxing the database server. You will have to appropriately plan for the amount of IDS traffic you expect to receive on your worst days. The database server needs to be able to receive the number of events and allow you to make queries. This means the server needs to have enough processing power, RAM, disk space, and network capacity. Also the network must have enough capacity, including any intermediary firewalls. In some cases, a completely separate network used to collect IDS data may be the solution.

Snort with PF

The firewall PF has the ability to forward packets to a specialized log interface, `pflog0`. Packets sent to `pflog0` are basically pcap*(3)* formatted and can be viewed or sniffed by pcap aware applications. Snort can be listen on the `pflog0` interface just like any other interface on the system. This capability opens up a variety of interesting possibilities.

If you are logging all denied traffic on your firewall, Snort will be able to identitfy attacks that are in this denied traffic. To log denied traffic, you can use the following in your *pf.conf* file:

```
block in log all
```

This sounds useful but may actually prevent you from seeing certain attacks. Snort will alarm on attacks and scans that only require one packet per session to be detected. For instance, a portscan or a packet that has strange header values will cause Snort to send an alert. However, most TCP-based attacks will not trigger a Snort event. The reason is simple: TCP-based attacks need to complete the TCP three-way handshake in order to send the malicious data. However, if the firewall blocks the initial connection request, thereby preventing the TCP session from being established, Snort will never see any malicious data.

As an example, consider a *Unicode* attack against a Microsoft IIS web server. The attack host needs to create a valid TCP session and then send a malformed HTTP request to the vulnerable server. If your firewall blocks the initial SYN packet and logs it to `pflog0`, the attack host will never get a chance to send the malformed HTTP request.

Conversely, your PF firewall could permit and log traffic to a host you are attempting to monitor. Snort could monitor this traffic and watch for attacks targeting that host. Since the traffic is allowed, you no longer have the problem with not detecting TCP-based attacks. In your *pf.conf* file you could add the following to capture all allowed traffic:

```
pass in log all from any to any keep state
```

Using Snort to monitor packets on `pflog0` is an interesting capability. Normally, you will not need to use Snort in this manner. However, there are times when this trick may come in very handy.

ACID

Digging through Snort alerts, regardless of how they are stored, can be a real headache. Beyond merely being difficult to manage, it can be even harder to recognize patterns, perform queries, and gather statistics. There are a number of tools that help with NIDS log analysis. One of the most popular tools is the Analysis Console for Intrusion Databases (ACID), a PHP-based system for querying and analyzing NIDS alerts.

ACID is designed to be a general-purpose intrusion detection analysis system. It is not focused simply on Snort; ACID can pull in firewall logs and raw TCP dumps as well. Although there are more input methods planned, development of ACID seems to have stalled. The last release as of the time of this writing was January 2003. Nevertheless, even with a slightly antiquated code base, ACID is still a valuable tool.

Installing ACID

FreeBSD administrators may install ACID from *ports/acid* or download ACID from the main ACID site, available at: *http://www.andrew.cmu.edu/user/rdanyliw/snort/snortacid.html*. OpenBSD administrators must fetch the compressed tarball and install by hand.

ACID has many dependencies including Apache, PHP, and MysSl. Given that normally you try to run your IDS sensors in a secure and locked-down configuration, it is advisable to run ACID on asystem other than your sensor host. ACID should be run on a backend host that has access to all your Snort logs. Ideally, you're using MySQL or some other database on a central server to store all the Snort alerts, and ACID can be pointed directly at this server, or even run on the same host.

Configuring ACID

Once ACID is installed, there are only a few small configuration changes left to make. The *acid_conf.php* file controls the behavior of ACID. In it, you can set the type of database ACID is running against and the specifics about how to access the database. In Example 9-1, ACID is running on the same host as the MySQL database server. Adjust the values in the *acid_conf.php* to match your environment.

Example 9-1. acid_conf.php

```
$dbtype             = "mysql";
$alert_dbname    = "snort";
```

Example 9-1. acid_conf.php (continued)

```
$alert_host     = "localhost";
$alert_port     = "";
$alert_user     = "root";
$alert_password = "MySQLrootpass";
$archive_dbname   = "snort_archive";
$archive_host     = "localhost";
$archive_port     = "";
$archive_user     = "root";
$archive_password = "MySQLrootpass";
```

There may be other configuration options that need to change based on your local environment. Be sure to check the entire configuration file to see if anything needs to be modified.

ACID does not provide any native security. If users have IP level access to your web server and you have no security protecting ACID, they will be able to view your IDS logs. This is an advantage you don't want to give an attacker. At the time this book was witten, querying Google for "Analysis Console for Intrusion Databases" and "queried on" (two strings on the main ACID page) resulted in over 70 publicly accessible ACID installations.

Put your ACID installation behind your external firewall and make sure users on the Internet at large cannot reach it. Also, consider using HTTP authentication available under Apache to provide a user/password based protection mechanism. You will also want to use SSL to protect the authentication credentials and subsequent data in transit. Configuring Apache to provide SSL encrypted content and authentication is covered in Chapter 6.

Running ACID

The screenshot of ACID in Figure 9-9 speaks volumes about its ability to display information about alerts Snort has generated. Prior to running ACID, we had flat files and database tables to dig through. While all the information was there, it was hard to determine what was really going on. ACID provides one-click views into the types of attacks occuring, the most frequent source and destination IPs and ports, and overall traffic makeup. It also has a search page that allows you to dig down into the data to find exactly what you want. ACID is largely GUI driven, so it is relatively self-explanatory. The best way to learn how to use ACID is to get a sensor up and running and watch as the attacks roll in.

HIDS on BSD

While not as glamorous as NIDS, HIDS can be extremely valuable in detecting an attack that has actually been successfully carried out. One of the big failings with most NIDS systems is their inability to recognize if an attack launched against a host

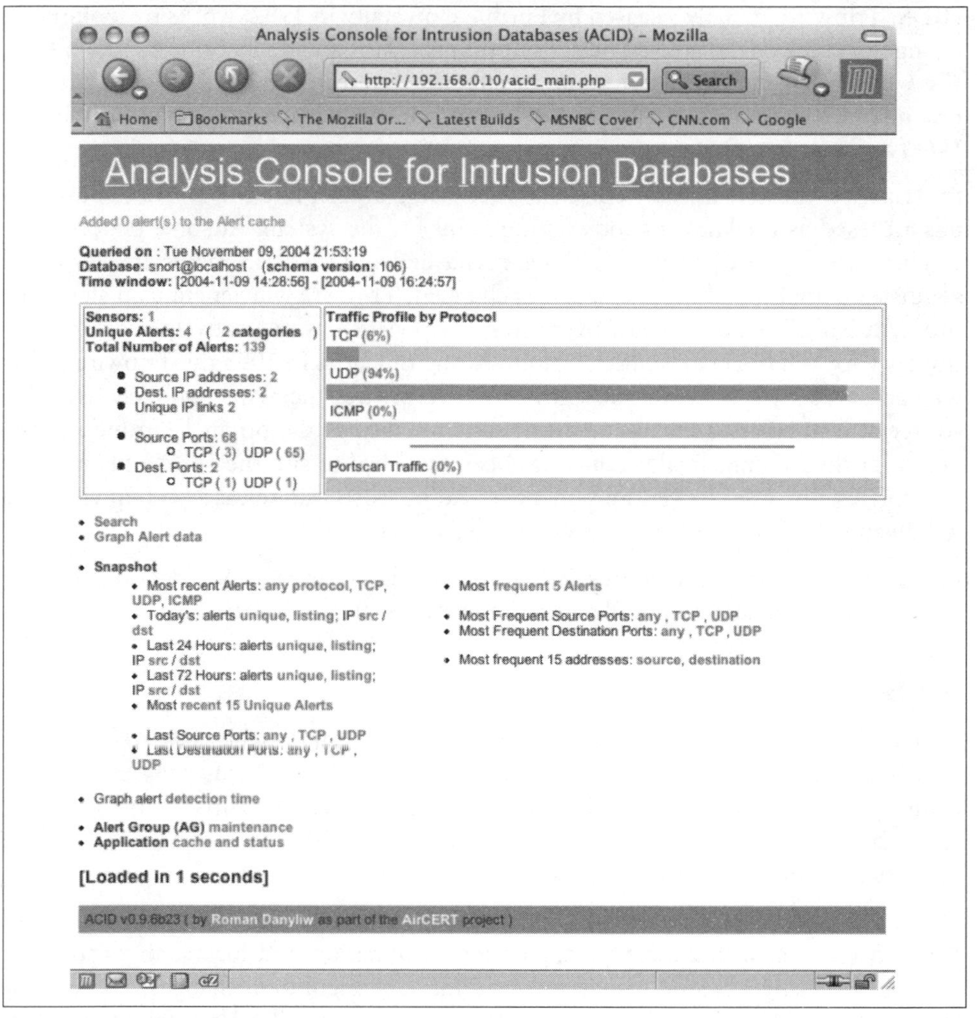

Figure 9-9. The main ACID screen

was successful in compromising the host. From the perspective of watching network traffic and assembling signatures for successful exploitation, NIDS have a long way to go.

However, once an attacker has broken in, he will likely leave footprints all over the system. Files will be created or modified. Processes will be terminated. Kernel parameters may be changed. A HIDS should be able to detect at least some of these footprints and alert youto the fact that something has gone very wrong.

HIDS come in many shapes and sizes on FreeBSD and OpenBSD. One of the most important features of HIDS in even the smallest networks is the ability to remotely manage and monitor the HIDS process. Tripwire is one of the oldest and best-known

HIDS. Tripwire, initially released by Purdue University in 1992, works by looking for changes to files on a system. The assumption is that if an attacker breaks into a host, she will modify core system files in an effort to leverage the host for more attacks. For instance, an attacker may install Trojan horses in place of system utilities like `ls(1)` and `netstat(1)`.

In Tripwire, files are initially checksummed using a hash like MD5. These hash values are used as the known good starting point for the system. At some periodic rate (nightly, weekly, and so on), the files are rehashed and the hash values are compared against the original values. If a hash has changed, Tripwire will generate an alert. The problem is that the open source version of Tripwire does not natively provide functionality for remote management or monitoring of alerts. In 1998 the Tripwire utility was acquired by a company now known as Tripwire, Inc. Their publicly available source still provides basically the same functionality as the original Purdue release. However their commercial product has been modified to suit the needs of large-scale enterprises. In order to centrally manage the open source release of Tripwire, you will need to roll your own form of centralized management.

Fear not! There are open source HIDS that provide Tripwire-like functionality and are manageable and monitorable on an enterprise scale.

Osiris

Osiris is a distributed host integrity verification program designed to detect changes to a host that may be the result of an intrusion. Unlike antivirus programs, which examine files on a host to look for specific traces of a virus, Osiris simply looks for any change. This allows a system administrator to decide if the change is due to a security problem or was expected.

Osiris utilizes a client/server model that allows it to scale. It has a central management daemon (`osirismd`) that stores configuration information and logs changes to client systems. By using a central management daemon, configuration changes can be made at a single location and pushed to remote clients automatically. Also, because the logs of what has changed on the client hosts are stored and compared locally on the central management server, patterns in changes are easy to recognize. For instance, if a new system administrator is hired and his user account is added to all your servers at once, the Osiris report will present this change in an easy to understand fashion. The management server is controlled by the management utility (`osiris`) that allows real-time updates to the configuration of the management daemon.

Whatever host integrity tool you are running, it is of little use if you do not have a known good starting point. Your initial scan of a host should be performed when it is in a secure state and you are sure none of the files you want to monitor have been maliciously altered. This may be easier said than done, however, especially if you have a large, preexisting server base. So, sometimes you just have to take a leap of faith on your initial scan. The author of Osiris maintains an online database of known good checksums for many versions of various operating systems. If you have a checksum of a binary that you don't know if it has been modified, check out *http://www.knowngoods.org/*.

On the client side, Osiris has a scan agent (`osirisd`) that retrieves its configuration from the management server, scans the local host, and returns results. Figure 9-10 shows the relationship between the components of Osiris.

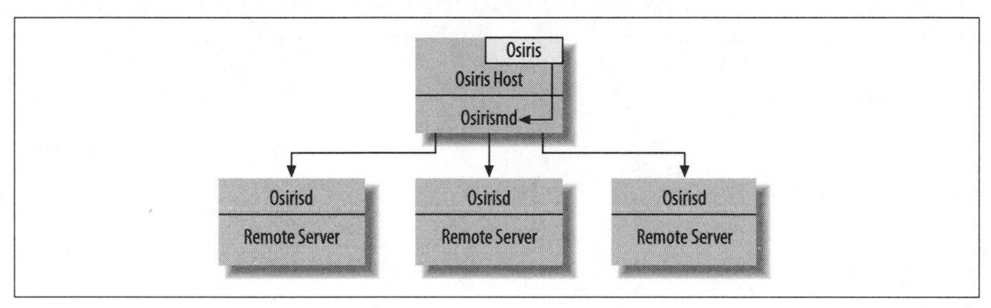

Figure 9-10. Structure of Osiris

Installing and Configuring Osiris

Like many other popular utilities, Osiris is in the FreeBSD ports tree. OpenBSD administrators must obtain the source directly from *http://osiris.shmoo.com/*. Not only can you install Osiris, you can also make a tarball of the Osiris management console software or agent software. In the Osiris source directory, use **`make console`** to create the management console package and **`make agent`** to make the agent package. The agent package is particularly useful as it allows you to have a complete package that can be deployed to multiple hosts rapidly.

Once Osiris is installed, start `osirismd` and point it towards the directory where it will store information. By default, this is */usr/local/osiris*.

```
% sudo osirismd -r /usr/local/osiris
```

The first time the management console starts, it automatically creates certificates to use for secure communication with the scan agents. Once this is done, you are prompted as to whether or not you want to trust the newly created certificate. Select yes and you find yourself at a username prompt. Enter a username of **`admin`** and an empty password to access Osiris. At the `osiris` prompt, run `edit-mhost` to set up variables on the management console. Edit the values in the configuration to suit your needs as shown in Example 9-2.

Example 9-2. Using edit-mhost to set up Osiris

```
osiris-4.0.5-release: edit-mhost
[ edit management host (localhost) ]
  > syslog facility [DAEMON]:
  > control port [2266]:
  > http host name (uses system name by default) []:
  > http control port [2267]:
  > notify email (default for hosts) []: sysadmin@test.com
  > admin email (gets all mail)[]:  uberadmin@test.com
  > notification smtp host [127.0.0.1]: mail.test.com
  > notification smtp port [25]:
  > authorized hosts:
   127.0.0.1
  Modify authorization list (y/n)? [n]
[ management config (localhost) ]
syslog_facility = DAEMON
control_port = 2266
http_port = 2267
http_host =
notify_email =  sysadmin@test.com
admin_email =  uberadmin@test.com
notify_smtp_host = mail.test.com
notify_smtp_port = 25
hosts_directory =
allow = 127.0.0.1
```

Once these changes are made, they take effect with `osirismd` automatically.

Now you need to bring up the scan agents on the hosts you wish to monitor. A good starting point is the host that `osirismd` is running on. Untar the tarball you made in the install process and execute the **`install.sh`** script within the created directory. Once the scan agent is installed and started, go back to the management console prompt and run the `new-host` command, as shown in Example 9-3. `new-host` needs to be run for each scan agent that is brought online. The options in the `new-host` script are relatively straightforward and are easily tailored to your environment. At the end the configuration, Osiris pushes a default configuration to the scan agent based on the OS of the host and then starts the baseline scan.

Example 9-3. Running new-host for every host you want to mointor

```
Is this correct (y/n)? y
 >>> new host (management) has been created.
Initialize this host? (yes/no): yes
Initializing a host will push over a configuration, start
a scan, and set the created database to be the
trusted database.
Are you sure you want to initialize this host (yes/no): yes
```

Example 9-3. Running new-host for every host you want to mointor (continued)

```
OS Name: FreeBSD
OS Version: 5.2.1-RELEASE

use the default configuration for this OS? (yes/no): yes
 >>> configuration (default.freebsd) has been pushed.
 >>> scanning process was started on host: management
```

At this point, the scan kicks off and Osiris returns to its prompt. Repeat this process for all the hosts you wish to scan and you'll have a functioning Osiris environment.

There are a variety of configuration (and reconfiguration) commands available at the Osiris prompt. A simple question mark (?) at the prompt brings up the listing including commands to list databases, modify agent configurations, and manually kick off scans.

Running Osiris

Osiris will automatically scan hosts based on the scheduling information you supplied during the agent configuration. If a change is detected, an email will be sent to the notification email address. It is then up to the person notified to determine if the change was a valid one. For instance, Example 9-4 shows an email from Osiris alerting that the netstat utility has changed.

Example 9-4. Sample Osiris alert about netstat

```
If these changes are approved, visit the URL below to set the
latest scan database to be the trusted database. Or, login to the
management console and set the trusted database to 60.If these
notifications persist, you may need to modify the scan config for
this host.

    <https://management.test.com:2267/?host=management&base_db=60>

Change Statistics:
-----------------------------------
        checksums: 1
       SUID files: 0
 root-owned files: 0
 file permissions: 0
        new files: 0
    missing files: 0
total differences: 4
     compare time: Fri Sep 19 23:27:37 2003
             host: management
         log file: no log file generated, see system log.
          base db: 59
       compare db: 60

[management][cmp][/usr/sbin/osirismd][checksum][ db717c99abad90ab290f40b157cca2c9,
22f6408a505991a8a7a69d9bffe93611]
```

Example 9-4. Sample Osiris alert about netstat (continued)

```
[management][cmp][/usr/sbin/osirismd][mtime][Mon Feb 23 16:34:04 2004,Mon Nov 1 13:12:52
2004]
[management][cmp][/usr/sbin/osirismd][ctime][ Mon Feb 23 16:34:04 2004, Mon Nov 1 13:12:52
2004]
[management][cmp][/usr/sbin/osirismd][bytes][ 106344,6073419]
```

On the face of it, this change seems pretty suspect. The `netstat` binary should only change with a system upgrade or if it's patched for some reason. Further, it has been replaced by a binary that is 6 megabytes in size, versus the 106 kilobytes it originally was. This incident is definitely worth exploring.

A quick word on system updating. When performing a large-scale upgrade, such as upgrading FreeBSD from source, tools such as Osiris can really become unwieldy. Many system libraries and utilities will be modified creating a massive number of deltas that need to be examined. It is usually impossible to validate all the changes made by the system during an upgrade. This is one of those times when you may need to take a leap of faith and create a new database assuming the new host is still trusted to be safe.

Wrapping Up

This chapter has only scratched the surface of IDS. It is a complicated topic with many tools and techniques available to help detect intrusions and manage your IDS system at a large scale. However, be wary that IDS is not for everyone. Deploying, administering, and monitoring an IDS system can be time consuming and may take you away from other, more important, security-related tasks. If you decide IDS is for you, then the BSD-based operating systems provide an excellent foundation. With their speed and maintainability, FreeBSD and OpenBSD are solid operating systems on which you can support a robust IDS infrastructure.

Resources

Snort Users' Guide
: The *Snort Users' Guide* is available online at *http://www.snort.org/docs/snort_manual/*. It is a valuable resource, especially as you become more familiar with Snort and how it functions on your network.

Osiris Users' Handbook (http://osiris.shmoo.com/docs/handbook.html)
: The *Osiris Users' Handbook* describes the ins and outs of how to deploy and maintain Osiris.

PART III

Auditing and Incident Response

Auditing and incident response are topics in system administration theory that are critical but often overlooked. They are not specific services that you run as much as concerns you keep in the back of your mind all the time.

- Chapter 10, *Managing the Audit Trails*
- Chapter 11, *Incident Response and Forensics*

CHAPTER 10

Managing the Audit Trails

Raspberry. There's only one man who would dare give me the raspberry: Lone Star!
—Dark Helmet
Spaceballs

The word audit usually makes people a little nervous; even when they have nothing to hide. An audit, in the world of accountants, is to examine an individual or organization's financial records formally. The goal of an audit is either to validate that people or organizations have followed the letter of the law, or uncover their horrible misdeeds. The success of an audit must be based upon *records* of transactions. Without these records, performing an audit requires far more detective work or is rendered impossible.

In the computing world, audits can be formal or informal interrupt-driven processes performed by system administrators to answer questions. A question like "Why haven't we received the mail our client sent?" sends administrators scurrying through mail logs. A more difficult question to answer might be, "Why didn't that dynamic web page load right?" because web server access logs, error logs, and database query logs may need to be consulted to build a complete picture of what transpired. In a security context, an incident response team conducts an audit to try to uncover any transgressions and perform root cause analysis. All these questions and mysteries can be solved...as long as you have a record of the transactions, or *logs*.

A part of our job as system administrators is to keep an eye on the systems we have built and that we administer. We explored the topic of system health monitoring as one of the ways to do this in Chapter 4. An aspect of a system's overall health in some cases is useful as an indicator of security breaches. Likewise, a system's logs often contain events pertaining to the security of the system: unauthorized login attempts or connections, frequent application crashes, mail relay attempts, and attempts to write to read-only FTP folders are examples of events that might spur an investigation. Automated monitoring of logs helps us guarantee that these events will be noticed and an investigation, or audit, can then ensue.

This chapter is about monitoring our systems through log analysis and ensuring that we're able to answer questions that might arise. To accomplish this task we must first ensure that our systems are generating the logs in which we're interested. The logfiles themselves are of moderate use already, but consolidating them on a single host helps ensure their integrity and perform audits more effectively. Finally, with a single storage location for logfiles, we can deploy a log monitoring system to alert us when unusual events occur. We cover each of these topics in turn.

System Logging

Logging is the process of recording events as they transpire. All operating systems generate events based on a system administrator's (or a default) configuration. Fortunately, both FreeBSD and OpenBSD give us a good starting point, with pretty reasonable default configurations. Applications installed on the operating system often also generate events and log them using the operating system's logging mechanism or in their own logfiles.

Logs help administrators diagnose problems with applications, provide instant warning and alert capability (which can be hooked into something that sends an email or page), and serve as fodder for forensic analysis. They help answer both trivial questions such as, "What errors did my application produce?" and help solve far more complex mysteries. It might take several logfiles, for example, to follow a user who logged into one system and, through some sequence of events, managed to gain escalated privileges on another.

The process of analyzing (often) disparate logfiles to determine how one event A eventually leads to another event Z is called auditing. The set of interrelated events that you identify between A and Z in the analysis is the audit trail. These audit trails don't really exist without a question you are trying to answer: it is the person or piece of data whose progress through systems you are trying to trace that defines these audit trails. Building these requires that you have set up logging appropriately on your system.

Logging, despite being a fairly well-understood concept, is frequently overlooked by administrators. Most administrators of Unix-based operating systems either minimally configure the logging functionality or they leave the default configuration intact. FreeBSD and OpenBSD administrators expect to find their *maillog*, *messages* log, and other logfiles in */var/log*, and some choose not to adjust the logging configuration. Unfortunately, without carefully examining the way your system and installed applications are set up to create logs, you probably will not have the information you need to build an audit trail when you need one.

As promised in Chapter 3, we revisit the topic of configuring `syslogd(8)` in this chapter. We explore some of the places we can send logfiles, and look at the factors that affect our decision-making process. Of course, no discussion about logging is complete without covering log rotation and retention. Finally, we examine some of the popular automated log-checking and system-monitoring tools available for the BSD operating systems.

Logging via syslogd

The syslog daemon, `syslogd`, is installed with the base distributions of FreeBSD and OpenBSD. `syslogd` accepts logs from the kernel (from */dev/klog*) and from applications running on the system via the logging socket it creates (*/var/run/log* on FreeBSD and */dev/log* on OpenBSD by default). It can also accept log messages from other systems over UDP port 514 (by default) when configured to do so. A machine running `syslogd` that accepts remote logs in this way is typically called a *loghost*. The configuration file for `syslogd`, */etc/syslog.conf*, controls what happens to log entries once they are received by the daemon.

syslog.conf Configuration

Several configuration parameters control how incoming logs are handled. The most basic elements are *facility* and *level*, which make up the selector field in the *syslog.conf* file. These facilities describe the part of the system generating the message, and the level describes the message severity. Syslog can then perform a variety of *actions* on the selected log messages. When an asterisk (*) is used in the place of either facility and/or level, it's understood to mean *all* facilities and/or levels.

The asterisk doesn't always mean all levels in other operating systems. In some operating systems, for example, an asterisk not only matches the levels from `debug` to `emerg`, it also matches the keyword `none`. As a result, *syslog.conf* files with an asterisk in the level field on this platform will cause the daemon to ignore all logs for the associated facility. If you have a secure file distribution scheme in a heterogeneous environment, take note.

Facilities and levels may also be specified for a subset of incoming logs through program and hostname specifications. We describe this in some detail later in this chapter. The action, the last important configuration element, is covered at the end of the section.

Syslog Facilities

OpenBSD includes the facilities `auth`, `authpriv`, `cron`, `daemon`, `ftp`, `kern`, `lpr`, `mail`, `mark`, `news`, `syslog`, `user`, `uucp`, and `local0` through `local7`. FreeBSD adds the facilities `console` and `security`. Other operating systems have a slightly different set of facilities. The specific variations between operating systems are not important. What is important is to remember that these differences exist and result in two issues: building software and remote logging.

When building software on BSD systems, bear in mind that although you may expect the software to use a given facility, the OS on which the software was designed may not have had that facility. Therefore the application programmer may log, by default, to another arbitrary facility. Software built out of ports generally "does the right thing." When building a loghost as described later in this chapter, you may find yourself accepting log messages from various operating systems. As a result, facility specification cannot be used as a means of capturing remote logs when the source operating system does not support a given facility.

Caveats aside, most applications allow for a user-configurable facility so you can choose something that makes sense in your environment. Let's look closely at the facilities present in the OpenBSD and FreeBSD operating systems.

`auth`
: For messages pertaining to authentication like those produced by `login(1)`, `su(1)`, `getty(8)`, and `sshd(8)`.

`authpriv`
: For messages like `auth` that should only be read by privileged individuals. For example, failed logins are logged to both `auth` and `authpriv`, but the attempted username is only logged to `authpriv`, as shown:

```
authpriv: Mar 28 18:31:56 dreadnaught login: 1 LOGIN FAILURE ON ttyp0, nobody
    auth: Mar 28 18:31:56 dreadnaught login: 1 LOGIN FAILURE ON ttyp0
```

`console` *(FreeBSD only)*
: This facility allows `syslogd` to capture log messages written to */dev/console* by the kernel console output driver.

`cron`
: For messages generated by the `cron(8)` daemon, and for when users run `crontab(1)`. If you write administrative scripts that are meant to run out of `cron`, you might want to send messages to this facility.

`daemon`
: For messages generated by system daemons like `routed(8)` that are not sent to other facilities.

`ftp`
: As the name implies, this facility is for the file transfer protocol daemon, `ftpd(8)`. You can expect the FTP daemon included in the base operating system to log to this facility. While most FTP daemons you use automatically configure themselves to log to this facility (especially when they are installed through the ports tree), make sure you check the application's logging behavior and ensure FTP logs don't show up under the `daemon` facility.

`kern`
: Kernel messages read from */dev/klog* are sent to this facility. User processes are not permitted to log kernel messages—any attempts to do so are quietly redirected to the `user` facility. Likewise, kernel messages from remote systems will end up in the `user` facility. FreeBSD administrators may force the daemon to accept events submitted to the `kern` facility by users by using the `–k` argument to `syslogd`.

`local0` *through* `local7`
: The manual page for *syslog.conf(5)* specifies that these facilities are for local use. This means that they may be defined locally by the organization in which they are used, not that they are somehow not usable by logs received from remote systems in a loghost context. You, the administrator, may define these seven facilities to provide consistent facilities per local policies. For instance, you might choose to use these levels in conjunction with EventReporter (formerly EventSLog), which sends Windows NT event logs to Unix systems' `syslogd`.

`lpr`
: For messages generated by `lpr(1)`, `lpc(8)`, `lpd(8)`. In other words, this facility is for messages relating to the line printing and spooling daemon.

`mail`
: As intuitively named as many of the other facilities, this facility is for messages pertaining to mail. Expect messages to show up here from Sendmail, Postfix, and other mail-related programs like the popular Courier IMAP and POP mail server software.

`mark`
: The `mark` facility is a pseudofacility and used only by `syslogd`. When specified, *mark* messages are generated. The frequency at which this occurs depends on the parameter given to the `–m` argument of `syslogd`. For logfiles that grow very slowly, it can be useful to add `mark` messages so that you have confidence that `syslogd` is still writing to logfiles. Mark messages follow the following form:

```
date/timestamp hostname -- MARK --
```

`news`
: Messages generated by the programs responsible for providing the network news system (`nntp`, for example) be assigned to this facility.

`security` *(FreeBSD only)*
: Security related subsystems like FreeBSD's `ipfw(4)` firewall will log to this facility.

`syslog`
: Syslog-related messages are sent to this facility. Generally this includes messages pertaining to `syslogd`'s startup and problems with its configuration.

`user`
: When no facility is specified, messages received by `syslogd` are sent to this facility. As mentioned earlier, messages from user processes with the kernel facility and messages from the kernel on remote systems are automatically assigned the user facility, though FreeBSD administrators may use the `-k` argument to `syslogd` to alter this behavior.

`uucp`
: For messages pertaining to the `uucp` system generated by `uucp`-related binaries.

Understanding Syslog facilities will get you well on the way to managing your logfiles. Before really understanding how logging works using Syslog, however, we need to examine logging levels and actions.

Syslog Levels

Syslog levels are a great deal simpler than facilities and consistent across operating systems. For one, there are only eight of them: `debug`, `info`, `notice`, `warning`, `err`, `crit`, `alert`, and `emerg`. There is little to contribute to the definition of these levels, so a slightly modified excerpt from the `syslog(3)` manpage is reproduced here:

`emerg`
: A panic condition. This is normally broadcast to all users.

`alert`
: A condition that should be corrected immediately, such as a corrupted system database.

`crit`
: Critical conditions, e.g., hard device errors.

`err`
: Errors.

`warning`
: Warning messages.

`notice`
: Conditions that are not error conditions, but should possibly be handled specially.

`info`
: Informational messages.

`debug`
: Messages that contain information normally of use only when debugging a program.

`none`
: The `none` pseudo-priority causes messages of the attached level to not be logged.

Syslog levels form the only other component required for complete specification of the selector field used in the *syslog.conf* file. This selector by default will apply to all messages handled by `syslogd`, but this behavior may be modified by using a program or hostname specification.

Program and Hostname Matching

The *syslog.conf* file may be broken into configuration blocks that apply to specific programs or hostnames. As discussed earlier, when dealing with Syslog messages arriving from other hosts on the network, a local facility may not be available on all remote systems. In this case, using a program specification, you can capture logs from this host even when the message originated from a remote system with a different facility. Example 10-1 shows a typical configuration for the capture of FTP logs on a system running `syslogd`.

Example 10-1. Basic syslog.conf to capture FTP logs

```
ftp.info                action1
```

This will work fine as long as the FTP program on this host and any other hosts that use this host as a loghost are configured to use the `ftp` facility. Some non-BSD operating systems, however, lack the `ftp` facility and instead log FTP messages to the `daemon` facility. If your BSD system is accepting logs from other systems, it may be useful to consolidate FTP logs into one file although if they are not distinguishable by facility, the problem is a little trickier.

To capture the FTP logs sent to the daemon facility along with your other FTP logs, specify the program `ftpd` after an exclamation mark (`!`) on a blank line as shown in Example 10-2. This matches all log entries with the `ftpd[`*`pid`*`]:` string.

Example 10-2. Capture FTP logs when facility may not be FTP

```
!ftpd
*.info                  action1
```

In FreeBSD, hostnames may be specified by using a plus sign (+). This specification is not supported in OpenBSD. Example 10-3 demonstrates how it's possible to segregate log entries on a host-by-host or host-group basis.

Example 10-3. Split logfiles based on hostname

```
+mailhost
mail.*                  action-A
auth.*                  action-B
+webserv1,webserv2
cron.notice             action-C
```

Syslog Actions

Now that we know a bit about log specification, it's time to examine how to configure syslogd to do something with log messages. On both FreeBSD and OpenBSD platforms, syslogd supports five log actions. Four of them are the same and likely to be familiar to even the novice administrator. They are as follows:

Log to a file/path
: When a pathname is specified as the log action, messages are appended to the file specified. When syslogd starts, these logfiles must already exist; syslogd does not create logfiles.

Log to the loghost
: To configure syslogd to send messages to another system, specify a hostname preceded by an at (@) sign. Typically all systems other than the loghost will log to @loghost. A canonical name (CNAME) entry is added to the local name servers to point requests for the hostname loghost to the appropriate system.

Logging to another host significantly improves your ability to build a successful audit trail for a variety of reasons. We go into more detail in the "Securing a Loghost" section, later in this chapter.

Log to specific users
: By specifying user accounts, separated by commas, log messages can be sent to specific users when they are logged in. This is useful for important administrative alerts.

Log to all logged-in users
: Specify an asterisk (*) and all logged-in users will receive the log message on their pseudo-terminal. This can be useful for critical system failures, disk space usage alerts, and so on.

Although the aforementioned four actions are familiar, there are a variety of non-file locations to which log messages may be sent using the pathname specification. These are as follows:

Log to the console
: It's possible to cause specific messages to be directed straight to the console by specifying the pathname as */dev/console*.

Log to the printer
: In high-security environments, it may be necessary to maintain physical paper logs. Adept intruders are often able to clean up any traces that they were on your system by modifying the system logs and other key files. Logging to the printer ensures that a log entry, once captured, is not lost. To capture log entries line by line, it might be useful to use a dot-matrix printer instead of a laser or inkjet printer. Bear in mind that printers can run out of paper and ink, ensure you also

record your logs elsewhere. Logging to the printer may be accomplished by either specifying the pathname of the printer device or piping log output to `lp(1)` when `lpd(8)` is running.

Log to virtual tty
: FreeBSD and OpenBSD systems support virtual *ttys* accessible from the console by pressing Alt-Fn (where *n* corresponds to the device */dev/ttyv(n-1)*). It's possible to send syslog messages to these virtual *ttys* by merely specifying the specific device. It may also be useful to turn the *tty* "off" so that nobody can log in as described in the manpage for *ttys(5)*.

OpenBSD offers a fifth action that writes log messages to an in-memory buffer. This will provide logged-in users access to logs even on systems with no local storage. This configuration must be used in conjunction with the `syslogc(8)` program that reads messages from the created buffer. For more information about this, consult the manpages for `syslogd` and `syslogc`.

FreeBSD's fifth option is to pipe selected messages to an external program. By specifying a vertical bar or pipe (|) symbol, the log message from `syslogd` is piped to the specified external program, much like the pipe symbol works on the command line. For more information about syslog actions, consult the manpage for *syslog.conf(5)*.

Debugging syslogd

Remember that Syslog facilities vary by operating system. This makes it tricky to reuse *syslog.conf* files between operating systems, and you will need to be extra diligent about testing your configuration to make sure it does what you want. As you are building your Syslog configuration, you may notice that by default, `syslogd` offers little in the way of debugging information, even when you have horribly misconfigured *syslog.conf*.

Fortunately there are ways to get useful debugging information from `syslogd`. FreeBSD administrators may run the daemon with the `-v` option, which will cause `syslogd` to log the numeric facility and priority of every locally generated message. Specify the `-v` flag twice to also log the name of the facility and level. OpenBSD administrators may run `syslogd` with the `-d` option to run `syslogd` in the foreground and send debugging output to the attached terminal. Of course, when debugging, you may also want to capture the output of *syslog.debug* on either platform. Finally, to inject messages into Syslog with arbitrary levels and facilities, use the `logger(1)` tool.

Running syslogd

The `syslogd` binaries on FreeBSD and OpenBSD behave differently. While the functionality they provide is equivalent, they have different command-line arguments and defaults. We will briefly examine the most important command-line arguments for `syslogd`.

Additional sockets

Don't forget to configure syslogd to receive messages from jailed and chrooted programs. To accomplish this, you will first need to configure syslogd to create additional log sockets. In FreeBSD, the path to this socket is specified as the parameter to the –l argument, and in OpenBSD, as the parameter to –a. For example, BIND chrooted in */var/named* will write system logs to */dev/log* within the chroot. Therefore, syslogd must be run with */var/named/dev/log* as the parameter to –l or –a. Unlike files specified in the action column in *syslog.conf*, these log sockets are created automatically when syslogd is run.

syslogd on FreeBSD

By default, syslogd on a FreeBSD system will run with the –s option. This tells it to operate in "secure mode," which causes the daemon to not listen for incoming UDP datagrams on port 514. This argument can be specified twice in the form –ss, which causes syslogd to not open a network socket at all. Doing this also disables syslogd's ability to log to other systems.

These defaults are specified in */etc/defauts/rc.conf*. To override these defaults, use the syslogd_flags variable in */etc/rc.conf*. Client syslogd systems should always have the –s argument specified. Loghost systems must not have the –s argument specified.

Finally, syslogd may also be configured to accept log messages from only certain systems specified either by IP address and mask or domain name. To activate this "allowed peer" functionality, use the –a option as described in the manpage for syslogd. This will prevent syslogd from performing actions on messages received from non-peers; –a does not act as a replacement for a local firewall, which will block the datagram at the host level preventing it from being received by the daemon.

syslogd on OpenBSD

syslogd on OpenBSD starts on boot. There is no good way to disable syslogd besides specifying invalid options in */etc/rc.conf.local*, like syslogd_flags="NO". The default OpenBSD configuration allows logging to remote systems but does not accept input from the UDP port. To enable loghost functionality, the –u (unsecure) argument must be specified as an argument to syslogd.

In OpenBSD 3.4, privilege separation was added to syslogd. This creates two instances of syslogd: the child runs as user _syslogd and listens for log requests from log sockets while the parent process gives the child access to write to logfiles and so on. Privilege separation ensures that when running as a loghost, a root-owned process is not exposed to network traffic.

Finally, the section in */etc/rc* that starts syslogd on OpenBSD systems will open up to two additional logging sockets. The first, */var/named/dev/log*, will be opened if named has been configured to run in */etc/rc.conf*. Since named can run chrooted, an additional logging socket is necessary. The second, */var/empty/dev/log*, is created if */var/empty* exists. This directory is used by a variety of system daemons that, like syslogd, fork a child process that listens on a network port and chroots itself in */var/empty*.

syslogd Drawbacks

syslogd has a long history as *the* system logger for Unix systems. Despite its prevalence, there are a number of inherent security concerns, which are as follows.

Lack of access control

Without the ability to limit at a granular level which users or applications may use syslogd, everyone has access to the local Syslog daemon (which may forward messages onto a loghost, in certain circumstances). In addition, unless protected by a firewall or network topology, anyone can send logs directly to the loghost. This may lead to denial of service attacks that consume disk space or throughput (CPU or network).

There are unfortunately no easy ways to prevent users from logging to a local system logger using the logger command or the *syslog* system call. In general, loghost systems should be protected by a local firewall. FreeBSD loghost servers may instead use the –a (allowed peer) argument to syslogd.

Denial of service attacks should be mitigated wherever possible by using a separate filesystem for logs and by monitoring CPU and network activity closely. See the "Monitoring System Health" section in Chapter 4 for options to monitor activity on FreeBSD and OpenBSD systems.

Lack of reliability

The use of UDP for message transport minimizes network overhead due to logging but makes a variety of problems possible. Messages are easily spoofed, injected, silently dropped, or significantly delayed. The UDP protocol has no provisions for ensuring datagrams reach the destination; this is the responsibility of the application, if the application cares. In this case, syslogd does not. Without a guarantee that messages that were sent are delivered, logs on a loghost system may be incomplete or incorrect without anyone's knowledge.

As with mitigating the risks associated with a lack of access control, it's important to monitor systems closely to ensure adequate CPU cycles and network bandwidth are available for the transmission of these messages.

Lack of integrity or confidentiality

Without cryptographically verifiable signatures, there is no way to guarantee that messages have not been modified before being received by syslogd. Without encryption, messages are easily observable while in transit to a loghost system.

One mitigation strategy is to use netcat in conjunction with cryptcat to send UDP log messages over an encrypted TCP stream. netcat is installed by default on OpenBSD and may be installed via ports on FreeBSD. cryptcat is available in the FreeBSD ports tree and may be installed on OpenBSD by hand. After installation, non-loghost servers can be configured to log via UDP to localhost with the following line in the file */etc/syslog.conf*:

```
*.info            @localhost
```

netcat must then collect UDP datagrams from local port 514 and send these over an encrypted tunnel created by cryptcat as follows:

```
% sudo nc -l -u -p 514 | sudo cryptcat loghost 12345
```

On the loghost server, *cryptcat* receives encrypted data from remote systems, converts it back into UDP traffic and sends this content to the local 514 port on the loghost. This is accomplished on the loghost side by a command similar to the following:

```
% sudo cryptcat -l -p 12345 | sudo nc -u localhost 514
```

While this approach works, it requires that all systems (not just the loghost) be configured to receive UDP datagrams. On FreeBSD systems, use the –b argument to syslogd to specify a bind address of 127.0.0.1, or localhost, thus preventing receipt of datagrams over the network. OpenBSD systems will need to be configured to use a local firewall. Since cryptcat uses twofish encryption, which relies on a symmetric key (both parties encrypt using the same key), you will have to modify the source code of cryptcat and replace the default key of "metallica" with something of your choosing.

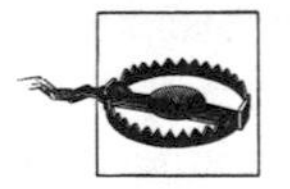

FreeBSD administrators should make a point to adjust the *Makefile* and remove the flag GAPING_SECURITY_HOLE. This will disable unneeded inetd-like functionality in netcat.

After this configuration is complete for each client, the loghost server accepts log messages over an encrypted connection. Because messages are only received over encrypted tunnels with a symmetric key, there is higher message integrity. There is still no guarantee that all messages that were sent were actually received. There is also no guarantee of in-order delivery or timeliness. Users who can log in on the clients can still send arbitrary log entries to the loghost.

As you can see, this mitigation strategy requires a great deal of upfront administration and does not scale well. Every change to the symmetric key (and this should change regularly) will require recompilation and/or automated distribution of a recompiled binary of `cryptcat`. It demonstrates, however, the extent to which some individuals will go to mitigate the risks associated with the lack of confidentiality in message transport.

Unfortunately other options are limited to transmitting log messages over a secure network (perhaps only for administrative data like log messages), or replacing `syslogd` with another daemon altogether. We consider replacing `syslogd` in next section of this chapter.

Monolithic

The `syslogd` binary is monolithic. It accepts messages over the network and locally, filters based on facility and level, and also can perform a variety of actions all from within a single binary. From a separation-of-duties perspective, this is not great design. Compare this with a program like Postfix, which has separate binaries to handle distinct tasks—some of these components need to run as root, others don't.

OpenBSD's support of privilege separation and chrooted behavior for `syslogd` mitigates most of the risk associated with this issue. Although still a single binary, the instance that communicates with external programs through sockets does not run as the root user and is carefully restricted from the rest of the filesystem.

There is little more that can be done about this security concern other than keeping an eye open for better-designed `syslogd` replacements.

syslogd Replacements

`syslogd`'s known security issues relating to lack of authentication, encryption, reliable delivery and message integrity have spawned several parallel efforts that attempt to solve this problem. For instance, an Internet Engineering Task Force (IETF) working group was formed to "document and address the security and integrity problems of the existing Syslog mechanism."* While this group has made some progress like the creation of RFC 3195, which describes reliable syslog transmission, it will be a little while until the standards they create can be implemented. In the meantime, other attempts have been made to solve the problems associated with `syslogd`.

syslog-ng

BalaBit, a Hungarian company, developed a "new generation" `syslogd` replacement in 1998, which was adopted by the Debian Linux distribution in 1999. `syslog-ng` boasts a variety of improvements over `syslogd`:

- Additional, more flexible, filtering options
- Communications over the more reliable, but less efficient, TCP protocol

* Chris Lonvick in May 2004. Available on the IETF Syslog Working Group home page (available at: *http://www.employees.org/~lonvick/index.shtml*).

- Support for TCP wrappers
- Logging of the complete chain of loghost relays to reach the destination loghost

Although this represents useful functionality, most of the security issues associated with syslogd as noted previously have not been addressed. Denial of service attacks are still possible without local access restrictions. syslog-ng's integration with TCP wrappers helps restrict hosts that can send logs to the loghost. However, the form of access control this provides can be accomplished, to a lesser extent, natively by syslogd on FreeBSD using the –a argument or by a firewall in either FreeBSD or OpenBSD. Finally, syslog-ng is an even larger daemon, which runs as root and relies on even more complex libraries to provide this additional functionality.

The major advantage provided by syslog-ng is its ability to use TCP instead of UDP. TCP support in itself increases reliability of log transport and unfortunately also decreases its ability to deal with large volumes of log messages. More importantly, TCP support means you can use syslog-ng in conjunction with a program like stunnel, which allows non-SSL aware TCP-based daemons to use SSL-based encrypted tunnels. This combination provides an effective solution to the confidentiality problem associated with sending logs in the clear over a potentially insecure network. It's not without tradeoffs, however, as throughput is further decreased with the overhead of encryption.

For more information about setting up syslog-ng, see the documentation at *balabit.com*. For detailed information about integrating syslog-ng and stunnel, see the examples page on *http://www.stunnel.org*.

minirsyslogd

The minirsyslogd project was driven by paranoia over the bloat associated with syslogd and the even larger syslog-ng. The daemon is small, advertised as "minimalistic," and low in flexibility and functionality; but it provides one key service that it does well.

minirsyslogd is a loghost daemon. It receives inbound log messages over a UDP port (by default 514) and performs as little processing as necessary to store messages in logfiles structured around the messages' source IP addresses. Because minirsyslogd refuses to create new directories, the existence of an IP-address named directory forms a rudimentary form of access control. This protects against arbitrary systems filling up disk space, but the daemon is still vulnerable to attack. This approach is less effective than using TCP wrappers, the –a argument to syslogd in FreeBSD, or a local firewall.

Nevertheless, the size and simplicity of the daemon makes a compelling case for a loghost or redundant high-security loghost system.

msyslog

The modular Syslog daemon (sometimes called `ssyslog` or Secure Syslog) is based on OpenBSD's Syslog daemon and is available in the FreeBSD ports tree (*ports/sysutils/msyslog*) but must be compiled by hand on OpenBSD. This daemon replaces the existing Syslog daemon and is designed as the name implies: separate modules are written to handle input, output, and file protection through encryption and hashing.

Installation of `msyslog` will result in the replacement of the `syslogd` binary, installation of the `peochk` utility to generate keys for file encryption and check the integrity of encrypted logfiles, and the installation of support for modular input/output specification (contained within */usr/local/lib/alat/libmsyslog.so.1*). Input modules provide support for reading messages from the BSD kernel, files and named pipes, UDP, and TCP. Likewise output modular support is available for typical `syslogd` functionality, a more flexible regular-expression based output specification, and the ability to send logs elsewhere via UDP or TCP.

Modular Syslog has even more flexibility and enhanced functionality than `syslog-ng` provides. One of the most important differentiators is the ability to encrypt logfiles and maintain a hash record of logfiles, which can be used to verify their integrity. While the modular design is good, the daemon and modular code will nevertheless always run as root.

There are, of course, more alternatives to `syslogd` available with new options appearing regularly. Visit the library at *http://www.loganalysis.org* for a current list of `syslogd` alternatives and additional information and resources.

Capturing Logs

What is captured varies from system to system, but in general there should be a log of all interactions with other systems. This certainly includes connection attempts (successes and failures), mail flow, FTP connections, and so on depending on the role of the system. Remember that `syslogd` discards any messages that do not match a known facility/level specification. A good rule of thumb is to ensure all messages in all facilities of higher importance than `debug` are logged (`*.info` in Syslog terms). This helps ensure that when the time comes to answer difficult questions, you have the information you need to reconstruct events and build an audit trail.

How precisely you capture all the logs in which you are interested will depend on the system in question. You may be very interested in `ftpd` logs access on an externally accessible FTP server or you may want to know whenever someone tries to transfer zones from your primary DNS server. In order to capture logs to build a successful audit trail, you need to carefully configure logging in every application. Look closely at the relevant documentation for more information on getting this done. If your applications are not producing appropriate logs, your job of building an audit trail will be much more difficult. Once this is done, make sure your applications are logging to an appropriate Syslog facility or level, if they use Syslog at all.

After having determined which facilities and levels interest you, it's straightforward to configure Syslog to capture these log messages and write them into appropriate logfiles. In most cases, it makes sense to write logs locally. This allows you to grant various administrators on different systems access to logs in which they are interested. Although this helps you answer questions about a given system, following a trail of logs across multiple systems can be very time consuming without also sending log messages to a central loghost.

Securing a Loghost

We have discussed `syslogd`'s ability to both send and receive messages across a network connection using UDP. While we have covered what a loghost is, what logs it should capture, and how it's configured, we still have not examined why they are useful, how to secure them, or where they fit into your network. We answer each of these questions next.

Benefits of a Loghost

First and foremost, a loghost consolidates logs for applications, network devices, firewalls, and other security appliances across potentially disparate networks. There is an obvious benefit here in terms of convenience: from a shell on one system you have access to logs for all systems from which the loghost accepts messages.

In addition to mere convenience, consolidating your logs also improves your security posture. Centralized logging makes it more difficult for intruders to tamper with or remove evidence of their actions. Having logs stored both locally and on one or more remote machines makes logfile tampering much more difficult. Consolidation also facilitates the work of an incident response team. It's easier for members of this team to correlate events and therefore build an audit trail. Increased log integrity brings with it a higher confidence in the results of an audit that this team conducts. Finally, consolidation of high-integrity logs in one location provides a good starting point for automated log monitoring. We talk more about this later in the chapter.

Loghost System Security

A loghost is a critical piece of your network. It contains a record of events across several systems and is the only authoritative source for event information. Capturing syslog messages is neither a CPU intensive nor a memory demanding task, so the temptation exists to couple this functionality with other system services. Keep in mind that the integrity of your logs is at stake. Build a server with redundant storage that does nothing more than collect, manage, and monitor `syslogd` messages.

In some circumstances a dedicated logging system is for some reason infeasible. Ensure at the very least that you maintain the "infrastructure server" concept as described in Chapter 3: any services provided should not require user accounts for non systems personnel. Bear in mind that every additional service provides another avenue for potential system compromise.

In environments with several systems personnel groups, it may be necessary to build a separate loghost for every group. If possible, avoid creating situations in which an audit trail you are likely to want will be split across multiple loghosts. If users or data can move between a given set of systems, all these systems should ideally use the same loghost.

Keeping in line with the idea that the loghost is a vital piece of systems infrastructure, it's important to protect this system in a variety of ways. The exact steps you take to do this at the network level are beyond the scope of this book. However, consider restricting access via a local firewall, disabling all services other than `ssh`, and tightening the configuration of `sshd`. If the machine is only available to select administrators via public/private key authentication, you have significantly increased the integrity of your logfiles.

Syslog Relay

When deploying a system to act as a loghost, it should be well protected from other systems, as described in the previous section. However, a loghost can only be protected so far—after all, UDP traffic must be able to get to the system. When dealing with disparate networks, it may seem necessary to permit UDP traffic from all local networks to the loghost on port 514. If you are the firewall administrator, this may make you uncomfortable. Otherwise, if you take this request to the firewall administrator at your organization, you may suddenly discover that she is unwilling to support your logging architecture.

Fortunately, you have options. Just because `syslogd` accepts UDP packets containing syslog messages, does not mean it must write them to disk. A server can both receive and send messages. In this context, it becomes a Syslog relay. In this case, only one system for each separate network needs to send traffic to the central loghost server. Figure 10-1 depicts a simple network with two distinct network segments.

The demilitarized zone (DMZ) houses systems to which people can connect over the Internet for vital services with one exception: the backup server. This server is not accessible via the Internet, and provides only backup services to the other systems on the DMZ. It's an ideal server to handle the task of being a syslog relay. All systems on the DMZ can send logs to the backup server, which in turn relays the logs to the loghost on the local area "intranet" network. The only firewall rule required to allow for

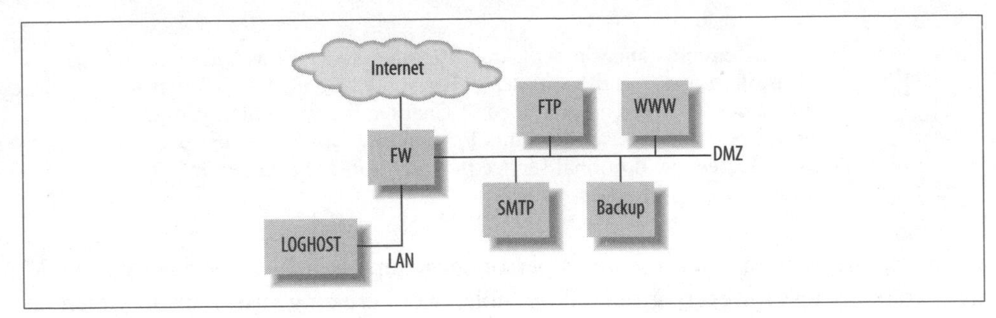

Figure 10-1. A simple network layout

completely centralized logging in this environment is one that permits UDP traffic from port 514 on the backup server to port 514 on the loghost.

Syslog relay configuration

Configuring a system to act as a Syslog relay is remarkably straightforward. In short, you must configure it to be a loghost, and also configure it to send logs to another loghost. On FreeBSD systems, be sure that the `-s` argument is not passed to `syslogd` in */etc/rc.conf*, allowing the daemon to listen for incoming UDP traffic on port 514. On OpenBSD, the relevant flag is `-u`, specified in */etc/rc.conf.local*. This achieves the "configure as loghost" part of the equation.

Second, adjust *syslog.conf* to send all logs to the loghost by adding a line as shown in Example 10-4. (We assume that your loghost is accessible via the hostname loghost.)

Example 10-4. Sending logs to a loghost

```
*.*                             @loghost
```

If your *syslog.conf* file contains no other entries, all logs will be transmitted to the loghost, whether they originate locally or on a remote system. In general, however, it's useful to keep a copy of your system's logs on the system itself. To do this, add lines similar to the following to your *syslog.conf* after the line specified in Example 10-4.

```
+myhostname.mydomain.tld
*.notice;auth,authpriv,cron,ftp,kern,lpr,mail,user.none /var/log/messages
auth.info                                               /var/log/authlog
mail.info                                               /var/log/maillog
# and so on...
```

Conclusion

Whether or not a Syslog relay is needed in your environment, building a loghost to consolidate logs is vital. Of course, after you have configured your systems to log locally and send logs to a central server, you can find yourself with a lot of logs sitting around with limited value. Moreover, dealing with the volume of logs on the loghost server can also be a challenge. Fortunately, there are solutions to the log management problem.

logfile Management

logfiles tend to grow quickly, accumulate steadily, and eventually become full of less immediately useful information. Log management practices need to come into play. Fortunately, FreeBSD and OpenBSD provide a tool to help manage logfiles: newsyslog(8). The newsyslog utility provides periodic, automated, logfile rotation and compression.

newsyslog Overview

In a nutshell, newsyslog provides the capability to take existing logfiles, rename and compress them, and create a new file to which syslogd can now write. This logfile rotation can happen based on the passage of time, or the size of the file in question. The behavior of newsyslog is controlled by its configuration file *newsyslog.conf*.

One important thing to keep in mind when looking over a *newsyslog.conf* file is that newsyslog is not a daemon. It's typically executed periodically through *cron(8)*. If you set up newsyslog to run once a week, you will never have a log containing less than a week's worth of information regardless of any size or date values in the configuration file. Make sure you configure newsyslog to run frequently enough to deal with the logs you need rotated most frequently. On most systems, running newsyslog every day is not considered out of the ordinary. The *newsyslog.conf* file in Example 10-5 provides a reasonable configuration for log rotation on a BSD system.

Example 10-5. A sample newsyslog.conf

```
# logfilename          [owner:group]     mode count size when [ZJB]
/var/log/cron                            600  3     100  *      J
/var/log/*.log                           600  7     100  *      JG
/var/log/lpd-errs                        644  7     100  *      J
/var/log/maillog        root:mailadmin   640  7     *    @T00   J
/var/log/sendmail.st    root:mailadmin   640  10    *    168     B
/var/log/messages                        640  5     100  *      J
/var/log/security                        600  10    100  *      J
/var/log/wtmp                            600  3     *    @01T05  B
```

It's important to understand what entries in this file mean to properly configure the servers under your jurisdiction, whether they are loghost systems or merely application servers. newsyslog has unique configuration options in FreeBSD 4.x, 5.x, and in OpenBSD, the details of which are beyond the scope of this book. For complete information about which options are supported, see the manpage for newsyslog on the platform of your choice. However, the basics are the same across platforms and we will endeavor to point out relevant differences.

`logfilename`
: This field holds the name of a file to be rotated. It may also contain a shell wildcard when the `G` option is specified (FreeBSD only).

`owner:group`
: The optional owner and group specification controls the file ownership of both rotated files and new files created after file rotation. In Example 10-5, both logs relating to mail will have their group set to *mailadmin*.

`mode`
: This field contains the octal representation of the mode bits of both rotated files and new files created after file rotation. In Example 10-5, both logs relating to mail will be readable by users in the *mailadmin* group based on the previous field. All files marked 600 will be readable only by root. Files with mode bits set to 640 but without specific owner and group specifications will be readable by root and any other users in the wheel group.

`count`
: The `count` field specifies the number of rotated logs to retain before replacing the oldest logs. Determining the number of files to retain depends on the conditions under which you are rotating logfiles and any security policies that exist in your organization pertaining to the preservation of logs.

`size`
: When the `size` field contains a value other than asterisk (*), it will be rotated if it is larger than the specified size in kilobytes when `newsyslog` runs. Note that logs nevertheless are rotated whenever `newsyslog` runs through `cron` and finds the file larger than the specified size. Since `newsyslog` is not a daemon that constantly runs monitoring files, it cannot rotate them the instant they reach a certain size.

`when`
: The `when` field specifies exactly what you think it does. The format is fully documented in the manpage for `newsyslog`, so we will not go into detail here. The same is true of the `when` field as with the `size` field: regardless of the date/time or interval specification, the log will only rotate when `newsyslog` runs and it's due.

`flags`
: The `flags` field varies among the various BSD platforms, and even varies among versions. The most commonly used flags are `Z` to compress the log via `gzip(1)`, `J` to compress the log using `bzip2(1)`, `B` to inform `newsyslog` that the file is a binary file (and therefore `newsyslog` should not add a `logfile turned over` message), and `G` to inform `newsyslog` that the value in the `logfilename` field is a shell pattern and should be expanded using `glob(3)` (FreeBSD only). Before using these flags or to learn about additional flags that may be available on your chosen platform, read the `newsyslog` manpage.

With a solid understanding of the options available in `newsyslog`, you are well prepared to start managing the collections of logs on your systems.

Configuring Log Rotation

If you have configured Syslog to log both locally and remotely, you now have several collections of logfiles to manage. When making decisions about configuring `newsyslog`, keep the following general guidelines in mind:

Make it easy on yourself
: Log management should be an issue you think about when you develop your logging configuration. Once you have instituted a management system, logfiles should be taken care of automatically—barring periodic checks to ensure the system is functioning as intended. Try to avoid making decisions that require manual intervention. You have better things to do than manage logfiles.

Develop a log retention policy
: A system administrator cannot develop policy on his own. Work with interested parties in the organization, the information security officer, and representatives of the corporate team to develop a log retention policy if you don't already have one. You should keep a log for at least a month so that you can isolate any reconnaissance activity that may have happened before a security incident was identified. For legal reasons, your organization may also need to ensure logs are not maintained beyond a certain point.

Rotate logs by date
: When you choose to rotate logfiles based on a size, it's often hard to track down log entries. When logfiles consist of entries during a known date span, tracking down specific events is much easier.

Keep smaller logs
: This sounds easy, but it can be a challenge on systems that generate a lot of messages. A wealth of log entries leads to large logfiles and increases the temptation to rotate based on size. Instead, either use the program specification in *syslog.conf* to split the logfiles into application specific files or rotate the logs more frequently. When logging both locally and to a centralized loghost, the local logs can be kept small by rotating them often while the logs on the loghost can be much larger if you don't plan to use them frequently.

Delete nonessential logs
: When a loghost exists on your network, logs on other systems can be considered nonessential. Configure these non-loghost systems to rotate appropriately and retain only as many compressed logfiles as is necessary to provide for local 30-day review.

Maintain redundant logs

Consider creating two identical loghost servers and maintaining independent replicas of logs on both systems. Access to one of these systems can be restricted even more than to the other.

Following these guidelines will help ensure that you have access to the information you need when tracking down problems and will also facilitate handling security incidents. Although most log rotation functionality can be handled by newsyslog, one minor problem remains: when logs are rotated and new files are created, archived files either remain in the directory with the original logs, or in another directory as specified as the argument to the –a parameter for newsyslog. Example 10-6 shows a script created to organize and manage these rotated logfiles.

Example 10-6. Example script to organize rotated logfiles

```
## Change these to suit your environment ##
base_syslog_dir="/var/log/syslogs"
rotated_dir="rotated"
all_msg_dir="logcheck"

## Date processing ##
if [ `date +%m` = "01" ] ; then  # If this is January, then
  thisyear=`date +%Y`# this is the current year,
  year=`expr $thisyear - 1`;    # but we want last year.
else                            # Otherwise,
  year=`date +%Y`               # we want this year
fi
month=`date -v-1m +%m`         # Last month

# First, create a directory for rotated logfiles if it doesn't
# already exist
dest_dir="$base_syslog_dir/$rotated_dir/$year/$month"
if [ ! -d $dest_dir ] ; then
  mkdir -p $dest_dir;
  chmod 700 $dest_dir;
fi

## Now move logfiles into the just-created directory ##
mv $base_syslog_dir/*.gz $dest_dir
```

This script, when run from cron immediately after newsyslog completes at the start of every month, will copy the compressed logfiles newsyslog created and move them into a rotated subdirectory structure. In this example, if $base_syslog_dir is */var/logs/syslogs* and $rotated_dir is rotated, then logs for any given month are located in */var/logs/syslogs/rotated/yyyy/mm*, where *mm* represents the month and *yyyy* represents the year.

Securing logfiles

Although we have already explored some of the aspects of logfile security during `newsyslog` configuration, we revisit the topic here—just as you should revisit the topic after configuring logfile rotation in your environment. With system logs, the need-to-know rule applies: only those who need access to system logs should be granted access. Whether this is granted through standard filesystem permissions or using ACLs will depend on your specific requirements and chosen operating system. The following guidelines should be applied:

Although tempting, remember that the *sappnd* flag cannot be used on logfiles that will eventually be rotated. See Chapter 2 for more details.

Remove world permissions
: In almost all cases, logfiles should not be world readable or writable. If possible, remove the world-execute bit so that nonprivileged users are kept out of the directory altogether. Any logfiles that require that they be world readable may be stored elsewhere.

Protect nonessential logfiles
: Whether or not logfiles are essential (stored on a loghost), they contain sensitive information. Limit access as much as possible. Certain groups of users may require access to certain logfiles, but the need-to-know rule should apply.

Lock down on rotate
: When logfiles are rotated, `newsyslog` creates new files with permissions you specify and enforces the same permissions on the rotated logfiles. Consider locking down permissions further so that only root is able to look at rotated logfiles. If your log rotation script is creating new directories for rotated logs and your system is in a kernel *securelevel* greater than 0, these new directories may be made immutable (via the *schg* filesystem flag) after the directory is created. Any parent directories (other than the log directory itself) may also have the *sappnd* flag set so that files and directories, once created, cannot be removed.

Although logfiles cannot easily be secured using filesystem flags, file-monitoring programs like Tripwire can ensure logfiles never shrink except at specific times when they are rotated.

Restrict access to the loghost
: Limit the number of administrators with access to the loghost(s). The logfiles administrators need should be made available on individual systems. Grant loghost access to incident response teams on a per-request basis. In the case of redundant loghost systems, one may be chosen as the "high-security" loghost with very limited access and draconian filesystem flags.

At this point, you know how to capture, consolidate logs, manage, and secure logfiles. Hopefully, with the steps you've taken, incident response teams will have an easier time correlating events and determining how a security incident occurred. Of course, something must prompt their investigation. It would certainly be preferable that an unusual event trigger this investigation rather than the head of your organization calling your department and asking why the external web site now reads "Hax0red 4 U."

Automated Log Monitoring

Monitoring the logs you collect is vital. A variety of programs exist that will monitor log messages as they come in and notify administrators when suspicious or unusual activity is detected. We will examine two such programs available for both FreeBSD and OpenBSD: `logcheck` and `swatch`.

Both these programs look for certain patterns in logfiles and then perform one or more given actions. To know what to look for, you will have to spend considerable time looking at system logs and determining what log entries you need to be notified about. It might be helpful to conduct some attacks against your systems to generate key events. Using tools like `nessus` and `nmap` and picking up a few exploits from the Security Focus web site (*http://www.securityfocus.com/*) will help you generate some of the logs you will want to capture. As new vulnerabilities are discovered, run them against your systems. Did they cause your log monitoring scripts to alert you in the way you desired? If not, adjust your configuration.

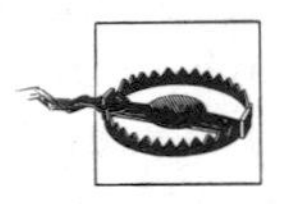

Regardless of the log monitoring solution you choose, configure the program to not need root access. In general, this requires little more than ensuring your logfiles are readable by some group to which the system user running your log monitoring application is a member.

Automated Auditing Using logcheck

`logcheck` is based upon a component of the Gauntlet firewall system by Trusted Information Systems, Inc. but later completely written by Craig Rowland of Psionic—at the time it was called `logsentry`. This is all ancient history. `logcheck` has not seen much development in more than seven years. Nevertheless, it requires very little effort to set up and its functionality continues to be useful. The way `logcheck` works is best described by its *README*:

> 1) By reporting everything you tell it to specifically look for via keywords.
>
> 2) By reporting everything you didn't tell it to ignore via keywords.

With this design, `logcheck` notifies administrators by email when key warning events occur, and when new, unexpected, log entries turn up. `logcheck` runs periodically through cron and reviews all messages since last execution. If there is anything to report, logcheck sends an email.

Installation

logcheck can be installed from *ports/security*; the name of the port is logcheck on FreeBSD and logsentry on OpenBSD. Both of these ports download the same compressed source tarball. As with other ports, logcheck is installed by running **make install** from the *logcheck* or *logsentry* ports directory. This will install the logtail binary and several sample configuration files and documents. Run **pkg_info -L** on the logcheck or logsentry package to determine exactly where the files have been installed on your system. Although the logcheck program has not been modified in years, the installation defaults do change from time to time.

Configuration

The heart of logcheck is *logcheck.sh*. This file contains key configuration elements like the address to which notifications should be sent, the location of additional configuration files, and the location of the logfiles to monitor. Each of these topics deserves some discussion as follows:

Email address
: The logcheck.sh script extracts "interesting" log entries and sends them to an email address. Given the sensitivity of log information, be sure you have protected the path this mail message will take in some way. How you accomplish this might involve encrypted tunnels, unencrypted traffic over an administrative network, or local delivery.

Location of keyword specification files
: There are four files that control how logcheck parses logs and determines what qualifies as interesting. These files are named *logcheck.hacking*, *logcheck.violations*, *logcheck.violations.ignore*, and *logcheck.ignore*. The former two enumerate keywords that, when found, identify log messages as interesting. The latter two contain longer phrases that more fully describe specific log messages which should be ignored.

Location of logfile(s)
: The easiest way to run logcheck is to point it at one single logfile. It's trivial on a loghost system to take all incoming logs and put them in a file for logcheck alone. This file will grow quickly and should therefore be truncated frequently. There is no need to keep compressed archives of this file.

For the sake of convenience and for a little added security, you may want to move the logcheck.sh script and configuration files into a directory under */usr/local/etc* accessible only as root. Whether you choose to take this approach or not, the next step is to tailor the additional configuration files for your environment—or at the very least review them.

logcheck.hacking
: When entries from the *logcheck.hacking* file are found in log messages, the subject line of the email `logcheck` sends will say "HOSTNAME DATE ACTIVE SYSTEM ATTACK!" Be careful about what keywords are found in this file.

logcheck.violations
: The *logcheck.violations* file is the second file containing keywords for interesting messages. Again, if you are too general, you will get too many false positives.

logcheck.ignore*
: Finally the *logcheck.[violations.]ignore* and *logcheck.ignore* files tell *logcheck* which log entries to ignore. Try to avoid merely using keywords in this file as you might be ignoring more than you bargained for.

Notice that being too general in either the hacking or violations configuration files will result in too many false positives whereas being too general in the ignore files will result in interesting log messages being missed. While `logcheck` is easy to configure, it's even easier to configure poorly. This phase of `logcheck` configuration is usually iterative, involving the following five steps.

1. Set up a single logfile that `logcheck` will parse. This file should be well protected from all users. Allow this file to accumulate several hours (or even a day's) worth of data.
2. Edit the hacking, violations, and two ignore files and remove both keywords and ignore lines you feel do not show up in your logfiles.
3. After you are comfortable with your changes, run `logcheck` and examine the output.
4. If you miss log entries you wanted to see or if you have too many log entries mailed to you, revise the hacking, violations, and two ignore files to compensate.
5. Repeat steps 3 and 4 until the four configuration files are producing output to your satisfaction.

Substrings in all the hacking and violations files are matched using case-insensitive `egrep(1)`. The ignore files specify patterns used by case-sensitive egrep. Bear this in mind when working with these configuration files. The manpage for `grep(1)` is a worthwhile read if you are not familiar with regular expressions.

Your goal in configuring `logcheck` this way is to be able to run `logcheck` very frequently but receive very little email. The more false positives you receive, the less likely you are to pay attention to the results produced by `logcheck`. Configure carefully, and configure well. As systems and applications are deployed in your network, revisit and revise your logging and `logcheck` configuration.

Drawbacks

logcheck is not perfect. It suffers from lack of active development, which means that you will need to move on to another piece of log monitoring software if you need additional functionality. While logcheck does a very good job monitoring logfiles, it can be inconvenient to deal with an additional logfile containing all messages. Moreover, if you choose to monitor logfiles from applications that cannot log via Syslog, you will need to make duplicates of these logs or inject them into Syslog using the -f flag of the logger command. This can quickly become an administrative headache. Fortunately, the log monitoring world is full of options. Next, we explore another popular log monitoring utility, swatch.

Automated Auditing Using swatch

swatch, the simple watcher, was originally designed to monitor logfiles written by syslogd but can now monitor arbitrary logfiles and is quite flexible. swatch expects a single configuration file that contains actions to perform when specified patterns have been found. swatch is almost as easy to install and configure as logcheck, but is more flexible and can perform a variety of actions besides sending email.

Installation

In OpenBSD and FreeBSD, the installation procedure for swatch on a loghost system is identical:

```
% cd /usr/ports/security/swatch
% make && sudo make install
```

On both platforms, this will install two binaries (swatch and swatch_oldrc2newrc) and the manpages for both. While example configuration files are included in the compressed *swatch* tarball, they are not installed during the install process. In OpenBSD the two example files are located in the *w-swatch-version/swatch-version/examples/* subdirectory of the *swatch* ports directory; in FreeBSD, check in the *work/swatch-version/examples/* subdirectory. Additional sample configuration files for swatch may be found at *http://www.loganalysis.org*.

Configuration

You can start using swatch with very little configuration, and getting things operational is trivial. As with logcheck however, fine-tuning swatch to work well in your environment will take some time. Before we get carried away, let's explore swatch's basic functionality.

swatch reads configuration from *${HOME}/.swatchrc* by default. You can, and usually should, change this behavior, by providing the –c argument and pointing to a configuration file you create, perhaps in */usr/local/etc/*. A contrived configuration file is provided in Example 10-7. As mentioned previously, swatch expects a series of patterns and actions in its configuration file. Patterns are provided as arguments to the watchfor and ignore statements, which do exactly what you think they do.

Example 10-7. Simple swatch configuration

```
ignore /refused connection from 10.1/
ignore /BAD SU john to root/

watchfor /inetd.* refused connection/
  echo normal
  throttle 01:00:00
  mail addresses=root,subject=Refused\ Connection,when=2-6,9-5

watchfor /file system full/
  echo bold
  throttle 00:05:00
  mail addresses=root,subject=FILE\ SYSTEM\ FULL,when=1-7,1-24

watchfor /BAD SU.*to root/
  echo bold
  throttle 00:01:00
```

ignore statements are best placed early in the configuration file to weed out logs that don't need to be parsed. This statement is followed by a regular expression, enclosed in slashes, which will cause log messages to be ignored if the pattern expressed matches the log message.

watchfor statements are also followed by a regular expression. When the expression matches a message, various actions are performed.

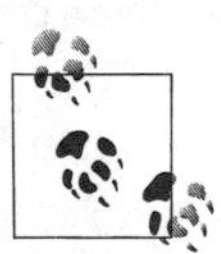

If you are unfamiliar with regular expressions, do not fear. A simple series of words is often enough for ignore and watchfor statements. If you would like more flexilibility, see the manpage for grep(1).

As the actions are fully documented in the manpage for swatch(1), we will not go into great detail here. However, the actions shown in Example 10-7 are the most popular and deserve some treatment as follows:

echo *modes*
: The echo action will result in the matched line being sent to standard output. A mode may be specified to change the color of the output, make it bold, and so on.

bell *N*
: When bell is specified as an action, a bell character will be sent to standard output.

`throttle`
: `throttle` tells `swatch` to limit notifications. When a `throttle` period of one hour is specified (as in the first `watchfor` statement in Example 10-7), a specific log message matched by this pattern will not be displayed until the hour is up. By default, `throttle` is done on a per-message basis so that other messages that also match the pattern, have their own `throttle` period. To make the `throttle` period apply to all messages that match the pattern, append `,use=regex` at the end of your `throttle` period specification. At the end of the `throttle` period, a summary is displayed listing the number of times the specific message was seen.

`mail`
: The `mail` action will, of course, send an email to the specified recipient(s) when messages are matched.

`when`
: The `when` option can be applied to any of `swatch`'s regular actions. This option restricts the action to a specific time period governed by days and hours. The first day of the week is Sunday and is expressed as the number 1. Hours must be specified in a 24-hour format.

At this point, you should have enough information to configure `swatch`. All that remains is that you know what to look for. For that, you'll need to study your logs, not this chapter.

Running swatch

After you have created a configuration file for `swatch`, you need to start it. `swatch` may be run on the command line or as a daemon by using the `--daemon` command-line argument. It might also be helpful to write a startup script that starts `swatch` as a daemon and redirects standard output to the console or a separate logfile. Be aware that `swatch` will need to be restarted whenever the logfile it reads is rotated. To do this, specify a restart time using the `--restart-time` command-line argument, which ensures the daemon restarts as soon after the log is rotated as possible.

Catching new messages

`swatch` is not designed to alert you when new messages show up in your logs. Whereas `logcheck` sends you alerts unless you tell it not to, `swatch` will only send you alerts when you tell it to. Fortunately, due to `swatch`'s flexibility, it's possible to configure it very much like `logcheck` using a series of `ignore` lines and `watchfor /.*/`. This expression will match all entries that have not been already ignored or caught by other `watchfor` statements.

Ongoing Monitoring

Once you have configured `logcheck` or `swatch` for your environment, you might be tempted to never evaluate your log monitoring capability again. If you used `logcheck` or have configured `swatch` to alert you of new messages, you will still have to return to log monitoring to cut down on unimportant messages that did not exist when you initially configured the log monitoring system.

Despite the fact that your logs are automatically monitored and you have little motivation to return to manually scanning them, you should nevertheless make a point to do so. A periodic manual scan or `tail` of logs in the background can help you catch activity that log scanners will not. You may notice certain entries appear that you would actually like to know about, yet somehow you have managed to configure your log scanner to ignore them. Watching logs scroll by periodically may also alert you to changes in the frequency with which certain log entries appear—a minor warning may not be a problem now and again, but several thousand warnings an hour might be worth examining. The point is, don't underestimate the value of periodic human scans of your logfiles.

Finally, make yourself revisit your log monitoring configuration. Continue running vulnerability test kits or sample exploits to help validate the configuration of your log monitoring solution.

Automated Auditing Scripts

Both FreeBSD and OpenBSD ship with auditing scripts that run daily through cron. Unlike the automated log monitoring tools discussed previously, these scripts examine various aspects of the filesystem. They notify administrators about the state of the system, notice changes in certain files, back up critical configuration files, and so on. The specific mechanisms behind these automated auditing scripts are vastly different in the two operating systems, however, and we must treat them independently.

OpenBSD's Security Script

OpenBSD runs the */etc/security* script from the */etc/daily* script, which runs every day, of course. The *security(8)* script performs numerous checks of files throughout the system including seeking out syntax errors in password and group files, checking various dotfiles in users' home directories, checking permissions throughout the filesystem, and even auditing changes to files. Most of this behavior is preconfigured and can only be adjusted by changing */etc/security* directly. This is typically not recommended.

Still, there are two ways in which you can affect what the *security* script will do for you. First, whenever you install applications that have important configuration files you should consider adding these files to */etc/changelist*. The *security* script detects and reports content changes for every file listed in *changelist(5)*. This helps keep you aware of configuration changes transpiring on your system.

Second, permission changes to files are closely audited against */etc/mtree/special* and any other files in */etc/mtree* with a *.secure* extension. These additional files may be created by using `mtree(8)` as follows:

```
# sudo mtree -cx -pdir -kcksum,gid,mode,nlink,size,link,time,uid \
  > /etc/mtree/dir.secure
% sudo chown root:wheel dir.secure
% sudo chmod 600 dir.secure
```

Creating *.secure* `mtree` files for file hierarchies containing chrooted services and important configuration files is a good idea. When you are done creating these `mtree` files and adjusting */etc/changelist*, you may want to make them all immutable.

Please remember, however, that the security script, *changelist* file, and `mtree` files are not the definitive answer for filesystem auditing, nor do they keep your system secure. The security script and associated files merely provide a small sanity check on a daily basis so that you, the administrator, can have an idea of what is changing on your system. There are innumerable ways in which your system could be compromised without the security script ever raising a red flag.

FreeBSD's Periodic Scripts

The `periodic(8)` utility runs scripts located in a specific directory. By default, */etc/crontab* on FreeBSD systems run periodic with three arguments: `daily`, `weekly`, and `monthly`. Each of these arguments corresponds to a directory within */etc/periodic* that contains scripts to run when `periodic` is run.

The behavior of the periodic system of scripts is controlled from *periodic.conf(5)*. It's in this file, that you may place directives that will affect which script will and will not run, and under what circumstances they will provide output. This flexibility is very important: most administrators who don't configure *periodic.conf* to provide only important output ignore all mail from root on a regular basis. Who can blame them? With default values, the signal-to-noise ratio from the periodic scripts is very high.

Take a moment to examine the default configuration for `periodic` in */etc/defaults/periodic.conf*. In most cases, you want to copy blocks of text into */etc/periodic.conf* and set success, info, and other verbose notifications to **NO**, while retaining notifications for errors and bad configuration. Example 10-8 provides a reasonable (and fairly quiet) default configuration for `periodic`.

Example 10-8. Sample /etc/periodic.conf

```
daily_show_success="NO"                # scripts returning 0
daily_show_info="NO"                   # scripts returning 1
daily_show_badconfig="YES"             # scripts returning 2
```

Example 10-8. Sample /etc/periodic.conf (continued)

```
weekly_show_success="NO"                # scripts returning 0
weekly_show_info="NO"                   # scripts returning 1
weekly_show_badconfig="YES"             # scripts returning 2

monthly_show_success="NO"               # scripts returning 0
monthly_show_info="NO"                  # scripts returning 1
monthly_show_badconfig="YES"            # scripts returning 2

daily_status_security_inline="YES"      # reduces number of messages

daily_clean_disks_verbose="NO"          # Mention files deleted
daily_clean_tmps_verbose="NO"           # Mention files deleted
daily_clean_preserve_verbose="NO"       # Mention files deleted
```

Of course, additional options may be relevant in your environment. The settings in the *periodic.conf* provided in Example 10-8 should at the very least reduce the informational mail you receive. Once you have periodic configured to only notify you for important events, you will find it far more useful.

Wrapping Up

Your system logs are like status reports. Without keeping a close eye on them, you are likely to miss something important and live to regret it. Fortunately, automated auditing tools make your job as a system administrator easier and help you be the instigator for incident response. When the incident response team conducts an audit, the care you take to configure logging across the systems you administer can make your life and their lives easier and facilitate getting answers, and getting back to the daily routine.

Resources

A list of resources follows.

Logging Tools

- minirsyslogd: *http://www.clueby4.org/minirsyslogd/*
- syslog-ng: *http://www.balabit.com/products/syslog_ng/*
- msyslog: *http://sourceforge.net/projects/msyslog/*

Secure Transport Providers for Logging

- stunnel: *http://www.stunnel.org/*
- cryptcat: *http://farm9.org/Cryptcat/*

Log Monitoring

- Swatch: *http://swatch.sourceforge.net/*
- Logcheck: *http://sourceforge.net/projects/logcheck/*

Selected Logging-Related Request for Comments (RFCs)

- RFC 3164: The BSD Syslog Protocol
- RFC 3195: Reliable Delivery for syslog

CHAPTER 11

Incident Response and Forensics

Go to a bookstore and take a look at the information security section. There will likely be shelves of books on how to hack, hacking techniques, tips on thinking like a hacker, and the glory of hacking into a system you own. Our industry has dedicated enormous resources on training security administrators and engineers to think like an attacker in an effort to make networks more secure. Although these types of books may indeed assist us in configuring and deploying more secure systems, they tend not to help us with the actual operation of these systems.

In the same bookstore, you're likely to only find a few books on incident response and forensics. Responding to incidents and performing forensic analysis are activities that are performed in the face of a compromised system or active attack. As much as we'd like to think we deploy unbreakable and totally secure hosts, this is simply not the case. Even after our best attempts, a security incident is inevitable. As a security professional, you need to be prepared for the worst and deal with incidents as they happen.

This dichotomy between building and deploying secure systems versus operating and maintaining secure systems is also evident in the BSD ports tree. In the *ports/security* directory, most of the tools are either vulnerability assessment tools or cryptographic libraries. There are a few HIDS tools designed assist in determining whether a compromise has occurred and there are a few tools designed for forensic analysis, but they are certainly not a majority.

So, the question becomes "why should I care about incident response and forensic analysis?" In short, one day you will be staring at a compromised system and unless you have prepared, you'll likely be at a loss for what to do.

Incident Response

A security incident can be reported in a number of ways. An IDS system may detect a compromised system. A user may report that she has had files deleted or modified.

And sometimes systems administrators will simply have a "bad feeling" about a host and ultimately realize it was victim of an attack. Regardless of how an incident is detected, the key to dealing with an incident is to be prepared and understand what your next steps are. Before an incident occurs, you need to prepare your tools, your process, and your coworkers for what needs to occur.

Incident response and forensics can be a detailed and difficult operation. For many, the activities and details discussed in this chapter will be sufficient. However, for those in more sensitive industries such as healthcare or finance, this chapter should serve only as a primer. Those who want a more rigorous treatment of incident response should consult the books and articles listed in the "Resources" section at the end of this chapter.

A good starting point is identifying your incident response process. This process, like the security-minded administration process, can be thought of in a lifecycle model. There are a variety of incident response lifecycles that different organizations have created over the years. Some are waterfalls while some are circles, some have seven states while others have four. The lifecycle presented in this chapter and shown in Figure 11-1 is a notional lifecycle. Think of it as a summary of other models; we use it for illustrative purposes. If, through your own research, you discover other lifecycle models that resonate better with you, by all means use them instead.

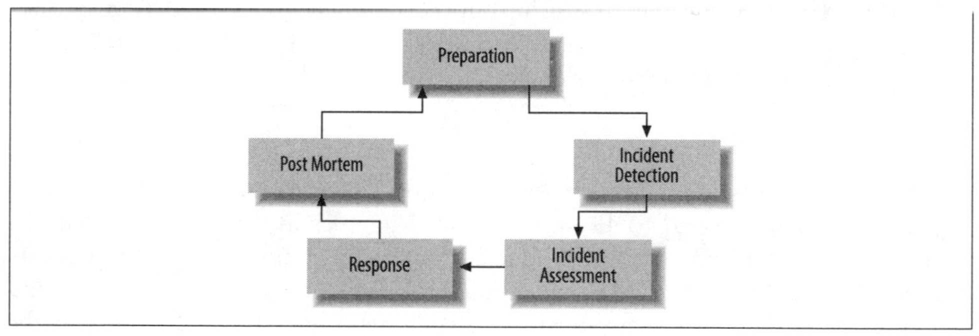

Figure 11-1. Incident response lifecycle

Preparation

Hopefully, you don't find yourself in the throes of responding to security incidents on a continuous basis. If you do, you should probably revisit your core security mechanisms. Most of the time, you should be in the preparation phase. Here, you update your forensics tools and training staff, and identify internal and external resources that play a part in the incident response process. The Boy Scout motto of "Be Prepared" is a good mantra for incident response.

Identifying resources

You must identify resources that will play a role in incident response. Potentially one of the most daunting resources to identify is simply the assets on your network. Keeping a current list of all your hosts, the operating system version each one is running, and physical location can be a full-time job depending on the size of your network. Having an up-to-date list of all your servers is vital because you never know when an incident will occur. For instance, if the physical location of a host has changed but has not been updated in your asset inventory, it can cause problems with your response. Running into a data center and unplugging the wrong host is at the very least embarrassing and probably makes a bad situation even worse for your organization. To prevent this problem, you should also consider labeling the front and back of each server and router to prevent confusion in the heat of an incident even if your inventory is up to date.

Other important resources are the people in your organization. You should maintain a current contact list so that you have easy access to important individuals when they are needed. Further, you should create an escalation procedure to be used during an incident. Most IT resources in a company have two managers that need to be dealt with, the business manager who wants the service to be online and the technical managers who actually manage the IT resources. Both these trees need to be identified and included in the escalation procedures. Also, you may wish to set time thresholds for upper management notification; for example, if an incident keeps a host offline for 10 hours, then higher ups in the company are notified. This is basically a recognition that an incident that results in an extended service outage will cause more damage to the business the longer it goes on.

Training staff

Incident response is not a one-person operation. Your technical staff should be trained in how to respond to an incident and their roles in the lifecycle should be clear. While the training does not need to be formal, it should be enough to educate the technical staff in the first steps they should take when they think they have found a compromised host. Also, any business owners who have been identified in the escalation procedure should be briefed as to expectations and actions they should take during an incident.

Creation of document templates

There may be documents you need to fill out during an incident. The most likely document you deal with is a *chain of custody*. The chain of custody document is used to reconstruct what has occurred to an asset during an incident. This can be particularly useful if law enforcement gets involved and you need to prove that a host was under constant control and evidence was not tampered with.

It's rare to have to create documents that will stand up in court. Most incidents end without going to court; many are only concerned with containing a compromise and not actually pursuing the attacker. However, if you find yourself in a situation where you need to create documents that will be used in a lawsuit or criminal investigation, you should examine the "Resources" section at the end of this chapter for more detailed direction.

A chain of custody document is filled out when acting on or transferring an asset during an incident. For instance, if you pull a drive from a compromised host and store it in a safe, you should document that activity on the chain of custody. A chain of custody template should include spaces for time, date, type of activity, name of asset acted upon, and spaces for two signatures. Capturing two signatures is important as a mechanism to prevent fraud. It's easy to get one person to lie about what has happened to an asset, it's much harder to get two.

Building your bag of tricks

To this point, our discussion of incident response has been a paper exercise. However, the technical preparation is just as important as the process and procedures we have talked about to this point. You should prepare your proverbial "bag of tricks" that you can reach into during an incident. This bag of tricks should include basic systems tools, forensic analysis aids, and some networking support. All of these tools should be placed on a bootable CD-ROM so they can be used independently of the host operating system.

There are a number of bootable CD images available that can provide a good starting point for you. Since this is a BSD book, and you will be dealing with BSD-based systems, we address the BSD-based bootable CD images. However, BSD is not your only option. For those with a Linux flair, the knoppix bootable CD image available from *http://www.knoppix.net* is a great live-CD image to start with.

FreeSBIE is based on FreeBSD. FreeSBIE provides tools for easily modifying the ISO image and creating customized CDs. While it's not explicitly a security-based distribution, it's actively developed and well supported. FreeSBIE is available from *http://www.freesbie.org/*.

Frenzy, another live CD based on FreeBSD, has the distinction of fitting on a mini-CD-ROM. Using a compressed filesystem, Frenzy actually has over 600MB of data that ends up getting shoved onto a 200MB CD. The mini-CD form factor is nice as it fits easily in a pocket and can be taken anywhere with you. However, Frenzy does not have the robust customization tools that FreeBSIE has. Frenzy is available from *http://frenzy.org.ua/eng/*.

Incident Detection

The next step of the incident response lifecycle is the actual detection of the incident. The detection may come from a variety of sources including an IDS sensor, log file analysis, user report, or simply odd host behavior. Whether it's an automated alert or a manual process, be prepared for incidents to be reported in a variety of ways. Don't expect something to jump up and say "This is a security incident." Some things may start as a simple host malfunction like excessive CPU usage or low memory situations. However, upon further inspection, you may discover the CPU utilization is due to a Trojan horse running on the host. At that point, the activity has moved from normal system administration to a security incident. Follow your gut feeling and be prepared to deal with incidents in a variety of forms. However, with that said, do not be overanxious to declare everything a security problem. Sometimes complicated situations can feel like a security compromise, but ultimately are system-level problems. A good question to ask your coworkers at this point is a simple "Did anyone change anything recently?" The answer to this simple question may be very enlightening.

Incident Assessment

Once you think you have a security issue, you need to determine the scope of the problem. Generally, time will be of the essence and the sooner you can make the proper assessment of what's happening, the better off you will be. Before you get started however, make a note of the time you started investigating so you have a trail to look back on.

Assessing the incident can be tricky. While you want to rapidly determine the scope of the problem, you do not want to cause further service interruption or disturb potential forensic data. At this stage, you want to examine log files, network traffic graphs, and IDS logs to help figure out the "blast radius." However, the whole time you are doing this, attempt to minimize change on the systems if possible. Avoid deleting files or writing to files if you can. This will make the after-the-fact forensic analysis easier.

In the course of your investigation, feel free to bring in the help of others that may be able to provide assistance. In particular, when doing your incident response preparation, you identified technical and business owners for each system in your network. If they can help troubleshoot or provide background information, give them a call and see if they can help assess the incident.

Response

Now things get sticky. You're sure you have a security problem, now you have to figure out what to do about it. In general, you have two goals: contain the compromise, and restore service as fast as possible.

> **False Alarms**
>
> One of the authors was a security manager for a large e-commerce company. During one Christmas vacation, he received a frantic phone call from his Network Operations Center indicating that the main web site was under attack and had been down for two hours. As part of the escalation procedure, the manager was notified after the on-call staff could not resolve the problem in the first two hours.
>
> Upon joining the teleconference that was set up to deal with the "attack," the author asked what type of attack it was and where it was coming from. No one knew or seemed to be able to describe what was going on besides high server load and potentially large amounts of traffic. After some troubleshooting and log analysis, the author determined that the referrers in the incoming web requests seemed to indicate that pop-up ads were accounting for a large portion of the web traffic.
>
> A quick phone call to a marketing manager verified that the marketing department had kicked off a new advertising initiative right before the Christmas vacation. The extra traffic caused by the advertising campaign had exceeded the capacity of the web servers. The marketing manager tuned down the number of pop-up ads being served, and the "security incident" ended.

Containing the compromise may be as simple as pulling the network cable from the compromised host. If you want to analyze the live system, leave the power on to the machine so you can run utilities from the CD drive and interact with the console. It should be noted that some attackers may install code that attempts to delete the attacker's tracks if the network interface goes down. While this makes for great Hollywood scripts and paranoid security administrators, it is not a common occurrence. Isolating a compromised host is usually better for the business than potentially losing data on the host.

Be sure you check hosts that are similar to the compromised host. For instance if you are examining a compromise on one web server in a cluster of web servers, it is entirely possible that the attacker used an automatic exploitation mechanism that could easily subvert all the web servers at once.

Restoring service can be tricky. If you have extra hardware and known good backups, you can usually restore the backup to extra hardware and place the machine in service. Be aware, however, that if you deploy a host with the same vulnerability that allowed the attacker to get in the first time, he will likely be able to compromise the new host. You may wish to wait to restore service until you know how the attacker got in. Moreover, if it's taken you a while to identify the security incident, recent backups may contain traces of malicious activity. In this case, it doesn't make sense to restore until you can identify exactly when the attacker got in.

If you don't have extra hardware and want to reuse the existing host, make a backup of the disk before you do anything. For information on copying disks, see "Forensics on BSD," later in this chapter. Then, reinstall the operating system from scratch. It is generally unwise to just reinstall applications on top of a compromised operating system. Unless you are 100% sure that the attacker did not leave any tools or processes in unknown places, you should just nuke the drive.

Postmortem Analysis

Even with the best attempts, you will have a security compromise periodically. It's important to learn from each and every one. Allowing a particular compromise to happen once is excusable; allowing it twice is not. After the events of the incident have finished and the parties have had some time to rest (approximately 24 hours is a reasonable amount of time) you should schedule a post mortem review of the incident.

If you wait too long, the people involved will likely have forgotten important details about the identification or response to the security incident. If you don't wait long enough, people will probably be too tired and want to "just get it over with" as soon as possible.

Through your review you should focus on two things: what went wrong and how to prevent it from happening again. The actions people take away from the meeting should be specific and have owners responsible for their execution.

Forensics on BSD

Once you have determined a host has been compromised, you may want to perform an analysis of the host to figure out what the attacker really did. This process, known as *forensic analysis,* can be a highly involved activity. Keeping track of evidence, performing highly technical tests against a host, and staying current on the latest attack trends can be a difficult job. However, the roots of forensic analysis are really simple common sense and investigation. Your detective work, ultimately, needs to be educational to you and help your enterprise learn from the compromise. Keep that goal in mind as you actually examine exploited hosts.

How Serious Are You?

The first thing you need to ask yourself is: what are you planning on doing with the data you gather from your analysis? If the break-in was severe and legal action may be taken against the attacker, you must perform a dramatically more detail-oriented analysis than if you are pursuing a minor-script driven attack that you are unlikely to follow up on. In some cases, you may find during the course of your incident response procedure that the vector of attack is obvious and your time is better spent bringing the host back online than actually performing forensics work. Just because a host was broken into does not mean you have to perform analysis on it, but if you are going to simply bring the host back into operation without determining how the attacker got in and how to stop him from doing it again, be prepared to rebuild the host every time it is compromised.

Quick Forensics

Sometimes, the avenue an attacker uses to gain access to a host is made obvious through a very cursory incident response procedure. In these cases, lengthy paperwork-driven procedures are more trouble than they are worth.

One of the authors was once involved in an incident where a Solaris FTP server appeared to have been compromised and was being used to distribute French pornography. Upon initial inspection of the FTP process that was running, it was clear that the compromise came as a result of flags that allowed anonymous write access to the public FTP directories. This excessive access was what the attackers were using to store and retrieve their pornography.

The system administrator who was responsible for the server was asked why he was allowing anonymous write access to the FTP server. As it turns out, the admin was a BSD administrator and used the flags appropriate for the BSD-based FTP server. Unfortunately, the same flags on the FTP server on the Solaris host allowed for world writable access. No further forensic analysis was performed.

Online and Offline Analysis

Depending on the state of the machine you're dealing with and the urgency with which you need to analyze the compromise, there are different types of analysis you may choose to do. At a high level, there are two types of forensic analysis;:online and offline.

Online analysis is performed against a running system. Using some manner of trusted media with forensic tools such as a CD-ROM, online analysis allows for the examination of the system as is operates. The advantage of online analysis is that you can examine what processes are running on a box and the characteristics of the running system. This type of analysis may result in a deep knowledge of how the box was compromised and what types of hacker tools are running on the host. Poking around after a reboot, or simply examining the static data on disk, may not provide a complete picture of what is going on.

The disadvantage of online analysis is that you may be disturbing and changing the host. Some attack tools detect when they are being "prodded" and may start deleting data or performing other malicious activities. Further, if you are investigating a host to which the attacker still has access (you have not unplugged the network cable) the attacker may begin changing things as you look at them.

Offline analysis is the act of performing forensics activities against a "dead" system. Rather than acting on a running host and examining processes and memory, an offline analysis deals with disk images and static files. The advantage of an offline analysis is that the data on the disk is relatively safe. Disks can be copied and write protected and all binaries can be made nonexecutable. This prevents some manner of logic bomb left by the attacker from changing the data on the compromised host. Also, multiple copies can be created allowing multiple individuals to analyze the data concurrently. If you want to do offline analysis but also want to examine what processes were running on the host, you can shut the host down using **`halt -d`**. This will force a crash dump and provide access to process tables and other kernel-level information.

Things to Look For

Forensic analysis is not a magic wand. There is no single tool that you can run that immediately returns "Host owned through OpenSSH exploit by Billy Bob with Social Security Number 123-45-6789."

Changed files

One of the first thing you should look for are changed files. An attacker may modify configuration files such as */etc/inetd.conf* to start new services or install a completely different binary specifically designed to hide her tracks. `netstat(1)` is a binary utility that is commonly modified by an attacker to hide new network connections. The Trojaned `netstat` will only show non-attacker connections to give the illusion that the network status is normal.

You may find changes in a variety of ways. Visual inspection of *inetd.conf* may help you find footprints of an attack. However, manual comparison of a binary is basically impossible. Ideally, you will have a HIDS like Osiris or Tripwire (covered in Chapter 9) running that will allow you to compare checksums of existing files and the original files on the host.

When performing an online analysis of a potentially compromised host, assume that all utilities on the machine are not trustworthy. Every utility you run should be launched from a trusted read-only media such as a CD-ROM. When viewing *inetd.conf*, for instance, use an editor or viewer from the CD-ROM, not the native `less` utility on the host.

Added users

Another popular maneuver by an attacker is to add new users to the system to allow remote logins and processes to be executed. Again, if you don't have a known good copy of the *passwd* file, you're at a disadvantage, especially if you have a large number of users on the system. Hopefully there are uncompromised hosts that have a similar user set that you can compare against.

When creating users, attackers like to create accounts with high privileges. A root-level account will allow an attacker to perform superuser activities on a host without having to do any other trickery. The dead giveaway is a user with UID of zero, the superuser UID. Any user with UID of zero that is not root or toor is likely not an authorized account.

Also, an attacker may attempt to create an account that looks like a system account but is really his gateway account into a box. For example, a typical FreeBSD installation has a number of system accounts preinstalled that are used for a variety of system functions. In Example 11-1, there's a user that shouldn't be there.

Example 11-1. /etc/passwd on a FreeBSD host

```
root:*:0:0:Charlie &:/root:/bin/csh
toor:*:0:0:Bourne-again Superuser:/root:
daemon:*:1:1:Owner of many system processes:/root:/sbin/nologin
operator:*:2:5:System &:/:/sbin/nologin
bin:*:3:7:Binaries Commands and Source:/:/sbin/nologin
tty:*:4:65533:Tty Sandbox:/:/sbin/nologin
kmem:*:5:65533:KMem Sandbox:/:/sbin/nologin
games:*:7:13:Games pseudo-user:/usr/games:/sbin/nologin
news:*:8:8:News Subsystem:/:/sbin/nologin
man:*:9:9:Mister Man Pages:/usr/share/man:/sbin/nologin
cron:*:10:10:Cron Admin User:/:/bin/csh
sshd:*:22:22:Secure Shell Daemon:/var/empty:/sbin/nologin
smmsp:*:25:25:Sendmail Submission User:/var/spool/clientmqueue:/sbin/nologin
```

Without looking carefully, you could easily overlook the illegitimate cron user with a shell of */bin/csh*.

Strange directories

Other tidbits to look for are oddly named directories. Attackers may try and hide data and tools in directories that are difficult to find or `cd` into. A directory named ... may blend in with the typical **`ls -al`** listing, but may contain traces of an attack.

```
% ls -al
total 636
drwxr-xr-x   6 root  wheel    512 May 16  2004 .
drwxr-xr-x  21 root  wheel    512 Jun 24 16:11 ..
-rwx------   1 root  wheel   6750 Oct 23 13:49 ...
-r--r--r--   1 root  wheel   8192 Feb 23  2004 boot
```

Also, directories with control characters or other nonprintable characters may be difficult to see or access. If you have problems accessing a file or directory (i.e., you try and change into a directory and get an error that there is no directory by that name) use **ls -q** to print the contents of the directory. The –q flag turns all nonprintable characters into question marks allowing you do determine that something really is amiss. In this example, ls -al returns a normal looking output, but ls -lq paints a different story.

```
% ls -al
total 2942
drwxr-xr-x   5 root  wheel      512 Nov 18 19:52 .
drwxr-xr-x  21 root  wheel      512 Jun 24 16:11 ..
drwx------   1 root  wheel     1024 Nov 17 17:21 testdirectory
drwxr-xr-x   3 501   501        512 Nov  4 12:04 osiris-4.0.6
-rw-r--r--   1 root  wheel  1882069 Nov  4 12:05 osiris-4.0.6.tar.gz
% ls -lq
total 2942
drwxr-xr-x   5 root  wheel      512 Nov 18 19:52 .
drwxr-xr-x  21 root  wheel      512 Jun 24 16:11 ..
drwx------   1 root  wheel     1024 Nov 17 17:21 test??directory
drwxr-xr-x   3 501   501        512 Nov  4 12:04 osiris-4.0.6
-rw-r--r--   1 root  wheel  1882069 Nov  4 12:05 osiris-4.0.6.tar.gz
```

Unknown processes and LKMs

Attackers may start new processes on a host or inject kernel modules to cause the host to perform unwanted activities such as network scanning, password cracking, and file sharing. A standard ps -auxww that is common in BSD administration can reveal if strange new processes are afoot. On a busy system, there may be quite a long process list and it may be difficult to determine what is legitimate and what is not. Take your time and do not jump to conclusions.

You may recall from Chapter 2 that running in a *securelevel* of 1 or greater will help ensure that kernel modules cannot be loaded.

Kernel modules can be checked with kldstat(8). Again, if you don't know what your baseline kernel modules are, it may be difficult to determine what is legitimate and what is the result of an attack. Osiris, discussed in Chapter 9, has the ability to monitor kernel modules and track when new modules are brought online.

In Example 11-2, kldstat shows a suspicious kernel module at ID 4. This is worth investigating.

Example 11-2. Running kldstat to see loaded modules

```
% kldstat
Id Refs Address    Size     Name
 1    7 0xc0400000 5e74fc   kernel
```

Example 11-2. Running kldstat to see loaded modules (continued)

```
 2    1 0xc09e8000 51ac8    acpi.ko
 3    1 0xc27ac000 19000    linux.ko
 4    1 0xc4200000 27e12    rootkit.ko
```

Known rootkits and hacker tools

The tools installed by an attacker who has broken into your system are generally not something specifically written by the attacker. There are a common set of tools used by attackers, and many times they are bundled into *rootkits*. The Wikipedia definition from *http://www.wikipedia.org/wiki/Rootkit* is as follows:

> A rootkit is a set of tools used after cracking a computer system that hide logins, processes, and logs as well as usually sniff terminals, connections, and the keyboard.
>
> Called "root" kit after the fact that originally it referred to a set of recompiled Unix tools such as "ps" "netstat" "w" "passwd" that would carefully hide any trace of the cracker that those commands would normally display, thus the cracker could maintain "root" on the system without the system administrator even seeing them.

That sounds daunting. Rootkits are specifically designed to evade detection and hide an attackers tracks. Thankfully, rootkits leave fingerprints on a system much like viruses do. Like viruses, there are tools designed to track down rootkits and help users identify what the rootkit does.

One of the better tools is called Rootkit Hunter and is available from *http://www.rootkit.nl/projects/rootkit_hunter.html*. Rootkit Hunter examines the md5 checksums of files on the system to see if they match known rootkits, looks for odd binary permissions, searches for hidden files, and tries to determine malicious kernel modules. Sounds convenient, huh?

Rootkit Hunter is straightforward to download and install. When you run Rootkit Hunter, you probably want to scan the entire host. It's hard to say where an attacker may or may not have left tools on the host. But using the –`checkall` flag, all Rootkit Hunter tests are run. Further, with –`skip-keypress` Rootkit Hunter will run non-interactively allowing you to run the tool and not have to babysit it.

When it's done, Rootkit Hunter will summarize the results. In Example 11-3, two vulnerable applications were found that should be patched. However, no rootkits were found. This does not necessarily mean there are no rootkits on the host, but simply that this tool didn't find any.

Example 11-3. Rootkit Hunter sample results

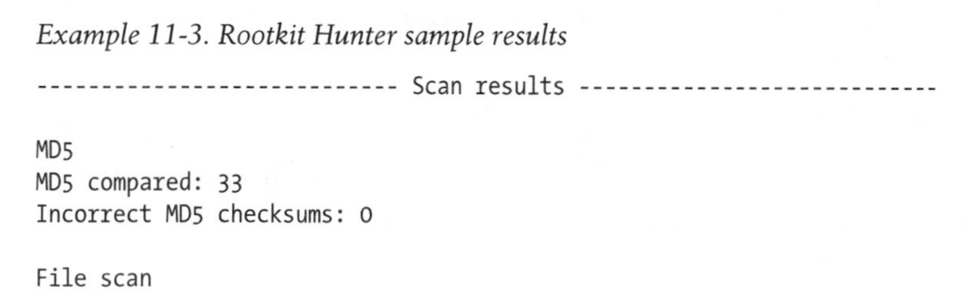

```
---------------------------- Scan results ----------------------------

MD5
MD5 compared: 33
Incorrect MD5 checksums: 0

File scan
```

Example 11-3. Rootkit Hunter sample results (continued)

```
Scanned files: 328
Possible infected files: 0

Application scan
Vulnerable applications: 2

Scanning took 97 seconds
```

Digging Deeper with the Sleuth Kit

You may reach a point where using basic system tools leads nowhere. There are several important open source forensics tools that are in common use today that provide low-level system information that can be useful to reconstruct what has occurred on a host. Many of them share common code or have changed names over time. It is important to understand the relationship between various toolkits, especially as you look for knowledge outside of this book.

History of the Sleuth Kit

In 1999, Wietse Venema (author of TCPWrappers and Postfix) and a small team created a set of tools called The Coroner's Toolkit (TCT) to aid in forensic analysis of a compromised Unix system. TCT was a great leap forward for open source forensics tools and put detailed, low-level analysis in the hands of the masses.

As good as TCT was, there were several weaknesses. The tools provided in TCT were very raw and low-level, necessitating the creation of supporting tools. Also, TCT was platform dependent and difficult to port. In response to this, @stake, a security service company, created the @stake Sleuth Kit (TASK). TASK unified third-party tools with TCT into one software package to provide a "one-stop shop" for UNIX forensic analysts. TASK also reworked internal code to make it more portable. TASK also broke tools apart according the layer at which they were operating on; filesystem, content, metadata, or human interface. This distinction between tools simplified use and helped analysts chose the right tool at the right time.

Finally, TASK was taken over by a group independent of industry or academic pressure. TASK became simply the Sleuth Kit (TSK) and is continually being developed to provide more utility and adapt to changes in supported operating systems. TSK source code and documentation is available from *http://www.sleuthkit.org/*.

Installing and Understanding TSK

TSK is in the ports tree and can be installed with relative ease. If you prefer, the Sleuth Kit can be compiled and installed from source after being downloaded from the *sleuthkit.org* web site. As mentioned previously, the tools in TSK are broken into four different layers; filesystem, content, metadata, and human interface.

The content (or data) layer is for the actual data of files and directories. Tools that operate on this layer directly interact with the data in files and directories. These tools start with the letter d.

The metadata layer contains information that describes the files and directory themselves. This includes *inode* information, FAT directory structures, access and modification times of files, and privilege information. These tools start with the letter i.

The human interface layer provides a more convenient way to interact with files. Rather than have to understand and track the metadata information, the human interface layer abstracts some of that information to make it easier on the analyst. Human interface tools start with the letter f.

Finally, the filesystem layer deals with (as you may have guessed) information about the filesystem such as volume name and when a volume was last mounted. These tools start with the letters fs.

Using TSK

When using the tools in TSK, the first thing you should do is make a copy of the disk with which you are interacting. *Never* interact directly with the compromised filesystem. Performing forensic analysis against the compromised filesystem may change the data in an unexpected and untraceable way. If you make changes to the original data, you will never really be sure of what an attacker has done as opposed to what you did.

Copying filesystems is relatively easy. On your forensics workstation you need to have at least twice as much free space as the filesystem you intend to copy from the compromised drive. Not only will you be making a copy of the compromised filesystem, you are also copying of all the free space on the filesystem as well.

Take the drive from the compromised host and attach it to the drive controller on your forensic workstation. Use the `dd(1)` utility to copy the compromised filesystem to an image file. So, assuming you wanted to examine the root filesystem of the compromised drive currently available as `ad1` to your home directory, you would execute the following.

```
% sudo dd if=/dev/ad1s1a of=/home/user/comp-root.dd
```

Depending on the size of the filesystem, this may take a while. `dd` is designed to be precise, not quick. You will probably see transfer speeds of 10–30MB a minute, so for a multi-gigabyte filesystem, you may consider getting some food or watching something on your TiVo.

If you are lucky enough not to have a compromised filesystem to deal with, you can still practice your forensics skills with your existing host. Hopefully you have enough space on one filesystem to hold the contents of another. Take the following host for example:

```
% df -k
Filesystem  1K-blocks    Used    Avail Capacity  Mounted on
/dev/ad0s1a    495726   85304   370764    19%    /
devfs               1       1        0   100%    /dev
/dev/ad0s1d  15231278 3099220 10913556    22%    /usr
/dev/ad0s1e   2697326   26902  2454638     1%    /var
```

The root filesystem is only 500MB and there is nearly 11GB of free space on the */usr* filesystem. In this setup, you can copy the root filesystem via dd to someplace in */usr* and perform your "analysis."

Once dd is complete, you have a bit-for-bit copy of the original filesystem that you can start doing your analysis against. You may, for the sake of safety, copy all the filesystems on the compromised disk, shut down your workstation, and remove the drive. This will ensure that you are not going to inadvertently modify the compromised disk.

Depending on the information you're looking for, you may want to use various tools in TSK. Normally, you want to build a timeline of when files were modified on the compromised host. Start this process by using the fls tool to gather data about allocated and unallocated files in the filesystem. Use fls with the –m flag to specify the mount point and –r to ensure the entire filesystem is examined. The –f flag specifies the filesystem type you are dealing with. This flag is used in nearly all TSK tools.

```
% fls -f freebsd -m / -r comp-root.dd > body
```

Next, use the ils tool to find information about unallocated *inodes*. With this information you can determine what files have been changed and deleted. Note that you are adding the output of the ils command to the body file, not overwriting it.

```
% ils -f freebsd -m comp-root.dd >> body
```

Finally, use the mactime command to create the timeline from the body file. mactime takes the input body file via the –b flag and requires a start date. mactime will only log changes that occurred after that date. In this example, we examine all changes on a host since January 1, 2000.

```
% mactime -b body 1/01/2000 > timeline
```

The timeline file now contains information on every file that has changed or been deleted since the start of the twenty-first century. You can examine the file using a pager like less or grep through it for strings you're interested in. In this case, we are interested in changes in *inetd.conf*. Using grep, we find the following entry

```
Thu Jul 24 2003 17:10:08 4939 m.c -/-rw-r--r-- 0 0 60159 /etc/inetd.conf
```

4939 is the size of the file. The `m.c` indicates that the file was modified and created at that time.

The timeline file can be very valuable when piecing together the events in an attack. File access, creation, and modification around the time of the attack may be pointers to indicate how an attacker broke in and what her motivations were.

Autopsy

Digging through the data generated by TSK by hand can be tedious and confusing. If you are performing analysis on a large number of hosts or are working as a team, the flat files and ad-hoc storage of TSK data can be cumbersome. Thankfully, there's Autopsy, a perl script that provides a web interface for interacting with data from the Sleuth Kit.

Autopsy can be installed from *sysutils* in the ports tree. Alternately, the code can be downloaded directly from *http://www.sleuthkit.org/* and configured manually. Note that the ports installation does not actually install Autopsy anywhere. You have to manually copy the script and supporting files to a directory of your choice, usually your home directory.

Once configured, Autopsy can be started simply with */path/to/autopsy*. Once started, Autopsy will direct you to a URL where you can access its functionality as shown in Example 11-4.

Example 11-4. Starting Autopsy

```
% sudo ./autopsy
============================================================================

                       Autopsy Forensic Browser
                             ver 1.73

============================================================================

Evidence Locker: /usr/home/gdead/evidence/
Start Time: Mon Dec 13 23:42:47 2004

Paste this as your browser URL on localhost:
        http://localhost:9999/37461905692459298670/autopsy
```

By default, Autopsy restricts connections to localhost only. If you want to change the port Autopsy runs on or allow remote access, you can start multiple instances of the program using the syntax autopsy *`port remote-host`*.

Autopsy does more than simply allow web access to TSK data. It aims to be a complete incident analysis tool that can be used from the beginning of the analysis process all the way through potential legal proceedings. Autopsy provides the ability for multiple analysts to work on one incident, multiple hosts to be associated with one incident, and even accounts for time drifts between hosts automatically. Further, notes can be entered for any piece of data within Autopsy allowing your analysis data to be stored with the raw information. Autopsy also automates the task of creating a timeline so you don't have to remember the awkward TSK commands. Figure 11-2 shows a timeline as viewed in Autopsy. Arguably, this is much nicer than viewing a flat text file from TSK.

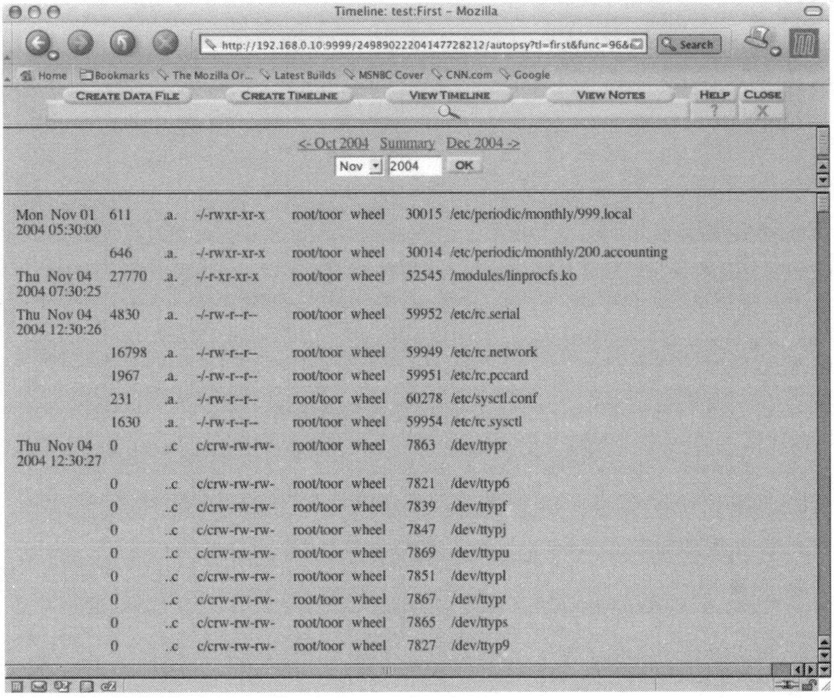

Figure 11-2. A sample timeline from Autopsy

TSK and Autopsy are complicated tools and we have only scratched the surface. With the test image you have, you should examine the other tools included with TSK to become familiar with their utility now...before you really need them.

Wrapping Up

Incident response and forensic analysis are (unfortunately) a fact of life. Even through your best efforts, eventually an attacker will cause you some real harm. There are many different ways to treat incident response and your needs will vary depending on your situation. However, having a clear understanding of how to respond and being prepared for it regardless of when it happens is the best way to ensure that your incident is handled as gracefully as possible.

Resources

Forensics List at SecurityFocus (http://www.securityfocus.com/incidents)
A general purpose forensics discussion list. Subscription information available at the link.

Incident Response, Ken van Wyk and Richard Forno (O'Reilly), 2001
A concise guide to all the ins and outs of incident response. Information available from *http://www.oreilly.com/catalog/incidentres/index.html*.

Investigating Computer-Related Crime, Peter Stephenson (CRC Press), 1999
A resource tailored to the corporate security specialist who needs detailed information on investigating attacks. This book provides a thorough coverage of the technical and legal aspects of computer crime.

Index

A

We'd like to hear your suggestions for improving our indexes. Send email to *index@oreilly.com*.

B

C

D

E

F

G

H

I

J

K

L

M

N

O

P

Q

R

S

T

U

V

W

X

Y

Z

About the Authors

Yanek Korff graduated with a bachelor's degree in computer science from the College of William and Mary and is currently a Certified Information Systems Security Professional (CISSP). Mr. Korff joined Bell Atlantic as a systems engineer where he played a role in the strategy, design, and deployment of a key northern Virginia test facility. He later joined Cigital, Inc., a software quality management company, where he helped design the system infrastructure. He is now a member of the information security division at America Online. During his career, Mr. Korff has been able to identify and mitigate information security risks particularly relating to host-based BSD security. By leveraging his experience, he has been able to apply security fundamentals to influence business and industry practices.

Paco Hope is a Senior Software Security Consultant with Cigital, Inc. His areas of expertise include software security, embedded systems, PKI, and host security. Mr. Hope has published articles on X.509 revocation and Unix host security features. Prior to joining Cigital, Inc., he served as director of product development for Tovaris, Inc., based in Charlottesville, Virginia, and as head systems administrator in the department of computer science at the University of Virginia. Mr. Hope was a double major in computer science and English at the College of William and Mary and received an M.S. in computer science from the University of Virginia.

Bruce Potter is a Senior Associate with Booz Allen Hamilton. Prior to working at Booz Allen, Mr. Potter served as a software security consultant for Cigital, Inc., in Dulles, Virginia. Mr. Potter is the founder of the Shmoo Group of security professionals. His areas of expertise include wireless security, large-scale network architectures, smartcards and promotion of secure software engineering practices. Mr. Potter coauthored the books *802.11 Security* (O'Reilly) and *Mac OS X Security* (New Riders). Mr. Potter was trained in computer science at the University of Alaska, Fairbanks.

Colophon

Our look is the result of reader comments, our own experimentation, and feedback from distribution channels. Distinctive covers complement our distinctive approach to technical topics, breathing personality and life into potentially dry subjects.

The image on the cover of *Mastering FreeBSD and OpenBSD Security* depicts fencers. Whether used for sport or for war, the art of fencing can be traced back to some of the earliest known civilizations. For example, fencers entertained Pharaohs in ancient Engypt. The Greeks and Romans, meanwhile, had systems of martial arts that included swordsmanship. The modern sport of fencing originated in the first Olympic Games, in 1896, and consists of three different weapons: foil, épée, and sabre. The lightest of these weapons is the foil. A foil fencer can only score hits by landing thrusts to the trunk of the body. A modern electrical scoring apparatus, worn by the fencer, will record a hit for any blow landed with a force of at least 4.90 newtons. Less flexible and heavier than the foil, the épée usually has a large hand guard. This bell-shaped guard is important because the épée fencer is not as limited in her targets—the entire body, including the hand, is considered a valid target to score hits. An épée fencer registers a hit with 7.35 newtons of force. The sabre differs from these first two swords in that it is an edge, rather than a point, weapon. A sabre fencer may land points to any part of the upper body (head, torso, and arms). A touch with the point, flat, or edge of the sword will register a hit.

Adam Witwer was the production editor, and Nancy Reinhardt was the copyeditor for *Mastering FreeBSD and OpenBSD Security*. Linley Dolby proofread the text. Sarah Sherman and Claire Cloutier provided quality control. Lucie Haskins wrote the index.

Emma Colby designed the cover of this book, based on a series design by Edie Freedman. The cover image is a 19th-century engraving from the Dover Pictorial Archive. Karen Montgomery produced the cover layout with Adobe InDesign CS using Adobe's ITC Garamond font.

David Futato designed the interior layout. This book was converted by Judy Hoer to FrameMaker 5.5.6 with a format conversion tool created by Erik Ray, Jason McIntosh, Neil Walls, and Mike Sierra that uses Perl and XML technologies. The text font is Linotype Birka; the heading font is Adobe Myriad Condensed; and the code font is LucasFont's TheSans Mono Condensed. The illustrations that appear in the book were produced by Robert Romano, Jessamyn Read, and Lesley Borash using Macromedia FreeHand MX and Adobe Photoshop CS. The tip and warning icons were drawn by Christopher Bing. This colophon was written by Adam Witwer.

Keep in touch with O'Reilly

1. Download examples from our books

To find example files for a book, go to:

www.oreilly.com/catalog

select the book, and follow the "Examples" link.

2. Register your O'Reilly books

Register your book at *register.oreilly.com*

Why register your books?
Once you've registered your O'Reilly books you can:

- Win O'Reilly books, T-shirts or discount coupons in our monthly drawing.
- Get special offers available only to registered O'Reilly customers.
- Get catalogs announcing new books (US and UK only).
- Get email notification of new editions of the O'Reilly books you own.

3. Join our email lists

Sign up to get topic-specific email announcements of new books and conferences, special offers, and O'Reilly Network technology newsletters at:

elists.oreilly.com

It's easy to customize your free elists subscription so you'll get exactly the O'Reilly news you want.

4. Get the latest news, tips, and tools

www.oreilly.com

- "Top 100 Sites on the Web"—PC Magazine
- CIO Magazine's Web Business 50 Awards

Our web site contains a library of comprehensive product information (including book excerpts and tables of contents), downloadable software, background articles, interviews with technology leaders, links to relevant sites, book cover art, and more.

5. Work for O'Reilly

Check out our web site for current employment opportunities:

jobs.oreilly.com

6. Contact us

O'Reilly Media
1005 Gravenstein Hwy North
Sebastopol, CA 95472 USA

TEL: 707-827-7000 or 800-998-9938
(6am to 5pm PST)

FAX: 707-829-0104

order@oreilly.com
For answers to problems regarding your order or our products. To place a book order online, visit:

www.oreilly.com/order_new

catalog@oreilly.com
To request a copy of our latest catalog.

booktech@oreilly.com
For book content technical questions or corrections.

corporate@oreilly.com
For educational, library, government, and corporate sales.

proposals@oreilly.com
To submit new book proposals to our editors and product managers.

international@oreilly.com
For information about our international distributors or translation queries. For a list of our distributors outside of North America check out:

international.oreilly.com/distributors.html

adoption@oreilly.com
For information about academic use of O'Reilly books, visit:

academic.oreilly.com